OPERATIONS MANAGEMENT

OPERATIONS MANAGEMENT

S Anil Kumar
Ex-Professor and Head
Department of Commerce & Management
NMKRV College for Women
Bangalore, Karnataka

N Suresh
Ex-Associate Professor and Head
Department of Industrial Engineering & Management
MVJ College of Engineering
Bangalore, Karnataka

NEW AGE MANAGEMENT

An Imprint of

NEW AGE INTERNATIONAL (P) LIMITED, PUBLISHERS
LONDON • NEW DELHI • NAIROBI
Bangalore • Chennai • Cochin • Guwahati • Hyderabad • Kolkata • Lucknow • Mumbai
Visit us at **www.newagepublishers.com**

Published by New Age International (P) Ltd., Publishers
First Edition: 2009
Reprint: 2018

GLOBAL OFFICES

- **New Delhi** **NEW AGE INTERNATIONAL (P) LIMITED, PUBLISHERS**
7/30 A, Daryaganj, New Delhi-110002, (INDIA)
Tel.: (011) 23253771, 23253472, **Telefax:** 23267437, 43551305
E-mail: contactus@newagepublishers.com • Visit us at www.newagepublishers.com
- **London** **NEW AGE INTERNATIONAL (UK) LTD.**
27 Old Gloucester Street, London, WC1N 3AX, UK
E-mail: info@newacademicscience.co.uk • Visit us at www.newacademicscience.co.uk
- **Nairobi** **NEW AGE GOLDEN (EAST AFRICA) LTD.**
Ground Floor, Westlands Arcade, Chiromo Road (Next to Naivas Supermarket)
Westlands, Nairobi, KENYA, **Tel.:** 00-254-713848772, 00-254-725700286
E-mail: kenya@newagepublishers.com

BRANCHES

- **Bangalore** 37/10, 8th Cross (Near Hanuman Temple), Azad Nagar, Chamarajpet, Bangalore- 560 018
Tel.: (080) 26756823, **Telefax:** 26756820, **E-mail: bangalore@newagepublishers.com**
- **Chennai** 26, Damodaran Street, T. Nagar, Chennai-600 017, **Tel.:** (044) 24353401, **Telefax:** 24351463
E-mail: chennai@newagepublishers.com
- **Cochin** CC-39/1016, Carrier Station Road, Ernakulam South, Cochin-682 016, **Tel.:** (0484) 2377303, **Telefax:** 4051304
E-mail: cochin@newagepublishers.com
- **Guwahati** Hemsen Complex, Mohd. Shah Road, Paltan Bazar, Near Starline Hotel, Guwahati-781 008,
Tel.: (0361) 2513881, **Telefax:** 2543669, **E-mail: guwahati@newagepublishers.com**
- **Hyderabad** 105, 1st Floor, Madhiray Kaveri Tower, 3-2-19, Azam Jahi Road, Near Kumar Theater, Nimboliadda Kachiguda, Hyderabad-500 027, **Tel.:** (040) 24652456, **Telefax:** 24652457
E-mail: hyderabad@newagepublishers.com
- **Kolkata** RDB Chambers (Formerly Lotus Cinema) 106A, 1st Floor, S N Banerjee Road, Kolkata-700 014
Tel.: (033) 22273773, **Telefax:** 22275247, **E-mail: kolkata@newagepublishers.com**
- **Lucknow** 16-A, Jopling Road, Lucknow-226 001, **Tel.:** (0522) 2209578, 4045297, **Telefax:** 2204098
E-mail: lucknow@newagepublishers.com
- **Mumbai** 142C, Victor House, Ground Floor, N.M. Joshi Marg, Lower Parel, Mumbai-400 013
Tel.: (022) 24927869, **Telefax:** 24915415, **E-mail: mumbai@newagepublishers.com**
- **New Delhi** 22, Golden House, Daryaganj, New Delhi-110 002, **Tel.:** (011) 23262368, 23262370, **Telefax:** 43551305
E-mail: sales@newagepublishers.com

ISBN: 978-81-224-2587-1
C-18-05-11395

Printed in India at Ajit Printing Press, Delhi.
Typeset at In-house, Delhi.

NEW AGE INTERNATIONAL (P) LIMITED, PUBLISHERS
7/30 A, Daryaganj, New Delhi-110002
Visit us at **www.newagepublishers.com**
(CIN: U74899DL1966PTC004618)

PREFACE

Operations management has been recognised as an important factor in a country's economic growth. The traditional view of manufacturing management is the concept of **Production Management** with the focus on economic efficiency in manufacturing. Later the new name **Operations Management** was identified, as service sector became more prominent. Rapid changes in technology have posed numerous opportunities and challenges, which have resulted in enhancement of manufacturing capabilities through new materials, facilities, techniques and procedures. Hence, managing a service system has become a major challenge in the global competitive environment. Operations Management has been a key element in the improvement and productivity in business around the world. Operations Management leads the way for the organisations to achieve its goals with minimum effort. Hence, the study of the subject at undergraduate and postgraduate level has more significance.

This book on 'Operations Management' covers the complete syllabus of Bachelor of Engineering of Visvesvaraya Technical University, Karnataka, however the coverage is wide enough to include the requirements of Bachelor and Master Degree courses of other Indian universities and professional courses like MBA, PGDCA, BBA.

Being student friendly is the unique feature of this book. The subject matter has been presented systematically in ten chapters, which can enable the reader master the topics covered without any additional guidance.

Complete care has been taken to make the book error free. However, mistakes might have crept inadvertently. Readers finding any error are requested to bring it to our notice, for enabling us to rectify them in our future editions.

We are grateful to **Mr. Saumya Gupta**, Managing Director and **Mr. Sudarshan** of New Age International (P) Limited Publishers for their commitment and encouragement in bringing out this book in time with good quality and for providing us the opportunity to share our knowledge with you.

The authors wish to express their sincere thanks to Principals and Managements of respective colleges. Our acknowledgements are also due to **Dr. Poornima Anil Kumar** and **Mrs. Bharathi Suresh** without whose support and sacrifice this work would not have been completed by the deadline.

Finally, our acknowledgement is due to the Almighty who has blessed us with the knowledge, required for writing this book.

S. Anil Kumar
N. Suresh

CONTENTS

1

OPERATIONS MANAGEMENT CONCEPTS

CHAPTER OUTLINE

1.1 INTRODUCTION

Operation is that part of as organization, which is concerned with the transformation of a range of inputs into the required output (services) having the requisite quality level. Management is the process, which combines and transforms various resources used in the operations subsystem of the organization into value added services in a controlled manner as per the policies of the organization.

The set of interrelated management activities, which are involved in manufacturing certain products, is called as **production management**. If the same concept is extended to services management, then the corresponding set of management activities is called as **operations management.**

1.2 HISTORICAL DEVELOPMENT

For over two centuries operations and production management has been recognized as an important factor in a country's economic growth.

The traditional view of manufacturing management began in eighteenth century when **Adam Smith** recognised the economic benefits of specialization of labour. He recommended breaking of jobs down into subtasks and recognises workers to specialized tasks in which they would become highly skilled and efficient. In the early twentieth century, F.W. Taylor implemented Smith's theories and developed scientific management. From then till 1930, many techniques were developed prevailing the traditional view. Brief information about the contributions to manufacturing management is shown in the Table 1.1.

Production Management becomes the acceptable term from 1930s to 1950s. As F.W. Taylor's works become more widely known, managers developed techniques that focused on economic efficiency in manufacturing. Workers were studied in great detail to eliminate wasteful efforts and achieve greater efficiency. At the same time, psychologists, socialists and other social scientists began to study people and human behaviour in the working environment. In addition, economists, mathematicians, and computer socialists contributed newer, more sophisticated analytical approaches.

With the 1970s emerge two distinct changes in our views. The most obvious of these, reflected in the new name **Operations Management** was a shift in the service and manufacturing sectors of the economy. As service sector became more prominent, the change from 'production' to 'operations' emphasized the broadening of our field to service organizations. The second, more suitable change was the beginning of an emphasis on synthesis, rather than just analysis, in management practices.

Table 1.1 Historical summary of operations management

Date	Contribution	Contributor
1776	Specialization of labour in manufacturing	Adam Smith
1799	Interchangeable parts, cost accounting	Eli Whitney & others
1832	Division of labour by skill; assignment of jobs by Skill; basics of time study	Charles Babbage
1900	Scientific management time study and work study Developed; dividing planning and doing of work	Frederick W.Taylor
1900	Motion of study of jobs	Frank B. Gilbreth
1901	Scheduling techniques for employees, machines Jobs in manufacturing	Henry L. Gantt
1915	Economic lot sizes for inventory control	F.W. Harris
1927	Human relations; the Hawthorne studies	Elton Mayo
1931	Statistical inference applied to product quality: quality control charts	W.A. Shewart
1935	Statistical Sampling applied to quality control: inspection sampling plans	H.F.Dodge & H.G.Roming
1940	Operations research applications in world war II	P.M.Blacker & others
1946	Digital Computer	John Mauchlly and J.P.Eckert
1947	Linear Programming	G.B.Dantzig, Williams & others
1950	Mathematical programming, on-linear and stochastic processes	A.Charnes, W.W.Cooper & others
1951	Commercial digital computer: large-scale computations available	Sperry Univac
1960	Organisational behaviour: continued study of people at work	L.Cummings, L.Porter
1970	Integrating operations into overall strategy and policy Computer applications to manufacturing, scheduling, and control, Material Requirement Planning (MRP)	W.Skinner J.Orlicky & G. Wright
1980	Quality and productivity applications from Japan: robotics, CAD-CAM	W.E. Deming & J.Juran

1.3 CONCEPT OF PRODUCTION

Production function is 'the part of an organisation, which is concerned with the transformation of a range of inputs into the required outputs (products) having the requisite quality level'.

Production is defined as 'the step-by-step conversion of one form of material into another form through chemical or mechanical process to create or enhance the utility of the product to the user'. Thus production is a value addition process. At each stage of processing, there will be value addition.

Edwood Buffa defines production as 'a process by which goods and services are created'.

Some examples of production are: manufacturing custom-made products like, boilers with a specific capacity, constructing flats, some structural fabrication works for selected customers, etc., and manufacturing standardized products like, car, bus, motor cycle, radio, television, etc.

1.4 PRODUCTION SYSTEM

The production system is 'that part of an organisation, which produces products of an organisation. It is that activity whereby resources, flowing within a defined system, are combined and transformed in a controlled manner to add value in accordance with the policies communicated by management'.

A simplified production system is shown below:

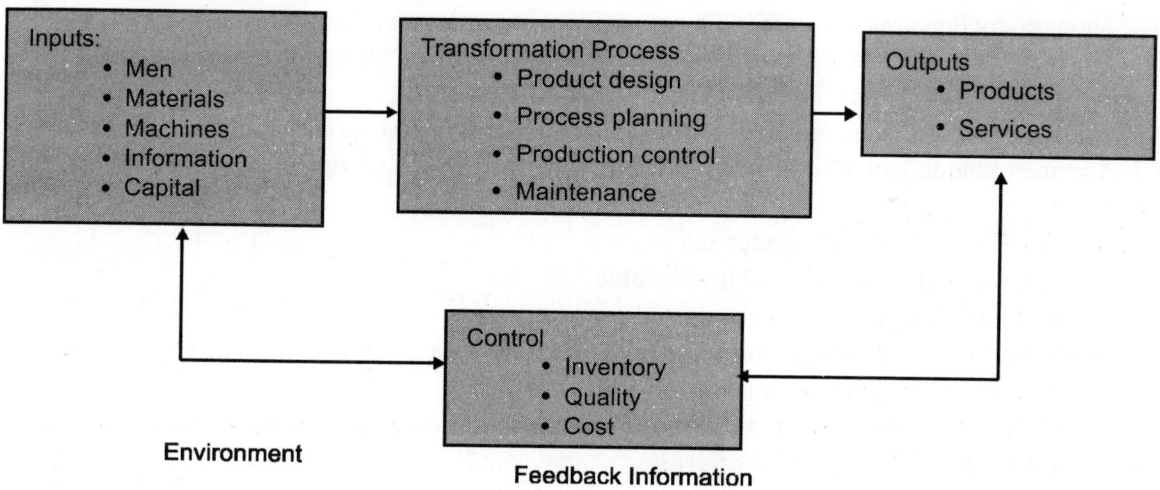

Fig.1.1 Schematic production system

The production system has the following characteristics:

1. Production is an organised activity, so every production system has an objective.
2. The system transforms the various inputs to useful outputs.
3. It does not operate in isolation from the other organisation system.
4. There exists a feedback about the activities, which is essential to control and improve system performance.

1.5 CLASSIFICATION OF PRODUCTION SYSTEM

Production systems can be classified as Job-shop, Batch, Mass and Continuous production systems.

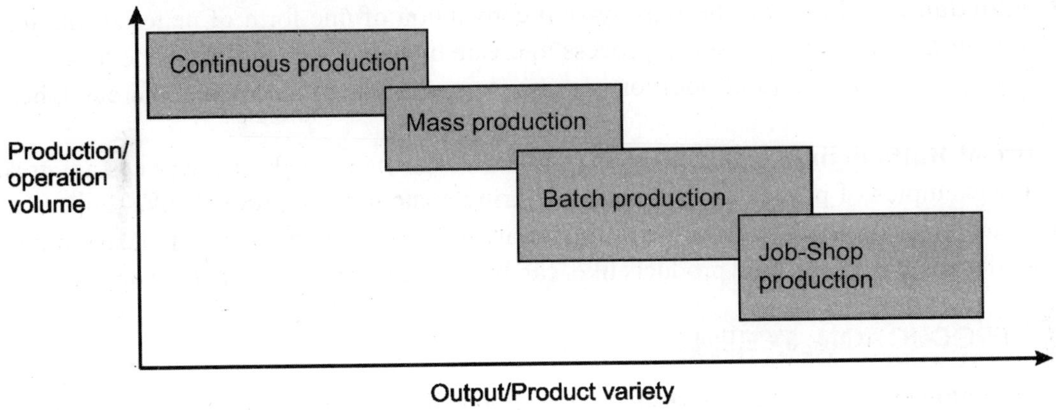

Fig. 1.2 Classifications of production systems

1.5.1 Job-Shop Production

Job-shop production are characterised by manufacturing one or few quantity of products designed and produced as per the specification of customers within prefixed time and cost. The distinguishing feature of this is low volume and high variety of products.

A job-shop comprises of general-purpose machines arranged into different departments. Each job demands unique technological requirements, demands processing on machines in a certain sequence.

Job-shop Production is characterised by

1. High variety of products and low volume.
2. Use of general purpose machines and facilities.
3. Highly skilled operators who can take up each job as a challenge because of uniqueness.
4. Large inventory of materials, tools, parts.
5. Detailed planning is essential for sequencing the requirements of each product, capacities for each work centre and order priorities.

Advantages

Following are the advantages of Job-shop Production:

1. Because of general purpose machines and facilities variety of products can be produced.
2. Operators will become more skilled and competent, as each job gives them learning opportunities.
3. Full potential of operators can be utilised.
4. Opportunity exists for Creative methods and innovative ideas.

Limitations

Following are the limitations of Job-shop Production:

1. Higher cost due to frequent set up changes.
2. Higher level of inventory at all levels and hence higher inventory cost.
3. Production planning is complicated.
4. Larger space requirements.

1.5.2 Batch Production

American Production and Inventory Control Society (APICS) defines Batch Production as a form of manufacturing in which the job pass through the functional departments in lots or batches and each lot may have a different routing. It is characterised by the manufacture of limited number of products produced at regular intervals and stocked awaiting sales.

Batch Production is characterised by

1. Shorter production runs.
2. Plant and machinery are flexible.
3. Plant and machinery set up is used for the production of item in a batch and change of set up is required for processing the next batch.
4. Manufacturing lead-time and cost are lower as compared to job order production.

Advantages

Following are the advantages of Batch Production:

1. Better utilisation of plant and machinery.
2. Promotes functional specialisation.
3. Cost per unit is lower as compared to job order production.
4. Lower investment in plant and machinery.
5. Flexibility to accommodate and process number of products.
6. Job satisfaction exists for operators.

Limitations

Following are the limitations of Batch Production:

1. Material handling is complex because of irregular and longer flows.
2. Production planning and control is complex.
3. Work in process inventory is higher compared to continuous production.
4. Higher set up costs due to frequent changes in set up.

1.5.3 Mass Production

Manufacture of discrete parts or assemblies using a continuous process are called *Mass Production*. This production system is justified by very large volume of production. The machines are arranged in a line or product layout. Product and process standardisation exists and all outputs follow the same path.

Mass Production is characterised by

1. Standardisation of product and process sequence.
2. Dedicated special purpose machines having higher production capacities and output rates.
3. Large volume of products.
4. Shorter cycle time of production.
5. Lower in process inventory.
6. Perfectly balanced production lines.
7. Flow of materials, components and parts is continuous and without any back tracking.
8. Production planning and control is easy.
9. Material handling can be completely automatic.

Advantages

Following are the advantages of Mass Production:

1. Higher rate of production with reduced cycle time.
2. Higher capacity utilisation due to line balancing.
3. Less skilled operators are required.
4. Low process inventory.
5. Manufacturing cost per unit is low.

Limitations

Following are the limitations of Mass Production:

1. Breakdown of one machine will stop an entire production line.
2. Line layout needs major change with the changes in the product design.
3. High investment in production facilities.
4. The cycle time is determined by the slowest operation.

1.5.4 Continuous Production

Production facilities are arranged as per the sequence of production operations from the first operations to the finished product. The items are made to flow through the sequence of operations through material handling devices such as conveyors, transfer devices, etc.

Continuous Production is characterised by

1. Dedicated plant and equipment with zero flexibility.
2. Material handling is fully automated.
3. Process follows a predetermined sequence of operations.
4. Component materials cannot be readily identified with final product.
5. Planning and scheduling is a routine action.

Advantages

Following are the advantages of Continuous Production:

1. Standardisation of product and process sequence.
2. Higher rate of production with reduced cycle time.
3. Higher capacity utilisation due to line balancing.
4. Manpower is not required for material handling as it is completely automatic.

5. Person with limited skills can be used on the production line.
6. Unit cost is lower due to high volume of production.

Limitations

Following are the limitations of Continuous Production:

1. Flexibility to accommodate and process number of products does not exist.
2. Very high investment for setting flow lines.
3. Product differentiation is limited.

1.6 PRODUCTION MANAGEMENT

Production management is 'a process of planning, organising, directing and controlling the activities of the production function. It combines and transforms various resources used in the production subsystem of the organization into value added product in a controlled manner as per the policies of the organization'.

E.S.Buffa defines production management as follows:

'**Production management** deals with decision-making related to production processes so that the resulting goods or services are produced according to specifications, in the amount and by the schedule demanded and out of minimum cost'.

1.6.1 Objectives of Production Management

The objective of the production management is 'to produce goods and services of Right Quality and Quantity at the Right time and Right manufacturing cost'.

1. **Right Quality:** The quality of product is established based upon the customers need. The right quality is not necessarily being the best quality. It is determined by the cost of the product and the technical characteristics as suited to the specific requirements.

2. **Right Quantity:** The manufacturing organisation should produce the products in right number. If they are produced in excess of demand the capital will block up in the form of inventory and if the quantity is produced in short of demand, leads to shortage of products.

3. **Right Time:** Timeliness of delivery is one of the important parameter to judge the effectiveness of production department. So, the production department has to make the optimal utilization of input resources to achieve its objective.

4. **Right Manufacturing Cost:** Manufacturing costs are established before the product is actually manufactured. Hence, all attempts should be made to produce the products at pre-established cost, so as to reduce the variation between actual and the standard (pre-established) cost.

1.7 OPERATIONS SYSTEM

An operation was defined in terms of the mission it serves for the organisation, technology it employs and the human and managerial processes it involves. Operations in an organisation can be categorised into Manufacturing Operations and Service Operations. Manufacturing Operations is a conversion process that includes manufacturing yields a tangible output: a product, whereas, a conversion process that includes service yields an intangible output: a deed, a performance, an effort.

Operations system converts inputs in order to provide outputs, which are required by a customer. It converts physical resources into outputs, the function of which is to satisfy customer wants.

Everett E. Adam & Ronald J. Ebert defines as 'An operating system is the part of an organisation that produces the organistion's physical goods and services'.

Ray Wild defines operations system as 'a configuration of resources combined for the provision of goods or services'.

In some of the organisation the product is a physical good (breakfast in hotels) while in others it is a service (treatment in hospitals). Bus and taxi services, tailors, hospital and builders are the examples of an operations system. The basic elements of an operation system show in Figure 1.3 with reference to departmental stores.

A departmental store's has an input like land upon which the building is located, labour as a stock clerk, capital in the form of building, equipment and merchandise, management skills in the form of the stores manager. Output will be serviced customer with desired merchandise. Random fluctuations will be from external or internal sources, monitored through a feedback system.

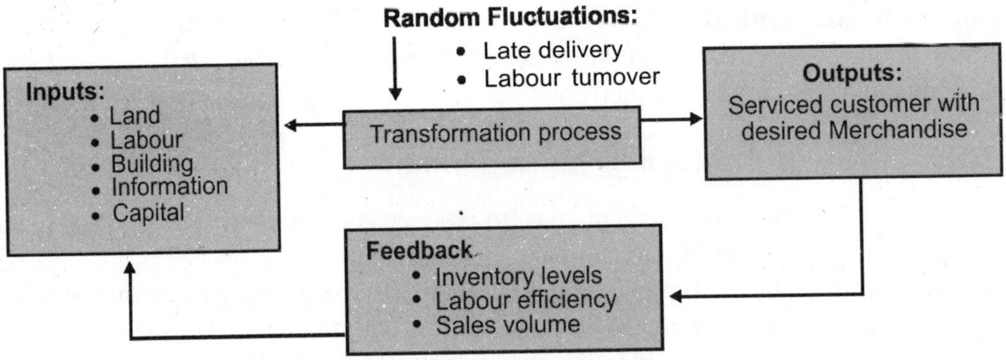

Fig.1.3 Operations system for department stores

1.7.1 A Framework of Managing Operations

Managing Operations can be enclosed in a frame of general management function as shown in figure 1.3. Operation managers are concerned with planning, organising, and controlling the activities, which affect human behaviour through models.

Planning is the activity that establishes a course of action and guide future decision-making. The operations manager defines the objectives for the operations subsystem of the organisation, and the policies, and procedures for achieving the objectives. This stage includes clarifying the role and focus of operations in the organization's overall strategy. It also involves product planning, facility designing and using the conversion process.

Organizing is the activities that establish a structure of tasks and authority. Operation managers establish a structure of roles and the flow of information within the operations subsystem. They determine the activities required to achieve the goals and assign authority and responsibility for carrying them out.

Controlling is the activities that assure the actual performance in accordance with planned performance. To ensure that the plans for the operations subsystems are accomplished, the operations manager must exercise control by measuring actual outputs and comparing them to planned operations management. Controlling costs, quality, and schedules are the important functions here.

1. **Behaviour:** Operations managers are concerned with the activities, which affect human behaviour through models. They want to know the behaviour of subordinates, which affects managerial activities. Their main interest lies in the decision-making behaviour.

2. **Models:** Models represents schematic representation of the situation, which will be used as a tool for decision-making. Following are some of the models used.

Aggregate planning models for examining how best to use existing capacity in short term, break-even analysis to identify break-even volumes, *Linear programming and computer simulation* for capacity utilisation, Decision tree analysis for long-term capacity problem of facility expansion, simple median model for determining best locations of facilities, etc.

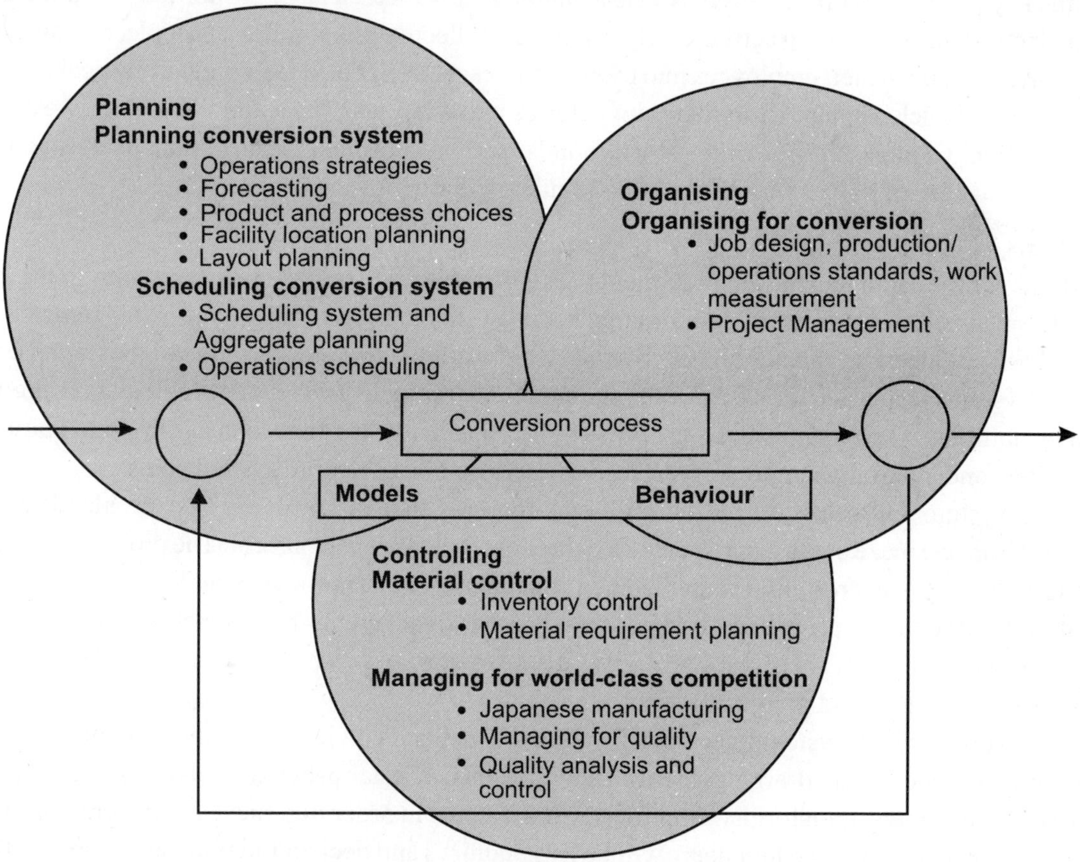

Fig. 1.4 General model for managing operations

1.8 OPERATIONS MANAGEMENT

Joseph G.Monks *defines* ***Operations Management*** *as the process whereby resources, flowing within a defined system, are combined and transformed by a controlled manner to add value in accordance with policies communicated by management.*

The operations managers have the prime responsibility for processing inputs into outputs. They must bring together under production plan that effectively uses the materials, capacity and knowledge available in the production facility. Given a demand on the system work must be scheduled and controlled to produce goods and/or services required. Control must be exercised over such parameters such as costs, quality and inventory levels.

The definition of the operations Management contains following keywords: Resources, Systems, transformation and Value addition Activities.

RESOURCES

Resources are the human, material and capital inputs to the production process. Human resources are the key assets of an organisation. As the technology advances, a large proportion of human input is in planning and controlling activities. By using the intellectual capabilities of people, managers can multiply the value of their employees into by many times. Material resources are the physical facilities and materials such as plant equipment, inventories and supplies. These are the major assets of an organisation. Capital in the form of stock, bonds, and/or taxes and contributions is a vital asset. Capital is a store of value, which is used to regulate the flow of the other resources.

SYSTEMS

Systems are the arrangement of components designed to achieve objectives according to the plan. The business systems are subsystem of large social systems. In turn, it contains subsystem such as personnel, engineering, finance and operations, which will function for the good of the organisation.

A systems approach to operations management recognises the hierarchical management responsibilities. If subsystems goals are pursued independently, it will results in sub-optimization. A consistent and integrative approach will lead to optimization of overall system goals.

The system approach to specific problems requires that the problem first be identified and isolated from the maze of the less relevant data that constitute the environment. The problem abstracted from the overall (macro) environment. Then it can be broken into manageable (micro) parts and analysed and solutions proposed. Doing this analysis is advantageous before making any changes. If the solution appears to solve the problem in a satisfactory way, changes can be made to the real system in an orderly and predictable way.

The ability of any system to achieve its objective depends on its design and its control. System design is a predetermined arrangement of components. It establishes the relationships that must exist between inputs, transformation activities and outputs in order to achieve the system objectives. With the most structured design, there will be less planning and decision-making in the operations of the system. System control consists of all actions necessary to ensure that activities conform to preconceived plans or goals. It involves following four essential elements:

1. Measurement by an accurate sensory device.
2. Feedback of information in a timely manner.
3. Comparison with standards such as time and cost standards.
4. Corrective actions by someone with the authority and ability to correct.

A closed loop control system can automatically function on the basis of data from within its own system.

TRANSFORMATION AND VALUE ADDING ACTIVITIES

The objective of combining resources under controlled conditions is to transform them into goods and services having a higher value than the original inputs. The transformation process applied will be in the form of technology to the inputs. The effectiveness of the production factors in the transformation process is known as productivity.

The productivity refers to the ratio between values of output per work hour to the cost of inputs. The firms overall ratio must be greater than 1, then we can say value is added to the product. Operations manager should concentrate improving the transformation efficiency and to increase the ratio.

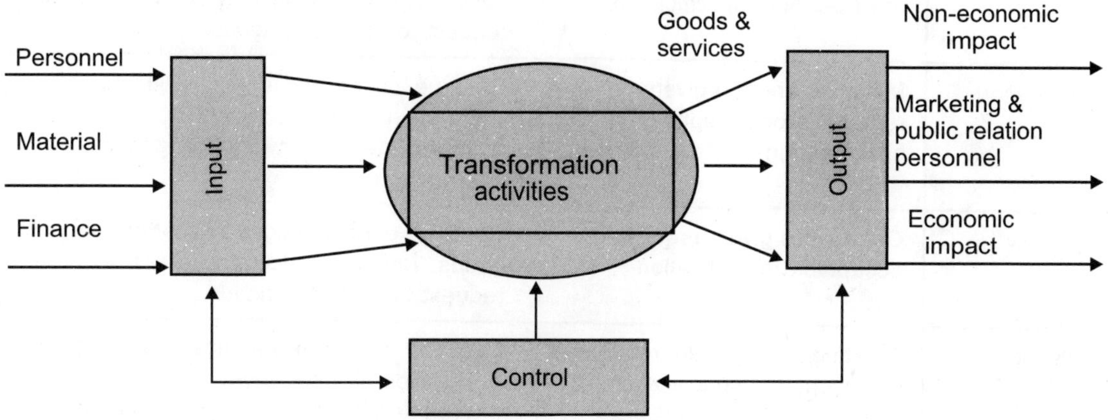

Fig. 1.5 Schematic model for operations/production system

1.9 OPERATIONS MANAGEMENT OBJECTIVES

***Joseph G. Monks** defines **Operations Management** as the process whereby resources, flowing within a defined system, are combined and transformed by a controlled manner to add value in accordance with policies communicated by management.*

Objectives of Operations Management can be categorized into Customer Service and Resource Utilisation.

CUSTOMER SERVICE

The first objective of operating systems is to utilize resources for the satisfaction of customer wants. Therefore, customer service is a key objective of operations management. The operating system must provide something to a specification, which can satisfy the customer in terms of cost and timing. Thus, providing the 'right thing at a right price at the right time' can satisfy primary objective.

These aspects of customer service – specification, cost and timing – are described for four functions in Table 1.1. They are the principal sources of customer satisfaction and must therefore be the principal dimension of the customer service objective for operations managers.

Generally, an organisation will aim reliably and consistently to achieve certain standards and operations manager will be influential in attempting to achieve these standards. Hence, this objective will influence the operations manager's decisions to achieve the required customer service.

Table 1.2 Aspects of customer service

Principal function	Principal customer wants	
	Primary considerations	**Other considerations**
Manufacture	Goods of a given, requested or acceptable specification	Cost, *i.e.* purchase price or cost of obtaining goods. Timing, *i.e.* delivery delay from order or request to receipt of goods.
Transport	Management of a given, requested or acceptable specification	Cost, *i.e.* cost of movements. Timing, *i.e.* 1. Duration or time to move. 2. Wait or delay from requesting to its commencement.
Supply	Goods of a given, requested or acceptable specification	Cost, *i.e.* purchase price or cost of obtaining goods. Timing, *i.e.* delivery delay from order or request to receipt of goods.
Service	Treatment of a given, requested or acceptable specification	Cost, *i.e.* cost of movements. Timing, *i.e.* 1. Duration or time required for treatment. 2. Wait or delay from requesting treatment to its commencement.

Resource Utilisation

Another major objective of operating systems is to utilize resources for the satisfaction of customer wants effectively. Customer service must be provided with the achievement of effective operations through efficient use of resources. Inefficient use of resources or inadequate customer service leads to commercial failure of an operating system.

Operations management is concerned essentially with the utilisation of resources, *i.e.* obtaining maximum effect from resources or minimising their loss, under utilisation or waste. The extent of the utilisation of the resources' potential might be expressed in terms of the proportion of available time used or occupied, space utilisation, levels of activity, etc. Each measure indicates the extent to which the potential or capacity of such resources is utilised. This is referred as the objective of resource utilisation.

Operations management is concerned with the achievement of both satisfactory customer service and resource utilisation. An improvement in one will often give rise to deterioration in the other. Often both cannot be maximized, and hence a satisfactory performance must be achieved on both objectives. All the activities of operations management must be tackled with these two objectives in mind, and because of this conflict, operations managers' will face many of the problems. Hence, operations managers must attempt to balance these basic objectives.

The Table 1.3 summarizes the twin objectives of operations management. The type of balance established both between and within these basic objectives will be influenced by market considerations, competitions, the strengths and weaknesses of the organization, etc. Hence, the operations managers should make a contribution when these objectives are set.

Table 1.3 The twin objectives of operations management

The customer service objective	The resource utilizations objective
i.e. to provide agreed/adequate levels of customer service (and hence customer satisfaction) by providing goods or services with the right specification, at the right cost and at the right time.	*i.e.* to achieve adequate levels of resource utilizations (or productivity) *e.g.* to achieve agreed levels of utilizations of materials, machines and labour.

1.10 THE STRATEGIC ROLE OF OPERATIONS

Primary goals of the organisations are related market opportunities. Economy and efficiency of conversion operations are the secondary goals, which will be predominant with the study and practice of operations management.

A Strategic Perspective

In figure 1.1 provides the basic downward flow of strategy influence leading to managing conversion operations and results. The general thrust of the process is guided by competitive and market conditions in the industry, which provide the basis for determining the organization's strategy. Where is the industry now, and where it will be in the future? What are the existing and potential markets? What market gaps exist, and what competencies do we have for filling them? A careful analysis of market segments and the ability of our competitors and ourselves to meet the needs of these segments will determine the best direction for focusing an organization's efforts.

After assessing the potential within an industry, an overall organizational strategy must be developed, including some basic choices of the primary basis for competing. In doing so, priorities are established among the following four characteristics:

- *Quality (product performance).*
- *Cost efficiency (low product price).*
- *Dependability (reliable, timely delivery of orders to customers).*
- *Flexibility (responding rapidly with new products or changes in volume).*

In recent years, most organizations cannot be best on all these dimensions and, by trying to do so, they end up doing nothing well. Furthermore, when a competency exists in one of these areas, an attempt to switch to a different one can lead to a downfall in effectiveness (meeting the primary objectives).

Time is emerging as a critical dimension of competition in both manufacturing and service industries. In any industry the firm with the fastest response to customer demands has the potential to achieve an overwhelming market advantage. In an era of time-based competition, a firm's competitive advantage is defined by the total time required to produce a product or service. Firms able to respond quickly have reported growth rates over three times the industry average and double the profitability. Thus the pay-off for quick response is market dominance. These basic strategic choices set the tone for the shape and content of the operations functions.

Operations Objectives

The overall objective of the operations subsystem is to provide conversion capabilities for meeting the organization's goals and strategy. The sub-goals of the operations subsystem, must specify the following:

1. Product/service characteristics.
2. Process characteristics.
3. Product/service quality.
4. Efficiency
    - Effective employee relations and cost control of labour.
    - Cost control of material.
    - Cost control in facility utilization.
5. Customer service (schedule)
    - Producing quantities to meet expected demand.
    - Meeting the required delivery date for goods or services.
6. Adaptability for future survival.

The priorities among these operations' sub-goals and their relative emphases should be direct reflections of the organization's mission. Relating these six operations sub-goals to the broader strategic choices above, it is clear that quality, efficiency, and dependability (customer service) are reflected in the sub-goals. Flexibility encompasses adaptability but also relates to product/service and process characteristics: Once choices about product and process are made, boundaries for meeting the other operations objectives are set.

Operations Alternatives and Tradeoffs

The operations sub-goals can be attained through the decisions that are made in the various operations areas. Each decision involves important tradeoffs between choices about product and process versus choices about quality, efficiency, schedule and adaptability.

Once a decision is made, it leads to many choices. Where should facilities be located? How large should they be? What degree of automation should be used? How skilled must labour be to operate the automated equipment? Will the product be produced on site? How do these decisions impact quality, efficiency, schedule (customer service), and adaptability? Are we prepared for changes in product or service, or do these decisions lock in our operations? These are examples of the tough, crucial tradeoffs that are at the heart of understanding the choices that must be made when planning strategically and tactically.

1.11 STRATEGIC PLANNING

Strategic planning is the process of thinking through the current mission of the organization and the current environmental conditions facing it, then setting forth a guide for tomorrow's decisions and results. Strategic planning is built on fundamental concepts: that current decisions are based on future conditions and results.

1.11.1 Strategic Planning for Production and Operations

In the production or operations function, strategic planning is the broad, overall planning that precedes the more detailed operational planning. Executives who head the production and operations function are actively involved in strategic planning, developing plans that are consistent with the firm's overall strategies as well as such functions as marketing, finance accounting and engineering. Production and operations strategic plans are the basis for (1) operational planning of facilities (design) and (2) operational planning for the use of these facilities.

1.11.2 Strategic Planning Approaches for Production/Operations

Henry Mintzberg suggests three contrasting modes of strategic planning: the entrepreneurial, the adaptive, and the planning modes. In the entrepreneurial mode, one strong, bold leader takes planning action on behalf of the production/operations function. In the adaptive mode, a manager's plan is formulated in a series of small, disjointed steps in reaction to a disjointed environment. The planning model uses planning essentials combined with the logical analysis of management science.

There are many approaches to strategic planning. The key point is that operations strategies must be consistent with the overall strategies of the firm. Operations typically utilize the overall corporate approach to strategic planning, with special modifications and a focus upon operations issues and opportunities. One general approach to strategic planning is a forced choice model given by Adam and Ebert.

1.11.3 Strategic Planning—Forced Choice Model

One of many planning models that have been used in strategic planning is a forced choice model, shown in Figure 1.6 (on page 16). In-group sessions or individually, analysts assess environmental considerations together with the organization's current production/operations position, thus forcing management to develop strategic options for operations.

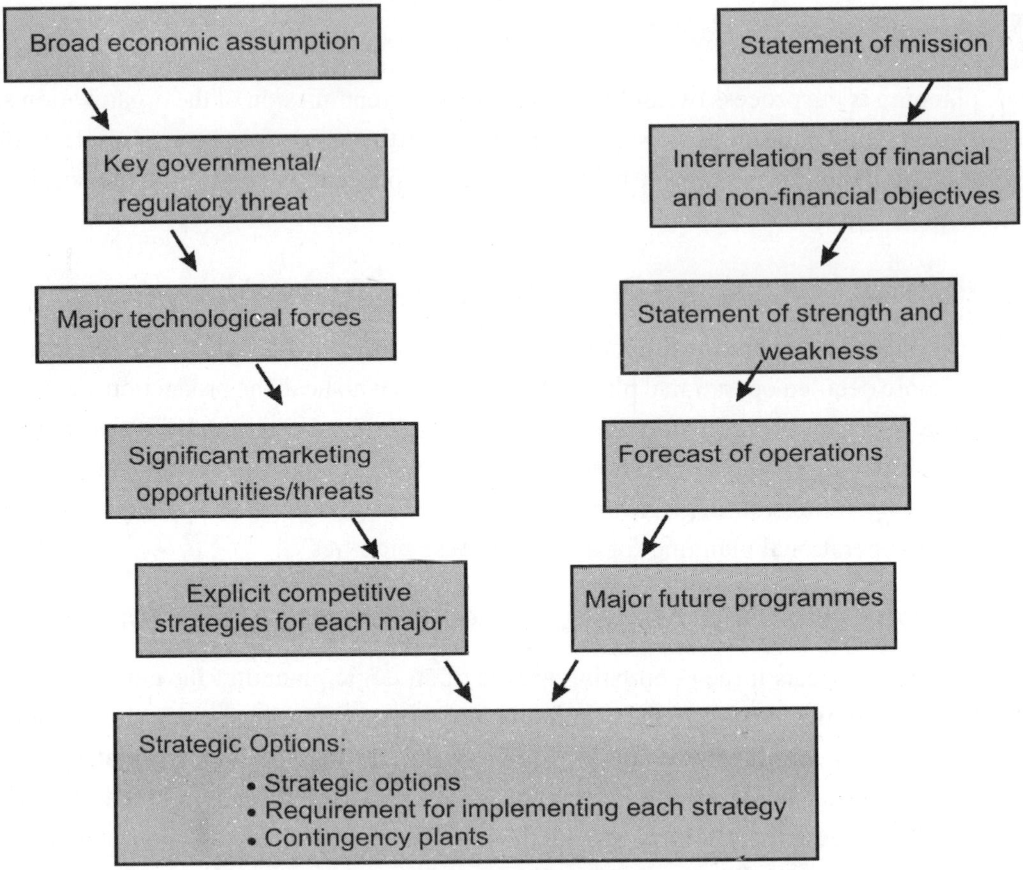

Fig.1.6 A forced choice model of strategic planning for operations

Source: Charles, N. Greene, Everett E. Adam, Jr., and Ronald J. Ebert, Management for Effective Performance (Prentice Hall 1985)

1.11.4 A Strategic Planning Operations Model

Professor Chris A. Voss of the London Business School, England, has set forth a framework for strategy and policy development in manufacturing. Concept is that manufacturing strategy tries to link the policy decisions associated with operations to the marketplace, the environment, and the company's overall goals. A simplified framework for examining operations strategy is shown in Figure 1.7.

One feature of this approach that is crucial to competitiveness is market-based view of strategic planning. It suggests that any strategic business unit of a company operates in the context of its corporate resources, the general and competitive industry environment, and the specific corporate goals of the company. In any area in which the company chooses to compete is a set of specific market-based criteria for success.

A low-cost, high productivity operation makes efficiency possible. Minimum use of scarce resources while sustaining high outputs is the key to productivity. Effectiveness is how well a company is able to meet specific criteria such as delivery schedules and technical capability. Quality is the degree to which the product or services meets customer and organisation expectations.

Quality reflects the 'goodness' of the product or services to the customer. Flexibility is the adoptability, the capability to change as business conditions change.

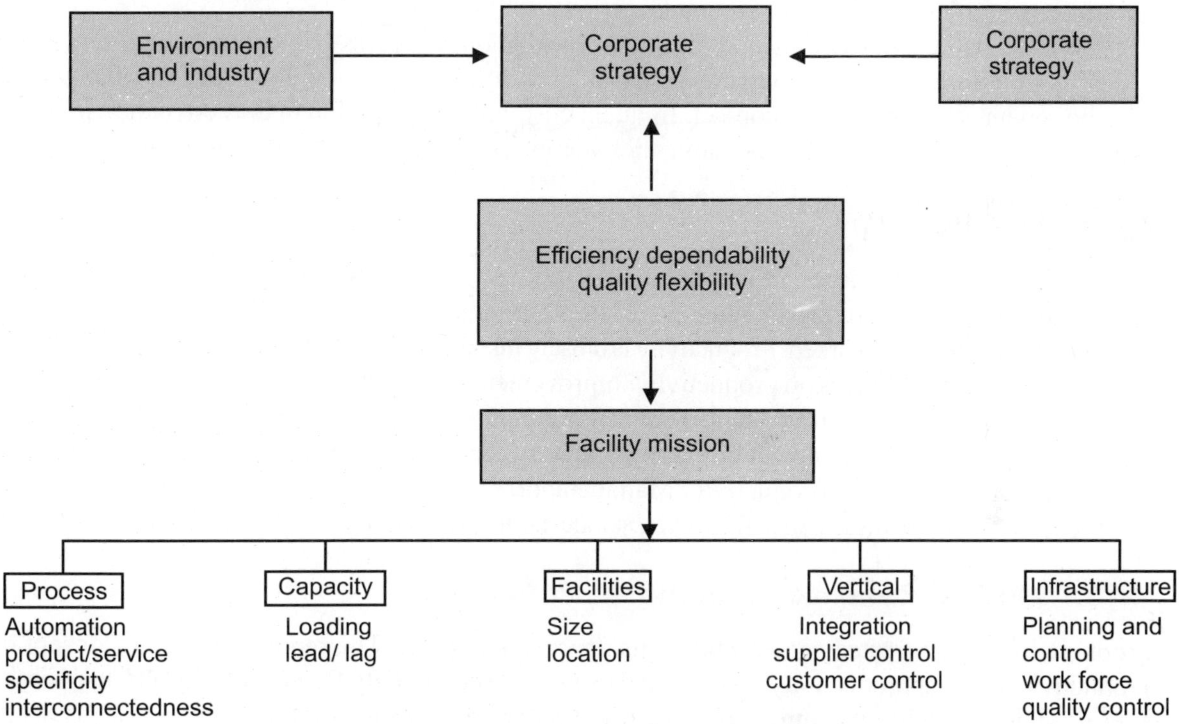

Fig. 1.7 Operations strategy framework

1.12 THE TREND: INFORMATION AND NON MANUFACTURING SYSTEMS

An increasingly significant trend in the Indian economy is the gradual shift of productive effort from manufacturing (industrial) to service and information based products. With this, the demand for communication and information based product is gradually restructuring the society. Traditional ways of doing things are being replaced by efficient methods. Computers play a major role in this transition along with fiber optics, microwaves, lasers and other communication technologies.

Following characteristics can be considered for distinguishing Manufacturing Operations with Service Operations:

1. Tangible/Intangible nature of output
2. Production and consumption
3. Nature of work (job)
4. Degree of customer contact
5. Customer participation in conversion
6. Measurement of performance
7. Quality of output
8. Inventory accumulated.

Manufacturing is characterized by tangible outputs (products). Consumption of outputs at overtime. Jobs useless labour and more equipment, little customer contact, no customer participation in the conversion process (in production). Sophisticated methods for measuring production activities and resource consumption as product are made.

Service is characterized by intangible outputs. In addition, it possess a potential for high variability in quality of output. Production and consumption occurs simultaneously. Jobs use more labour and less equipment, direct consumer contact, frequent customer participation in the conversion process. Elementary methods for measuring conversion activities and resource consumption are used.

1.13 PRODUCTIVITY

Productivity is defined in terms of utilization of resources, like material and labour. In simple terms, productivity is the ratio of output to input. For example, productivity of labour can be measured as units produced per labour hour worked. Productivity is closely inked with quality, technology and profitability. Hence, there is a strong stress on productivity improvement in competitive business environment.

Productivity can be improved by (*a*) controlling inputs, (*b*) improving process so that the same input yields higher output, and (*c*) by improvement of technology. These aspects are discussed in more detail in the lesson on Productivity Management.

Productivity can be measured at firm level, at industry level, at national level and at international level.

1.13.1 Modern Dynamic Concept of Productivity

Productivity can be treated as a multidimensional phenomenon. The modern dynamic concept of productivity looks at productivity as what may be called "productivity flywheel". The productivity is energized by competition. Competition leads to higher productivity, higher productivity results in better value for customers, this results in higher share of market for the organization, which results in still keener competition. Productivity thus forms a cycle, relating to design and products to satisfy customer needs, leading to improved quality of life, higher competition *i.e.* need for having still higher goals and higher share of market, and thereby leading to still better designs.

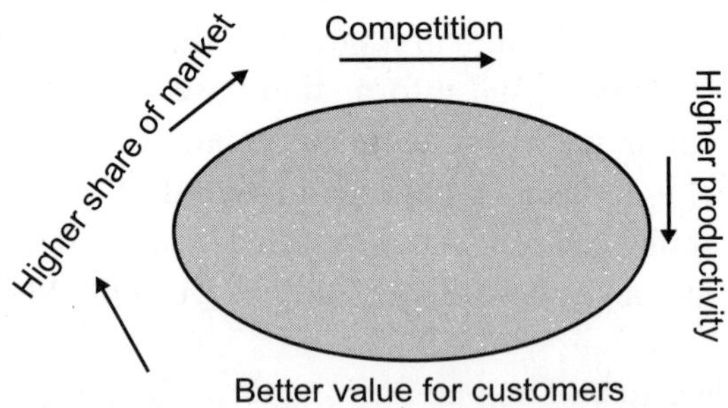

Fig. 1.8 Dynamic concept of productivity

1.13.2 Factor Productivity and Total Productivity

When productivity is measured separately for each input resource to the production process it is called factor productivity or partial productivity. When productivity is measured for all the factors of production together, it is called total factor productivity.

Generally factor productivity calculations are required at firm level and industry level, whereas total factor productivity calculations are made for measuring productivity at national and international level.

Productivity of materials can be measured as output units per unit material consumed. It can also be measured in terms of value generated per unit expenditure in materials.

For measuring productivity of different groups of operatives, different ratios can be used, which are indicative of output/input relationship. For example, the productivity of assembly line work can be measured as output units per man-hour or alternatively, the value of good produced per cost of labour on assembly line.

1.13.3 Productivity Analysis

For the purposes of studies of productivity for improvement purposes, following types of analysis can be carried out:

1. ***Trend analysis*:** Studying productivity changes for the firm over a period of time.
2. ***Horizontal analysis*:** Studying productivity in comparison with other firms of same size and engaged in similar business.
3. ***Vertical analysis*:** Studying productivity in comparison with other industries and other firms of different sizes in the same industry.
4. ***Budgetary analysis:*** Setting up a norm for productivity for a future period as budget, based on studies as above, and planning strategies to achieve it.

1.14 FACTORS AFFECTING PRODUCTIVITY

Economists site a variety of reasons for changes in productivity. However some of the principle factors influencing productivity rate are:

1. ***Capital/labour ratio*:** It is a measure of whether enough investment is being made in plant, machinery, and tools to make effective use of labour hours.
2. ***Scarcity of some resources*:** Resources such as energy, water and number of metals will create productivity problems.
3. ***Work-force changes*:** Change in work-force effect productivity to a larger extent, because of the labour turnover.
4. ***Innovations and technology*:** This is the major cause of increasing productivity.
5. ***Regulatory effects*:** These impose substantial constraints on some firms, which lead to change in productivity.
6. ***Bargaining power*:** Bargaining power of organized labour to command wage increases excess of output increases has had a detrimental effect on productivity.
7. ***Managerial factors*:** Managerial factors are the ways an organization benefits from the unique planning and managerial skills of its manager.
8. ***Quality of work life*:** It is a term that describes the organizational culture, and the extent to which it motivates and satisfies employees.

1.15 INTERNATIONAL DIMENSIONS OF PRODUCTIVITY

Industrialized nations are developing two strategies to remain competitive in the business.

1. Moving to a new and more advanced products, and
2. Employing better and more flexible system.

New Products

High Volume Products like steel, textiles, etc. with constitute an industrial base are not secure. Nations such as Japan, France and West Germany are shifting their industrial base towards products and processes that make better use of their research capabilities and skilled workers. Their future lies in microelectronics, precision manufactured castings, specialty steels, custom fabrics, fiber optics, lasers, etc.

Trend Towards More Flexible Systems

The production runs of these higher valued specialty items and custom designed products are often much shorter than for traditional mass produced goods. But the non-productive time (downtime) required to set up equipment for producing different options, new models and new products are very costly. So production facilities must be designed with the utmost flexibility to accommodate change overs in rapid fashion. This is where computers, robotics come into play.

German executives understand the need for a strong technological focus and the dangers of hierarchical bureaucracies and paper profits. Studies reveal that over 50 per cent of Germany's large manufacturing firms are managed by Ph.D.'s with technical backgrounds.

In recent years, the managerial techniques and productivity methods in Japanese firms have attracted worldwide attention. The following are some of the characteristics of the Japanese firm as compared with the American firms.

1. ***Corporate objectives*:** Employees and customers are given priority over shareholders. Honesty in business is important.
2. ***Time horizon*:** Long-term viability is more important than short-term profits.
3. ***Production systems*:** Automated systems with extensive use of microprocessors and robotics. Quality is paramount, and things happen on schedule.
4. ***Employment relations*:** Long-term employment of loyal workers. Unions cooperate to benefit total firm. Politeness and harmony are emphasized.
5. ***Materials*:** Resources are limited. Space is used efficiently and inventories are kept to a bare minimum.
6. ***Financing*:** More use is made of debt capital and less of equity capital.
7. ***Training*:** Employees are thoroughly trained and rotated to learn a variety of skills.
8. ***Worker participation*:** Employees are thoroughly trained and rotated to learn a variety of productivity improvements via suggestions, quality circles and consultation with supervisors.

1.16 THE ENVIRONMENT OF OPERATIONS

One of the most encompassing influences on productivity is the environment in which organization operates. The social impact of an organization is a reflection of the values held by top management.

It evolves from the religious and cultural norms of society, from childhood training, education, and reflection on the purpose of life and the value of one's self and of others. The preferred values of the society reflect purpose, integrity and a respect for the life and humanity of others.

Every facet of our economic and social environment regulated and controlled by law designed to protect general public. The figure illustrates some of the laws impact on the productivity of the firms.

1.17 SCOPE OF OPERATIONS MANAGEMENT

Operations Management concern with the conversion of inputs into outputs, using physical resources, so as to provide the desired utilities to the customer while meeting the other organizational objectives of effectiveness, efficiency and adoptability. It distinguishes itself from other functions such as personnel, marketing, finance, etc. by its primary concern for 'conversion by using physical resources'. Following are the activities, which are listed under Production and Operations Management functions:

1. Location of facilities.
2. Plant layouts and Material Handling.
3. Product Design.
4. Process Design.
5. Production and Planning Control.
6. Quality Control.
7. Materials Management.
8. Maintenance Management.

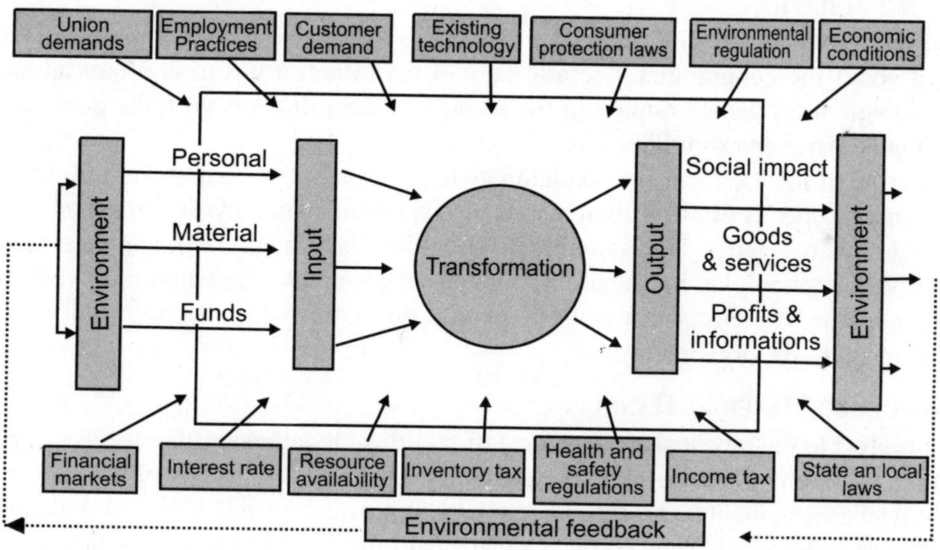

Fig. 1.9 Environment of operations

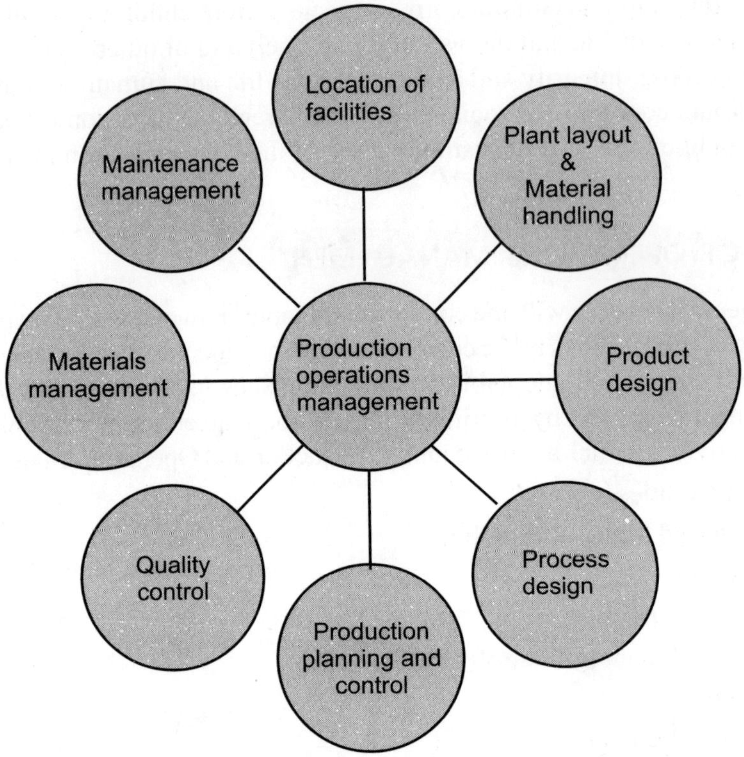

Fig. 1.10 Scope of production and operations management

Location of Facilities

Location of facilities for operations is a long-term capacity decision, which involves a long-term commitment about the geographically static factors that affect a business organisation. It is an important strategic level decision-making for an organisation. It deals with the questions such as 'where our main operations should be based?'

The selection of location is a key-decision as large investment is made in building plant and machinery. An improper location of plant may lead to waste of all the investments made in plant and machinery equipments. Hence, location of plant should be based on the company's expansion plan and policy, diversification plan for the products, changing sources of raw materials and many other factors. The purpose of the location study is to find the optimal location that will results in the greatest advantage to the organization.

Plant Layout and Material Handling

Plant layout refers to the physical arrangement of facilities. It is the configuration of departments, work centres and equipment in the conversion process. The overall objective of the plant layout is to design a physical arrangement that meets the required output quality and quantity most economically.

According to James More 'Plant layout is a plan of an optimum arrangement of facilities including personnel, operating equipment, storage space, material handling equipments and all other supporting services along with the design of best structure to contain all these facilities'.

'Material Handling' refers to the 'moving of materials from the store room to the machine and from one machine to the next during the process of manufacture'. It is also defined as the 'art and science of moving, packing and storing of products in any form'. It is a specialized activity for a modern manufacturing concern, with 50 to 75% of the cost of production. This cost can be reduced by proper section, operation and maintenance of material handling devices. Material handling devices increases the output, improves quality, speeds up the deliveries and decreases the cost of production. Hence, material handling is a prime consideration in the designing new plant and several existing plants.

PRODUCT DESIGN

Product design deals with conversion of ideas into reality. Every business organisation have to design, develop and introduce new products as a survival and growth strategy. Developing the new products and launching them in the market is the biggest challenge faced by the organizations. The entire process of need identification to physical manufactures of product involves three functions—Design and Marketing, Product, Development, and manufacturing. Product Development translates the needs of customers given by marketing into technical specifications and designing the various features into the product to these specifications. Manufacturing has the responsibility of selecting the processes by which the product can be manufactured. Product design and development provides link between marketing, customer needs and expectations and the activities required to manufacture the product.

PROCESS DESIGN

Process design is a macroscopic decision-making of an overall process route for converting the raw material into finished goods. These decisions encompass the selection of a process, choice of technology, process flow analysis and layout of the facilities. Hence, the important decisions in process design are to analyse the workflow for converting raw material into finished product and to select the workstation for each included in the workflow.

PRODUCTION PLANNING AND CONTROL

Production planning and control can be defined as the process of planning the production in advance, setting the exact route of each item, fixing the starting and finishing dates for each item, to give production orders to shops and to follow-up the progress of products according to orders.

The principle of production planning and control lies in the statement 'First Plan Your Work and then Work on Your Plan'. Main functions of production planning and control include Planning, Routing, Scheduling, Dispatching and Follow-up.

Planning is deciding in advance what to do, how to do it, when to do it and who is to do it. Planning bridges the gap from where we are, to where we want to go. It makes it possible for things to occur which would not otherwise happen.

Routing may be defined as the selection of path, which each part of the product will follow, which being transformed from raw material to finished products. Routing determines the most advantageous path to be followed for department to department and machine to machine till raw material gets its final shape.

Scheduling determines the programme for the operations. Scheduling may be defined as 'the fixation of time and date for each operation' as well as it determines the sequence of operations to be followed.

Dispatching is concerned with the starting the processes. It gives necessary authority so as to start a particular work, which has been already been planned under 'Routing' and 'Scheduling'. Therefore, dispatching is 'Release of orders and instruction for the starting of production for any item in acceptance with the Route sheet and Schedule Charts'.

The function of **Follow-up** is to report daily the progress of work in each shop in a prescribed proforma and to investigate the causes of deviations from the planned performance.

Quality Control (QC)

Quality Control may be defined as 'a system that is used to maintain a desired level of quality in a product or service'. It is a systematic control of various factors that affect the quality of the product. Quality Control aims at prevention of defects at the source, relies on effective feedback system and corrective action procedure.

Quality Control can also be defined as 'that Industrial Management technique by means of which product of uniform acceptable quality is manufactured'. It is the entire collection of activities, which ensures that the operation will produce the optimum quality products at minimum cost.

The main objectives of Quality Control are:

1. To improve the companies income by making the production more acceptable to the customers *i.e.* by providing longlife, greater usefulness, maintainability, etc.
2. To reduce companies cost through reduction of losses due to defects.
3. To achieve interchangeability of manufacture in large-scale production.
4. To produce optimal quality at reduced price.
5. To ensure satisfaction of customers with productions or services or high quality level, to build customer good will, confidence and reputation of manufacturer.
6. To make inspection prompt to ensure quality control.
7. To check the variation during manufacturing.

Materials Management

Materials Management is that aspect of management function, which is primarily concerned with the acquisition, control, and use of materials needed and flow of goods and services connected with the production process having some predetermined objectives in view.

The main objectives of Material Management are:

1. To minimise material cost.
2. To purchase, receive, transport and store materials efficiently and to reduce the related cost.
3. To cut down costs through simplification, standardisation, value analysis, import substitution, etc.
4. To trace new sources of supply and to develop cordial relations with them in order to ensure continuous supply at reasonable rates.
5. To reduce investment tied in the inventories for use in other productive purposes and to develop high inventory turnover ratios.

MAINTENANCE MANAGEMENT

In modern industry, equipment and machinery are a very important part of the total productive effort. Therefore their idleness or downtime becomes are very expensive. Hence, it is very important that the plant machinery should be properly maintained.

The main objectives of Maintenance Management are:

1. To achieve minimum breakdown and to keep the plant in good working condition at the lowest possible cost.
2. To keep the machines and other facilities in such a condition that permits them to be used at their optimal capacity without interruption.
3. To ensure the availability of the machines, buildings and services required by other sections of the factory for the performance of their functions at optimal return on investment.

EXERCISE

1. Define Operations management. Explain the key concepts of Operations management with a schematic diagram.
2. Distinguish between manufacturing and service operation with example.
3. What is strategic planning? Explain the role of models in strategic planning.
4. Define the term operations management. Briefly explain the strategic role of operations.
5. Write a note on system view of operations.
6. Explain, how the considerations of environtnental assessment and organisational position provide a modeling framework for the strategic planning of operations.
7. Briefly explain how service producers differ from goods producers in important aspects of their operations.
8. State the important objectives of production management.
9. Define the term productive system.
10. Give two examples for the productive systems concerned to service and manufacturing respectively.
11. "Operations strategy"—A key element in corporate strategy. Briefly explain.
12. Explain what do you understand by product-focused systems and process-focused systems.
13. Differentiate between Production Management and Operations Management.
14. Explain the historical evaluation of production function up to 21st century.
15. What are the various decisions and their applications made by operations manager in a POM system?
16. Briefly explain the importance of operations management in the corporate management.
17. Explain the concept of productivity.

REFERENCES

1. Everett, E. Adam, Jr.Ronald J.Ebert, *Production and Operations Management,* Prentice-Hall of India Private Limited, 5th Edition, 1994.
2. R. Pannerselvam, *Production and Operations Management,* Prentice-Hall of India Private Limited, 9th print, 2004.
3. Joseph, G. Monks, *Theory and Problems of Operations Management,* Tata McGraw-Hill Publishing Company Limited, 2nd Edition, 2004.
4. Joseph, G. Monks, *Operations Management,* McGraw-Hill International Edition, 3rd Edition.
5. S. Anil Kumar, N. Suresh, *Production and Operations Management,* New Age International (P) Limited Publishers, 2nd Edition, 2008.

2

OPERATIONS DECISION-MAKING

CHAPTER OUTLINE

2.1 INTRODUCTION

Thousand of business decisions are made everyday. Not all the decisions will make or break the organisation. But each one adds a measure of success or failure to the operations. Hence decision-making essentially involves choosing a particular course of action, after considering the possible alternatives. This chapter examines management as a science and the characteristics of decisions. The use of economic and statical models is discussed along with decision trees.

2.2 MANAGEMENT AS A SCIENCE

Management scientists hold that, education, scientific training and experience can improve a person's ability to make decisions. Scientific decision-making rests upon organized principles of knowledge and depends largely upon the collection of empirical data and analysis of the data in a way that repeatable results will be obtained.

The association of management with the scientific method involves drawing objective conclusions from the facts. Facts come from the analysis of data, which must be gathered, compiled and digested into meaningful form, such as graphs and summary statistics. Computers are helpful in these tasks because they can easily store data and us with the more sophisticated and statistical analysis. But not all variables are quantifiable, so decision-makers must still use some value-based judgments in a decision process.

Thus management as a science is characterised by

- Organised principle of knowledge.

- Use of empirical data.
- Systematic analysis of data.
- Repeatable results.

2.3 CHARACTERISTICS OF DECISIONS

Operations decision range from simple judgments to complex analyses, which also involves judgment. Judgment typically incorporates basic knowledge, experience, and common sense. They enable to blend objectives and sub-objective data to arrive at a choice.

The appropriateness of a given type of analysis depends on

- The significant or long lasting decisions,
- The time availability and the cost of analysis, and
- The degree of complexity of the decision.

The significant or long lasting decisions deserve more considerations than routine ones. Plant investment, which is a long-range decision, may deserve more thorough analysis. *The time availability and the cost of analysis* also influence the amount of analysis. *The degree of complexity of the decision increases when* many variables are involved, variables are highly independent and the data describing the variables are uncertain.

Business decision-makers have always had to work with incomplete and uncertain data. Fig. 2.1 below depicts the information environment of decisions. In some situations a decision-maker has complete information about the decision variables; at the other extremes, no information is available. Operations management decisions are made all along this continuum.

Complete certainty in decision-making requires data on all elements in the population. If such data are not available, large samples lend more certainty than do small ones. Beyond this, subjective information is likely to be better than no data at all.

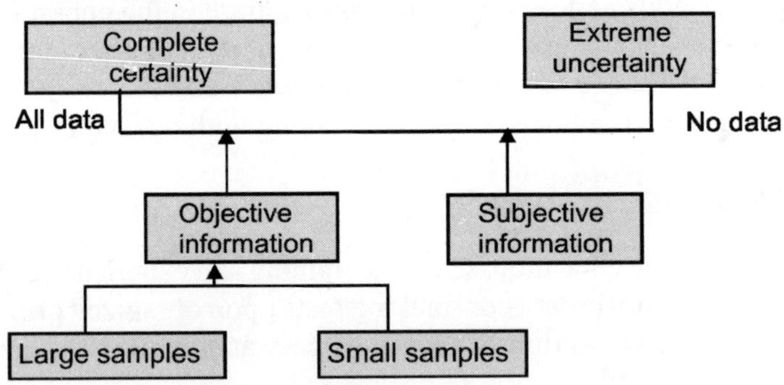

Fig. 2.1 Information continuum

2.4 FRAMEWORK FOR DECISION-MAKING

An analytical and scientific framework for decision implies the following systematic steps

- Defining the problem.
- Establish the decision criteria.
- Formulation of a model.
- Generating alternatives .

- Evaluation of the alternatives.
- Implementation and monitoring.

DEFINING THE PROBLEM

Defining the problem enables to identify the relevant variables and the cause of the problem. Careful definition of the problem is crucial. Finding the root cause of a problem needs some questioning and detective work. If a problem defined is too narrow, relevant variable may be omitted. If it is broader, many tangible aspects may be included which leads to the complex relationships.

ESTABLISH THE DECISION CRITERIA

Establish the decision criterion is important because the criterion reflects the goals and purpose of the work efforts. For many years profits served as a convenient and accepted goal for many organisations based on economic theory. Nowadays organisation will have multiple goals such as employee welfare, high productivity, stability, market share, growth, industrial leadership and other social objectives.

FORMULATION OF A MODEL

Formulation of a model lies at the heart of the scientific decision-making process. Model describes the essence of a problem or relationship by abstracting relevant variables from the real world situation. Models are used to simplify or approximate reality, so the relationships can be expressed in tangible form and studied in isolation.

Modeling a decision situation usually requires both formulating a model and collecting the relevant data to use in the model. Mathematical and statistical models are most useful models for understanding the complex business of the problem. Mathematical models can incorporate factor that cannot readily be visualized. With the aid of computers and simulation techniques, these quantitative models reflexible.

GENERATING ALTERNATIVES

Alternatives are generated by varying the values of the parameters. Mathematical and statistical models are particularly suitable for generating alternatives because they can be easily modified. The model builder can experiment with a model by substituting different values for controllable and uncontrollable variable.

EVALUATION OF THE ALTERNATIVES

Evaluation of the alternatives is relatively objective in an analytical decision process because the criteria for evaluating the alternatives have been precisely defined. The best alternative is the one that most closely satisfies the criteria. Some models like LPP model automatically seek out a maximising or minimising solution. In problems various heuristic and statical techniques can be used to suggest the best course of action.

IMPLEMENTATION AND MONITORING

Implementation and monitoring are essential for completing the managerial action. The best course of action or the solution to a problem determined through a model is implemented in the business world. Other managers have to be convinced of the merit of the solution. Then the follow-up procedures are required to ensure about appropriate action taken. This includes an analysis and evaluation of the solution along with the recommendations for changes or adjustments.

2.5 DECISION METHODOLOGY

The kind and amount of information available helps to determine which analytical methods are most appropriate for modeling a given decision. Figure 2.2 illustrates some useful quantitative methods that are classified according to the amount of certainty that exists with respect to the decision variables and possible outcomes. These analytical techniques often serve as the basis for formulating models, which help to reach operational decisions.

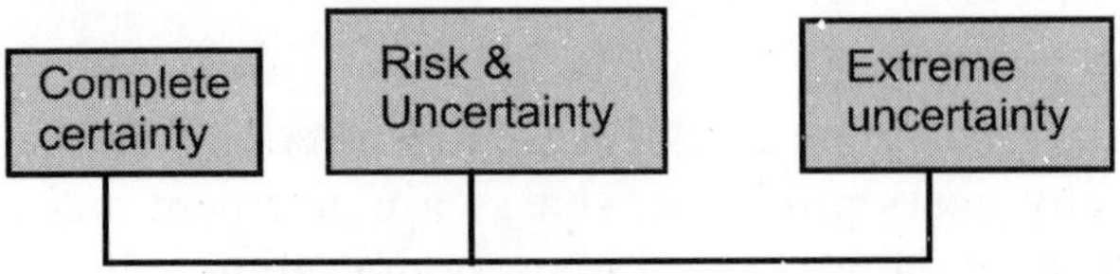

(All information)
Algebra:
Break-even
Benefit/cost
Calculus
Mathematical programming:
Linear
Non-linear
Integer
Dynamic
Goal

(Some information)
Statistical analysis:
- Objective and subjective probabilities
- Estimation and tests of hypothesis
- Bayesian statistics
- Decision theory
- Correlation and regression
- Analysis of variance
- Non-parametric methods

Queuing theory
Simulation
Heuristic methods
Network analysis techniques:
Decision trees
PERT and CPM
Utility theory

(No information)
Game theory
Flip coin

Fig. 2.2 Quantitative methods as a function of degree of certainty

The degree of certainty is classified as complete certainty, risk and uncertainty and extreme uncertainty.

2.5.1 Complete Certainty Methods

Under complete certainty conditions, all relevant information about the decision variables and outcomes is known or assumed to be known. Following are some of the methods used:

- ***Algebra***: This basic mathematical logic is very useful for both certainty and uncertainty analysis. With valid assumptions, algebra provides deterministic solutions such as break-even analysis and benefit cost analysis.
- ***Calculus***: The branch of mathematics provides a useful tool for determining optimal value where functions such as inventory costs, are to be maximised or minimised.
- ***Mathematical programming***: Programming techniques have found extensive applications in making a product mix decisions; minimising transportation costs, planning and scheduling production and other areas.

2.5.2 Risk and Uncertainty Methods

In risk and uncertainty situations, information about the decision variables or the outcomes is probabilistic. Following are some of the useful approaches:

- **Statistical analysis:** Objective and subjective probabilities with the use of probability and probability distribution, Estimation and tests of hypothesis, Bayesian statistics, Decision theory, Correlation and regression technique for forecasting demand and Analysis of variance are some of the techniques used for decision-making.
- **Queuing theory:** The analysis of queues in terms of waiting-time length and mean waiting time is useful in analysing service systems, maintenance activities, and shop floor control activities.
- **Simulation:** Simulation duplicates the essence of an activity. Computer simulations are valuable tools for the analysis of investment outcomes, production processes, scheduling and maintenance activities.
- **Heuristic methods:** Heuristic methods involve set of rules, which facilitate solutions of scheduling, layout and distribution problems when applied in a consistent manner.
- **Network analysis techniques:** Network approaches include decision trees, CPM and PERT methods. They are helpful in identifying alternative course of action and controlling the project activities.
- **Utility theory:** Utility theory or preference theory allows decision-makers to incorporate their own experience and values into a relatively formalized decision structure.

2.5.3 Extreme Uncertainty Methods

Under extreme uncertainty, no information is available to assess the likelihood of alternative outcomes. Following are some of strategies to solve this:

- **Game theory:** Game theory helps decision-makers to choose course of action when there is no information about what conditions will prevail.
- **Coin flip:** Flipping a coin is sometimes used in situation where the decision-makers are wholly indifferent.

2.5.4 Decision-Making Under Uncertainty

No information is available on how likely the various states of nature are under those conditions. Four possible decision criteria are Maximin, Maximax, Laplace, and Minimax regret. These approaches can be defined as follows:

- **Maximin:** Determine the worst possible pay-off for each alternative, and choose the alternative that has the "best worst." The Maximin approach is essentially a pessimistic one because it takes into account only the worst possible outcome for each alternative. The actual outcome may not be as bad as that, but this approach establishes a "guaranteed minimum."
- **Maximax:** Determine the best possible pay-off, and choose the alternative with that pay-off. The Maximax approach is an optimistic, "go for it" strategy; it does not take into account any pay-off other than the best.
- **Laplace:** Determine the average pay-off for each alternative, and choose the alternative with the best average. The Laplace approach treats the states of nature as equally likely.
- **Minimax regret:** Determine the worst regret for each alternative, and choose the alternative with the "best worst." This approach seeks to minimize the difference between the pay-off that is realized and the best pay-off for each state of nature.

ILLUSTRATION 1: *Referring to the pay-off table, determine which alternative would be chosen under each of these strategies:*
(*a*) *Maximin,* (*b*) *Maximax, and* (*c*) *Laplace.*

	Possible future demand in Rs.		
Alternatives	Low	Moderate	High
Small facility	10	10	10
Medium facility	7	12	12
Large facility	(4)	2	16

SOLUTION

(*a*) Using Maximin, the worst pay-offs for the alternatives are:
Small facility: Rs.10 million
Medium facility: 7 million
Large facility: –4 million
Hence, since Rs.10 million is the best, choose to build the small facility using the maximum strategy.

(*b*) Using Maximax, the best pay-offs are:
Small facility: Rs.10 million
Medium facility: 12 million
Large facility: 16 million
The best overall pay-off is the Rs.16 million in the third row. Hence, the Maximax criterion leads to building a large facility.

(*c*) For the Laplace criterion, first find the row totals, and then divide each of those amounts by the number of states of nature (three in this case). Thus, we have:

	Raw total (Rs.Million)	**Raw average (Rs.Million)**
Small facility	30	10.00
Medium facility	31	10.33
Large facility	14	4.67

Because the medium facility has the highest average, it would be chosen under the Laplace criterion.

ILLUSTRATION 2: *Determine which alternative would be chosen using a Minimax regret approach to the capacity-planning programme.*

SOLUTION: The first step in this approach is to prepare a table of opportunity losses, or regrets. To do this, subtract every pay-off in each column from the best pay-off in that column. For instance, in the first column, the best pay-off is 10, so each of the three numbers in that column must be subtracted from 10. Going down the column, the regrets will be 10 – 10 = 0, 10 – 7 = 3, and 10 – (– 4) = 14. In the second column, the best pay-off is 12. Subtracting each pay-off from 12 yields 2, 0, and 10. In the third column, 16 is the best pay-off. The regrets are 6, 4, and 0. These results are summarized in a regret table:

	Regrets (in Rs. million)			
Alternative	Low	Medium	High	Worst
Small facility	0	2	6	6
Medium facility	3	0	4	4
Large facility	14	10	0	14

The second step is to identify the worst regret for each alternative. For the first alternative, the worst is 6; for the second, the worst is 4; and for the third, the worst is 14. The best of these worst regrets would be chosen using Minimax regret. The lowest regret is 4, which is for a medium facility. Hence, that alternative would be chosen.

2.5.5 Decision-Making Under Risk

Between the two extremes of certainty and uncertainty lies the case of risk: The probability of occurrence for each state of nature is known. (Note that because the states are mutually exclusive and collectively exhaustive, these probabilities must add to 1.00.) A widely used approach under such circumstances is the expected monetary value criterion.

The expected value is computed for each alternative, and the one with the highest expected value is selected. The expected value is the sum of the pay-offs for an alternative where each pay-off is weighted by the probability for the relevant state of nature.

ILLUSTRATION 3: *Determine the expected pay-off of each alternative, and choose the alternative that has the best-expected pay-off. Using the expected monetary value criterion, identify the best alternative for the previous pay-off table for these probabilities: low = 0.30, moderate = 0.50, and high = 0.20. Find the expected value of each alternative by multiplying the probability of occurrence.*

	Possible future demand in Rs.		
Alternatives	Low	Moderate	High
Small facility	10	10	10
Medium facility	7	12	12
Large facility	(4)	2	16

SOLUTION: For each state of nature by the pay-off for that state of nature and summing them:

EV_{small} = 0.30 (Rs.10) + 0.50 (Rs.10) + 0.20 (Rs.10) = Rs.10

EV_{medium} = 0.30 (Rs.7) + 0.50 (Rs.12) + 0.20 (Rs.12) = Rs.10.5

EV_{large} = 0.30 (–4) + 0.50 (Rs.2) + 0.20 (Rs.16) = Rs. 3

Hence, choose the medium facility because it has the highest expected value.

ILLUSTRATION 4: *Global Telecom Corp. must choose one of three partnering firms (X Co., Y Co., or Z Co.) with which to develop a personal communicator. The possible states of nature are that future demand may be low, medium, or high. Estimated dollar pay-offs (in net present value terms) for each alternative under each state of nature are shown in the accompanying Table. Which partnering firm should be chosen under the criterion of (a) maximax, (b) Maximin, and (c) Laplace?*

SOLUTION

(*a*) *Maximax:* Choose the alternative that offers the best possible (highest) pay-off. The highest pay-off is Rs.140 million with Z Co. Therefore choose Z Co.

(*b*) *Maximin:* For each alternative, locate the worst possible pay-off. Then choose the best of these "worst" values. The best of the worst is X Co. with a minimum profit of Rs.10 million.

(*c*) *Laplace:* Find the average pay-off for each alternative, and choose the alternative with the best. The highest average is Z Co. [(0 + 20 + 140)/3 = Rs.0.53.3 m]. Choose Z Co.

Pay-off Table

Alternatives	Profit (Rs. million) If Future Demand Is		
	Low	Medium	High
X Co. partner	10	50	70
Y Co. partner	–10	44	120
Z Co. partner	0	20	140

When probability values, $P(X)$, are assigned to the states of nature of a pay-off table, two additional decision criteria can be considered: maximum probability and expected monetary value. The expected monetary value approach utilizes the highest average, or expected value, $E(X)$.

$$E(X) = \Sigma\ [X.P(X)].$$

ILLUSTRATION 5: *For the data in illustration 8, assume probabilities of:*

P (low demand) = 0.3 P(medium demand) = 0.5P (high demand) = 0.2

Which partnering firm should be chosen under the criterion of (a) maximum probability and (b) Expected Monetary Value (EMY)?

SOLUTION

(*a*) *Maximum probability:* Find the most likely state of nature, and choose the best alternative within that state. Most likely is [P(medium demand) = 0.5]. Choose *X* Co., where pay-off is Rs.50 m.

(*b*) *Expected monetary value:* For each alternative, multiply the value of each possible outcome (*X*) by its probability of occurrence, *P* (*X*). Then sum across all outcomes, *i.e.*, *L* [*X*. *P*(*X*)] to get the expected value, E(X), of each alternative. The alternative with the highest expected outcome is designated the expected monetary value, EMV*.

$$E(X\text{ Co.}) = 10(0.3) + 50(0.5) + 70(0.2) = 42$$

$$E(Y\text{ Co.}) = -10(0.3) + 44(0.5) + 120(0.2) = 43$$

$$EMY^* = \text{Rs. } 43 \text{ m}$$

$$E(Z\text{ Co.}) = 0(0.3) + 20(0.5) + 140(0.2) = 38$$

2.6 DECISION SUPPORT SYSTEM

Decision support system (DSS) is computer-based systems designed to aid decision-makers of any stage of the decision process in the development of alternatives and evaluation of possible course of action. Their purpose is to provide the information and analytical support that enables managers to better control and guide the decision process. Emphasis is given for giving useful information and appropriate quantitative models that support the manager's skills. Thus, DSS are a logical extension of the managerial decision processes. This helps the managers to learn better, how to apply data processing and modeling capabilities of computers to the analysis of ill-structured and value based decisions.

2.7 ECONOMIC MODELS

Break-even Analysis is an economic model describing cost-price-volume relationships. It is a complete certainty type of model because costs and revenues are known quantities.

2.7.1 Break-even Analysis

One of the techniques to study the total cost, total revenue and output relationship is known as Break-even Analysis. 'A Break-even Analysis indicates at what level of output, cost and revenue are in equilibrium'. In other words, it determines the level of operations in an enterprise where the undertaking neither gains a profit nor incurs a loss.

NOTATIONS AND TERMINOLOGY AS USED IN BREAK-EVEN ANALYSIS

- **Break-even chart (BEC):** It is a graph showing the variation in total costs at different levels of output (cost line) as well as the variation in the total revenues at various levels of output.
- **Break-even point:** It is that point of activity (sales volume) where total revenues and total expenses are equal. It is point of zero profit, *i.e.* stage of no profit and no loss. BEP can be used to study the impact of variations in volume of sales and cost of production on profits.
- **Angle of incidence:** It is an angle at which total revenue line intersects total cost line. The magnitude, of this angle indicates the level of profit. Larger the angle of incidence, higher will be the profits per unit increase in sales and vice versa.

- ***Margin of safety***: It is excess of budgeted or actual sales over the break-even sales volume *i.e.* margin of safety = (actual sales minus sales at BEP)/actual sales. A high margin of safety would mean that even with a lean period, where sales go down, the company would not come in loss area. A small margin of safety means a small reduction in sale would take company to cross BEP and come in red zone.

CALCULATION OF BEP

Relationship between costs and activity level (AL) is also assumed to be linear. For every elemental cost, actual cost figures at different activity levels are plotted, and by 'least square analysis' a 'line of best fit' is obtained. This would give a fixed cost component and a variable cost component for the elemental cost.

This analysis is carried out for all elemental costs. The total cost function would give total fixed cost and total variable cost for the company. The Break-even Point is that volume where the fixed and variable costs are covered. But no profit exists. Thus at BEP, the total revenues equal to the total costs.

If F – Fixed Costs, which are independent on quantity produced
a – Variable Cost per unit
b – Selling Price per unit
Q – Quantity (Volume of output)

The total costs are given by

$$\text{Total Cost (TC)} = \text{Fixed Cost} + \text{Variable Cost}$$

$$\text{TC} = (F + a \cdot Q)$$

$$\text{Sales Revenue (SR)} = \text{Selling price per unit} \times \text{Quantity}$$

$$\text{SR} = \text{b.Q}$$

The point of Intersection of Total Cost line and the sales revenue is the Break-even Point

i.e. at Break-even Point, Total Cost (TC) = Sales Revenue (SR)

$$F + a \cdot Q = b \cdot Q$$

$$F = Q\,(b - a)$$

$$Q = \frac{F}{(b-a)} \text{ in units} \qquad ...(1)$$

In terms of the number of units sold the break-even point is given by :

$$Q_{\text{BEP}} = \frac{F}{(b-1)} \text{Unit}$$

Profit volume ratio (PVR) is defined as the ratio between Contribution Margin and Sales Revenue.

$$\textit{i.e.}\ \text{Profit Volume Ratio } (f) = \frac{Contribution \cdot Margin}{Sales.\, Revenue}$$

$$= \frac{Sales.\, Revenue - Total \times Variable \times Cost}{Sales.\, Revenue}$$

$$\phi = \frac{(b \cdot Q - a \cdot Q)}{b \cdot Q} = \frac{Q(b-a)}{b \cdot Q} \qquad (2)$$

From Equation 1, $F = Q \cdot (b - a)$, Hence Equation 2 can be written as

$$\phi = \frac{Q \cdot (b-a)}{b \cdot Q} = \frac{F}{b \cdot Q}$$

$$i.e.\ b \cdot Q = \frac{F}{Q}$$

So BEP can also be given by

$$Q_{BEP} = \frac{F}{PV \cdot \text{Ratio}} = \frac{F}{\phi} \qquad (3)$$

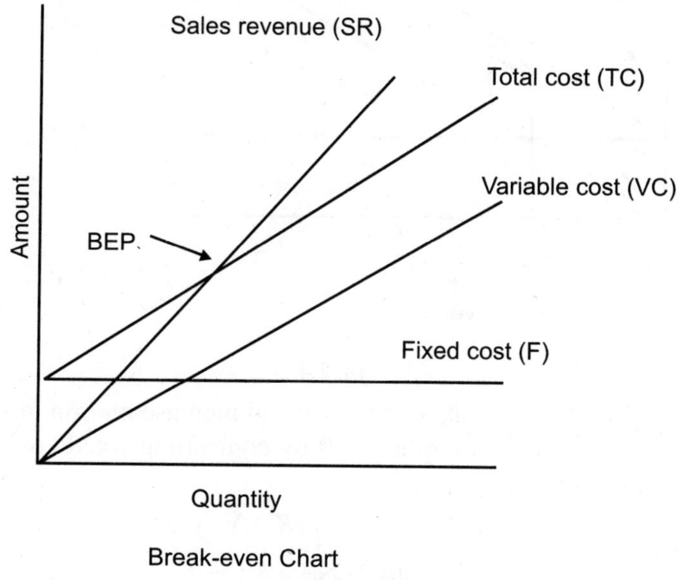

Fig. 2.3

Margin of safety (MOS) is defined as the ratio between Operating Profit and Contribution Margin. It signifies the fractional reduction in the current activity level required to reach the break-even point.

Sales turnover (STO) is defined as ratio between Sales Revenue and the Capital Employed. It represents the number of times capital employed is turned over to reach the sales revenue level that is called **Operating management performance [OMP]**.

IMPROVING OMP

A company interested in improving its OMP will have to improve its operating profit. Following any of the strategies given below or a combination of them can do this:

(*a*) By reducing variable costs

(*b*) By reducing fixed costs

(*c*) By increasing sales price

(*d*) By increasing the activity level.

(*a*) **A reduction in variable costs** will bring down BEP, increase PV ratio and increase margin of safety. To achieve a required Targeted Profit (Z), variable cost would have to be controlled at

$$V=SR-(F+Z)$$

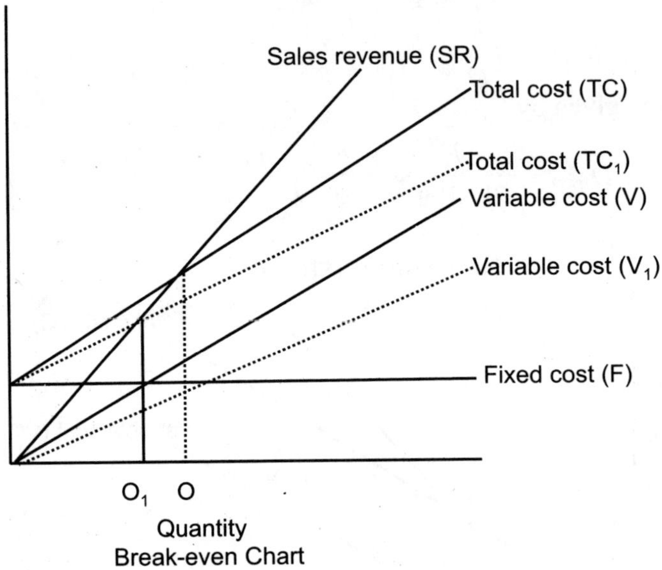

Fig. 2.4

(*b*) **A reductin in fixed costs** will bring down BEP and increase margin of safety. It will have no effect on PV ratio. To achieve a required TP by controlling fixed cost alone, the fixed cost would have to be controlled as

$$F=(SR-V)-Z$$

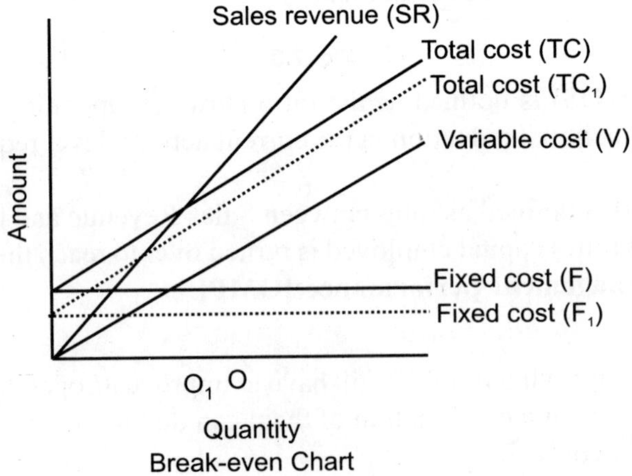

Fig. 2.5

(*c*) **An increase in selling price** will bring BEP down, it will increase PV ratio and it will also increase the margin of safety. To get the targeted profit level the increase required in selling price is given by

$$b' = \frac{(F+Z)}{(b-a)} \times b$$

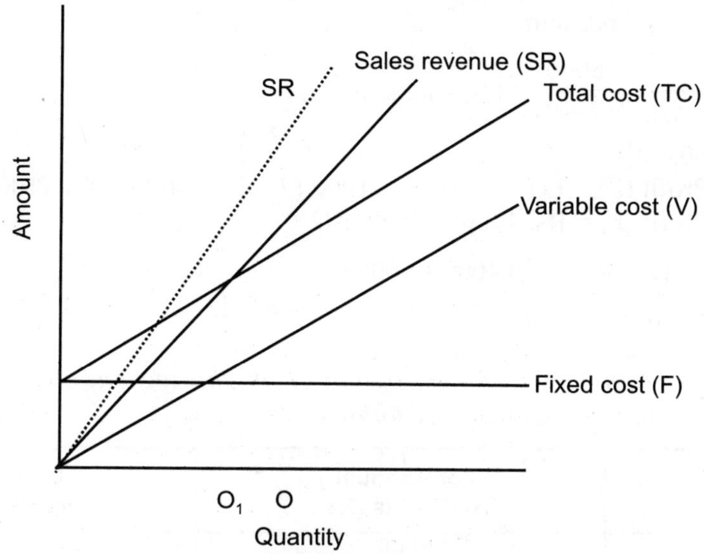

Break-even Chart

Fig. 2.6

(*d*) **An increase in activity level** will of course have no effect on BEP, it will not change PV ratio, but will increase the margin of safety. The new activity level required to achieve the desired TP is given by

$$\text{New SR} = \frac{(F+Z)}{PV\ Ratio} \text{ or } \frac{(F+Z)}{(SR-V)} \times SR$$

If now is the existing activity level, the activity level required in terms of number of units N_{new} to achieve a targeted profit is given by

$$N_{\text{New}} = \frac{(F+Z)}{\text{CM}} \text{ or } \frac{(F+Z)}{(\text{SR}-V)} \times N_{\text{New}}$$

With the help of this analysis, discreet decisions regarding control of variable costs, fixed costs, fixing sales price and activity level can be taken to achieve the desired targeted profit.

ILLUSTRATION 6: *The owner of shop is contemplating adding a new product, which will require additional monthly payment of Rs. 6,000. Variable costs would be Rs. 2.00 per new product, and its selling price is Rs. 7.00 each.*

(*a*) How many new products must be sold in order to break-even?

(*b*) What would the profit (loss) be if 1,000 units were sold in a month?

(*c*) How many units must be sold to realize a profit of Rs.4,000?

SOLUTION

Fixed Cost (F) = Rs. 6,000, Variable Cost (a) = Rs. 2 per unit,
Sales Price (b) = Rs.7 per unit

(*a*) $Q_{\text{BEP}} = \dfrac{F}{(b-a)} = \dfrac{6000}{(7-2)} = 1200$ units/month

(*b*) For $Q = 1000$,
Operating Profit (Z) = $Q\,(b-a) - F = 1000\,(7-2) - 6000$ = Rs. (1000)

(*c*) Operating Profit (Z) = Rs. 4000: solve for Q

$$Q = \frac{(Z+F)}{(b-a)} = \frac{(4000+6000)}{(7-2)} = 2000 \text{ units.}$$

ILLUSTRATION 7: *A manager has the option of purchasing one, two, or three machines. Fixed costs and potential volumes are as follows:*

Number of machines	Total annual fixed costs (Rs.)	Corresponding range of output
1	9600	0 to 300
2	15000	301 to 600
3	20000	601 to 900

Variable cost is Rs.10 per unit, and revenue is Rs.40 per unit.

(a) Determine the break-even point for each range.

(b) If projected annual demand is between 580 and 660 units, how many machines should the manager purchase?

SOLUTION

(*a*) Compute the break-even point for each range using the formula

$$Q_{BEP} = \frac{F}{(b-a)}$$

For one machine $Q_{\text{BEP}} = \dfrac{F}{(b-a)} = \dfrac{9600}{(40-10)} = 320$ units

[Not in range, so there is no BEP]

For two machines $Q_{\text{BEP}} = \dfrac{F}{(b-a)} = \dfrac{15000}{(40-10)} = 500$ units

For three machines $Q_{\text{BEP}} = \dfrac{F}{(b-a)} = \dfrac{20000}{(40-10)} = 666.67$ units (*b*) Comparing the projected range of demand to the two ranges for which a break-even point occurs, we can see that the break-even point is 500, which is in the range 301 to 600. This means that even if demand were at the low end of the range, it would be above the break-even point and thus yield a profit. That is not true of range 601 to 900. At the top end of projected demand, the volume would still be less than the break-even point for that range, so there would be no profit. Hence, the manager should choose two machines.

ILLUSTRATION 8: *For an existing product that sells for SP = Rs.650 per unit, FC = Rs.82,000 and VC = Rs. 240 per unit. (a) What is the BEP? (b) What volume is needed to generate a profit of Rs.10,250?*

SOLUTION

(*a*)

$$Q_{BEP} = \frac{F}{(b-a)} = \frac{82000}{(650-240)} = 200 \text{ units}$$

(*b*) The volume needed for a specific profit can be computed as:

$$Q_{BEP} = \frac{Z+F}{b-a} = \frac{10250+82000}{(650-240)} = 225 \text{ units}$$

Note: For volumes > BEP, all contribution of (Rs.650 – 240 = Rs.410/unit) goes into profit. Thus the additional volume needed is Rs.10,250 ÷ Rs.410/unit = 25 units.

ILLUSTRATION 9: *Process X has fixed costs of Rs. 20,000 per year and variable costs of Rs. 12 per unit, whereas process Y has fixed costs of Rs. 8,000 per year and variable costs of Rs. 22 per unit. At what production quantity (Q) are the total costs of X and Y equal?*

SOLUTION

$$\begin{aligned} X &= Y \\ F_x + V_x \cdot Q &= F_y + V_y \cdot Q \\ \text{Rs. } 20{,}000 + \text{Rs. } 12Q &= \text{Rs. } 8{,}000 + \text{Rs. } 22Q \\ \text{Rs. } 10Q &= \text{Rs. } 12{,}000 \\ Q &= 1{,}200 \text{ units.} \end{aligned}$$

ILLUSTRATION 10: *Cover-the-Globe Paint Co. produces 9,000 paint sprayers per year and obtains Rs. 675, 000 revenue from them. Fixed costs are Rs. 210,000 per year, and total costs are Rs. 354,000 per year. How much does each sprayer contribute to fixed costs and profit?*

SOLUTION

$$\text{Contribution Margin(CM)} = \text{SP} - \text{VC}$$

Where $\text{Sales} \times \text{Price} = \frac{675000}{9000} = \text{Rs. 75 per unit and } VC = \frac{\text{Total Variable Cost}}{\text{Quantity}}$

Where $TVC = \text{Total Cost} - \text{Fixed Cost} = \text{Rs. } 354{,}000 - \text{Rs. } 210{,}000 = \text{Rs. } 144{,}000$

$$= \frac{144000}{9000} = \text{Rs. } 16 \text{ per unit}$$

Therefore, C = Rs. 75 – Rs.16 = Rs. 59/unit

ILLUSTRATION 11: *A firm has annual fixed costs of Rs.3.2 million and variable costs of Rs.7 per unit. It is considering an additional investment of Rs. 800,000, which will increase the fixed costs by Rs. 150,000 per year and will increase the contribution by Rs. 2 per unit. No change is anticipated in the sales volume or the sales price of Rs.15 per unit. What is the break-even quantity if the new investment is made?*

SOLUTION: The Rs. 2 increase in contribution will decrease variable cost to Rs.7 – Rs.2 = Rs. 5 per unit. The addition to fixed cost makes them Rs. 3.2 million + Rs.150,000 = Rs. 3,350,000.

$$Q_{\text{BEP}} = \frac{F}{b-a} = \frac{3350000}{(15-5)} = 335000 \text{ units.}$$

ILLUSTRATION 12: *A producer of air conditioners sells the industrial model for Rs. 175 each. The production costs at volumes of 2,000 and 4,000 units are as shown in Table. The company does not know the fixed cost at zero volume and realizes that some of its costs are "semivariable." Nevertheless, it wishes to prepare a break-even chart and determine the BEP.*

	2,000 units	**4,000 units**
Labour	Rs. 40,000	Rs. 80,000
Materials	90,000	180,000
Overhead	70,000	80,000
Selling and administrative	80,000	90,000
Depreciation and other FC	70,000	70,000
Total	Rs. 350,000	Rs. 500,000

SOLUTION: This is a more realistic situation, because the fixed cost and variable cost are determined from actual production volumes. Plot the total cost at both volumes as seen in Fig. 2.7. The slope of the total cost line ($\Delta Y / \Delta X$) is the estimated variable cost per unit.

$$\text{Variable Cost } (a) = \frac{\text{Change in Cost}}{\text{Change in Units}} = \frac{500000 - 350000}{4000 - 2000} = \text{Rs.75 unit}$$

By subtracting 2,000 units of variable cost from the total cost at 2,000 units, we can evaluate the implied fixed costs as follows:

$$\text{FC} = \text{total cost @ 2,000 volume} - \text{(2,000 units) (variable cost/unit)}$$

$$= \text{Rs. } 350{,}000 - 2{,}000 \text{ units (Rs.75 unit)} = \text{Rs. } 200{,}000.$$

Therefore, $$\text{BEP} = \frac{\text{Fixed Cost}}{\text{Contribution per Unit}} = \frac{2,00,000}{(175-75)} = 1000 \text{ units}$$

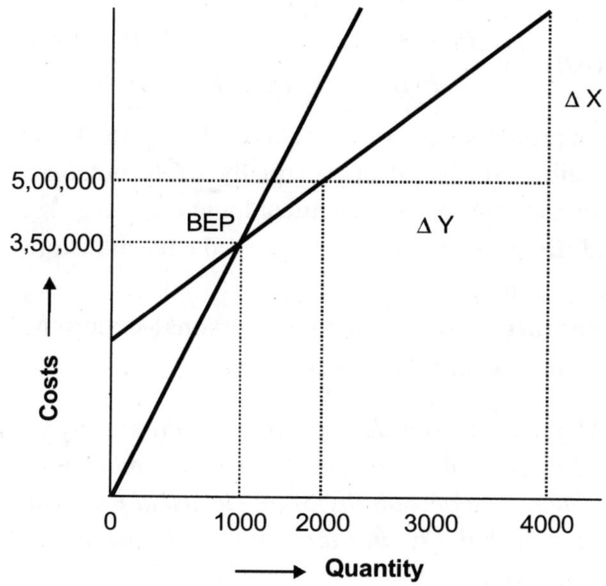

Fig. 2.7

ILLUSTRATION 13: *A professional sports promoter leases a 40,000 seat stadium for soccer games. Tickets sell for an average of Rs.14 each. If fixed costs per season (four games) are Rs.1720,000 and variable costs are Rs. 2 per spectator, what is the break-even point in number of seats filled per game?*

SOLUTION

$$Q_{BEP} = \frac{F}{b-a} = \frac{720000}{(14-2)} = 60000 \text{ seats/season}$$

$$Q_{BEP} = \frac{60000}{4} \frac{\text{seats}}{\text{games}} = 15000 \text{ seats/games}$$

2.8 STATISTICAL MODELS

Most business decisions are made with only limited or incomplete information. Statistical theory can help to control error associated with the amount of data used in the decision process. Decision makers utilize probabilities, which are the most basic measures of uncertainty. Probabilities attach a quantitative value (between 0 and 1) to the occurrence of an event. Events are called independent if the occurrence of one in no way affects any other one. Mutually exclusive events automatically preclude each other, such as classifying an item as good or defective. Following are the rules for applying probabilities.

$$\text{Complement } P(A) = 1 - P(\dddot{A})$$
$$\text{Multiplication } P(A \text{ and } B) = P(A)\,P(B/A) = P(A) \cdot P(B) \text{ (if independent)}$$
$$\text{Addition } P(A \text{ or } B) = P(A) + P(B) \text{ (if mutually exclusive)}$$

$$\text{Bayes' rule P (A/B)} = \frac{P(A \text{ and } B)}{P(B)} = \frac{P(A)\,P(B/A)}{P(A)\,P(B/A) + P(\dddot{A})\,P(B/\dddot{A})}$$

There are three types of probabilities. Namely classical, empirical, and subjective probabilities.

(*a*) **Classical probabilities** are based upon equally likely outcomes that can be calculated prior to an event on the basis of mathematical logic.

(*b*) **Empirical probabilities** are based upon observed data and express the relative frequency of an event in the long run.

(*c*) **Subjective probabilities** are based upon personal experience or judgment and are sometimes used to analyse one-time occurrences.

ILLUSTRATION 14: *Market research data on a company's product has shown that during the first 3 years of use, 10 per cent of the products had a mechanical difficulty and 40 per cent had an electrical problem. The probability of an electrical problem, given some mechanical difficulty, is 0.6. What is the probability that a product will have either a mechanical difficulty or an electrical problem, or both?*

SOLUTION

Probability of Mechanical defect is $P(M) = 0.10$

Probability of Electrical defect is $P(E) = 0.40$

Probability of an electrical problem, with mechanical defect $P(E/\mathrm{M}) = 0.60$

Probability that a product will have either a mechanical difficulty or an electrical problem is given by $P(M \text{ or } E) = P(M) + p(E) - P(M \text{ and } E)$

Where $P(M \text{ and } E) = P(M)\,P(E/M) = (0.10)(0.60) = 0.06$

$P(M \text{ or } E) = 0.10 + 0.40 - 0.06 = 0.44.$

ILLUSTRATION 15: *Three molding machines (X, Y and Z) are used to produce 600 computer terminal keys that are rushed (without inspection) to a customer. The number of good (G) and defective (0) keys from each machine is as shown in Table.*

	Machine X	Machine Y	Machine Z	Row total
Good (G)	45	225	270	540
Not good (G)	5	25	30	60
Total	50	250	300	600

When customer receives the keys, they are randomly selected for installation at the probability that a key selected (*a*) is defective, (*b*) was produced by machine *Z* and good, (*c*) was either produced by machine *Z* or is good? (*d*) Is the probability of selecting a good key independent of the machine from which the key was made?

SOLUTION: Given the data, we can estimate the empirical probabilities as follows:

$$P(G) = \frac{\text{Number of good}}{\text{Total number keys}} = \frac{540}{600} = 0.900$$

$$P(Z) = \frac{\text{Number from Z}}{\text{Total number keys}} = \frac{300}{600} = 0.500$$

$P(G\,l\,Z)$, which is read "Good, given it is from Z," is found as follows:

$$P(G/Z) = \frac{\text{Number from Z that are good}}{\text{Total number from Z}} = \frac{270}{300} = 0.900$$

Now, using the rules of probability we have:

(*a*) $P\,(G)\ =1-P\,(g)=1-0.90=0.10$

(*b*) $P\,(Z \text{ and } G)=P\,(Z)\,P\,(G/Z)=(0.50)(0.90)=0.45$

(*c*) $P\,(Z \text{ or } G)=P\,(Z)+P\,(G)-P\,(Z \text{ and } G)\ =0.50+0.90-0.45=0.95$

(*d*) The P (G) does not depend on whether the key is from machine X, Y, or Z:
$P\,(G)=P\,(G/X)=P\,(G/Y)=P\,(G/Z)=540/600=225/250=0.90$

2.8.1 Equations for Discrete and Continuous Data

Frequency data that are grouped into classes and used to express probabilities are either discrete or continuous. Discrete data stem from countable populations and are often expressed in terms of proportions (p's). Continuous data are obtained from measurable populations and are often classified as variables data (designated x). Discrete probabilities-result from summations (Σ) of individual event probabilities, whereas continuous probabilities are obtained from an integration $\left(\int\right)$ of the area under a continuous probability function. The distinction between discrete and continuous distributions is important because it affects the sample sizes and the risks of error associated with work sampling, quality control, and other productive activities.

Following table give the Summary of the statistical equations used for computing measures of central value and dispersion for populations, samples, and sampling distributions.

	Discrete (countable: attributes data)	**Continuous (measurable: variables data)**
Population		
Central value	Proportion π	Mean μ
Standard deviation	$\delta = \sqrt{\pi(1-\pi)}$	$\delta = \sqrt{\frac{\sum (X-\bar{X})^2}{N}}$
Sample		
Central value	Proportion p	Mean $\bar{X}$

contd.

Standard deviation	$S=\sqrt{pq}$	$S=\sqrt{\dfrac{\sum(X-\bar{X})^2}{n-1}}$
	Where q = 1 – p	
Sampling distribution		
Central value	Average proportion $\bar{p}$	Mean of Mean $\bar{X}$
Standard error	$S_p=\sqrt{\dfrac{pq}{n}}$	$S_X=\dfrac{S}{\sqrt{n}}$

ILLUSTRATION 16: *In 400 observations of a computer operator, an analyst found him idle 32 times. Find (a) the sample proportion and (b) the standard error of proportion.*

SOLUTION

(*a*) $$\bar{P} = \frac{\text{no. idle}}{\text{total no.}} = \frac{32}{400} = 0.08$$

(*b*) $$S_p = \sqrt{\frac{pq}{n}} = \sqrt{\frac{(0.08)(0.92)}{400}} = 0.014.$$

ILLUSTRATION 17: *In a study to find the time to service customers, a bank teller worked 60 minutes and served 36 customers. A record of the individual service times showed* $\Sigma(X-X)^2$ *= (0.79 minutes)*^{2}*. Find (a) the sample mean time and (b) the standard error of the mean.*

(*a*) $$\text{Mean } \bar{X} = \frac{60}{36} = 1.67 \text{ min/customer}$$

(*b*) $$S_X = \frac{S}{\sqrt{n}} \text{ where } S = \sqrt{\frac{\sum(X-\bar{X})^2}{n-1}} = \sqrt{\frac{79}{36-1}} = 0.15 \text{ min}$$

Therefore, $$S_X = \frac{S}{\sqrt{n}} = \frac{0.15}{\sqrt{36}} = 0.025 \text{ min.}$$

2.9 DECISION TREE

A decision tree is a schematic representation of the alternatives available to a decision maker and their possible consequences. The term gets its name from the tree like appearance of the diagram (see Figure 2.8 below). Although tree diagrams can be used in place of a pay-off table, they are particularly useful for analyzing situations that involve sequential decisions.

A decision tree is composed of a number of nodes that have branches emanating from them (see Figure 2.8 below). Square nodes denote decision points, and circular nodes denote chance events. Read the tree from left to right. Branches leaving square nodes represent alternatives; branches leaving circular nodes represent chance events (*i.e.*, the possible states of nature).

After the tree has been drawn, it is analyzed from right to left; that is, starting with the last decision that might be made. For each decision, choose the alternative that will yield the greatest return (or the lowest cost). If chance events follow a decision, choose the alternative that has the highest expected monetary value (or lowest expected cost).

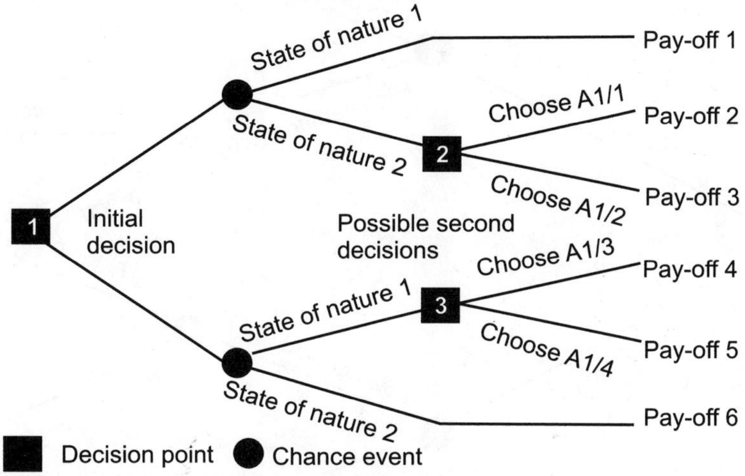

Fig. 2.8 A schematic representation of the available alternatives and their possible consequences

ILLUSTRATION 18: *A manager must decide on the size of a video arcade to construct. The manager has narrowed the choices to two: large or small. Information has been collected on pay-offs, and a decision tree has been constructed. Analyze the decision tree and determine which initial alternative (build small or build large) should be chosen in order to maximize expected monetary value.*

SOLUTION: Analyze the decisions from right to left:

1. Determine which alternative would be selected for each possible second decision. For a small facility with high demand, there are three choices: do nothing, work overtime, and expand. Because expand has the highest payoff, you would choose it. Indicate this by placing a double slash through each of the other alternatives. Similarly, for a large facility with low demand, there are two choices: do nothing and reduce prices. You would choose reduce prices because it has the higher expected value, so a double slash is placed on the other branch.
2. Determine the product of the chance probabilities and their respective pay-offs for the remaining branches:

   Build small

   Low demand 0.4 (Rs.40) = Rs.16: High demand 0.6(Rs. 55) = 33

   Build large

   Low demand 0.4 (Rs.50) = 20: High demand 0.6 (Rs.70) = 42
3. Determine the expected value of each initial alternative:

   Build small Rs. 16 + Rs. 33 = Rs. 49

   Build large Rs. 20 + Rs. 42 = Rs. 62

Hence, the choice should be to build the large facility because it has a larger expected value than the small facility.

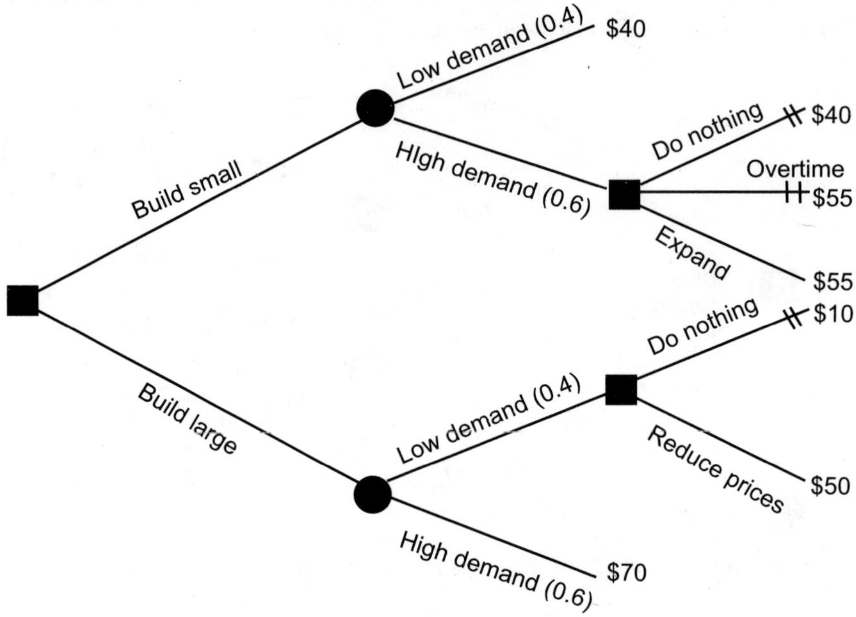

Fig. 2.9 Decision tree diagram

ILLUSTRATION 19: *A manufacturer of small power tools is faced with foreign competition, which necessitates that it either modify (automate) its existing product or abandon it and market a new product. Regardless of which course of action it follows, it will have the opportunity to drop or raise prices if it experiences a low initial demand.*

Pay-off and probability values associated with the alternative courses of action are shown in Fig. 2.10. Analyze the decision tree, and determine which course of action should be chosen to maximize the expected monetary value. (Assume monetary amounts are present-value profits.)

SOLUTION: Analyze the tree from right to left by calculating the expected values for all possible courses of action and choosing the branch with the highest expected value. Begin with the top (modify product) branch.

At chance event 2

Drop price branch: $E(X)$ = Rs. 20,000(0.2) + Rs.150,000(0.8) = Rs.124,000

Raise price branch: $E(X)$ = Rs. 40,000(0.9) + Rs. 200,000(0.1) = Rs.56,000

Therefore, choose to drop price and use Rs.124,000 as the value of this branch at Decision 2.

Note: The Rs.124,000 is an expected monetary value (EMV) and can be entered above the square box under Decision 2. Place slash marks through the other (non-usable) alternative.

At chance event 1

If low demand: Rs. 124, 000 (0.3) = Rs. 37,200

If high demand: 400,000 (0.7) = Rs. 280, 000

E (*X*) = Rs. 317, 200

Therefore, use Rs. 317,200 as the value of this branch at Decision 1. Similarly, for the bottom (new product) branch, the values are Rs. 86,000 at Decision 2 and [Rs. 86,000 (0.5) + Rs. 600,000 (0.5)] Rs. 343,000 at Decision 1. The new product branch thus has a higher expected value and is selected as the best course of action under the expected value criteria.

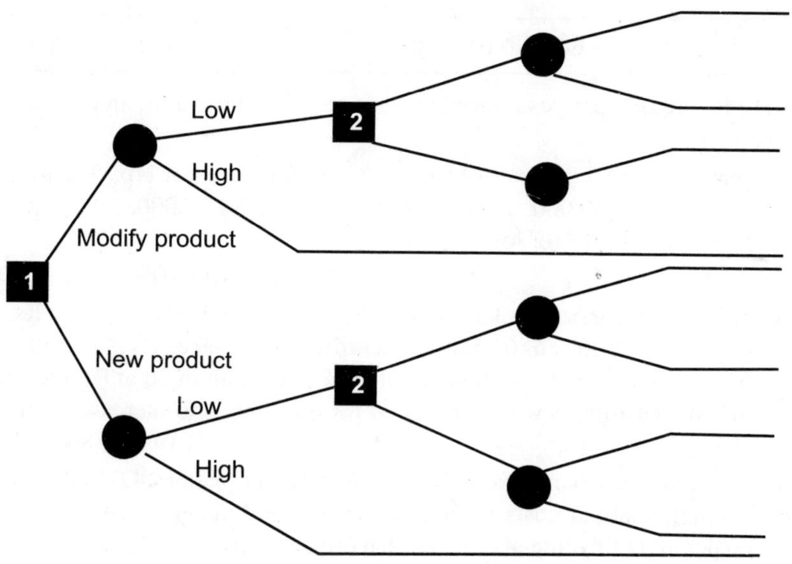

Fig. 2.10 Decision tree diagram

EXERCISE

1. List the steps in a systematic decision-making process.
2. Identify some major advantages of using models.
3. What types of models are most useful for operations management decision-making?
4. How do the characteristics of the decision situation affect the choice of a technique to use in decision analysis?
5. What factors contribute most to the complexity of a decision situation?
6. What is break-even analysis?
7. What is contribution?
8. What is a decision tree?
9. What kinds of decision situations are particularly well suited to analysis by the use of decision analysis?

10. Distinguish between (*a*) classical, (*b*) empirical, and (*c*) subjective probabilities.
11. Explain the two concepts underlying statistical inference of (*a*) sampling distribution and (*b*) the central limit theorem.
12. What is the difference between the standard error of proportion and standard error of mean?
13. Ten observations taken of the time required to assemble a sofa frame in a furniture plant were as shown below (min). Find the (*a*) mean time, (*b*) standard deviation, and (*c*) standard error of the mean.

Observation	4.7	4.2	5.1	4.8	5.5	5.4	5.8	4.8	5.0	4.7	50.0
$(X-X)$	– 0.3	– 0.8	0.1	–0.2	0.5	0.4	0.8	– 0.2	0.0	–0.3	
$(X-X)^2$	0.09	0.64	0.01	0.04	0.25	0.16	0.64	0.04	0.00	0.09	1.96

14. Fixed costs are Rs. 40,000 per year, variable costs are Rs. 50 per unit, and the selling price is Rs. 90 each. Find the BEP. **[Ans.** 1,000 units]
15. Florida Citrus produced 40,000 boxes of fruit that sold for Rs. 3 per box. The total variable costs for the 40,000 boxes were Rs. 60,000, and the fixed costs were Rs.75,000. (*a*) What was the break-even quantity? (*b*) How much profit (or loss) resulted?
[Ans. (*a*) 50,000 boxes and (*b*) Rs.15, 000 loss]
16. A travel agency has an excursion package that sells for Rs. 125. Fixed costs are Rs. 80,000; and at the present volume of 1,000 customers, variable costs are Rs. 25,000 and profits are Rs. 20,000. (*a*) What is the break-even point volume? (*b*) Assuming that fixed costs remain constant, how many additional customers will be required for the agency to increase profit by Rs.1000?
[Ans. (*a*) 800 units (*b*) 10 customers]
17. Last year, Dever Furniture Co. produced 200 maple dressers (pattern 427) that sold for Rs. 210 each. The company included labour costs of Rs. 42 per unit and material costs of Rs.18 per unit, and it allocated Rs. 80 per unit of overhead costs to each dresser. Cost records reveal that overhead costs are 60 per cent fixed and 40 per cent variable. What was the total annual contribution from pattern 427?
[Ans. Rs.118 per unit, or Rs. 23, 600 total]
18. Given the pay-off table below showing the profit (present value Rs.in lakhs), a firm might expect in a foreign country for three alternative factory investments (X, Y, and Z) under different levels of inflation. Economists have assigned probabilities of 0.2, 0.3, 0.4, and 0.1 to the possible inflation levels A, B, C and D, respectively. Find the preferred investment alternative using criteria of (*a*) Maximax, (*b*) Maximin, (*c*) Laplace, (*d*) Maximum probability, and (*e*) Expected monetary value. Finally, (*f*) use your "judgment."

		State of nature: Amount of inflation		
	A = 2%	B = 5%	C =10%	D =15%
Build factory X	10	30	50	120
Build factory Y	40	50	60	70
Lease plant Z	10	40	80	10

19. Frozen Pizza Co. is considering whether it should allocate funds for research on an instant freeze-dry process for home use. If the research is successful (and the R&D manager feels there is a 75 per cent chance it will be), the firm could market the product at a Rs.4 million profit. However, if the research

is unsuccessful, the, firm will incur a Rs.6 million loss. What is the expected monetary value (EMV) of proceeding with the research? **[Ans.** Rs.1.5 million]

20. The operations manager of a large airport is concerned with the problem of having adequate personnel to offer individual assistance to handicapped passengers during rush hours. Data were collected on the number of requests for assistance during 20 randomly selected rush hours and revealed the information shown in Table.

Hour no.	1	2	3	4	5	6	7	8	9	10
No. of requests	40	42	42	30	38	48	42	44	37	38
Hour no.	11	12	13	14	15	16	17	18	19	20
No. of requests	49	47	34	57	42	52	56	44	50	48

Determine (*a*) Mean, (*b*) Standard Deviation, and (*c*) Standard Error of the mean.

Ans. (*a*) 44 requests per hour (*b*) 7 requests per hour (*c*) 1.57

REFERENCES

1. Joseph, G. Monks, *Theory and Problems of Operations Management,* Tata McGraw-Hill Publishing Company Limited, 2nd Edition, 2004.
2. Joseph, G. Monks, *Operations Management,* McGraw-Hill International Edition, 3rd Edition.
3. S.Anil Kumar, N. Suresh, *Production and Operations Management,* New Age International (P) Limited Publishers, 2nd Edition, 2008.

3

SYSTEMS DESIGN AND CAPACITY

CHAPTER OUTLINE

3.1 INTRODUCTION

Before products can flow into a market, someone must design and invest in the facilities and organisation to produce them. This chapter concerns the planning of the systems needed to produce goods and services. Capacity Planning for manufacturing and service systems are different. Both must be designed with capacity limitations in mind. The approaches for long-term and short-term capacity planning will help the managers to make best use of resources.

3.2 MANUFACTURING AND SERVICE SYSTEMS

Manufacturing and service systems are arrangements of facilities, equipment, and people to produce goods and services under controlled conditions.

Manufacturing systems produce standardized products in large volumes. This plant and machinery have a finite capacity and contribute fixed costs that must be borne by the products produced. Variable costs are added as labour is employed to combine or process the raw materials and other components. Value addition will takes place during the production process for the product. The cost of output relative to the cost of input can be measured, as the actual cost is known *i.e.* productivity is measurable quantity.

Service systems present more uncertainty with respect to both capacity and costs. Services are produced and consumed in the presence of the customer and there is little or no opportunity to store value, as in a finished goods inventory. As a result capacity of service systems like hospitals, restaurants and many other services must be sufficiently flexible to accommodate a highly variable demand. In addition, many services such as legal and medical involves professional or intellectual services judgments that are not easily standardized. This makes more difficult to accumulate costs and measure the productivity of the services.

3.3 DESIGN AND SYSTEMS CAPACITY

Production systems design involves planning for the inputs, transformation activities, and outputs of a production operation. Design plays a major role because they entail significant investment of funds and establish cost and productivity patterns that continue in future.

The capacity of the manufacturing unit can be expressed in number of units of output per period. In some situations measuring capacity is more complicated when they manufacture multiple products. In such situations, the capacity is expressed as man-hours or machine hours. The relationship between capacity and output is shown in the Figure 3.1.

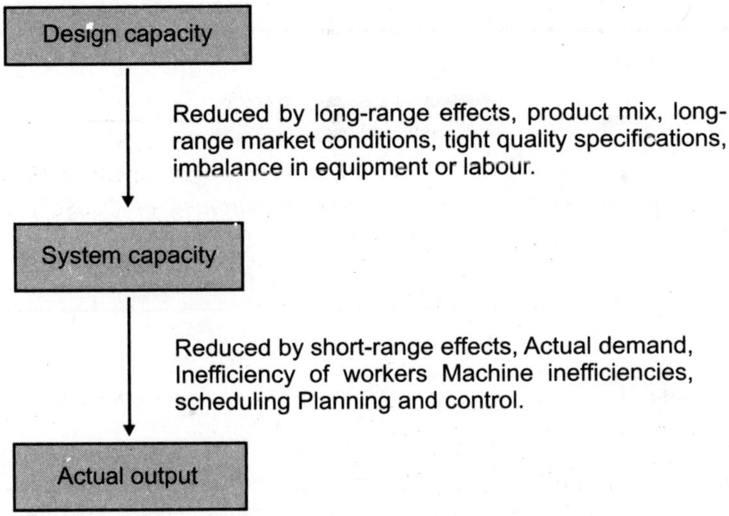

Fig. 3.1 Capacity and output relationship

DESIGN CAPACITY

Designed capacity of a facility is the planned or engineered rate of output of goods or services under normal or full scale operating conditions. For example, the designed capacity of the cement plant is 100 TPD (Tonnes per day). Capacity of the sugar factory is 150 tonnes of sugarcane crushing per day. The uncertainty of future demand is one of the most perplexing problems faced by new facility planners.

Organisation does not plan for enough regular capacity to satisfy all their immediate demands. Design for a minimum demand would result in high utilisation of facilities but results in inferior service and dissatisfaction of customers because of inadequate capacity. The design capacity should reflect management's strategy for meeting the demand. The best approach is to plan for some in-between level of capacity.

System/effective capacity: System capacity is the maximum output of the specific product or product mix the system of workers and machines is capable of producing as an integrated whole. System capacity is less than design capacity or at the most equal it because of the limitation of product mix, quality specification, and breakdowns. The actual is even less because of many factors affecting the output such as actual demand, downtime due to machine/equipment failure, unauthorized absenteeism.

The system capacity is less than design capacity because of long-range uncontrollable factors. The actual output is still reduced because of short-term effects such as breakdown of equipment, inefficiency of labour. The system efficiency is expressed as ratio of actual measured output to the system capacity.

These different measures of capacity are useful in defining two measures of system effectiveness: efficiency and utilization. *Efficiency* is the ratio of actual output to effective capacity. *Utilization* is the ratio of actual output to design capacity.

$$\text{Efficiency} = \frac{\text{Actual output}}{\text{Effective capacity}}$$

$$\text{Utilization} = \frac{\text{Actual output}}{\text{Design capacity}}$$

It is common for managers to focus exclusively on efficiency, but in many instances, this emphasis can be misleading. This happens when effective capacity is low compared with design capacity. In those cases, high efficiency would seem to indicate effective use of resources when it does not.

3.4 CAPACITY PLANNING

Design of the production system involves planning for the inputs, conversion process and outputs of production operation. The effective management of capacity is the most important responsibility of production management. The objective of capacity management *(i.e.* planning and control of capacity) is to match the level of operations to the level of demand.

Capacity planning is to be carried out keeping in mind future growth and expansion plans, market trends, sales forecasting, etc. It is a simple task to plan the capacity in case of stable demand. But in practice the demand will be seldom stable. The fluctuation of demand creates problems regarding the procurement of resources to meet the customer demand. Capacity decisions are strategic in nature. Capacity is the rate of productive capability of a facility. Capacity is usually expressed as volume of output per period of time.

Production managers are more concerned about the capacity for the following reasons:

- Sufficient capacity is required to meet the customers demand in time.
- Capacity affects the cost efficiency of operations.
- Capacity affects the scheduling system.
- Capacity creation requires an investment.

Capacity planning is the first step when an organisation decides to produce more or new products.

3.5 PROCESS OF CAPACITY PLANNING

Capacity planning is concerned with defining the long-term and the short-term capacity needs of an organisation and determining how those needs will be satisfied. Capacity planning decisions are taken based upon the consumer demand and this is merged with the human, material and financial resources of the organisation.

Capacity requirements can be evaluated from two perspectives—long-term capacity strategies and short-term capacity strategies.

1. **Long-term capacity strategies:** Long-term capacity requirements are more difficult to determine because the future demand and technology are uncertain. Forecasting for five or ten years

into the future is more risky and difficult. Even sometimes company's today's products may not be existing in the future. Long-range capacity requirements are dependent on marketing plans, product development and life-cycle of the product. Long-term capacity planning is concerned with accommodating major changes that affect overall level of the output in long-term. Marketing environmental assessment and implementing the long-term capacity plans in a systematic manner are the major responsibilities of management. Following parameters will affect long-range capacity decisions.

- **Multiple products**: Company's produce more than one product using the same facilities in order to increase the profit. The manufacturing of multiple products will reduce the risk of failure. Having more than on product helps the capacity planners to do a better job. Because products are in different stages of their life cycles, it is easy to schedule them to get maximum capacity utilisation.
- **Phasing in capacity:** In high technology industries, and in industries where technology developments are very fast, the rate of obsolescence is high. The products should be brought into the market quickly. The time to construct the facilities will be long and there is no much time, as the products should be introduced into the market quickly. Here the solution is phase in capacity on modular basis. Some commitment is made for building funds and men towards facilities over a period of 3-5 years. This is an effective way of capitalizing on technological breakthrough.
- **Phasing out capacity:** The outdated manufacturing facilities cause excessive plant closures and down time. The impact of closures is not limited to only fixed costs of plant and machinery. Thus, the phasing out here is done with humanistic way without affecting the community. The phasing out options makes alternative arrangements for men like shifting them to other jobs or to other locations, compensating the employees, etc.

2. **Short-term capacity strategies:** Managers often use forecasts of product demand to estimate the short-term workload the facility must handle. Managers looking ahead up to 12 months, anticipate output requirements for different products, and services. Managers then compare requirements with existing capacity and then take decisions as to when the capacity adjustments are needed.

For short-term periods of up to one year, fundamental capacity is fixed. Major facilities will not be changed. Many short-term adjustments for increasing or decreasing capacity are possible. The adjustments to be required depend upon the conversion process like whether it is capital intensive or labour intensive or whether product can be stored as inventory.

Capital-intensive processes depend on physical facilities, plant and equipment. Short-term capacity can be modified by operating these facilities more or less intensively than normal. In labour intensive processes short-term capacity can be changed by laying off or hiring people or by giving overtime to workers. The strategies for changing capacity also depend upon how long the product can be stored as inventory.

The short-term capacity strategies are:

1. **Inventories:** Stock finished goods during slack periods to meet the demand during peak period.
2. **Backlog:** During peak periods, the willing customers are requested to wait and their orders are fulfilled after a peak demand period.
3. **Employment level (hiring or firing):** Hire additional employees during peak demand period and layoff employees as demand decreases.

4. **Employee training:** Develop multi skilled employees through training so that they can be rotated among different jobs. The multi skilling helps as an alternative to hiring employees.
5. **Subcontracting:** During peak periods, hire the capacity of other firms temporarily to make the component parts or products.
6. **Process design:** Change job contents by redesigning the job.

3.6 IMPORTANCE OF CAPACITY DECISIONS

1. Capacity decisions have a real impact on the ability of the organisation to meet future demands for products and services; capacity essentially limits the rate of output possible. Having capacity to satisfy demand can allow a company to take advantage of tremendous opportunities.
2. Capacity decisions affect operating costs. Ideally, capacity and demand requirements will be matched, which will tend to minimize operating costs. In practice, this is not always achieved because actual demand either differs from expected demand or tends to vary (*e.g.,* cyclically). In such cases, a decision might be made to attempt to balance the costs of over and under capacity.
3. Capacity is usually a major determinant of initial cost. Typically, the greater the capacity of a productive unit, the greater its cost. This does not necessarily imply a one for-one relationship; larger units tend to cost *proportionately* less than smaller units.
4. Capacity decisions often involve long-term commitment of resources and the fact that, once they are implemented, it may be difficult or impossible to modify those decisions without incurring major costs.
5. Capacity decisions can affect competitiveness. If a firm has excess capacity, or can quickly add capacity, that fact may serve as a barrier to entry by other firms. Then too, capacity can affect *delivery speed,* which can be a competitive advantage.
6. Capacity affects the ease of management; having appropriate capacity makes management easier than when capacity is mismatched.

ILLUSTRATION 1: *Given the information below, compute the efficiency and the utilization of the vehicle repair*

Department: Design capacity = 50 trucks per day
Effective capacity = 40 trucks per day
Actual output = 36 trucks per day

SOLUTION

$$\text{Efficiency} = \frac{\text{Actual output}}{\text{Effective capacity}} = \frac{36 \text{ trucks per day}}{40 \text{ trucks per day}} = 90\%$$

$$\text{Utilisation} = \frac{\text{Actual output}}{\text{Design capacity}} = \frac{36 \text{ trucks per day}}{50 \text{ trucks per day}} = 72\%$$

ILLUSTRATION 2: *The design capacity for engine repair in our company is 80 trucks per day. The effective capacity is 40 engines per day and the actual output is 36 engines per day. Calculate the utilization and efficiency of the operation. If the efficiency for next month is expected to be 82%, what is the expected output?*

SOLUTION

$$\text{Utilization} = \frac{\text{Actual output}}{\text{Design capacity}} = \frac{36}{40} = 45\%$$

$$\text{Efficiency} = \frac{\text{Actual output}}{\text{Effective capacity}} = \frac{36}{40} = 90\%$$

$$\text{Expected output} = (\text{Effective capacity})(\text{Efficiency})$$
$$= (40)(0.82) = 32.8 \text{ engines per day}$$

ILLUSTRATION 3: *Given: F = Fixed Cost = Rs. 1000, V = Variable cost = Rs. 2 per unit and P = Selling price = Rs. 4 per unit, Find the break-even point in Rs. and in units. Develop the break-even chart.*

SOLUTION

$$\text{Break-even point(\$)} = \text{BEP(\$)} = \frac{F}{1-\dfrac{V}{P}} = \frac{1000}{1-\dfrac{2}{4}} = \frac{1000}{0.5} = \$2{,}000$$

$$\text{Break-even point}(x) = \text{BEP}(x) = \frac{F}{P-V} = \frac{1000}{4-2} = 500$$

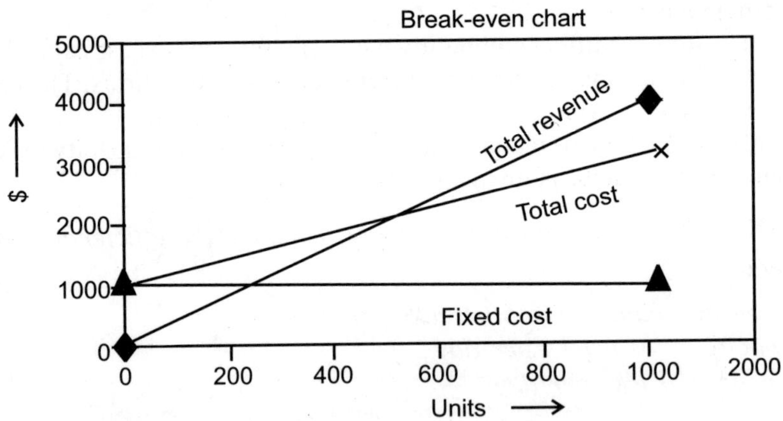

Fig. 3.2

ILLUSTRATION 4: *Jack's Grocery is manufacturing a "store brand" item that has a variable cost of Rs. 0.75 per unit and a selling price of Rs. 1.25 per unit. Fixed costs are Rs. 12,000. Current volume is 50,000 units. The Grocery can substantially improve the product quality by adding a new piece of equipment at an additional fixed cost of Rs. 5,000. Variable cost would increase to Rs. 1.00, but their volume should increase to 70,000 units due to the higher quality product. Should the company buy the new equipment? What are the break-even points (Rs. and units) for the two processes? Develop a break-even chart.*

SOLUTION

Profit = $TR - TC$

Option A: Current Equipment
BEP Sales in value (Rs.)
BEP Sales in Quantity (Units)

Option B: Adding New Equipment
BEP Sales in value (Rs.)
BEP Sales in Quantity (Units)
Profit = 50000 * (1.25 – 0.75) –12000 = Rs.13000.
Option B: Add equipment:
Profit = 70000 * (1.25 – 1.00) – 17000 = Rs.500.

Therefore, the company should continue as is with the present equipment as this returns a higher profit.

Using current equipment:

$$\text{BEP(sales is value)} = \frac{F}{1-\frac{V}{P}} = \frac{12,000}{1-\frac{0.75}{1.25}} = \frac{12,000}{1-0.60} = \frac{12,000}{0.40} = \text{Rs. } 30,000$$

$$\text{BEP(is quality)} = \frac{F}{P-V} = \frac{12,000}{1.25-0.75} = 24,000 \text{ units}$$

Adding a new equipment:

$$\text{BEP (sales is value)} = \frac{F}{1-\frac{V}{P}} = \frac{17,000}{1-\frac{1.00}{1.25}} = \frac{17,000}{1-0.80} = \frac{17,000}{0.2} = \text{Rs. } 85,000.$$

$$\text{BEP(is quality)} = \frac{F}{P-V} = \frac{17,000}{1.25-1.00} = \frac{17,000}{0.25} = 68,000 \text{ units}$$

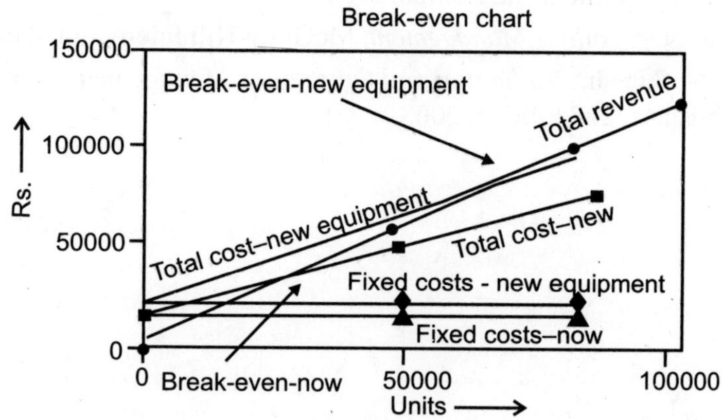

Fig. 3.3

EXERCISE

1. What is meant by 'phasing in' capacity?
2. Distinguish between design capacity and system capacity.
3. How the following organizations adjust to the daily fluctuations in demand?
   (*a*) Airlines, (*b*) Restaurants, (*c*) Dentists.
4. A manufacturer of TV watches uses three TRS7 electronic chips in each TV watches produced. Demand estimates for the number of TV watches that could be sold next year are shown

Demand X	20000	40000	50000
P (X)	0.30	0.50	0.20

   (*a*) Assuming the firm decides to produce on an expected value basis, how many TRS7 chips should they plan to produce for next year's sales?
   (*b*) What capacity is required to meet 150 percent of expected demand?
5. The individual component capacities (in units per day) for an assembly line that consists of five activities are as shown in the accompanying diagram.
   (*a*) What is the system capacity?
   (*b*) What is the efficiency of the system?
6. An automatic drive-in teller at American National Bank has the capacity of handling 2,000 entries per regular banking day (according to the firm that sold it to the bank). However, because of limitations imposed by automobile access, the teller is available only 60 per cent of the time. It is actually being used for about 800 entries per day. What is the system efficiency?

REFERENCES

1. Joseph, G. Monks, *Theory and Problems of Operations Management*, Tata McGraw-Hill Publishing Company Limited, 2nd Edition, 2004.
2. Joseph, G. Monks, *Operations Management,* McGraw-Hill International Edition, 3rd Edition.
3. S. Anil Kumar, N. Suresh, *Production and Operations Management,* New Age International (P) Limited Publishers, 2nd Edition, 2008.

4

FACILITY LOCATION AND LAYOUT

CHAPTER OUTLINE

4.1 INTRODUCTION AND MEANING

Plant location or the facilities location problem is an important strategic level decision-making for an organisation. One of the key features of a conversion process (manufacturing system) is the efficiency with which the products (services) are transferred to the customers. This fact will include the determination of where to place the plant or facility.

The selection of location is a key-decision as large investment is made in building plant and machinery. It is not advisable or not possible to change the location very often. So an improper location of plant may lead to waste of all the investments made in building and machinery, equipment.

Before a location for a plant is selected, long range forecasts should be made anticipating future needs of the company. The plant location should be based on the company's expansion plan and policy, diversification plan for the products, changing market conditions, the changing sources of raw materials and many other factors that influence the choice of the location decision. The purpose of the location study is to find an optimum location one that will result in the greatest advantage to the organization.

4.2 NEED FOR SELECTING A SUITABLE LOCATION

The need for selecting a suitable location arises because of three situations.

I. When starting a new organisation, *i.e.*, location choice for the first time.

II. In case of existing organisation.

III. In case of Global Location.

I. In Case of Location Choice for the First Time or New Organisations

Cost economies are always important while selecting a location for the first time, but should keep in mind the cost of long-term business/organisational objectives. The following are the factors to be considered while selecting the location for the new organisations:

1. **Identification of region:** The organisational objectives along with the various long-term considerations about marketing, technology, internal organisational strengths and weaknesses, region-specific resources and business environment, legal-governmental environment, social environment and geographical environment suggest a suitable region for locating the operations facility.

2. **Choice of a site within a region:** Once the suitable region is identified, the next step is choosing the best site from an available set. Choice of a site is less dependent on the organisation's long-term strategies. Evaluation of alternative sites for their tangible and intangible costs will resolve facilities-location problem.

The problem of location of a site within the region can be approached with the following cost-oriented non-interactive model, *i.e.*, dimensional analysis.

3. **Dimensional analysis:** If all the costs were tangible and quantifiable, the comparison and selection of a site is easy. The location with the least cost is selected. In most of the cases intangible costs which are expressed in relative terms than in absolute terms. Their relative merits and demerits of sites can also be compared easily. Since both tangible and intangible costs need to be considered for a selection of a site, dimensional analysis is used.

Dimensional analysis consists in computing the relative merits (cost ratio) for each of the cost items for two alternative sites. For each of the ratios an appropriate weightage by means of power is given and multiplying these weighted ratios to come up with a comprehensive figure on the relative merit of two alternative sites, *i.e.*,

$C_1^M, C_2^M, \ldots, C_z^M$ are the different costs associated with a site M on the 'z' different cost items.

$C_1^N, C_2^N, \ldots, C_z^N$ are the different costs associated with a site N and $W_1, W_2, W_3, \ldots, W_z$ are the weightage given to these cost items, then relative merit of the M and site N is given by:

$$\left(C_1^M / C_1^N\right)^{W_1} \times \left(C_2^M / C_2^N\right)^{W_2}, \ldots, \left(C_z^M / C_z^N\right)^{W_z}$$

If this is > 1, site N is superior and vice-versa.

When starting a new factory, plant location decisions are very important because they have direct bearing on factors like, financial, employment and distribution patterns. In the long run, relocation of plant may even benefit the organization. But, the relocation of the plant involves stoppage of production, and also cost for shifting the facilities to a new location. In addition to these things, it will introduce some inconvenience in the normal functioning of the business. Hence, at the time of starting any industry, one should generate several alternate sites for locating the plant. After a critical analysis, the best site is to be selected for commissioning the plant. Location of warehouses and other facilities are also having direct bearing on the operational performance of organizations.

The existing firms will seek new locations in order to expand the capacity or to place the existing facilities. When the demand for product increases, it will give rise to following decisions:

Whether to expand the existing capacity and facilities.

Whether to look for new locations for additional facilities.

Whether to close down existing facilities to take advantage of some new locations.

II. In Case of Location Choice for Existing Organisation

In this case a manufacturing plant has to fit into a multi-plant operations strategy. That is, additional plant location in the same premises and elsewere under following circumstances:

1. Plant manufacturing distinct products.
2. Manufacturing plant supplying to specific market area.
3. Plant divided on the basis of the process or stages in manufacturing.
4. Plants emphasizing flexibility.

The different operations strategies under the above circumstances could be:

1. **Plants manufacturing distinct products:** Each plant services the entire market area for the organization. This strategy is necessary where the needs of technological and resource inputs are specialized or distinctively different for the different product-lines.

For example, a high quality precision product-line should not be located along with other product-line requiring little emphasis on precision. It may not be proper to have too many contradictions such as sophisticated and old equipment, highly skilled and semi-skilled personnel, delicates processes and those that could permit rough handlings, all under one roof and one set of managers. Such a setting leads to much confusion regarding the required emphasis and the management policies.

Product specialization may be necessary in a highly competitive market. It may be necessary to exploit the special resources of a particular geographical area. The more decentralized these pairs are in terms of the management and in terms of their physical location, the better would be the planning and control and the utilization of the resources.

2. **Manufacturing plants supplying to a specific market area:** Here, each plant manufactures almost all of the company's products. This type of strategy is useful where market proximity consideration dominates the resources and technology considerations. This strategy requires great deal of coordination from the corporate office. An extreme example of this strategy is that of soft drinks bottling plants.

3. **Plants divided on the basis of the process or stages in manufacturing:** Each production process or stage of manufacturing may require distinctively different equipment capabilities, labour skills, technologies, and managerial policies and emphasis. Since the products of one plant feed into the other plant, this strategy requires much centralized coordination of the manufacturing activities from the corporate office that are expected to understand the various technological aspects of all the plants.

4. **Plants emphasizing flexibility:** This requires much coordination between plants to meet the changing needs and at the same time ensure efficient use of the facilities and resources. Frequent changes in the long-term strategy in order to improve be efficiently temporarily, are not healthy for the organization. In any facility location problem the central question is: 'Is this a location at which the company can remain competitive for a long time?'

For an established organization in order to add on to the capacity, following are the ways:

(*a*) *Expansion of the facilities at the existing site:* This is acceptable when it does not violate the basic business and managerial outlines, *i.e.*, philosophies, purposes, strategies and capabilities. For example, expansion should not compromise quality, delivery, or customer service.

(*b*) *Relocation of the facilities (closing down the existing ones):* This is a drastic step which can be called as 'Uprooting and Transplanting'. Unless there are very compelling reasons, relocation is not done. The reasons will be either bringing radical changes in technology, resource availability or other destabilization.

All these factors are applicable to service organizations, whose objectives, priorities and strategies may differ from those of hardcore manufacturing organizations.

III. In Case of Global Location

Because of globalisation, multinational corporations are setting up their organizations in India and Indian companies are extending their operations in other countries. In case of global locations there is scope for virtual proximity and virtual factory.

VIRTUAL PROXIMITY

With the advance in telecommunications technology, a firm can be in virtual proximity to its customers. For a software services firm much of its logistics is through the information/ communication pathway. Many firms use the communications highway for conducting a large portion of their business transactions. Logistics is certainly an important factor in deciding on a location—whether in the home country or abroad. Markets have to be reached. Customers have to be contacted. Hence, a market presence in the country of the customers is quite necessary.

VIRTUAL FACTORY

Many firms based in USA and UK in the service sector and in the manufacturing sector often out sources part of their business processes to foreign locations such as India. Thus, instead of one's own operations, a firm could use its business associates' operations facilities. The Indian BPO firm is a foreign-based company's 'virtual service factory'. So a location could be one's own or one's business associates. The location decision need not always necessarily pertain to own operations.

REASONS FOR A GLOBAL/FOREIGN LOCATION

A. Tangible Reasons

The tangible reasons for setting up an operations facility abroad could be as follows:

Reaching the customer: One obvious reason for locating a facility abroad is that of capturing a share of the market expanding worldwide. The phenomenal growth of the GDP of India is a big reason for the multinationals to have their operations facilities in our country. An important reason is that of providing service to the customer promptly and economically which is logistics-dependent. Therefore, cost and case of logistics is a reason for setting up manufacturing facilities abroad. By logistics set of activities closes the gap between production of goods/services and reaching of these intended goods/services to the customer to his satisfaction. Reaching the customer is thus the main objective. The tangible and intangible gains and costs depend upon the company defining for itself as to what that 'reaching' means. The tangible costs could be the logistics related costs; the intangible costs may be the risk of operating is a foreign country. The tangible gains are the immediate gains; the intangible gains are an outcome of what the company defines the concepts of reaching and customer for itself.

The other *tangible reasons* could be as follows:

(*a*) The host country may offer substantial tax advantages compared to the home country.

(*b*) The costs of manufacturing and running operations may be substantially less in that foreign country. This may be due to lower labour costs, lower raw material cost, better availability of the inputs like materials, energy, water, ores, metals, key personnel etc.

(*c*) The company may overcome the tariff barriers by setting up a manufacturing plant in a foreign country rather than exporting the items to that country.

B. Intangible Reasons

The intangible reasons for considering setting up an operations facility abroad could be as follows:

1. Customer-related Reasons

(*a*) With an operations facility in the foreign country, the firm's customers may feel secure that the firm is more accessible. Accessibility is an important 'service quality' determinant.

(*b*) The firm may be able to give a personal tough.

(*c*) The firm may interact more intimately with its customers and may thus understand their requirements better.

(*d*) It may also discover other potential customers in the foreign location.

2. Organisational Learning-related Reasons

(*a*) The firm can learn advanced technology. For example, it is possible that cutting-edge technologies can be learn by having operations in an technologically more advanced country. The firm can learn from advanced research laboratories/universities in that country. Such learning may help the entire product-line of the company.

(*b*) The firm can learn from its customers abroad. A physical location there may be essential towards this goal.

(*c*) It can also learn from its competitors operating in that country. For this reason, it may have to be physically present where the action is.

(*d*) The firm may also learn from its suppliers abroad. If the firm has a manufacturing plant there, it will have intensive interaction with the suppliers in that country from whom there may be much to learn in terms of modern and appropriate technology, modern management methods, and new trends in business worldwide.

3. Other Strategic Reasons

(*a*) The firm by being physically present in the host country may gain some 'local boy' kind of psychological advantage. The firm is no more a 'foreign' company just sending its products across international borders. This may help the firm in lobbying with the government of that country and with the business associations in that country.

(*b*) The firm may avoid 'political risk' by having operations in multiple countries.

(*c*) By being in the foreign country, the firm can build alternative sources of supply. The firm could, thus, reduce its supply risks.

(*d*) The firm could hunt for human capital in different countries by having operations in those countries. Thus, the firm can gather the best of people from across the globe.

(*e*) Foreign locations in addition to the domestic locations would lower the market risks for the firm. If one market goes slow the other may be doing well, thus lowering the overall risk.

4.3 FACTORS INFLUENCING PLANT LOCATION/FACILITY LOCATION

Facility location is the process of determining a geographic site for a firm's operations. Managers of both service and manufacturing organizations must weigh many factors when assessing the desirability of a particular site, including proximity to customers and suppliers, labour costs, and transportation costs.

Location conditions are complex and each comprises a different Characteristic of a tangible (i.e. Freight rates, production costs) and non-tangible (i.e. reliability, Frequency security, quality) nature.

Location conditions are hard to measure. Tangible cost based factors such as wages and products costs can be quantified precisely into what makes locations better to compare. On the other hand non-tangible features, which refer to such characteristics as reliability, availability and security, can only be measured along an ordinal or even nominal scale. Other non-tangible features like the percentage of employees that are unionized can be measured as well. To sum this up non-tangible features are very important for business location decisions.

It is appropriate to divide the factors, which influence the plant location or facility location on the basis of the nature of the organisation as:

1. **General locational factors**, which include controllable and uncontrollable factors for all type of organisations.
2. **Specific locational factors** specifically required for manufacturing and service organisations.

Location factors can be further divided into two categories:

Dominant factors are those derived from competitive priorities (cost, quality, time, and flexibility) and have a particularly strong impact on sales or costs. Secondary factors also are important, but management may downplay or even ignore some of them if other factors are more important.

4.3.1 General Locational Factors

Following are the general factors required for location of plant in case of all types of organisations.

Controllable Factors

1. Proximity to markets
2. Supply of materials
3. Transportation facilities
4. Infrastructure availability
5. Labour and wages

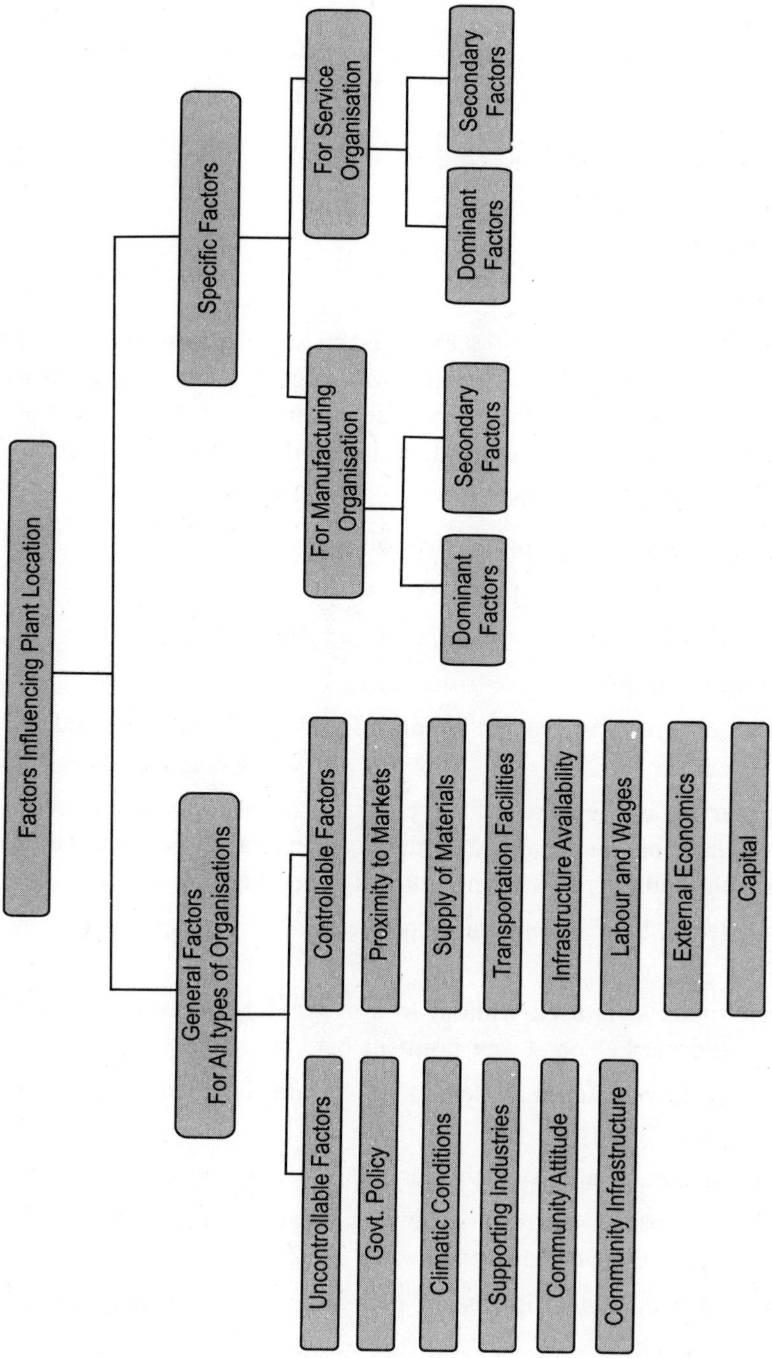

Fig. 4.1 Factors influencing plant location

6. External economies
7. Capital.

UNCONTROLLABLE FACTORS

8. Government policy
9. Climate conditions
10. Supporting industries and services
11. Community and labour attitudes
12. Community Infrastructure.

CONTROLLABLE FACTORS

1. **Proximity to markets:** Every company is expected to serve its customers by providing goods and services at the time needed and at reasonable price organizations may choose to locate facilities close to the market or away from the market depending upon the product. When the buyers for thc product are concentrated, it is advisable to locate the facilities close to the market.

Locating nearer to the market is preferred if

- The products are delicate and susceptible to spoilage.
- After sales services are promptly required very often.
- Transportation cost is high and increase the cost significantly.
- Shelf life of the product is low.

Nearness to the market ensures a consistent supply of goods to customers and reduces the cost of transportation.

2. **Supply of raw material:** It is essential for the organization to get raw material in right qualities and time in order to have an uninterrupted production. This factor becomes very important if the materials are perishable and cost of transportation is very high.

General guidelines suggested by Yaseen regarding effects of raw materials on plant location are:

- When a single raw material is used without loss of weight, locate the plant at the raw material source, at the market or at any point in between.
- When weight loosing raw material is demanded, locate the plant at the raw material source.
- When raw material is universally available, locate close to the market area.
- If the raw materials are processed from variety of locations, the plant may be situated so as to minimize total transportation costs.

Nearness to raw material is important in case of industries such as sugar, cement, jute and cotton textiles.

3. **Transportation facilities:** Speedy transport facilities ensure timely supply of raw materials to the company and finished goods to the customers. The transport facility is a prerequisite for

the location of the plant. There are five basic modes of physical transportation, air, road, rail, water and pipeline. Goods that are mainly intended for exports demand a location near to the port or large airport. The choice of transport method and hence the location will depend on relative costs, convenience, and suitability. Thus transportation cost to value added is one of the criteria for plant location.

4. **Infrastructure availability:** The basic infrastructure facilities like power, water and waste disposal, etc., become the prominent factors in deciding the location. Certain types of industries are power hungry e.g., aluminum and steel and they should be located close to the power station or location where uninterrupted power supply is assured throughout the year. The non-availability of power may become a survival problem for such industries. Process industries like paper, chemical, cement, etc., require continuous. Supply of water in large amount and good quality, and mineral content of water becomes an important factor. A waste disposal facility for process industries is an important factor, which influences the plant location.

5. **Labour and wages:** The problem of securing adequate number of labour and with skills specific is a factor to be considered both at territorial as well as at community level during plant location. Importing labour is usually costly and involve administrative problem. The history of labour relations in a prospective community is to be studied. Prospective community is to be studied. Productivity of labour is also an important factor to be considered. Prevailing wage pattern, cost of living and industrial relation and bargaining power of the unions' forms in important considerations.

6. **External economies of scale:** External economies of scale can be described as urbanization and locational economies of scale. It refers to advantages of a company by setting up operations in a large city while the second one refers to the "settling down" among other companies of related Industries. In the case of urbanization economies, firms derive from locating in larger cities rather than in smaller ones in a search of having access to a large pool of labour, transport facilities, and as well to increase their markets for selling their products and have access to a much wider range of business services.

Location economies of scale in the manufacturing sector have evolved over time and have mainly increased competition due to production facilities and lower production costs as a result of lower transportation and logistical costs. This led to manufacturing districts where many companies of related industries are located more or less in the same area. As large corporations have realized that inventories and warehouses have become a major cost factor, they have tried reducing inventory costs by launching "Just in Time" production system (the so called Kanban System). This high efficient production system was one main factor in the Japanese car industry for being so successful. Just in time ensures to get spare parts from suppliers within just a few hours after ordering. To fulfill these criteria corporations have to be located in the same area increasing their market and service for large corporations.

7. **Capital:** By looking at capital as a location condition, it is important to distinguish the physiology of fixed capital in buildings and equipment from financial capital. Fixed capital costs as building and construction costs vary from region to region. But on the other hand buildings can also be rented and existing plants can be expanded. Financial capital is highly mobile and does not very much influence decisions. For example, large Multinational Corporations such as Coca-

Cola operate in many different countries and can raise capital where interest rates are lowest and conditions are most suitable.

Capital becomes a main factor when it comes to venture capital. In that case young, fast growing (or not) high tech firms are concerned which usually have not many fixed assets. These firms particularly need access to financial capital and also skilled educated employees.

UNCONTROLLABLE FACTORS

8. **Government policy:** The policies of the state governments and local bodies concerning labour laws, building codes, safety, etc., are the factors that demand attention.

In order to have a balanced regional growth of industries, both central and state governments in our country offer the package of incentives to entrepreneurs in particular locations. The incentive package may be in the form of exemption from a safes tax and excise duties for a specific period, soft loan from financial institutions, subsidy in electricity charges and investment subsidy. Some of these incentives may tempt to locate the plant to avail these facilities offered.

9. **Climatic conditions:** The geology of the area needs to be considered together with climatic conditions (humidity, temperature). Climates greatly influence human efficiency and behaviour. Some industries require specific climatic conditions e.g., textile mill will require humidity.

10. **Supporting industries and services:** Now a day the manufacturing organisation will not make all the components and parts by itself and it subcontracts the work to vendors. So, the source of supply of component parts will be the one of the factors that influences the location.

The various services like communications, banking services professional consultancy services and other civil amenities services will play a vital role in selection of a location.

11. **Community and labour attitudes:** Community attitude towards their work and towards the prospective industries can make or mar the industry. Community attitudes towards supporting trade union activities are important criteria. Facility location in specific location is not desirable even though all factors are favouring because of labour attitude towards management, which brings very often the strikes and lockouts.

12. **Community infrastructure and amenity:** All manufacturing activities require access to a community infrastructure, most notably economic overhead capital, such as roads, railways, port facilities, power lines and service facilities and social overhead capital like schools, universities and hospitals.

These factors are also needed to be considered by location decisions as infrastructure is enormously expensive to build and for most manufacturing activities the existing stock of infrastructure provides physical restrictions on location possibilities.

4.3.2 Specific Locational Factors for Manufacturing Organisation

DOMINANT FACTORS

Factors dominating location decisions for new manufacturing plants can be broadly classified in six groups. They are listed in the order of their importance as follows.

1. Favourable labour climate
2. Proximity to markets
3. Quality of life
4. Proximity to suppliers and resources
5. Utilities, taxes, and real estate costs

1. **Favourable labour climate:** A favorable labour climate may be the most important factor in location decisions for labour-intensive firms in industries such as textiles furniture and consumer electronics. Labour climate includes wage rates, training requirements attitudes toward work, worker productivity and union strength. Many executives consider weak unions or al low probability of union organizing efforts as a distinct advantage.

2. **Proximity to markets:** After determining where the demand for goods and services is greatest, management must select a location for the facility that will supply that demand. Locating near markets is particularly important when the final goods are bulky or heavy and outbound transportation rates are high. For example, manufacturers of products such as plastic pipe and heavy metals all emphasize proximity to their markets.

3. **Quality of life:** Good schools, recreational facilities, cultural events, and an attractive lifestyle contribute to quality of life. This factor is relatively unimportant on its own, but it can make the difference in location decisions.

4. **Proximity to suppliers and resources:** In many companies, plants supply parts to other facilities or rely on other facilities for management and staff support. These require frequent coordination and communication, which can become more difficult as distance increases.

5. **Utilities, taxes, and real estate costs:** Other important factors that may emerge include utility costs (telephone, energy, and water), local and state taxes, financing incentives offered by local or state governments, relocation costs, and land costs.

SECONDARY FACTORS

There are some other factors needed to be considered, including room for expansion, construction costs, accessibility to multiple modes of transportation, the cost of shuffling people and materials between plants, competition from other firms for the workforce, community attitudes, and many others. For global operations, firms are emphasizing local employee skills and education and the local infrastructure.

4.3.3 Specific Locational Factors for Service Organisation

DOMINANT FACTORS

The factors considered for manufacturers are also applied to service providers, with one important addition — the impact of location on sales and customer satisfaction. Customers usually look about how close a service facility is, particularly if the process requires considerable customer contact.

Proximity to Customers

Location is a key factor in determining how conveniently customers can carry on business with a firm. For example, few people would like to go to remotely located dry cleaner or supermarket if another is more convenient. Thus the influence of location on revenues tends to be the dominant factor.

Transportation Costs and Proximity to Markets

For warehousing and distribution operations, transportation costs and proximity to markets are extremely important. With a warehouse nearby, many firms can hold inventory closer to the customer, thus reducing delivery time and promoting sales.

Location of Competitors

One complication in estimating the sales potential at different location is the impact of competitors. Management must not only consider the current location of competitors but also try to anticipate their reaction to the firm's new location. Avoiding areas where competitors are already well established often pays. However, in some industries, such as new-car sales showrooms and fast-food chains, locating near competitors is actually advantageous. The strategy is to create a critical mass, whereby several competing firms clustered in one location attract more customers than the total number who would shop at the same stores at scattered locations. Recognizing this effect, some firms use a follow –the leader strategy when selecting new sites.

Secondary Factors

Retailers also must consider the level of retail activity, residential density, traffic flow, and site visibility. Retail activity in the area is important, as shoppers often decide on impulse to go shopping or to eat in a restaurant. Traffic flows and visibility are important because businesses customers arrive in cars. Visibility involves distance from the street and size of nearby buildings and signs. High residential density ensures night time and weekend business when the population in the area fits the firm's competitive priorities and target market segment.

4.4 LOCATION THEORIES

Alfred Weber's Theory of the Location of Industries

Alfred Weber (1868–1958), with the publication of Theory of the Location of Industries in 1909, put forth the first developed general theory of industrial location. His model took into account several spatial factors for finding the optimal location and minimal cost for manufacturing plants.

The point for locating an industry that minimizes costs of transportation and labour requires analysis of three factors:

1. The point of optimal transportation based on the costs of distance to the 'material index'—the ratio of weight to intermediate products (raw materials) to finished product.
2. The labour distortion, in which more favourable sources of lower cost of labour may justify greater transport distances.
3. Agglomeration and degglomerating.

Agglomeration or concentration of firms in a locale occurs when there is sufficient demand for support services for the company and labour force, including new investments in schools and hospitals. Also supporting companies, such as facilities that build and service machines and financial services, prefer closer contact with their customers.

Degglommeration occurs when companies and services leave because of over concentration of industries or of the wrong types of industries, or shortages of labour, capital, affordable land, etc. Weber also examined factors leading to the diversification of an industry in the horizontal relations between processes within the plant.

The issue of industry location is increasingly relevant to today's global markets and trans-national corporations. Focusing only on the mechanics of the Weberian model could justify greater transport distances for cheap labour and unexploited raw materials. When resources are exhausted or workers revolt, industries move to different countries.

4.5 LOCATION MODELS

Various models are available which help to identify the ideal location. Some of the popular models are:

1. Factor rating method
2. Weighted factor rating method
3. Load-distance method
4. Centre of gravity method
5. Break-even analysis.

4.5.1 Factor Rating Method

The process of selecting a new facility location involves a series of following steps:

1. Identify the important location factors.
2. Rate each factor according to its relative importance, *i.e.*, higher the ratings is indicative of prominent factor.
3. Assign each location according to the merits of the location for each factor.
4. Calculate the rating for each location by multiplying factor assigned to each location with basic factors considered.
5. Find the sum of product calculated for each factor and select best location having highest total score.

ILLUSTRATION 1: *Let us assume that a new medical facility, Health-care, is to be located in Delhi. The location factors, factor rating and scores for two potential sites are shown in the following table. Which is the best location based on factor rating method?*

Sl. No.	Location factor	Factor rating	Rating	
			Location 1	Location 2
1.	Facility utilization	8	3	5
2.	Total patient per month	5	4	3
3.	Average time per emergency trip	6	4	5
4.	Land and construction costs	3	1	2
5.	Employee preferences	5	5	3

SOLUTION

Sl. No.	Location factor	Factor rating (1)	Location 1		Location 2	
			(Rating) (2)	Total= (1) . (2)	(Rating) (3)	Total = (1) . (3)
1.	Facility utilization	8	3	24	5	40
2.	Total patient per month	5	4	20	3	15
3.	Average time per emergency trip	6	4	24	5	30
4.	Land and construction costs	3	1	3	2	6
5.	Employee preferences	5	5	25	3	15
			Total	96	Total	106

The total score for location 2 is higher than that of location 1. Hence location 2, is the best choice.

4.5.2 Weighted Factor Rating Method

In this method to merge quantitative and qualitative factors, factors are assigned weights based on relative importance and weightage score for each site using a preference matrix is calculated. The site with the highest weighted score is selected as the best choice.

ILLUSTRATION 2: *Let us assume that a new medical facility, Health-care, is to be located in Delhi. The location factors, weights, and scores (1 = poor, 5 = excellent) for two potential sites are shown in the following table. What is the weighted score for these sites? Which is the best location?*

Sl. No.	Location factor	Weight	Scores	
			Location 1	Location 2
1.	Facility utilization	25	3	5
2.	Total patient km per month	25	4	3
3.	Average time per emergency trip	25	3	3
4.	Land and construction costs	15	1	2
5.	Employee preferences	10	5	3

SOLUTION: The weighted score for this particular site is calculated by multiplying each factor's weight by its score and adding the results:

$$\text{Weighted score location 1} = 25 \times 3 + 25 \times 4 + 25 \times 3 + 15 \times 1 + 10 \times 5$$
$$= 75 + 100 + 75 + 15 + 50 = 315$$
$$\text{Weighted score location 2} = 25 \times 5 + 25 \times 3 + 25 \times 3 + 15 \times 2 + 10 \times 3$$
$$= 125 + 75 + 75 + 30 + 30 = 335$$

Location 2 is the best site based on total weighted scores.

4.5.3 Load-distance Method

The load-distance method is a mathematical model used to evaluate locations based on proximity factors. The objective is to select a location that minimizes the total weighted loads moving into and out of the facility. The distance between two points is expressed by assigning the points to grid coordinates on a map. An alternative approach is to use time rather than distance.

DISTANCE MEASURES

Suppose that a new warehouse is to be located to serve Delhi. It will receive inbound shipments from several suppliers, including one in Ghaziabad. If the new warehouse were located at Gurgaon, what would be the distance between the two facilities? If shipments travel by truck, the distance depends on the highway system and the specific route taken. Computer software is available for calculating the actual mileage between any two locations in the same county. However, for load-distance method, a rough calculation that is either Euclidean or rectilinear distance measure may be used. Euclidean distance is the straight-line distance, or shortest possible path, between two points.

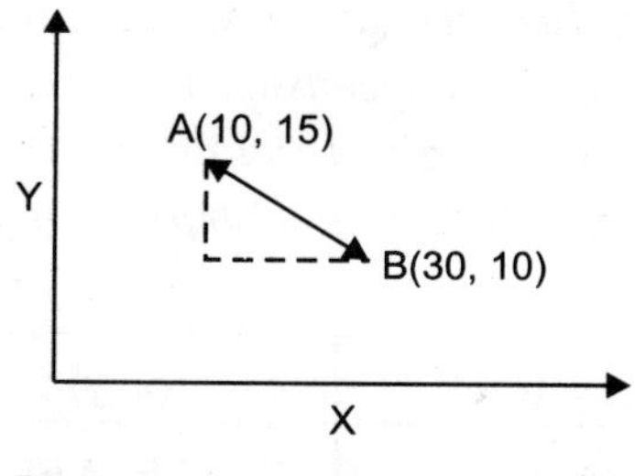

Fig. 4.2 Distance between point A and point B

The point A on the grid represents the supplier's location in Ghaziabad, and the point B represents the possible warehouse location at Gurgaon. The distance between points A and B is the length of the hypotenuse of a right triangle, or

$$d_{AB} = \text{Sqrt}\left((X_A - X_B)^2 + (Y_A - Y_B)^2\right)$$

where d_{AB} = distance between points A and B

X_A = x-coordinate of point A

Y_A = y-coordinate of point A

X_B = x-coordinate of point B

Y_B = y-coordinate of point B

Rectilinear distance measures distance between two points with a series of 90° turns as city blocks. Essentially, this distance is the sum of the two dashed lines representing the base and side of the triangle in figure. The distance travelled in the *x*-direction is the absolute value of the difference in *x*-coordinates. Adding this result to the absolute value of the difference in the *y*-coordinates gives

$$D_{AB} = |X_A - X_B| + |Y_A - Y_B|$$

CALCULATING A LOAD-DISTANCE SCORE

Suppose that a firm planning a new location wants to select a site that minimizes the distances that loads, particularly the larger ones, must travel to and from the site. Depending on the industry, a load may be shipments from suppliers, between plants, or to customers, or it may be customers or employees travelling to or from the facility. The firm seeks to minimize its load-distance, generally by choosing a location so that large loads go short distances.

To calculate a load-distance for any potential location, we use either of the distance measures and simply multiply the loads flowing to and from the facility by the distances travelled. These loads may be expressed as tones or number of trips per week.

This calls for a practical example to appreciate the relevance of the concept. Let us visit a new Health-care facility, once again.

ILLUSTRATION 3: *The new Health-care facility is targeted to serve seven census tracts in Delhi. The table given below shows the coordinates for the centre of each census tract, along with the projected populations, measured in thousands. Customers will travel from the seven census tract centres to the new facility when they need health-care. Two locations being considered for the new facility are at (5.5, 4.5) and (7, 2), which are the centres of census tracts C and F. Details of seven census tract centres, co-ordinate distances along with the population for each centre are given below. If we use the population as the loads and use rectilinear distance, which location is better in terms of its total load-distance score?*

Sl. No.	Census tract	(x, y)	Population (l)
1	A	(2.5, 4.5)	2
2	B	(2.5, 2.5)	5
3	C	(5.5, 4.5)	10
4	D	(5, 2)	7
5	E	(8, 5)	10
6	F	(7, 2)	20
7	G	(9, 2.5)	14

SOLUTION: Calculate the load-distance score for each location. Using the coordinates from the above table. Calculate the load-distance score for each tract.

Using the formula $D_{AB} = |X_A - X_B| + |Y_A - Y_B|$

Census tract	(x, y)	Population (l)	Locate at (5.5, 4.5)		Locate at (7, 2)	
			Distance (d)	Load-distance	Distance (d)	Load-distance
A	(2.5, 4.5)	2	3 + 0 = 3	6	4.5 + 2.5 = 7	14
B	(2.5, 2.5)	5	3 + 2 = 5	25	4.5 + 0.5 = 5	25
C	(5.5, 4.5)	10	0 + 0 = 0	0	1.5 + 2.5 = 4	40
D	(5, 2)	7	0.5 + 2.5 = 3	21	2 + 0 = 2	14
E	(8, 5)	10	2.5 + 0.5 = 3	30	1 + 3 = 4	40
F	(7, 2)	20	1.5 + 2.5 = 4	80	0 + 0 = 0	0
G	(9, 2.5)	14	3.5 + 2 = 5.5	77	2 + 0.5 = 2.5	35
			Total	239	Total	168

Summing the scores for all tracts gives a total load-distance score of 239 when the facility is located at (5.5, 4.5) versus a load-distance score of 168 at location (7, 2). Therefore, the location in census tract F is a better location.

4.5.4 Centre of Gravity

Centre of gravity is based primarily on cost considerations. This method can be used to assist managers in balancing cost and service objectives. The centre of gravity method takes into account the locations of plants and markets, the volume of goods moved, and transportation costs in arriving at the best location for a single intermediate warehouse.

The centre of gravity is defined to be the location that minimizes the weighted distance between the warehouse and its supply and distribution points, where the distance is weighted by the number of tones supplied or consumed. The first step in this procedure is to place the locations on a coordinate system. The origin of the coordinate system and scale used are arbitrary, just as long as the relative distances are correctly represented. This can be easily done by placing a grid over an ordinary map. The centre of gravity is determined by the formula.

$$C_X = \frac{\sum D_{ix}.W_i}{\sum W_i} \qquad C_Y = \frac{\sum D_{iy}.W_i}{\sum W_i}$$

where C_x = x-coordinate of the centre of gravity

C_y = y-coordinate of the centre of gravity

D_{ix} = x-coordinate of location i

D_{iy} = y-coordinate of location i

ILLUSTRATION 4: *The new Health-care facility is targeted to serve seven census tracts in Delhi. The table given below shows the coordinates for the centre of each census tract, along with the projected populations, measured in thousands. Customers will travel from the seven census tract centres to the new facility when they need health-care. Two locations being considered for the new facility are at (5.5, 4.5) and (7, 2), which are the centres of census tracts C and F. Details of seven census tract centres, coordinate distances along with the population for each centre are given below. Find the target area's centre of gravity for the Health-care medical facility.*

Sl. No.	Census tract	(x, y)	Population (I)
1	A	(2.5, 4.5)	2
2	B	(2.5, 2.5)	5
3	C	(5.5, 4.5)	10
4	D	(5, 2)	7
5	E	(8, 5)	10
6	F	(7, 2)	20
7	G	(9, 2.5)	14

SOLUTION: To calculate the centre of gravity, start with the following information, where population is given in thousands.

Sl. No.	Census tract	(x, y)	Population (I)	Lx	Ly
1	A	(2.5, 4.5)	2	5	9
2	B	(2.5, 2.5)	5	12.5	12.5
3	C	(5.5, 4.5)	10	55	45
4	D	(5, 2)	7	35	14
5	E	(8, 5)	10	80	50
6	F	(7, 2)	20	140	40
7	G	(9, 2.5)	14	126	35
		Total	68	453.50	205.50

Next we find C_x and C_y.

$$C_x = 453.5/68 = 6.67$$

$$C_y = 205.5/68 = 3.02$$

The centre of gravity is (6.67, 3.02). Using the centre of gravity as starting point, managers can now search in its vicinity for the optimal location.

4.5.5 Break-even Analysis

Break even analysis implies that at some point in the operations, total revenue equals total cost. Break even analysis is concerned with finding the point at which revenues and costs agree exactly. It is called 'Break-even Point'. The Fig. 4.3 portrays the Break Even Chart:

Break even point is the volume of output at which neither a profit is made nor a loss is incurred.

The Break Even Point (BEP) in units can be calculated by using the relation:

$$\text{BEP} = \frac{\text{Fixed Cost}}{\text{Contribution per unit}} = \frac{\text{Fixed Cost}}{\text{Selling Price} - \text{Variable Cost per unit}} = \frac{F}{S-V} \text{ units}$$

The Break Even Point (BEP) in Rs. can be calculated by using the relation:

$$\text{BEP} = \frac{\text{Fixed Cost}}{\text{PV Ratio}} = \frac{\text{Fixed Cost}}{\left\{\frac{\text{Sales} - \text{Variable Cost}}{\text{Sales}}\right\}} = \frac{F}{\phi} \text{ Rs.}$$

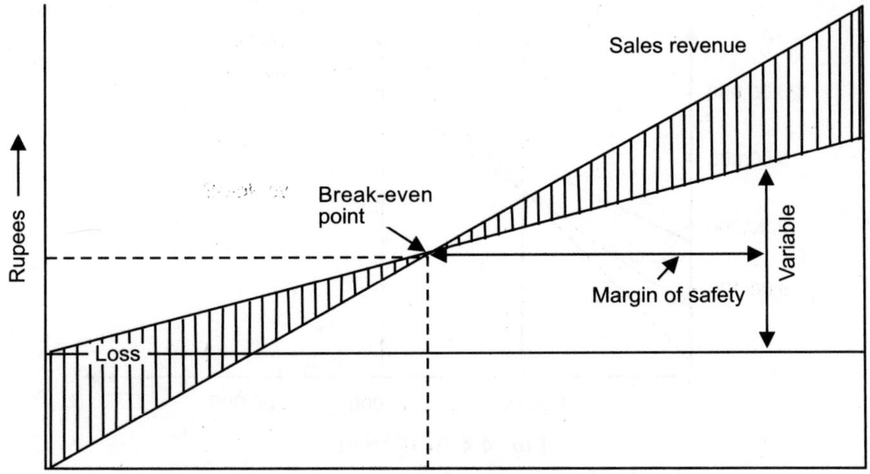

Fig. 4.3 Units of output or percentage of capacity

Plotting the break even chart for each location can make economic comparisons of locations. This will be helpful in identifying the range of production volume over which location can be selected.

ILLUSTRATION 5: *Potential locations X, Y and Z have the cost structures shown below. The ABC company has a demand of 1,30,000 units of a new product. Three potential locations X, Y and Z having following cost structures shown are available. Select which location is to be selected and also identify the volume ranges where each location is suited?*

	Location X	Location Y	Location Z
Fixed Costs	Rs. 150,000	Rs. 350,000	Rs. 950,000
Variable Costs	Rs. 10	Rs. 8	Rs. 6

SOLUTION: Solve for the crossover between X and Y:

$$10X + 150{,}000 = 8X + 350{,}000$$
$$2X = 200{,}000$$
$$X = 100{,}000 \text{ units}$$

Solve for the crossover between Y and Z:

$$8X + 350{,}000 = 6X + 950{,}000$$
$$2X = 600{,}000$$
$$X = 300{,}000 \text{ units}$$

Therefore, at a volume of 1,30,000 units, Y is the appropriate strategy.

From the graph (Fig. 4.4) we can interpret that location X is suitable up to 100,000 units, location Y is suitable up to between 100,000 to 300,000 units and location Z is suitable if the demand is more than 300,000 units.

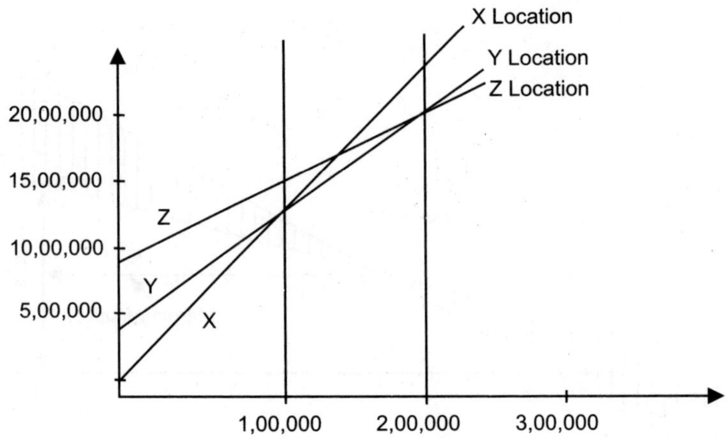

Fig. 4.4 BEP chart

4.6 LOCATIONAL ECONOMICS

An ideal location is one which results in lowest production cost and least distribution cost per unit. These costs are influenced by a number of factors as discussed earlier. The various costs which decide locational economy are those of land, building, equipment, labour, material, etc. Other factors like community attitude, community facilities and housing facilities will also influence the selection of best location. Economic analysis is carried out to decide as to which locate best location.

The following illustration will clarify the method of evaluation of best layout selection.

ILLUSTRATION 6: *From the following data select the most advantageous location for setting a plant for making transistor radios.*

	Site X Rs.	*Site Y* Rs.	*Site Z* Rs.
(*i*) Total initial investment	2,00,000	2,00,000	2,00,000
(*ii*) Total expected sales	2,50,000	3,00,000	2,50,000
(*iii*) Distribution expenses	40,000	40,000	75,000
(*iv*) Raw material expenses	70,000	80,000	90,000
(*v*) Power and water supply expenses	40,000	30,000	20,000
(*vi*) Wages and salaries	20,000	25,000	20,000
(*vii*) Other expenses	25,000	40,000	30,000
(*viii*) Community attitude	Indifferent	Want business	Indifferent
(*ix*) Employee housing facilities	Poor	Excellent	Good

SOLUTION

Total expenses	*Site X* Rs.	*Site Y* Rs.	*Site Z* Rs.
[Add (*iii*) (*iv*) (*v*) (*vi*) and (*vii*)]	1,95,000	2,15,000	2,35,000

$$\text{Rate of return (RoR), \%} = \frac{\text{Total sales} - \text{Total expenses}}{\text{Total investment}} \times 100$$

$$\text{RoR for Site X} = \frac{2,50,000 - 1,95,000}{2,00,000} \times 100$$

$$= \mathbf{27.5\%}$$

$$\text{RoR for Site Y} = \frac{3,00,000 - 2,15,000}{2,00,000} \times 100$$

$$= \mathbf{42.5\%}$$

$$\text{RoR for Site Z} = \frac{2,50,000 - 2,35,000}{2,00,000} \times 100$$

$$= \mathbf{7.5\%}$$

Location Y can be selected because of higher rate of return.

4.7 PLANT LAYOUT

Plant layout refers to the physical arrangement of production facilities. It is the configuration of departments, work centres and equipment in the conversion process. It is a floor plan of the physical facilities, which are used in production.

According to Moore "*Plant layout is a plan of an optimum arrangement of facilities including personnel, operating equipment, storage space, material handling equipment and all other supporting services along with the design of best structure to contain all these facilities*".

4.7.1 Objectives of Plant Layout

The primary goal of the plant layout is to maximise the profit by arrangement of all the plant facilities to the best advantage of total manufacturing of the product.

The objectives of plant layout are:

1. Streamline the flow of materials through the plant.
2. Facilitate the manufacturing process.
3. Maintain high turnover of in-process inventory.
4. Minimise materials handling and cost.
5. Effective utilisation of men, equipment and space.
6. Make effective utilisation of cubic space.
7. Flexibility of manufacturing operations and arrangements.
8. Provide for employee convenience, safety and comfort.
9. Minimize investment in equipment.
10. Minimize overall production time.
11. Maintain flexibility of arrangement and operation.
12. Facilitate the organizational structure.

4.7.2 Principles of Plant Layout

1. **Principle of integration:** A good layout is one that integrates men, materials, machines and supporting services and others in order to get the optimum utilisation of resources and maximum effectiveness.

2. **Principle of minimum distance:** This principle is concerned with the minimum travel (or movement) of man and materials. The facilities should be arranged such that, the total distance travelled by the men and materials should be minimum and as far as possible straight line movement should be preferred.

3. **Principle of cubic space utilisation:** The good layout is one that utilise both horizontal and vertical space. It is not only enough if only the floor space is utilised optimally but the third dimension, *i.e.,* the height is also to be utilised effectively.

4. **Principle of flow:** A good layout is one that makes the materials to move in forward direction towards the completion stage, *i.e.,* there should not be any backtracking.

5. **Principle of maximum flexibility**: The good layout is one that can be altered without much cost and time, *i.e.,* future requirements should be taken into account while designing the present layout.

6. **Principle of safety, security and satisfaction:** A good layout is one that gives due consideration to workers safety and satisfaction and safeguards the plant and machinery against fire, theft, etc.

7. **Principle of minimum handling:** A good layout is one that reduces the material handling to the minimum.

4.8 CLASSIFICATION OF LAYOUT

Layouts can be classified into the following five categories:

1. Process layout
2. Product layout
3. Combination layout
4. Fixed position layout
5. Group layout

4.8.1 Process Layout

Process layout is recommended for batch production. All machines performing similar type of operations are grouped at one location in the process layout *e.g.,* all lathes, milling machines, etc. are grouped in the shop will be clustered in like groups.

Thus, in process layout the arrangement of facilities are grouped together according to their functions. A typical process layout is shown in Fig. 4.5. The flow paths of material through the facilities from one functional area to another vary from product to product. Usually the paths are long and there will be possibility of backtracking.

Process layout is normally used when the production volume is not sufficient to justify a product layout. Typically, job shops employ process layouts due to the variety of products manufactured and their low production volumes.

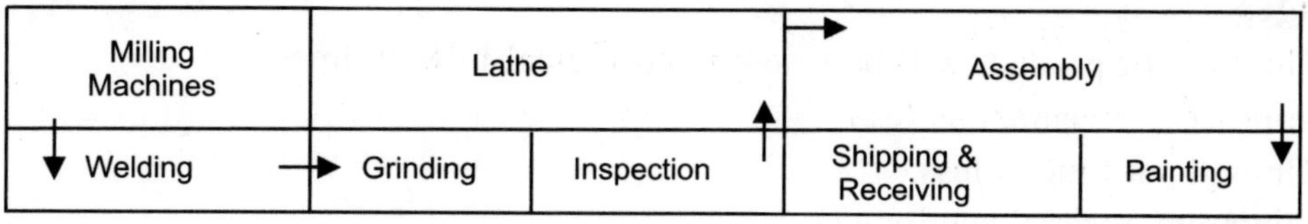

Fig. 4.5 Process layout

Advantages

1. In process layout machines are better utilized and fewer machines are required.
2. Flexibility of equipment and personnel is possible in process layout.
3. Lower investment on account of comparatively less number of machines and lower cost of general purpose machines.
4. Higher utilisation of production facilities.
5. A high degree of flexibility with regards to work distribution to machineries and workers.
6. The diversity of tasks and variety of job makes the job challenging and interesting.
7. Supervisors will become highly knowledgeable about the functions under their department.

Limitations

1. Backtracking and long movements may occur in the handling of materials thus, reducing material handling efficiency.
2. Material handling cannot be mechanised which adds to cost.
3. Process time is prolonged which reduce the inventory turnover and increases the in-process inventory.
4. Lowered productivity due to number of set-ups.
5. Throughput (time gap between in and out in the process) time is longer.
6. Space and capital are tied up by work-in-process.

4.8.2 Product Layout

In this type of layout, machines and auxiliary services are located according to the processing sequence of the product. If the volume of production of one or more products is large, the facilities can be arranged to achieve efficient flow of materials and lower cost per unit. Special purpose machines are used which perform the required function quickly and reliably.

The product layout is selected when the volume of production of a product is high such that a separate production line to manufacture it can be justified. In a strict product layout, machines are not shared by different products. Therefore, the production volume must be sufficient to achieve satisfactory utilisation of the equipment. A typical product layout is shown in Fig. 4.6.

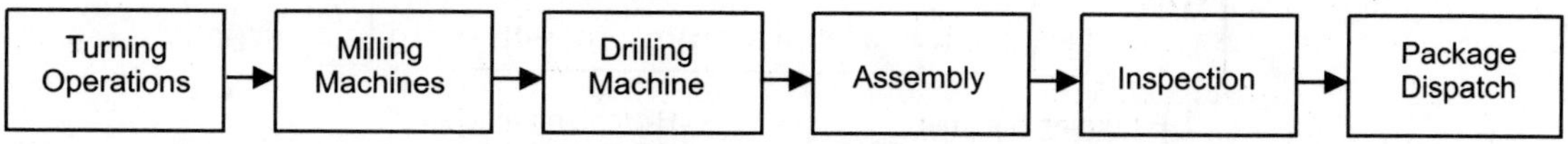

Fig. 4.6 Product layout

Advantages

1. The flow of product will be smooth and logical in flow lines.
2. In-process inventory is less.
3. Throughput time is less.
4. Minimum material handling cost.
5. Simplified production, planning and control systems are possible.
6. Less space is occupied by work transit and for temporary storage.
7. Reduced material handling cost due to mechanised handling systems and straight flow.
8. Perfect line balancing which eliminates bottlenecks and idle capacity.
9. Manufacturing cycle is short due to uninterrupted flow of materials.
10. Small amount of work-in-process inventory.
11. Unskilled workers can learn and manage the production.

Limitations

1. A breakdown of one machine in a product line may cause stoppages of machines in the downstream of the line.
2. A change in product design may require major alterations in the layout.
3. The line output is decided by the bottleneck machine.
4. Comparatively high investment in equipments is required.
5. *Lack of flexibility.* A change in product may require the facility modification.

4.8.3 Combination Layout

A combination of process and product layouts combines the advantages of both types of layouts. A combination layout is possible where an item is being made in different types and sizes. Here machinery is arranged in a process layout but the process grouping is then arranged in a sequence to manufacture various types and sizes of products. It is to be noted that the sequence of operations remains same with the variety of products and sizes. Figure 4.7 shows a combination type of layout for manufacturing different sized gears.

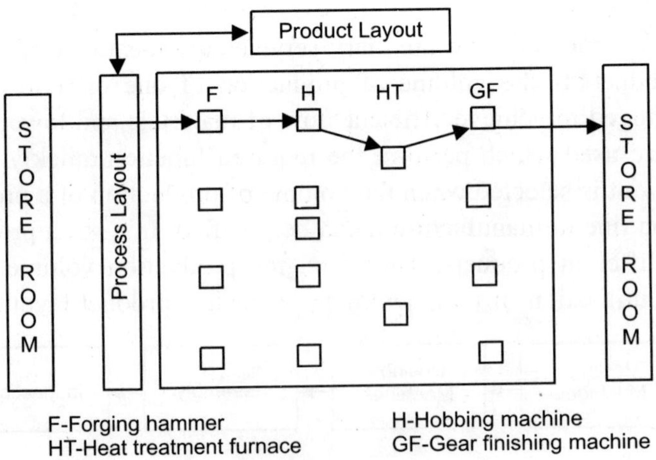

Fig. 4.7 Combination layout for making different types and sizes of gears

4.8.4 Fixed Position Layout

This is also called the **project type** of layout. In this type of layout, the material, or major components remain in a fixed location and tools, machinery, men and other materials are brought to this location. This type of layout is suitable when one or a few pieces of identical heavy products are to be manufactured and when the assembly consists of large number of heavy parts, the cost of transportation of these parts is very high.

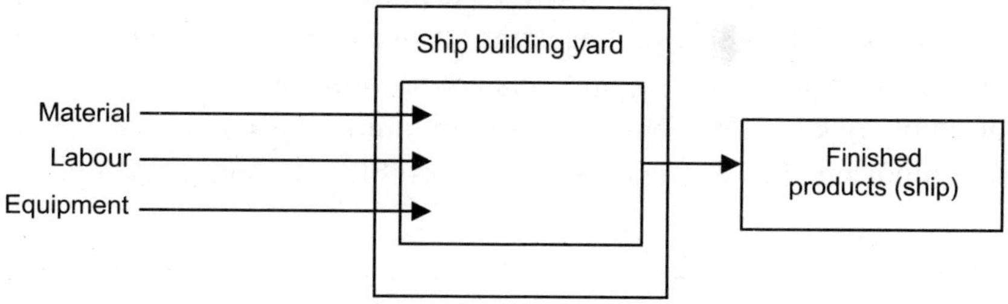

Fig. 4.8 Fixed position layout

Advantages

The major advantages of this type of layout are:

1. Helps in job enlargement and upgrades the skills of the operators.
2. The workers identify themselves with a product in which they take interest and pride in doing the job.
3. Greater flexibility with this type of layout.
4. Layout capital investment is lower.

4.8.5 Group Layout (or Cellular Layout)

There is a trend now to bring an element of flexibility into manufacturing system as regards to variation in batch sizes and sequence of operations. A grouping of equipment for performing a sequence of operations on family of similar components or products has become all the important.

Group Technology (GT) is the analysis and comparisons of items to group them into families with similar characteristics. GT can be used to develop a hybrid between pure process layout and pure flow line (product) layout. This technique is very useful for companies that produce variety of parts in small batches to enable them to take advantage and economics of flow line layout.

The application of group technology involves two basic steps; first step is to determine component families or groups. The second step in applying group technology is to arrange the plants equipment used to process a particular family of components. This represents small plants within the plants. The group technology reduces production planning time for jobs. It reduces the set-up time.

Thus **group layout** is a combination of the product layout and process layout. It combines the advantages of both layout systems. If there are *m*-machines and *n*-components, in a group layout (Group-Technology Layout), the *m*-machines and *n*-components will be divided into distinct number of machine-component cells (group) such that all the components assigned to a cell are almost processed within that cell itself. Here, the objective is to minimize the intercell movements.

The basic aim of a group technology layout is to identify families of components that require similar of satisfying all the requirements of the machines are grouped into cells. Each cell is capable of satisfying all the requirements of the component family assigned to it.

The layout design process considers mostly a single objective while designing layouts. In process layout, the objective is to minimize the total cost of materials handling. Because of the nature of the layout, the cost of equipments will be the minimum in this type of layout. In product layout, the cost of materials handling will be at the absolute minimum. But the cost of equipments would not be at the minimum if the equipments are not fully utilized.

In-group technology layout, the objective is to minimize the sum of the cost of transportation and the cost of equipments. So, this is called as multi-objective layout. A typical process layout is shown in Fig. 4.9.

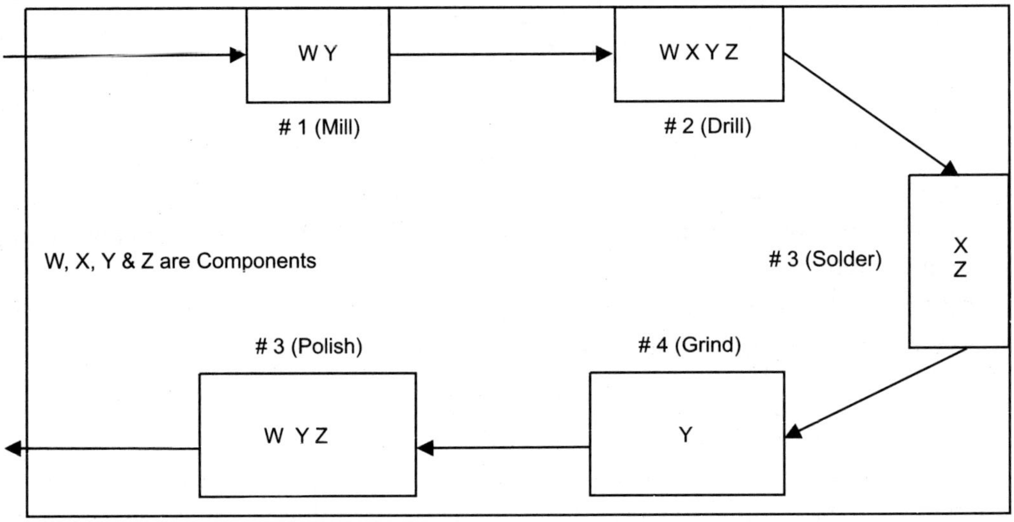

Fig. 4.9 Group layout or Cellular layout

Advantages of Group Technology Layout

Group Technology layout can increase—

1. Component standardization and rationalization.
2. Reliability of estimates.
3. Effective machine operation and productivity.
4. Customer service.

It can decrease the—

1. Paper work and overall production time.
2. Work-in-progress and work movement.
3. Overall cost.

Limitations of Group Technology Layout

This type of layout may not be feasible for all situations. If the product mix is completely dissimilar, then we may not have meaningful cell formation.

4.9 DESIGN OF PRODUCT LAYOUT

In product layout, equipment or departments are dedicated to a particular product line, duplicate equipment is employed to avoid backtracking, and a straight-line flow of material movement is achievable. Adopting a product layout makes sense when the batch size of a given product or part is large relative to the number of different products or parts produced.

Assembly lines are a special case of product layout. In a general sense, the term assembly line refers to progressive assembly linked by some material-handling device. The usual assumption is that some form of pacing is present and the allowable processing time is equivalent for all workstations. Within this broad definition, there are important differences among line types. A few of these are material handling devices (belt or roller conveyor, overhead crane); line configuration (U-shape, straight, branching); pacing (mechanical, human); product mix (one product or multiple products); workstation characteristics (workers may sit, stand, walk with the line, or ride the line); and length of the line (few or many workers). The range of products partially or completely assembled on lines includes toys, appliances, autos, clothing and a wide variety of electronic components. In fact, virtually any product that has multiple parts and is produced in large volume uses assembly lines to some degree.

A more-challenging problem is the determination of the optimum configuration of operators and buffers in a production flow process. A major design consideration in production lines is the assignment of operation so that all stages are more or less equally loaded. Consider the case of traditional assembly lines illustrated in Fig. 4.10.

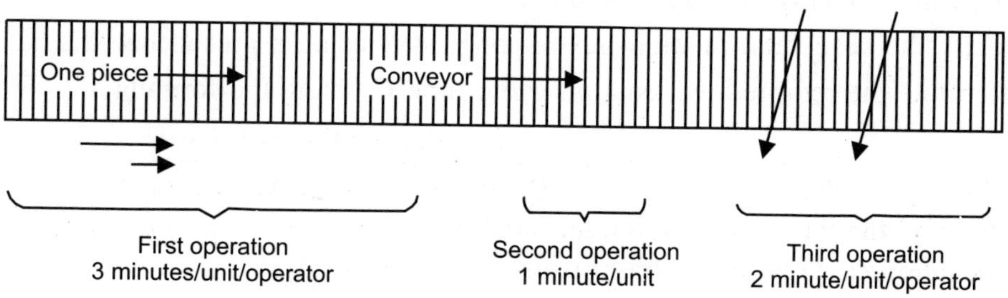

Fig. 4.10 Traditional assembly line

In this example, parts move along a conveyor at a rate of one part per minute to three groups of workstations. The first operation requires 3 minutes per unit; the second operation requires 1 minute per unit; and the third requires 2 minutes per unit. The first workstation consists of three operators; the second, one operator; and the third, two operators. An operator removes a part from the conveyor and performs some assembly task at his or her workstation. The completed part is returned to the conveyor and transported to the next operation. The number of operators at each workstation was chosen so that the line is balanced. Since three operators work simultaneously at the first workstation, on the average one part will be completed each minute. This is also true for other two stations. Since the parts arrive at a rate of one per minute, parts are also completed at this rate.

Assembly-line systems work well when there is a low variance in the times required to perform the individual subassemblies. If the tasks are somewhat complex, thus resulting in a higher assembly-time variance, operators down the line may not be able to keep up with the flow of parts from the preceding workstation or may experience excessive idle time. An alternative to a conveyor-paced assembly-line is a sequence of workstations linked by gravity conveyors, which act as buffers between successive operations.

Line Balancing

Assembly-line balancing often has implications for layout. This would occur when, for balance purposes, workstation size or the number used would have to be physically modified.

The most common assembly-line is a moving conveyor that passes a series of workstations in a uniform time interval called the **workstation cycle time** (which is also the time between successive units coming off the end of the line). At each workstation, work is performed on a product either by adding parts or by completing assembly operations. The work performed at each station is made up of many bits of work, termed tasks, elements, and work units. Such tasks are described by motion-time analysis. Generally, they are grouping that cannot be subdivided on the assembly-line without paying a penalty in extra motions.

The total work to be performed at a workstation is equal to the sum of the tasks assigned to that workstation. The line-balancing problem is one of assigning all tasks to a series of workstations so that each workstation has no more than can be done in the workstation cycle time, and so that the unassigned (idle) time across all workstations is minimized.

The problem is complicated by the relationships among tasks imposed by product design and process technologies. This is called the precedence relationship, which specifies the order in which tasks must be performed in the assembly process.

The steps in balancing an assembly line are:

1. Specify the sequential relationships among tasks using a precedence diagram.
2. Determine the required workstation cycle time C, using the formula

$$C = \frac{\text{Production time per day}}{\text{Required output per day (in units)}}$$

3. Determine the theoretical minimum number of workstations (N_t) required to satisfy the workstation cycle time constraint using the formula

$$N_t = \frac{\text{Sum of task times (T)}}{\text{Cycle time (C)}}$$

4. Select a primary rule by which tasks are to be assigned to workstations, and a secondary rule to break ties.
5. Assign tasks, once at a time, to the first workstation until the sum of the task times is equal to the workstation cycle time, or no other tasks are feasible because of time or sequence restrictions. Repeat the process for workstation 2, workstation 3, and so on until all tasks are assigned.
6. Evaluate the efficiency of the balance derived using the formula

$$\text{Efficiency} = \frac{\text{Sum of task times (T)}}{\text{Actual number of workstations } (N_a) \times \text{Workstations cycle time (C)}}$$

7. If efficiency is unsatisfactory, rebalance using a different decision rule.

ILLUSTRATION 7: *The MS 800 car is to be assembled on a conveyor belt. Five hundred cars are required per day. Production time per day is 420 minutes, and the assembly steps and times for the wagon are given below. Find the balance that minimizes the number of workstations, subject to cycle time and precedence constraints.*

Task	Task time (in seconds)	Description	Tasks that must precede
A	45	Position rear axle support and hand fasten	-
B	11	Four screws to nuts	A
C	9	Insert rear axle	B
D	50	Tighten rear axle support screws to nuts	-
E	15	Position front axle assembly and hand	D
F	12	Fasten with four screws to nuts	C
G	12	Tighten front axle assembly screws	C
H	12	Position rear wheel 1 and fasten hubcap	E
I	12	Position rear wheel 2 and fasten hubcap	E
J	8	Position front wheel 1 and fasten hubcap	F, G, H, I
K	9	Position front wheel 2 and fasten hubcap	J

SOLUTION

1. Draw a precedence diagram as follows:

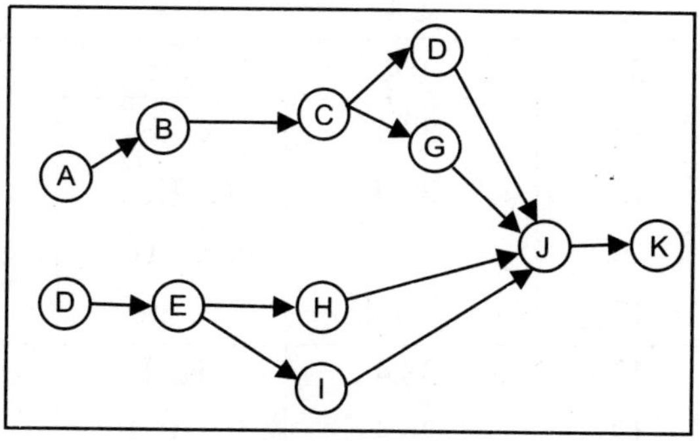

2. Determine workstation cycle time. Here we have to convert production time to seconds because our task times are in seconds

$$C = \frac{\text{Production time per day}}{\text{Required output per day (in units)}}$$

$$= \frac{420 \text{ min} \times 60 \text{ sec}}{500 \text{ cars}} = \frac{25200}{500} = 50.4 \text{ secs}$$

3. Determine the theoretical minimum number of workstations required (the actual number may be greater)

$$N_t = \frac{T}{C} = \frac{195 \text{ seconds}}{50.4 \text{ seconds}} = 3.87 = 4 \text{ (rounded up)}$$

4. Select assignment rules.

(*a*) Prioritize tasks in order of the largest number of following tasks:

Task	Number of following tasks
A	6
B or D	5
C or E	4
F, G, H, or I	2
J	1
K	0

Our secondary rule, to be invoked where ties exist from our primary rule, is (*b*) Prioritize tasks in order of longest task time. Note that D should be assigned before B, and E assigned before C due to this tie-breaking rule.

5. Make task assignments to form workstation 1, workstation 2, and so forth until all tasks are assigned. It is important to meet precedence and cycle time requirements as the assignments are made.

Station	Task	Task time (in sec)	Remaining unassigned time (in sec)	Feasible remaining tasks	Task with most followers	Task with longest operation time
Station 1	A	45	5.4	Idle	None	
Station 2	D	50	0.4	Idle	None	
Station 3	B	11	39.4	C, E	C, E	E
	E	15	24.4	C, H, I	C	
	C	9	15.4	F, G, H, I	F, G, H, I	F, G, H, I
	F	12	3.4 idle	None		
Station 4	G	12	38.4	H, I	H, I	H, I
	H	12	26.4	I		
	I	12	14.4	J		
	J	8	6.4 idle	None		
Station 5	K	9	41.4 idle	None		

6. Calculate the efficiency.

$$\text{Efficiency} = \frac{T}{N_a C} = \frac{195}{5 \times 50.4} = .77 \text{ or } 77\%$$

7. Evaluate the solution. An efficiency of 77 per cent indicates an imbalance or idle time of 23 per cent (1.0 – .77) across the entire line.

In addition to balancing a line for a given cycle time, managers must also consider four other options: pacing, behavioural factors, number of models produced, and cycle times.

Pacing is the movement of product from one station to the next after the cycle time has elapsed. Paced lines have no buffer inventory. Unpaced lines require inventory storage areas to be placed between stations.

Behavioural Factors

The most controversial aspect of product layout is behavioural response. Studies have shown that paced production and high specialization lower job satisfaction. One study has shown that productivity increased on unpaced lines. Many companies are exploring job enlargement and rotation to increase job variety and reduce excessive specialization. For example, New York Life has redesigned the jobs of workers who process and evaluate claims applications. Instead of using a production line approach with several workers doing specialized tasks, New York Life has made each worker solely responsible for an entire application. This approach increased worker responsibility and raised morale. In manufacturing, at its plant in Kohda, Japan, Sony Corporation dismantled the conveyor belts on which as many as 50 people assembled camcorders. It set up tables for workers to assemble an entire camera themselves, doing everything from soldering to testing. Output per worker is up 10 per cent, because the approach frees efficient assemblers to make more products instead of limiting them to conveyor belt's speed. And if something goes wrong, only a small section of the plant is affected. This approach also allows the line to match actual demand better and avoid frequent shutdown because of inventory buildups.

Number of Models Produced

A mixed-model line produces several items belonging to the same family. A single-model line produces one model with no variations. Mixed model production enables a plant to achieve both high-volume production and product variety. However, it complicates scheduling and increases the need for good communication about the specific parts to be produced at each station.

Cycle Times

A line's cycle time depends on the desired output rate (or sometimes on the maximum number of workstations allowed). In turn, the maximum line efficiency varies considerably with the cycle time selected. Thus, exploring a range of cycle times makes sense. A manager might go with a particularly efficient solution even if it does not match the output rate. The manager can compensate for the mismatch by varying the number of hours the line operates through overtime, extending shifts, or adding shifts. Multiple lines might even be the answer.

4.10 DESIGN OF PROCESS LAYOUT

The analysis involved in the design of production lines and assembly lines relates primarily to timing, coordination, and balance among individual stages in the process.

For process layouts, the relative arrangement of departments and machines is the critical factor because of the large amount of transportation and handling involved.

Procedure for Designing Process Layouts

Process layout design determines the best relative locations of functional work centres. Work centres that interact frequently, with movement of material or people, should be located close together, whereas those that have little interaction can be spatially separated. One approach of designing an efficient functional layout is described below.

1. List and describe each functional work centre.
2. Obtain a drawing and description of the facility being designed.
3. Identify and estimate the amount of material and personnel flow among work centres
4. Use structured analytical methods to obtain a good general layout.
5. Evaluate and modify the layout, incorporating details such as machine orientation, storage area location, and equipment access.

The first step in the layout process is to identify and describe each work centre. The description should include the primary function of the work centre; drilling, new accounts, or cashier; its major components, including equipment and number of personnel; and the space required. The description should also include any special access needs (such as access to running water or an elevator) or restrictions (it must be in a clean area or away from heat).

For a new facility, the spatial configuration of the work centres and the size and shape of the facility are determined simultaneously. Determining the locations of special structures and fixtures such as elevators, loading docks, and bathrooms becomes part of the layout process. However, in many cases the facility and its characteristics are given. In these situations, it is necessary to obtain a drawing of the facility being designed, including shape and dimensions, locations of fixed structures, and restrictions on activities, such as weight limits on certain parts of a floor or foundation.

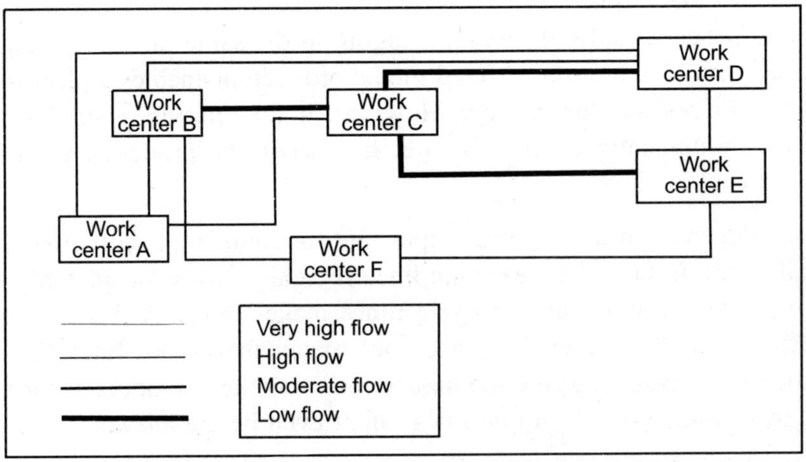

Fig 4.11 Relationship flow diagram

To minimize transport times and material-handling costs, we would like to place close together those work centres that have the greatest flow of materials and people between them.

To estimate the flows between work centres, it is helpful to begin by drawing relationship diagram as shown in Fig. 4.11.

For manufacturing systems, material flows and transporting costs can be estimated reasonably well using historical routings for products or through work sampling techniques applied to workers or jobs. The flow of people, especially in a service system such as a business office or a university administration building, may be difficult to estimate precisely, although work sampling can be used to obtain rough estimates.

The amounts and/or costs of flows among work centres are usually presented using a flow matrix, a flow-cost matrix, or a proximity chart.

1. Flow Matrix

A flow matrix is a matrix of the estimated amounts of flow between each pair of work centres. The flow may be materials (expressed as the number of loads transported) or people who move between centres. Each work centre corresponds to one row and one column, and the element f_{ij} designates the amount of flow from work centre (row) I to work centre (column) j. Normally, the direction of flow between work centres is not important, only the total amount, so f_{ij} and f_{ji} can be combined and the flows represented using only the upper right half of a matrix.

Flow Matrix Table

	Work centre									
	A	B	C	D	E	F	G	H	I	
A	-	25	32	0	80	0	30	5	15	
B	-	-	20	10	30	75	0	7	10	Daily flows
C	-	-	-	0	10	50	45	60	0	between
D	-	-	-	-	35	0	25	90	120	work
E	-	-	-	-	-	20	80	0	70	centres
F	-	-	-	-	-	-	0	150	20	
G	-	-	-	-	-	-	-	50	45	
H	-	-	-	-	-	-	-	-	80	
I	-	-	-	-	-	-	-	-	-	

2. Flow-cost Matrix

A basic assumption of facility layout is that the cost of moving materials or people between work centers is a function of distance travelled. Although more complicated cost functions can be accommodated, often we assume that the per unit cost of material and personnel flows between work centres is proportional to the distance between the centres. So for each type of flow between each pair of departments, i and j, we estimate the cost per unit per unit distance, c_{ij}.

Flow-cost Matrix Table

	Work centre									
	A	B	C	D	E	F	G	H	I	
A	-	25	32	0	80	0	30	5	15	
B	-	-	40	10	90	75	0	7	10	Daily cost
C	-	-	-	0	10	50	45	60	0	for flows
D	-	-	-	-	35	0	50	90	240	between
E	-	-	-	-	-	20	80	0	70	work centres
F	-	-	-	-	-	-	0	150	20	(Rs. per day
G	-	-	-	-	-	-	-	150	45	per 100 ft)
H	-	-	-	-	-	-	-	-	80	
I	-	-	-	-	-	-	-	-	-	

3. Proximity Chart

Proximity charts (relationship charts) are distinguished from flow and flow-cost matrices by the fact that they describe qualitatively the desirability or need for work centres to be close together, rather than providing quantitative measures of flow and cost. These charts are used when it is difficult to measure or estimate precise amounts or costs of flow among work centres. This is common when the primary flows involve people and do not have a direct cost but rather an indirect cost, such as when employees in a corporate headquarters move among departments (payroll, printing, information systems) to carry out their work.

4.11 SERVICE LAYOUT

The major factors considered for service providers, is an impact of location on sales and customer satisfaction. Customers usually look about how close a service facility is, particularly if the process requires considerable customer contact. Hence, service facility layouts should provide for easy entrance to these facilities from the freeways. Well-organized packing areas, easily accessible facilities, well designed walkways and parking areas are some of the requirements of service facility layout.

Service facility layout will be designed based on degree of customer contact and the service needed by a customer. These service layouts follow conventional layouts as required. For example, for car service station, product layout is adopted, where the activities for servicing a car follows a sequence of operation irrespective of the type of car. Hospital service is the best example for adaptation of process layout. Here, the service required for a customer will follow an independent path. The layout of car servicing and hospital is shown in Figs. 4.12 and 4.13.

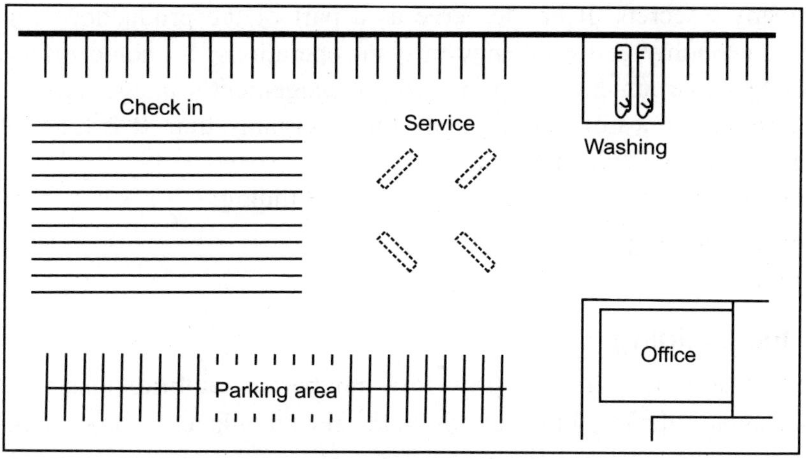

Fig. 4.12 Service layout for car servicing

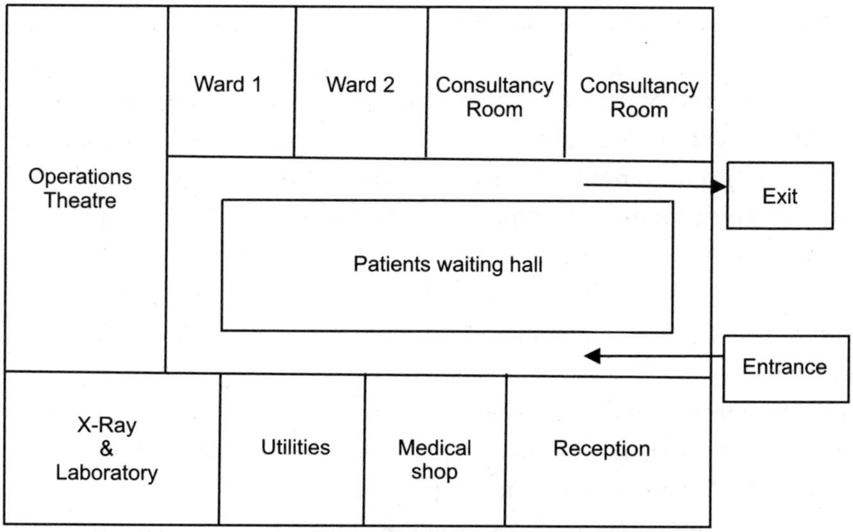

Fig. 4.13 Layout for hospitality service

4.12 ORGANISATION OF PHYSICAL FACILITIES

The following are the most important physical facilities to be organised:

1. Factory building
2. Lighting
3. Claimatic conditions
4. Ventilation
5. Work-related welfare facilities.

I. FACTORY BUILDING

Factory building is a factor which is the most important consideration for every industrial enterprise. A modem factory building is required to provide protection for men, machines, materials, products or even the company's secrets. It has to serve as a part of the production facilities and as a factor to maximise economy and efficiency in plant operations. It should offer a pleasant and comfortable working environment and project the management's image and prestige. Factory building is like skin and bones of a living body for an organisation. It is for these reasons that the factory building acquires great importance.

Following factors are considered for an Industrial Building:

A. Design of the building.

B. Types of buildings.

A. Design of the Building

The building should designed so as to provide a number of facilities—such as lunch rooms, cafeteria, locker rooms, crèches, libraries, first-aid and ambulance rooms, materials handling facilities, heating, ventilation, air-conditioning, etc. Following factors are considerations in the designing of a factory building:

1. **Flexibility:** Flexibility is one of thc important considerations because the building is likely to become obsolete and provides greater operating efficiency even when processes and technology change. Flexibility is necessary because it is not always feasible and economical to build a new plant, every time a new firm is organised or the layout is changed. With minor alternations, the building should be able to accommodate different types of operations.

2. **Product and equipment:** The type of product that is to be manufactured, determines column-spacing, type of floor, ceiling, heating and air-conditioning. A product of a temporary nature may call for a less expensive building and that would be a product of a more permanent nature. Similarly, a heavy product demands a far more different building than a product which is light in weight.

3. **Expansibility:** Growth and expansion are natural to any manufacturing enterprises. They are the indicators of the prosperity of a business. The following factors should be borne in mind if the future expansion of the concern is to be provided for:

(*i*) The *area of the land* which is to be acquired should be large enough to provide for the future expansion needs of the firm and accommodate current needs.

(*ii*) The *design of the building* should be in a rectangular shape. Rectangular shapes facilitate expansion on any side.

(*iii*) If *vertical expansion* is expected, strong foundations, supporters and columns must be provided.

(*iv*) If *horizontal expansion* is expected, the side walls must be made non-load-bearing to provide for easy removal.

4. **Employee facilities and service area:** Employee facilities must find a proper place in the building design because they profoundly affect the morale, comfort and productivity. The building plan should include facilities for lunch rooms, cafeteria, water coolers, parking area and the like. The provision of some of these facilities is a legal requirement. Others make good working conditions possible. And a good working condition is good business.

Service areas, such as the tool room, the supervisor's office, the maintenance room, receiving and dispatching stations, the stock room and facilities for scrap disposal, should also be included in the building design.

B. Types of Buildings

Industrial buildings may be grouped under two types:

1. Single-storey buildings,
2. Multi-storey buildings.

The decision on choosing a suitable type for a particular firm depends on the manufacturing process and the area of land and the cost of construction.

1. Single-storey Buildings

Most of the industrial buildings manufacturing which are now designed and constructed are single storeyed, particularly where lands are available at reasonable rates. Single-storey buildings offer several operating advantages. A single-storey construction is preferable when materials handling is difficult because the product is big or heavy, natural lighting is desired, heavy floor loads are required and frequent changes in layout are anticipated.

Advantages

Advantages of single-storey building are:

1. There is a greater flexibility in layout and production routing.
2. The maintenance cost resulting from the vibration of machinery is reduced considerably because of the housing of the machinery on the ground.
3. Expansion is easily ensured by the removal of walls.
4. The cost of transportation of materials is reduced because of the absence of materials handling equipment between floors.
5. All the equipment is on the same level, making for an easier and more effective layout supervision and control.
6. Greater floor load-bearing capacity for heavy equipment is ensured.
7. The danger of fire hazards is reduced because of the lateral spread of the building.

Limitations

Single-storey buildings suffer from some limitations. These are:

1. High cost of land, particularly in the city.
2. High cost of heating, ventilating and cleaning of windows.
3. High cost of transportation for moving men and materials to the factory which is generally located far from the city.

2. Multi-storey Buildings

Schools, colleges, shopping complexes, and residences, and for service industries like Software, BPO etc. multi-storey structures are generally popular, particularly in cities. Multi-storey buildings are useful in manufacture of light products, when the acquisition of land becomes difficult and expensive and when the floor load is less.

Advantages

When constructed for industrial use, multi-storey buildings offer the following advantages:

1. Maximum operating floor space (per sq. ft. of land). This is best suited in areas where land is very costly.
2. Lower cost of heating and ventilation.
3. Reduced cost of materials handling because the advantage of the use of gravity for the flow of materials.

Limitations

Following are the disadvantages of multi-storey building:

1. Materials handling becomes very complicated. A lot of time is wasted in moving them between floors.
2. A lot of floor space is wasted on elevators, stairways and fire escapes.
3. Floor load-bearing capacity is limited, unless special construction is used, which is very expensive.
4. Natural lighting is poor in the centres of the shop, particularly when the width of the building is somewhat great.
5. Layout changes cannot be effected easily and quickly.

Generally speaking, textile mills, food industries, detergent plants, chemical industries and software industry use these types of buildings.

II. LIGHTING

It is estimated that 80 per cent of the information required in doing job is perceived visually. Good visibility of the equipment, the product and the data involved in the work process is an essential factor in accelerating production, reducing the number of defective products, cutting down waste and preventing visual fatigue and headaches among the workers. It may also be added that both inadequate visibility and glare are frequently causes accidents.

In principle, lighting should be adapted to the type of work. However, the level of illumination, measured in should be increased not only in relation to the degree of precision or miniaturization of the work but also in relation to the worker's age. The accumulation of dust and the wear of the light sources cut down the level of illumination by 10–50 per cent of the original level. This gradual drop in the level should therefore be compensated for when designing the lighting system. Regular cleaning of lighting fixture is obviously essential.

Excessive contrasts in lighting levels between the worker's task and the general surroundings should also be avoided. The use of natural light should be encouraged. This can be achieved by installing windows that open, which are recommended to have an area equal to the time of day, the distance of workstations from the windows and the presence or absence of blinds. For this reason it is essential to have artificial lighting, will enable people to maintain proper vision and will ensure that the lighting intensity ratios between the task, the surrounding objects and the general environment are maintained.

Control of Lighting

In order to make the best use of lighting in the work place, the following points should be taken into account:

1. For uniform light distribution, install an independent switch for the row of lighting fixtures closest to the windows. This allows the lights to be switched on and off depending on whether or not natural light is sufficient.
2. To prevent glare, avoid using highly shiny, glossy work surfaces.
3. Use localized lighting in order to achieve the desired level for a particular fine job.
4. Clean light fixtures regularly and follow a maintenance schedule so as to prevent flickering of old bulbs and electrical hazards due to worn out cables.
5. Avoid direct eye contact with the light sources. This is usually achieved by positioning them properly. The use of diffusers is also quite effective.

III. CLIMATIC CONDITIONS

Control of the climatic conditions at the workplace is paramount importance to the workers health and comfort and to the maintenance of higher productivity. With excess heat or cold, workers may feel very uncomfortable, and their efficiency drops. In addition, this can lead to accidents.

This human body functions in such a way as to keep the central nervous system and the internal organs at a constant temperature. It maintains the necessary thermal balance by continuous heat exchange with the environment. It is essential to avoid excessive heat or cold, and wherever possible to keep the climatic conditions optimal so that the body can maintain a thermal balance.

Working in a Hot Environment

Hot working environments are found almost everywhere. Work premise in tropical countries may, on account of general climatic conditions, be naturally hot. When source of heat such as furnaces, kilns or hot processes are present, or when the physical workload is heavy, the human body may also have to deal with excess heat. It should be noted that in such hot working environments sweating is almost the only way in which the body can lose heat. As the sweat evaporates, the body cools. There is a relationship between the amount and speed of evaporation and a feeling of comfort. The more intense the evaporation, the quicker the body will cool and feel refreshed. Evaporation increases with adequate ventilation.

Working in a Cold Environment

Working in cold environments was once restricted to non-tropical or highly elevated regions. Now as a result of modern refrigeration, various groups of workers, even in tropical countries, are exposed to a cold environment.

Exposure to cold for short periods of time can produce serious effects, especially when workers are exposed to temperatures below 10°C. The loss of body heat is uncomfortable and quickly affects work efficiency. Workers in cold climates and refrigerated premises should be well protected against the cold by wearing suitable clothes, including footwear, gloves and, most importantly, a hat. Normally, dressing in layers traps dead air and serves as an insulation layer, thus keeping the worker warmer.

Control of the Thermal Environment

There are many ways of controlling the thermal environment. It is relatively easy to assess the effects of thermal conditions, especially when excessive heat or cold is an obvious problem. To solve the problem, however, consistent efforts using a variety of available measures are usually necessary. This is because the problem is linked with the general climate, which greatly affects the workplace climate, production technology, which is often the source of heat or cold and varying conditions of the work premises as well as work methods and schedules. Personal factors such as clothing, nutrition, personal habits, and age and individual differences in response to the given thermal conditions also need to be taken into account in the attempt to attain the thermal comfort of workers.

In controlling the thermal environment, one or more of the following **principles** may be applied:

1. Regulating workroom temperature by preventing outside heat or cold from entering (improved design of the roof, insulation material or installing an air-conditioned workroom. Air-conditioning is costly, especially in factories. But it is sometimes a worthwhile investment if an appropriate type is chosen);
2. provision of ventilation in hot workplaces by increasing natural ventilating through openings or installing ventilation devices;
3. separation of heat sources from the working area, insulation of hot surfaces and pipes, or placement of barriers between the heat sources and the workers;
4. control of humidity with a view to keeping it at low levels, for example by preventing the escape of steam from pipes and equipment;
5. Provision of adequate personal protective clothing and equipment for workers exposed to excessive radiant heat or excessive cold (heat-protective clothing with high insulation value may not be recommended for jobs with long exposure to moderate or heavy work as it prevents evaporative heat loss);
6. Reduction of exposure time, for example, by mechanization, remote control or alternating work schedules;
7. Insertion of rest pauses between work periods, with comfortable, if possible air-conditioned, resting facilities;
8. Ensuring a supply of cold drinking-water for workers in a hot environment and of hot drinks for those exposed to a cold environment.

IV. VENTILATION

Ventilation is the dynamic parameter that complements the concept of air space. For a given number of workers, the smaller the work premises the more should be the ventilation.

Ventilation differs from air circulation. Ventilation replaces contaminated air by fresh air, whereas as the air-circulation merely moves the air without renewing it. Where the air temperature and humidity are high, merely to circulate the air is not only ineffective but also increases heat absorption. Ventilation disperses the heat generated by machines and people at work. Adequate ventilation should be looked upon as an important factor in maintaining the worker's health and productivity.

Except for confined spaces, all working premises have some minimum ventilation. However, to ensure the necessary air flow (which should not be lower than 50 cubic metres of air per hour per worker), air usually needs to be changed between four to eight times per hour in offices or for sedentary workers, between eight and 12 times per hour in workshops and as much as 15 to 30 or more times per hour for public premises and where there are high levels of atmospheric pollution or humidity. The air speed used for workplace ventilation should be adapted to the air temperature and the energy expenditure: for sedentary work it should exceed 0.2 metre per second, but for a hot environment the optimum speed is between 0.5 and 1 metre per second. For hazardous work it may be even higher. Certain types of hot work can be made tolerable by directing a stream of cold air at the workers.

Natural ventilation, obtained by opening windows or wall or roof airvents, may produce significant air flows but can normally be used only in relatively mild climates. The effectiveness of this type of ventilation depends largely on external conditions. Where natural ventilation is inadequate, artificial ventilation should be used. A choice may be made between a blown-air system, an exhaust air system or a combination of both ('push-pull' ventilation). Only 'push-pull' ventilation systems allow for better regulation of air movement.

V. WORK-RELATED WELFARE FACILITIES

Work-related welfare facilities offered at or through the workplace can be important factors. Some facilities are very basic, but often ignored, such as drinking-water and toilets. Others may seem less necessary, but usually have an importance to workers far greater than their cost to the enterprise.

1. Drinking Water

Safe, cool drinking water is essential for all types of work, especially in a hot environment. Without it fatigue increases rapidly and productivity falls. Adequate drinking water should be provided and maintained at convenient points, and clearly marked as "Safe drinking water". Where possible it should be kept in suitable vessels, renewed at least daily, and all practical steps taken to preserve the water and the vessels from contamination.

2. Sanitary Facilities

Hygienic sanitary facilities should exist in all workplaces. They are particularly important where chemicals or other dangerous substances are used. Sufficient toilet facilities, with separate facilities for men and women workers, should be installed and conveniently located. Changing-rooms and cloakrooms should be provided. Washing facilities, such as washbasins with soap and towels, or showers, should be placed either within changing-rooms or close by.

3. First-aid and Medical Facilities

Facilities for rendering first-aid and medical care at the workplace in case of accidents or unforeseen sickness are directly related to the health and safety of the workers. First-aid boxes should be clearly marked and conveniently located. They should contain only first-aid requisites of a prescribed standard and should be in the charge of qualified person. Apart from first-aid boxes, it is also desirable to have a stretcher and suitable means to transport injured persons to a centre where medical care can be provided.

4. Rest Facilities

Rest facilities can include seat, rest-rooms, waiting rooms and shelters. They help workers to recover from fatigue and to get away from a noisy, polluted or isolated workstation. A sufficient number of suitable chairs or benches with backrests should be provided and maintained, including seats for occasional rest of workers who are obliged to work standing up. Rest-rooms enable workers to recover during meal and rest breaks.

5. Feeding Facilities

It is now well recognized that the health and work capacity of workers to have light refreshments are needed. A full meal at the workplace in necessary when the workers live some distance away and when the hours of work are so organized that the meal breaks are short. A snack bar, buffet or mobile trolleys can provide tea, coffee and soft drinks, as well as light refreshments. Canteens or a restaurant can allow workers to purchase a cheap, well-cooked and nutritious meal for a reasonable price and eat in a clean, comfortable place, away from the workstation.

6. Child-care Facilities

Many employers find that working mothers are especially loyal and effective workers, but they often face the special problems of carrying for children. It is for this reason that child-care facilities, including crèches and day-care centres, should be provided. These should be in secure, airy, clean and well lit premises. Children should be looked after properly by qualified staff and offered food, drink education and play at very low cost.

7. Recreational Facilities

Recreational facilities offer workers the opportunity to spend their leisure time in activities likely to increase physical and mental well-being. They may also help to improve social relations within the enterprise. Such facilities can include halls for recreation and for indoor and outdoor sports, reading-rooms and libraries, clubs for hobbies, picnics and cinemas. Special educational and vocational training courses can also be organized.

EXERCISE

Section A

1. What do you mean by plant location?
2. What is virtual proximity?
3. What is virtual factory?
4. What is agglomeration?
5. What is degglomeration?
6. What is plant layout?
7. Mention any four objectives of plant layout.

Section B

1. Explain different operations strategies in case of location choice for existing organisation.
2. Explain the factors to be considered while selecting the location for the new organisation.

3. Explain the reasons for global or foreign location.
4. Explain the Alfred Weber's theory of the location of industries.
5. Explain the objectives of plant layout.
6. Explain the main principles of plant layout.
7. Explain the factors considered for an industrial building.

Section C

1. Explain the need for selecting a suitable location.
2. Explain the factors influencing plant location.
3. Explain the different types of layouts.
4. Explain the physical facilities required in an organisation/factory.

5

FORECASTING DEMAND

CHAPTER OUTLINE

5.1 INTRODUCTION

Forecasts are essential for the smooth operations of business organizations. They provide information that can assist managers in guiding future activities toward organizational goals.

5.2 FORECASTING OBJECTIVES AND USES

Forecasts are estimates of the occurrence, timing, or magnitude of uncertain future events. Forecasts are essential for the smooth operations of business organizations. They provide information that can assist managers in guiding future activities toward organizational goals.

Operations managers are primarily concerned with forecasts of demand—which are often made by (or in conjunction with) marketing. However, managers also use forecasts to estimate raw material prices, plan for appropriate levels of personnel, help decide how much inventory to carry, and a host of other activities. This results in better use of capacity, more responsive service to customers, and improved profitability.

5.3 FORECASTING DECISION VARIABLES

Forecasting activities are a function of (1) the type of forecast (*e.g.*, demand, technological), (2) the time horizon (short, medium, or long range), (3) the database available, and (4) the methodology employed (qualitative or quantitative). Forecasts of demand are based primarily on non-random trends and relationships, with an allowance for random components. Forecasts for groups of products tend to be more accurate than those for single products, and short-term forecasts are more accurate than long-term forecasts (greater than five years). Quantification also enhances the objectivity and precision of a forecast.

5.4 FORECASTING METHODS

There are numerous methods to forecasting depending on the need of the decision-maker. These can be categorized in two ways:

1. Opinion and Judgmental Methods or Qualitative Methods.
2. Time Series or Quantitative Forecasting Methods.

5.4.1 Opinion and Judgmental Methods

Some opinion and judgment forecasts are largely intuitive, whereas others integrate data and perhaps even mathematical or statistical techniques. Judgmental forecasts often consist of (1) forecasts by individual sales people, (2) Forecasts by division or product-line managers, and (3) combined estimates of the two. *Historical analogy* relies on comparisons; *Delphi* relies on the best method from a group of forecasts. All these methods can incorporate experiences and personal insights. However, results may differ from one individual to the next and they are not all amenable to analysis. So there may be little basis for improvement over time.

5.4.2 Time Series Methods

A *time series* is a set of observations of a variable at regular intervals over time. In *decomposition analysis,* the components of a time series are generally classified as trend *T*, cyclical *C*, seasonal *S*, and random or irregular *R*. *(Note:* Autocorrelation effects are sometimes included as an additional factor.)

Time series are tabulated or graphed to show the nature of the time dependence. The forecast value (Ye) is commonly expressed as a multiplicative or additive function of its components; examples here will be based upon the commonly used multiplicative model.

$$Y_c = T.\ S.\ C.\ R \text{ multiplicative model} \quad (5.1)$$

$$Y_c = T + S + C + R \text{ additive model} \quad (5.2)$$

where *T* is Trend, *S* is Seasonal, *C* is Cyclical, and *R* is Random components of a series.

Trend is a gradual long-term directional movement in the data (growth or decline).

Seasonal effects are similar variations occurring during corresponding periods, e.g., December retail sales. Seasonal can be quarterly, monthly, weekly, daily, or even hourly indexes.

Cyclical factors are the long-term swings about the trend line. They are often associated with business cycles and may extend out to several years in length.

Random component are sporadic (unpredictable) effects due to chance and unusual occurrences. They are the residual after the trend, cyclical, and seasonal variations are removed.

SUMMARY OF FORECASTING METHODS

Method	Description	Time horizon	Relative cost
Opinion and judgment (qualitative)			
Sales force composites	Estimates from field sales people are aggregated	SR-MR	L-M
Executive opinion (and/or panels)	Marketing, finance, and production managers jointly prepare forecast	SR-LR	L-M

contd.

Field sales and product-line management	Estimates from regional sales people are reconciled with national projections from product-line managers	MR	M
Historical analogy	Forecast from comparison with similar product previously introduced	SR-LR	L-M
Delphi	Experts answer a series of questions (anonymously), receive feedback, and revise estimates	LR	M-H
Market surveys	Questionnaires/interviews for data to learn about consumer behaviour	MR-LR	H
Time series (quantitative)			
Naive	Forecast equals latest value or latest plus or minus some percentage	SR	L
Moving average	Forecast is average of *n* most recent periods (can also be weighted)	SR	L
Trend projection	Forecast is linear, exponential, or other projection of past trend	MR-LR	L
Decomposition	Time series is divided into trend, seasonal, cyclical, and random components	SR-LR	L
Exponential smoothing	Forecast is an exponentially weighted moving average, where latest values carry most weight	SR	L
Box-Jenkins	A time-series-regression model is proposed, statistically tested, modified, and retested until satisfactory	MR-LR	M-H
Associative (quantitative)			
Regression and correlation (and leading indicators)	Use one or more associate variables to forecast via a least-squares equation (regression) or via a close association (correlation) with an explanatory variable	SR-MR	M-H
Econometric	Use simultaneous solution of multiple regression equations that relate to broad range of economic activity	SR-LR	H
Time series (quantitative)			
Naive	Forecast equals latest value or latest plus or minus some percentage	SR	L
Moving average	Forecast is average of *n* most recent periods (can also be weighted)	SR	L
Trend projection	Forecast is linear, exponential, or other projection of past trend	MR-LR	L
Decomposition	Time series is divided into trend, seasonal, cyclical, and random components	SR-LR	L
Exponential smoothing	Forecast is an exponentially weighted moving average, where latest values carry most weight	SR	L
Box-Jenkins	A time-series-regression model is proposed, statistically tested, modified, and retested until satisfactory	MR-LR	M-H
Associative (quantitative)			
Regression and correlation (and leading indicators)	Use one or more associate variables to forecast via a least-squares equation (regression) or via a close association (correlation) with an explanatory variable	SR-MR	M-H
Econometric	Use simultaneous solution of multiple regression equations that relate to broad range of economic activity	SR-LR	H

Key: L = low, M = medium, H = high, SR = short range, MR = medium range, LR = long range.

FORECASTING PROCEDURE FOR USING TIME SERIES

Following are the steps in time series forecasting:

1. Plot historical data to confirm relationship (*e.g.*, linear, exponential).
2. Develop a trend equation (*T*) to describe the data.
3. Develop a seasonal index (*SI*, *e.g.*, monthly index values).
4. Project trend into the future (*e.g.*, monthly trend values).
5. Multiply trend values by corresponding seasonal index values.
6. Modify projected values by any knowledge of:

   (*C*) Cyclical business conditions,

   (*R*) Anticipated irregular effects.

   Trend: Three methods for describing trend are: (1) Moving average, (2) Hand fitting, and (3) Least squares.

1. MOVING AVERAGE

A centered moving average (MA) is obtained by summing and averaging the values from a given number of periods repetitively, each time deleting the oldest value and adding a new value. Moving averages can smooth out fluctuations in any data, while preserving the general pattern of the data (longer averages result in more smoothing). However, they do not yield a forecasting equation, nor do they generate values for the ends of the data series.

$$\text{MA} = \frac{\sum x}{\text{Number of Period}}$$

A weighted moving average (MAw) allows some values to be emphasized by varying the weights assigned to each component of the average. Weights can be either percentages or a real number.

$$\text{MA}_{wt} = \frac{\sum (Wt)X}{\sum Wt}$$

ILLUSTRATION 1: *Shipments (in tons) of welded tube by an aluminum producer are shown below:*

Year	1	2	3	4	5	6	7	8	9	10	11
Tons	2	3	6	10	8	7	12	14	14	18	19

(a) Graph the data, and comment on the relationship. *(b)* Compute a 3-year moving average, plot it as a dotted line, and use it to forecast shipments in year 12. *(c)* Using a weight of 3 for the most recent data, 2 for the next, and 1 for the oldest, forecast shipments in year 12.

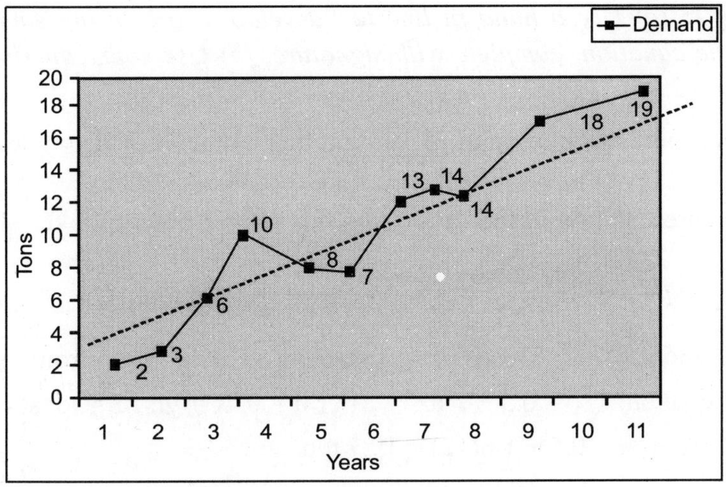

Table 5.1 3-year moving average

Year	Shipments (tonns)	3-year moving total	3-year moving average
1	2	-	-
2	3	11	3.7
3	6	19	6.3
4	10	24	8.0
5	8	25	8.3
6	7	27	9.0
7	13	33	11.0
8	14	40	13.3
9	14	46	15.3
10	18	51	17.0
11	19	-	-

(*a*) The data points appear relatively linear. (*b*) See Table 5.1 for computations and Fig. 5.2 for plot of the MA. The MA forecast for year 12 would be that of the latest average, 17.0 tons.

(*c*)
$$MA_{wt} = \frac{\sum (Wt)X}{\sum Wt} = \frac{(1)(14)+(2)(18)+(3)(19)}{1+2+3} = 17.8 \text{ tons}$$

2. HAND FITTING

A hand fit or freehand curve is simply a plot of a representative line that (subjectively) seems to best fit the data points. For linear data, the forecasting equation will be of the form:

$$Y_c = a + b\,(X) \text{ (signature)}$$

where Y_c is the trend value, a is the intercept (where line crosses the vertical axis), b is the slope (the rise, Δy, divided by the run, Δx), and X is the time value (years, quarters, etc.). The "signature" identifies the point in time when $X = 0$, as well as the X and Y units.

ILLUSTRATION 2: *(a) Use a hand fit line to "develop a forecasting equation for the data in Fig. 5.2. State the equation, complete with signature. (b) Use your equation to forecast tube shipments for year 12.*

(*a*) Select points some distance apart. A straight line connecting the values for years 3 and 8 might be a good

Free hand representation of the data. From this we can determine the slope and intercept:

$$Slope: b \;=\; \frac{\Delta Y}{\Delta X} = \frac{Y_2 - Y_1}{X_2 - X_1} = \frac{14-6}{8-3} = 1.6 \text{ tons}$$

Intercept: $a = 0.5$ tons (*Note:* This is the estimated Y value at $X = 0$ from graph.)

Equation: $Y_C = 0.5 + 1.6X$ (Yr 0 = 0, X = yrs, Y = tons)

(*b*) For year 12: $Yc = 0.5 + 1.6(12) = 19.7$ tons.

3. Least squares

Least squares arc a mathematical technique of fitting a trend to data points. The resulting *line of best fit* has the following properties: (1) the summation of all vertical deviations about it is zero, (2) the summation of all vertical deviations squared is a minimum, and (3) the line goes through the means X and Y. For linear equations, the line of best fit is found by the simultaneous solution for a and b of the following two *normal equations:*

$$\sum Y = na + b\sum X$$

$$\sum XY = a\sum X + b\sum X^2$$

The above equations can be used in the form shown above and are used in that form for regression. However, with time series, the data can also be coded so that $\sum X = 0$. Two terms then dropout, and the equations are simplified to:

$$\sum Y = na \qquad a = \frac{\sum Y}{n}$$

$$\sum XY = b\sum X^2 \qquad b = \frac{\sum XY}{\sum X^2}.$$

To code the time series data, designate the center of the time span as X = 0 and let each successive period be ±1 more unit away. (For an even number of periods, use values of ±0.5, 1.5, 2.5, etc.).

ILLUSTRATION 3: *Use the least square method to develop a linear trend equation for the data from illustration 1. State the equation and forecast a trend value for year 16.*

Table 5.2

Year	X year coded	Y shipments (tons)	XY	X²
1	– S	2	– 10	25
2	– 4	3	– 12	16
3	– 3	6	– 18	9
4	– 2	10	– 20	4
5	– 1	8	– 8	1
6	0	7	0	0
7	1	12	12	1
8	2	14	28	4
9	3	14	42	9
10	4	18	72	16
11	5	19	95	25
	0	113	181	110

we have:

$$a = \frac{\sum Y}{n} = \frac{113}{11} = 10.30 \qquad b = \frac{\sum XY}{\sum X^2} = \frac{181}{110} = 1.6$$

The forecasting equation is of the form $Y = a + bX$.

$$Y = 10.3 + 1.6\ X \text{ (year } 6 = 0,\ X = \text{years},\ Y = \text{tons).}$$

Seasonal indexes: A seasonal index *(SI)* is a ratio that relates a recurring seasonal variation to the corresponding trend value at the given time. In the *ratio-to-moving average* method of calculation monthly (or quarterly) data are typically used to compute a 12-month (or 4-quarter) moving average.

(This dampens out all seasonal fluctuations.) Actual monthly (or quarterly) values are then *divided by the moving average value* centered on the actual month. In the *ratio-to-trend* method, the actual values are *divided by the trend value* centered on the actual month. The ratios obtained for several of the same months (or quarters) are then averaged to obtain the seasonal index values. The indexes can be used to obtain seasonalized forecast values, Y_{sz} (or to deseasonalize actual data). $Y_{sz} = (SI)\ Yc$.

ILLUSTRATION 4: *Snowsport International has experienced low snowboard sales in July, as shown in Table 5.3. Using the ratio-to-trend values, calculate a seasonal index value for July and explain its meaning.*

Table 5.3

	Yr 5	Yr 6	Yr 7	Yr 8	Yr 9	Yr 10	Yr 11	Yr I2
July actual sales	22	30	18	26	45	36	40	
July trend value, *Yc*	170	190	210	230	250	270	290	
Ratio (actual ÷ trend)	0.13	0.16	0.09	0.11	0.18	0.13	0.14	

Total = 0.94.

(*a*) A third row has been added to Table 5.3 to show the ratio of actual to trend values for July. Using a simple average, the July index is $SI_{July} = 0.94 \div 7 = 0.13$. This means that July is typically only 13 per cent of the trend value for July in any given year. Winter months are likely quite high.

ILLUSTRATION 5: *The forecasting equation for the previous example, centered in July of year 4 with X units in months, was Yc = 1800 + 20X (July 15, Yr 4 = 0, X = mo, Y = units/yr).*

* Use this equation and the July seasonal index of 0.13 to compute (*a*) the trend (deseasonalized) value for July of year 12 and (*b*) the forecast of actual (seasonalized) snowboard sales in July of year 12.

(*a*) July of year 12 is (8)(12) = 96 months away from July of year 4, so the/trend value is:

Yc = 1800 + 20(96) = 3,240 units/yr or 3,240 units/yr 12 mo/yr = 310 units/mo

(*b*) The actual (seasonalized) forecast is *Ysz* = (SI) *Yc* = (0.13)(310) = 40 units.

5.5 EXPONENTIAL SMOOTHING

Exponential smoothening is a moving-average forecasting technique that weights past data in an Exponential manner so that most recent data carry more weight in the moving average.

With simple Exponential smoothening, the forecast F_t is made up of the last period forecast F_{t-1} plus a portion, α, of the difference between the last periods actual demand A_{t-1} and last period forecast F_{t-1}.

$$F_t = F_{t-1} + (A_{t-1} - F_{t-1}).$$

ILLUSTRATION 6: *A firm uses simple exponential smoothing with α = 0.1 to forecast demand. The forecast for the week of February 1 was 500 units, whereas actual demand turned out to be 450 units.*

(*a*) *Forecast the demand for the week of February 8.*

(*b*) *Assume that the actual demand during the week of February 8 turned out to be 505 units. Forecast the demand for the week of February 15, Continue forecasting through March 15, assuming that subsequent demands were actually 516, 488, 467, 554 and 510 units.*

SOLUTION

(*a*)

$$F_t = F_{t-1} + \alpha (A_{t-1} - F_{t-1})$$

$$= 500 + 0.1(450 - 500) = 495 \text{ unit}$$

(*b*) Arranging the procedure in tabular form, we have

Table 5.4

Week	Actual demand A_{t-1}	Old forecast F_{t-1}	Forecast error $A_{t-1} - F_{t-1}$	Correction $\alpha (A_{t-1} - F_{t-1})$	New forecast $(F_t) F_{t-1} + (A_{t-1} - F_{t-1})$
Feb. 1	450	500	– 50	– 5	495
8	505	495	10	1	496
15	516	496	20	2	498
22	488	498	– 10	– 1	497
Mar. 1	467	497	– 30	– 3	494
8	554	494	60	6	500
15	510	500	10	1	501

The smoothing constant, α, is a number between 0 and 1 that enters multiplicatively into each forecast but whose influence declines exponentially as the data become older. Typical values range from 0.01 to 0.40. An Ion α gives more weight to the past average and will effectively dampen high random variation. High α values are more responsive to changes in demand (*e.g.*, from new-product introductions, promotional campaigns). An α of 1 would reflect total adjustment to recent demand, and the forecast would be last period's actual demand. A satisfactory α can generally be determined by trial-and-error modeling (on computer) to see which value minimizes forecast error.

Simple exponential smoothing yields only an average. It does not extrapolate for trend effects. No α value will fully compensate for a trend in the data. An α value that yields an approximately equivalent degree of smoothing as a moving average of n periods is:

$$\alpha = \frac{2}{n+1}$$

5.5.1 Adjusted Exponential Smoothing

Adjusted exponential smoothing models have all the features of simple exponential smoothing models, plus they project into the future (for example, to time period $t + 1$) by adding a trend correction increment, T_t, to the current period smoothed average, $\hat{F}_t$.

$$\hat{F}_{t+1} = \hat{F}_t + T_t$$

Figure 5.1 depicts the components of a trend-adjusted forecast that utilizes a second smoothing coefficient β. The β value determines the extent to which the trend adjustment relies on the latest difference in forecast amounts $(\hat{F}_t - \hat{F}_{t-1})$ versus the previous trend T_{t-1} Thus:

$$\hat{F}_t = \alpha A_{t-1} + (1-\alpha)\left(\hat{F}_{t-1} + T_{t-1}\right)$$

$$T_t = \beta(\hat{F}_t - \hat{F}_{t-1}) + (1-\beta)T_{t-1}$$

A low β gives more smoothing of the trend and may be useful if the trend is not well-established. A high β will emphasize the latest trend and be more responsive to recent changes in trend. The initial trend adjustment T_{t-1} is sometimes assumed to be zero.

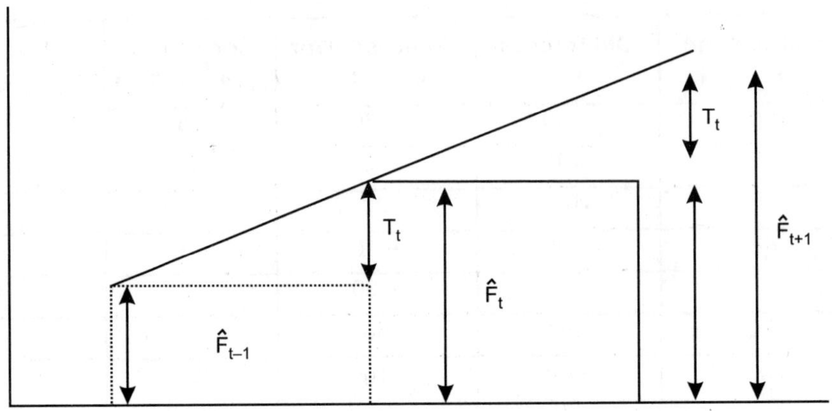

Fig. 5.1 Components of trend adjusted forecast

Self-adaptive models: Self-adjusting computer models that change the values of the smoothing coefficients α s and β s in an adaptive fashion have been developed; these models help to minimize the amount of forecast error.

5.6 REGRESSION AND CORRELATION METHODS

Regression and correlation techniques quantify the statistical association between two or more variables.

(*a*) ***Simple regression*** expresses the relationship between a dependent variable Y and a independent variable X in terms of the slope and intercept of the line of best fit relating the two variables.

(*b*) ***Simple correlation*** expresses the degree or closeness of the relationship between two variables in terms of a correlation coefficient that provides an indirect measure of the variability of points from the line of best fit. Neither regression nor correlation gives proof of a cause-effect relationship.

5.6.1 Regression

The simple linear regression model takes the form $Y_c = a + bX$, where Yc is the dependent variable and X the independent variable. Values for the slope b and intercept α are obtained by using the *normal equations* written in the convenient form:

$$b = \frac{\sum XY - n\overline{X}\overline{Y}}{\sum X^2 - nX^2} \tag{1}$$

$$a = \overline{Y} - b\overline{X} \tag{2}$$

In Equations. (1) and (2), $\overline{X} = (\sum X)/n$ and $\overline{Y} = (\sum Y)/n$ Y are the means of the independent and dependent variables respectively, and n is the number of pairs of observations made.

ILLUSTRATION 7: *The general manager of a building materials production plant feels that the demand for plasterboard shipments may be related to the number of construction permits issued in the county during the previous quarter. The manager has collected the data shown in Table 5.5.*

(a) *Compute values for the slope b and intercept a.*

(b) *Determine a point estimate for plasterboard shipments when the number of construction permits is 30.*

Table 5.5

Construction permits (X)	Plasterboard shipments (Y)
15	6
9	4
40	16
20	6
25	13
25	9
15	10
35	16

SOLUTION: (*a*)

Table 5.6

X	Y	XY	X^2	Y^2
15	6	90	225	36
9	4	36	81	16
40	16	640	1,600	256
20	6	120	400	36
25	13	325	625	169
25	9	225	625	81
15	10	150	225	100
35	16	560	1,225	256
184	**80**	**2,146**	**5,006**	**950**

$n = 8$ pairs of observations $\quad \bar{X} = \left(\sum X\right)/n \quad$ or $\quad \bar{X} = \dfrac{184}{8} = 23$

$$\bar{Y} = \left(\sum Y/n\right) \quad \text{or} \quad \bar{Y} = \frac{80}{8} = 10$$

$$b = \frac{\sum XY - n\bar{X}\bar{Y}}{\sum X^2 - nX^2} \quad \text{or} \quad b = \frac{2146 - 8(23)(10)}{5006 - 8(23)(23)} = 0.395$$

$$a = \bar{Y} - b\bar{X} \quad \text{or} \quad a = 10 - 0.395(23) = 0.91$$

(*b*) The regression equation is

$$Y_c = 0.91 + 0.395\,X \;(X = \text{permits, } Y = \text{shipments})$$

Then, letting $X = 30$,

$$Y_c = 0.91 + 0.395(30) = 12.76 \sim 13 \text{ shipments.}$$

STANDARD DEVIATION OF REGRESSION

A regression line describes the relationship between a given value of the independent variable X and μ_{y-x} the mean of the corresponding probability distribution of the dependent variable *Y.* We assume the distribution of *Y* values is normal for any given X value. The point estimate, or forecast, is the mean of that distribution for any given value of X.

The *standard deviation* of *regression* S_{y-x} is a measure of the dispersion of data points around the regression line. For simple regression, the computation of S_{y-x} has $n - 2$ degrees of freedom.

$$S_{y-x} = \sqrt{\frac{\sum Y^2 - a\sum Y - b\sum XY}{n-2}}.$$

ILLUSTRATION 8: *Using the data from illustration 7, compute the Standard Deviation of Regression.*

SOLUTION

$$S_{y-x} = \sqrt{\frac{\sum Y^2 - a\sum Y - b\sum XY}{n-2}}$$

$$S_{y-x} = \sqrt{\frac{950 - (0.91)(80) - (0.396)(2146)}{8-2}} = 2.2 \text{ shipments.}$$

ILLUSTRATION 9: *Using the data from illustrations 7 and 8,develop a 95 per cent prediction interval estimate for the specific number of shipments to be made when 30 construction permits were issued during the previous quarter.*

Note: $X = 23$ for the $n = 8$ observations, and $\Sigma\,(X - X)^2 = 774$. Also, from Illustration 7, $Y_c = 13$ shipments, where $X = 30$; and from Illustration 8, $S_{y-x} = 2.2$ shipments.

SOLUTION

$$\text{Prediction interval} = Y_c \pm t\text{S}_{\text{ind}} \qquad (3)$$

where the *t*-value for $n - 2 = 8 - 2 = 6$ degrees of freedom = 2.45 and where

$$S_{ind} = S_{y-x}\sqrt{1 + \frac{1}{n} + \frac{(X - \bar{X})^2}{\sum (X - \bar{X})^2}}$$

$$S_{ind} = 2.2\sqrt{1 + \frac{1}{8} + \frac{(30-23)^2}{774}} = 2.4 \text{ shipments}$$

∴ Production interval = 13 ± 2.45 (2.4) = 7.1 to 18.90 (use 7 to 19 shipments).

For large samples ($n \geq 100$), Equation 3 can be approximated by using the normal (*Z*) distribution rather than the *t*, in the form of $Y_c \pm ZS_{y-x}$ (*Note:* For 95 per cent confidence, the Z value is the same as *t* with ∞ df, which from Table 5.7 (given below) equals 1.96.) Also, the significance of the regression line slope coefficient (*b*) can be tested using the expression:

$$t_{calc} = \frac{b}{S_b}$$

where $$S_b = S_{y-x}\sqrt{\frac{1}{\sum(X-\bar{X})^2}}$$

If the value of $t_{calc} > t_{df}$ from the *t*-table, the relationship between the *X* and *Y* variables is statistically significant.

Table 5.7 *t*-Distribution values (for 90 per cent and 95 per cent confidence)

df	5	6	7	8	9	10	12	15	20	30	00
t_{05} (90%) t_{10} (95%)	2.02 2.57	1.94 2.45	1.90 2.37	1.86 2.31	1.83 2.26	1.81 2.23	1.78 2.17	1.75 2.13	1.73 2.08	1.70 2.04	1.65 1.96

5.6.2 Correlation

The simple linear *correlation coefficient r* is a number between –1 and + 1 that tells how well a linear equation describes the relationship between two variables. As illustrated in Fig. 5.2 *r* is designated as positive if *Y* increases as *X* increases, and negative if *Y* decreases as *X* increases. An *r* of zero indicates an absence of any relationship between the two variables.

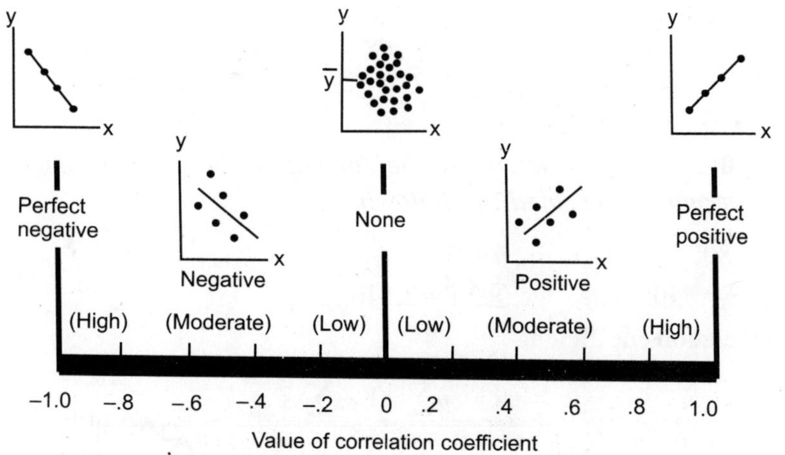

Fig. 5.2 Interpretation of correlation coefficient

The deviation of all points (*Y*) from the regression line (Y_c) consists of deviation accounted for by the regression line (explained) and random deviation (unexplained). Fig. 5.3 illustrates this for one point, *Y*. Squaring the deviation we have variation.

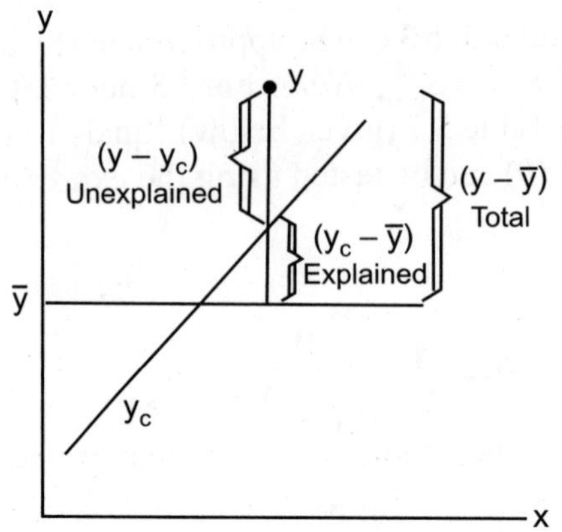

Fig. 5.3 Deviation of dependent variable

$$\text{Total variation} = \text{explained} + \text{unexplained}$$

$$\sum(Y-\bar{Y})^2 = \sum(Y_C-\bar{Y})^2 + \sum(Y-Y_C)^2$$

The *coefficient of determination* r^2 is the ratio of explained variation to total variation:

$$r^2 = \frac{\sum(Y_C-\bar{Y})^2}{\sum(Y-\bar{Y})^2}$$

The *coefficient of correlation* r is the square root of the coefficient of determination:

$$r = \sqrt{\frac{\sum(Y_C-\bar{Y})^2}{\sum(Y-\bar{Y})^2}}$$

When the sample size is sufficiently large (*e.g.*, greater than 50), the value of r can be computed more directly form:

$$r = \frac{n\sum XY - \sum X.\sum Y}{\sqrt{\left(n\sum X^2 - (\sum X)^2\right)\left[n\sum Y^2 - (\sum Y)^2\right]}}$$

ILLUSTRATION 10: *A study to determine the correlation between plasterboard shipments X and construction permits Y revealed the following:*

$\sum X = 184$ $\sum Y = 80$' $n = 8$

$\sum X^2 = 5{,}006$ $\sum Y^2 = 950$ $\sum XY = 2{,}146$

Compute the correlation coefficient.

$$r = \frac{n\sum XY - \sum X.\sum Y}{\sqrt{\left(n\sum X^2 - (\sum X)^2\right)\left[n\sum Y^2 - (\sum Y)^2\right]}}$$

$$r = \frac{8\,(2146) - (184)\,(80)}{\sqrt{[8(5006)-(184)^2][8(950)-80^2]}} = \frac{2448}{\sqrt{7430{,}400}} = 0.90.$$

The significance of any value of r can be statistically tested under a hypothesis of no correlation.

To test, the computed value of r is compared with a tabled value of r for a given sample size and significance level. If the computed value exceeds the tabled value, the correlation is significant.

5.7 APPLICATIONS AND CONTROL OF FORECAST

5.7.1 Forecast Controls

A simple measure of forecast error is to compute the deviation of the actual from the forecast values. Deviations will vary from plus to minus, but they should tend to average out near zero if the forecast is on target.

Forecast error = actual demand – forecast demand.

The individual forecast errors are usually summarized in a statistic such as average error, mean squared error, or mean absolute deviation (MAD).

$$\text{MAD} = \frac{\sum|\text{Error}|}{n}$$

The estimate of the MAD can be continually updated by using an exponential smoothing technique. Thus the current MAD_t is:

$$\text{MAD}_t = \propto (\text{actual} - \text{forecast}) + (1 - \propto)\ \text{MAD}_{t-1}$$

where $\propto$ is a smoothing constant. Higher values of α will make the current MAD, more responsive to current forecast errors.

When the average deviation (MAD) is divided into the cumulative deviation [$\sum$(Actual – forecast)], the result is a *tracking signal:*

$$\text{Tracking signal} = \frac{\sum(\text{Actual} - \text{forecast})}{MAD}$$

Tracking signals are one way of monitoring how well a forecast is predicting actual values. They express the cumulative deviation (also called the running sum of forecast error, RSFE) in terms of the number of average deviations (MADs). Action limits for tracking signals commonly range from three to eight. When the signal goes beyond this range, corrective action may be required.

ILLUSTRATION 11: *A high-valued item has a tracking-signal-action limit of 4 and has been forecast as shown in Table 5.8. Compute the tracking signal, and indicate whether some corrective action is appropriate.*

Table 5.8

Period	Actual	Forecast	Error (A – F)	|Error|	$(\text{Error})^2$ (A– F)
1	80	78	2	2	A
2	92	79	13	13	169
3	71	83	–12	12	144
4	83	79	4	4	16
5	90	80	10	10	100
6	102	83	19	19	361
		Totals	36	60	794

$$\text{MAD} = \frac{\sum|\text{Error}|}{n} = \frac{60}{6} = 10$$

$$\text{Tracking signal} = \frac{\sum(\text{Actual} - \text{forecast})}{\text{MAD}} = \frac{36}{10} = 3.6$$

Action limit of 4 is not exceeded. Therefore, no action is necessary.

Control charts are a second way of monitoring forecast error. Variations of actual from forecast (or average) values are quantified in terms of the estimated standard deviation of forecast S_F.

$$S_F = \sqrt{\frac{\sum(\text{Actual} - \text{Forecast}t)^2}{n-1}}$$

Control limits are then set, perhaps at two or three standard deviations away from the forecast average $\bar{X}$ or the $2S_F$ or $3S_F$ limits are used as maximum acceptable limits for forecast error. Note that the limits are based on individual forecast values, so you assume that the errors are normally distributed around the forecast average.

ILLUSTRATION 12

(*a*) *Compute the $2S_F$ control limits for the data given in Illustration 11.*

(*b*) *Are all forecast errors within these limits?*

(*a*) Control limits about the mean CL = $\bar{X} \pm 2S_F$

Where

$$\bar{X} = \frac{78 + 79 + 83 + 79 + 80 + 83}{6} = 80$$

$$S_F = \sqrt{\frac{\sum(\text{Actual} - \text{Forecast})^2}{n-1}} = \sqrt{\frac{794}{6-2}} = \sqrt{196} = 14$$

Therefore, CL = 80 ± 2(14) = 52 to 108 (rounded to integer values).

(*b*) All forecast errors (as calculated in Illustration 5.11) are within the ::t:: 28 error limit.

Note: Since *n* is less than 30, this distribution of forecast errors does not wholly satisfy the normality assumption.

Forecast Application

Forecasts should be sufficiently accurate to plan for future activities. Low-accuracy methods may suffice; higher accuracy usually costs more to design and implement. *Long-term forecasts*—used for location, capacity, and new-product decisions-require techniques with long-term horizons. *Short-term forecasts*— such as those for production-and-inventory control, labour levels, and cost controls–can rely more on recent history.

ILLUSTRATION 13: *A food processing company uses a moving average to forecast next month's demand. Past actual demand (in units) is as shown in Table 5.9.*

(*a*) *Compute a simple 5-month moving average to forecast demand for month 52.*

(*b*) *Compute a weighted 3-month moving average, where the weights are highest for the latest months and descend in order of 3, 2 and 1.*

Table 5.9

Month	Actual demand
43	105
44	106
45	110
46	110
47	114
48	121
49	130
50	128
51	137

SOLUTION

(*a*) $$\text{MA} = \frac{\sum X}{\text{Number of Period}} = \frac{114+121+130+128+137}{5} = 126 \text{ units}$$

(*b*) $$\text{MA}_{wt} = \frac{\sum (wt)X}{\sum Wt} = \frac{3\times 137+2\times 128+1\times 130}{6} = \frac{797}{6} = 133 \text{ units}$$

ILLUSTRATION 14: *For N = 7 years of (Coded) time series data,* $\sum Y = 56$, $\sum XY = 70$, *and* $\sum X^2 = 28$.

(*a*) Find the intercept and slope of the linear trend line.

(*b*) Forecast the *Y*-value for 6 years distant from the origin.

SOLUTION

(*a*) $$\text{Intercept} = \frac{\sqrt{Y}}{N} = \frac{56}{7} = 8.0 \quad \text{Slope} = \frac{\sum XY}{\sum X^2} = \frac{70}{28} = 2.5$$

(*b*) $$Y_c = a + b\,(X) = 8.0 + 2.5\,(6) = 23.0.$$

ILLUSTRATION 15: *The following forecasting equation has been derived by a least-squares method to describe the shipments of welded aluminum tube.*

$$Y_c = 10.27 + 1.65X \ \ (1996 = O, X = \text{years}, Y = \text{tons/yr})$$

Rewrite the equation by (a) shifting the origin to 2001; (b) expressing X units in months, retaining Y in tons per year; (c) expressing X units in months, and Y in tons per month.

SOLUTION

(*a*) $Y_c = 10.27 + 1.65(X + 5)$

$= 18.52 + 1.65X$ (yr 2001 = 0, X = years, Y = tons per year)

(*b*) $Y_c = 10.27 + \dfrac{1.65X}{12}$

$= 10.27 + 0.14X$ (July 1, 1996 = 0, X = months, Y = tons per year)

(*c*) $Y_c = \dfrac{10.27 + 0.14X}{12}$

$= 0.86 + 0.01X$ (July 1, 1996 = 0, X = months, Y = tons per month)

ILLUSTRATION 16: *Quarterly trend values for units demanded have been computed as $Q_1 = 620$, $Q_2 = 655$, $Q_3 = 690$, and $Q_4 = 725$. The corresponding seasonal indexes for the quarters are 0.72, 1.33, 1.05, and 0.90, respectively. Forecast the actual (seasonalized) sales for Q_3 and Q_4.*

SOLUTION

For *Q3*: Y_{sz} = (*SI*) *Yc* = (1.05)(690) = 725 units

For *Q4*: Y_{sz} = (*SI*) *Yc* = (0.90)(725) = 653 units.

ILLUSTRATION 17: *A sportswear manufacturer wishes to use data from a 5-year period to develop seasonal indexes. Trend values and ratios of actual A to trend T for most months have already been computed as shown in Table 5.10. April and May actual and trend values are shown in Tables 5.11 and 5.12.*

Table 5.10

Month	Jan.	Feb.	Mar.	April	May	June	July	Aug.	Sept.	Oct.	Nov.	Dec.
Ratio AIT	0.72	0.58	0.85			1.43	1.21	1.05	0.98	0.92	0.88	1.12

Compute the seasonal relatives for April and May, correct the total to equal 12.00, and determine the resulting seasonal indexes. See Tables 5.11 and 5.12.

Table 5.11 **Table 5.12**

Year	1	2	3	4	5	Year	I	2	3	4	5
April actual	382	401	458	480	533	May actual	485	530	560	592	656
April trend	400	436	472	508	544	May trend	403	439	475	511	547
April A/T	0.96	0.92	0.97	0.94	0.98	May A/T	1.20	1.21	1.18	1.16	1.20

SOLUTION

April total = 4.77

April average = 4.77 ÷ 5 = 0.95

May total = 5.95

May average = 5.95 ÷ 5 = 1.19

Month	Jan.	Feb.	Mar.	April	May	June	July	Aug.	Sept.	Oct.	Nov.	Dec.	12 month.
Ratio A/T	0.72	0.58	0.85	0.95	1.19	1.43	1.21	1.05	0.98	0.92	0.88	1.12	11.88

$$\text{Correction factor} = \frac{12}{11.88} = 1.01$$

Multiplying each month's ratio by the correction factors, we get

Month	Jan.	Feb.	Mar.	April	May	June	July	Aug.	Sept.	Oct.	Nov.	Dec.	12 month.
Ratio A/T	0.73	0.59	0.86	0.96	1.20	1.44	1.22	1.06	0.99	0.93	0.89	1.13	12.00

ILLUSTRATION 18: *The production manager of the sportswear firm in the previous problem has projected trend values for next summer (June, July, August) of 586, 589 and 592. Using the seasonal indexes given (1.44, 1.22, 1.60), what actual seasonalized production should the manager plan for?*

SOLUTION

$$\text{June: } Y_{sz} = \text{SI } Y_c = (1.44)(586) = 844$$
$$\text{July: } Y_{sz} = (1.22)(589) = 719$$
$$\text{August: } Y_{sz} = (1.06)(592) = 628$$

ILLUSTRATION 19: *Lakeside Hospital has used a 9-month, moving-average forecasting method to predict drug and surgical dressing inventory requirements. The actual demand for one item is as shown in Table 5.13 Using the previous moving-average data, convert to an exponential smoothing forecast for month 33.*

Table 5.13

Month	24	25	26	27	28	29	30	31	32
Demand	78	65	90	71	80	101	84	60	73

SOLUTION

$$\text{MA} = \frac{\sum X}{\text{Number of Period}} = \frac{78+65+\ldots.+73}{9} = 78 \text{ units}$$

Thus, assume the previous forecast was $F_{t-1} = 78$.

$$\text{Then estimate} \propto \text{as } \alpha = \frac{2}{n+2} = \frac{2}{9+1} = 0.2$$

$$\text{So, } F_t = F_{t-1} + \propto (A_{t-1} - F_{t-1}) = 78 + 0.2\,(73 - 78) = 77 \text{ units.}$$

ILLUSTRATION 20: *A shoe manufacturer, using exponential smoothing with ∝ = 0.1, has developed a January trend forecast of 400 units for a ladies' shoe. This brand has seasonal indexes of 0.80, 0.90, and 1.20, respectively, for the first 3 months of the year. Assuming that* *actual sales were 344 units in January and 414 units in February, what would be the seasonalized (adjusted) March forecast?*

SOLUTION

(*a*) Deseasonalize actual January demand.

$$\text{Demand} = \frac{344}{0.80} = 430 \text{ units}$$

(*b*) Compute the deseasonalized forecast.

$$F_t = F_{t-1} + \alpha\,(A_{t-1} - F_{t-1})$$
$$= 400 + 0.1\,(430 - 400) = 403$$

(*c*) Seasonalized (adjusted) February forecast would be:

$$F_{t(sz)} = 403\,(0.90) = 363$$

Repeating for February, we have:

(*a*) $$\text{Demand} = \frac{414}{0.90} = 460$$

(*b*) $$F_t = 403 + 0.1(460 - 403) = 409$$

(*c*) $$F_{t(sz)} = 409\,(1.20) = 491$$

ILLUSTRATION 21: *Develop an adjusted exponential forecast for the week of 5/14 for a firm with the demand shown in Table 5.14. Let* $\alpha = 0.1$ *and* $\beta = 0.2$*. Begin with a previous average of* $\hat{F}_{t-1} = 650$*, and let the initial trend adjustment,* $T_{t-1} = 0$*.*

Table 5.14

Week	3/19	3/26	4/2	4/9	4/16	4/23	/30	5/7
Demand	700	685	648	717	713	728	754	762

SOLUTION

We have:

Week 3/19:
$$F_t = \propto A_{t-1} + (1 - \propto)\,(F_{t-1} + T_{t-1})$$
$$= 0.1(700) + 0.9(650 + 0) = 655.00$$
$$T_t = \beta\,(F_t - F_{t-1}) + (1 - \beta)\,T_{t-1}$$
$$F_{t+1} = F_t + T_t = 655 + 1 = 656.000$$

The 656.00 is the adjusted forecast for week 3/26.

Week 3/26:
$$F_t = 0.1(685) + 0.9(655 + 1.0) = 658.90$$

$$T_t = 0.2(658.9\text{-}655) + 0.8(1.0) = 1.58$$

Therefore $$F_{t+1} = 658.9 + 1.58 = 660.48$$

The remainder of the calculations is in Table 5.15. The trend-adjusted forecast for the week of 5/14 is 711.89 = 712 units

Table 5.15

(1) Week	(2) Previous average $\hat{F}_{t-1}$	(3) Actual demand A_t-1	(4) Smoothed average $\hat{F}_t$	(5) Smoothed trend T_t T_t	(6) Next-period projection $\hat{F}_{t-1}$
Mar19	650.00	700	655.00	1.00	656.00
26	655.00	685	658.90	1.58	660.48
Apr. 2	658.90	648	659.23	1.33	660.56
9	659.23	717	666.20	2.46	669.06
16	660.20	713	673.09	3.35	676.44
23	673.09	728	681.60	4.39	685.99
30	681.60	754	691. 79	5.74	698.53
May 7	692.79	762	704.88	7.01	711.89
14		770			

EXERCISE

1. What are forecasts?
2. What are the costs associated with forecasting–or not forecasting?
3. Summarize the key features of the more commonly used forecasting method.
4. What is a time series, and what are the components of a time series?
5. Explain the (*a*) trend, (*b*) seasonal, (*c*) cyclical, and (*d*) random components of a series.
6. What steps are involved in using time series data to make a forecast?
7. What is exponential smoothing?
8. Distinguish between, (*a*) simple regression, and (*b*) simple correlation.
9. Forecast demand for March was 950 units, but actual demand turned out to be only 820. If the firm is using a simple exponential smoothing technique with a = 0.2, what is the forecast for April? **[Ans.** 924 units]
10. Using the results from Problem 1, assume the April demand was actually 980 units. Now what is the forecast for May? **[Ans.** 935 units]
11. A forecaster is using an exponential smoothing model with a = 0.4 and wishes to convert to a moving average. What length of moving average is approximately equivalent? **[Ans.** 4 periods]

12. A university registrar has adopted a simple exponential smoothing model (a = 0.4) to forecast enrollments during the three regular terms (excluding summer). The results are shown in Table 5.16 (*a*) Use the data to develop an enrollment forecast for the third quarter of year 2. (*b*) What would be the effect of increasing the smoothing constant to 1.0?

Table 5.16

Year	Quarter	Actual Enrollment (000)	Old Forecast (000)	Forecast Error (000)	Correction (000)	New Forecast (000)
1	1st	20.50	20.00	0.5	0.20	20.20
	2nd	21.00				
	3rd	19.12				
2	1st	20.06				
	2nd	22.00				
	3rd					

[**Ans.** (*a*) 20,800, (*b*) Forecast would reflect the total amount of variation of previous demand from previous forecast—therefore, no smoothing.]

13. A firm producing photochemical has a weekly demand pattern as shown in Table 5.17. Using a smoothing constant of = 0.5 for both original data and trend, and beginning with week I, (*a*) compute the simple exponentially smoothed forecast and (*b*) compute the trend-adjusted exponentially smoothed forecast for the first five periods.

Table 5.17

Week	1	2	3	4	5	6	7	8	9	10	11	12	13	14	15
Demand	30	34	22	16	10	10	14	20	30	36	30	10	12	20	30

14. Find the regression equation resulting from the values $\sum X = 70$, $\sum Y = 90$, $\sum XY = 660$, $\sum X^2 = 514, n = 10$. [**Ans.** $Y_c = 0.25 + 1.25X$]

15. A producer of roofing materials has collected data relating interest rates to sales of asphalt shingles and found that the unexplained variation = 680, and explained variation = 2840. (*a*) Find the correlation coefficient. (*b*) Explain its meaning.

[**Ans.** (*a*) $r = 0.90$ (*b*) 81 per cent of the variation in shingle sales is associated with interest-rate levels.]

16. The Carpet Cleaner Co. is attempting to do a better job of inventory management by predicting the number of vacuums the company will sell per week on the basis of the number of customers who respond to magazine advertisements in an earlier week. On the basis of a sample of $n = 102$ weeks, the following data were obtained:

$$a = 25 \qquad \sum (Y - Y_c)^2 = 22{,}500$$

$$b = 0.10 \qquad \sum (Y - Y_c)^2 = 45{,}000$$

(*a*) Provide a point estimate of the number of vacuums sold per week when 80 inquiries were received in the earlier week. (*b*) Estimate (at the 95.5 per cent level) the number of vacuums sold per week when 80 inquiries were received the week earlier. (*c*) State the value of the coefficient of determination. (*d*) Explain the meaning of your r^2 value.

[Ans. (*a*) 33, (*b*) Using the large-sample approximation, the interval is 3 to 63 because S_{y-x}=15 (*c*) 0.5 (*d*) 50 per cent of the variation in number of vacuums sold is explained by the magazine advertisements.]

17. A recreation operations planner has had data collected on automobile traffic at a selected location *Y* on an interstate highway in hopes that the information can be used to predict weekday demand for state: operated camposites 200 miles away. Random samples of 32 weekdays during the camping season resulted in data from which the following expression was developed: $Y_c = 18 + 0.02X$.

where *X* is the number of automobiles passing the location and *Y* is the number of camposites demanded that day. In addition, the unexplained variation is $\sum (Y - Y_c)^2$ = 1,470, and the total variation is $\sum (Y - \bar{Y})^2$ = 4,080. (*a*). What is the value of the coefficient of determination? (*b*) Explain, in words; the meaning of the coefficient of determination. (*c*) What is the value of the coefficient of correlation?

[Ans.(*a*) 0.64 (*b*) It tells the percentage of variation in camposites demanded that is associated with automobile traffic at the selected site. (*c*) 0.80.]

18. Allan's Underground Systems installs septic systems for new houses constructed outside the city limits. To help forecast his demand, Mr. Allan has collected the data shown in Table on the number of country building permits issued per month, along with the corresponding number of bid requests he has received over a 15-month period.

Table 5.18

Month	1	2	3	4	5	6	7	8	9	10	11	12	13	14	15
No. Building permits	8	20	48	60	55	58	50	45	34	38	10	5	12	29	50
No. Bid requests	20	7	8	4	18	40	48	54	47	42	30	22	10	4	3

(*a*) Compute the simple correlation coefficient *r* between the number of building permits issued and the number of bid requests received in that month. Use all 15 periods of data.

(*b*) Use the first 12 months of data for building permits, and compute *r* between the number of building permits issued in a month and the number of bid requests received 2 months later (*i.e., a* 2-month lag). (*c*) Repeat (*b*), but use *a* 3-month lag. (*d*) Which type of regression model would be best to forecast bid requests: a same-month model, a 2-month lag model, or *a* 3-month lag model?

[Ans. (*a*) 0.08 (*b*) 0.84 (*c*) 0.96 (*d*) A 3-month lag model is best. It permits Allan to explain 93 per cent of the variation in number of bid requests.]

19. Two experienced managers have resisted the introduction of a computerized exponential smoothing system, claiming that there judgmental forecast are "much better than any impersonal computer could do." There past record of prediction is as shown in Table 5.19.

Table 5.19

Week	Actual Demand	Forecast
1	4,000	4500
2	4,200	5,000
3	4,200	4,000
4	3,000	3,800
5	3,800	3,600
6	5,000	4,000
7	5,600	5,000
8	4,400	4,800
9	5,000	4,000
10	4,800	5,000

(*a*) Compute the MAD. (*b*) Compute the tracking signal. (*c*) On the basis of your calculations, is the judgmental system performing satisfactorily?

[Ans. (*a*) 570 (*b*) 0.53 (*c*) yes]

REFERENCES

1. Joseph, G. Monks, *Theory and Problems of Operations Management*, Tata McGraw-Hill Publishing Company Limited, 2nd Edition, 2004.
2. Joseph, G. Monks, *Operations Management*, McGraw-Hill International Edition, 3rd Edition.
3. S. Anil Kumar, N. Suresh, *Production and Operations Management,* New Age International (P) Limited Publishers, 2nd Edition, 2008.

6

PRODUCT DEVELOPMENT AND DESIGN

CHAPTER OUTLINE

6.1 INTRODUCTION

Product design is the mother of all operations processes in an organisation. The processes for manufacture, the planning of production, the processes and checks for quality depend upon the nature of the product. One may say that it all starts with the design of the product. Even the logistics or plain shipment of the product depends upon how or what the product has been designed for. Design gives the blueprint. When the design engineer keys in the computer aided design or when a product design artist draws lines on a sheet of paper, it starts a train of activities.

6.2 PURPOSE OF A PRODUCT DESIGN

Is product design a creative designer's fancy? In popular perception, the term designer conjures up images of a maverick yet highly creative artist who in his fits of imagination comes up with a hitherto not seen product. What is design without creativity in it? Indeed, designs are 'creative' in nature and they should be so. However, in an organisational context, the design should serve the organisational objectives while being creative. Since an organisation has a purpose, the product design should help to serve that larger purpose.

Design starts with conceptualisation which has to have a basis. Providing value to the customer, the return on investment to the company and the competitiveness of the company should form the basis of the product design effort. What separates a product designer from a freelance artist is the former's orientation towards these organisational objectives.

A product's design has tremendours impact on what materials and components would be used, which suppliers will be included, what machines or what type of processes will be used to manufacture it, where it will be stored, how it will be transported. Since a customer does not necessarily imply an already tied-up customer, but also a potential one, what and how will the general yet target customer community be informed depends upon what the design of the product is. For instance, a simple product like toothpaste which is also designed to act as a mouth freshner needs to be placed, advertised, promoted and priced differently. Thus, marketing is also impacted by product design. A product design reflects a company's overall strategy.

Product development and design is primarily governed by management decisions with respect to quality and pricing policy. A development programme and a market survey can provide information as to market potentialities as well as functional, operational, dependability, and durability requirements and possibilities. Selection of the functional scope and application of standardization, simplification, and specialization principles are closely related to plant efficiency and to its net profit and must therefore be an integral part of management policy. The economics of a proposed new product or new model have to be analyzed in order to establish the market size that would justify production. Aesthetic considerations come normally at an advanced stage, but may sometimes be a dominant factor in design, especially with consumer goods. Finally, product development and design must be carried out with close liaison with the production departments, in order to ensure that the right materials and processes are utilized and that their implications are considered at a fairly early stage.

6.3 PRODUCT ANALYSIS

Many factors have to be analyzed in connection with development and design, factors varying in character and complexity, factors affiliated with different fields in production and industrial engineering. Some of these may be grouped as follows:

1. Marketing aspect
2. Product characteristics
   (*i*) Functional aspect,
   (*ii*) Operational aspect,
   (*iii*) Durability and dependability aspects, and
   (*iv*) Aesthetic aspect.
3. Economic analysis
   (*i*) The profit consideration,
   (*ii*) The effect of stardardization, simplification, and specialization, and
   (*iii*) The break-even analysis.
4. Production aspect

All these factors are interrelated and each presents many issues that have to be carefully considered, as indicated by Figure 6.1. Market research may guide product engineers in their work to improve existing products or to develop new ones. The design and its characteristics have to undergo an economic analysis and must be studied in the light of available production facilities and techniques. A costing analysis is naturally dependent on the sales volume; hence the suggested design has to be re-evaluated by market research so that a sales forecast can be worked out. This expected sales volume provides the basis for a further study from the production methods aspect, and the economic analysis has to be rechecked and perhaps modified. Thus product development and design is an excellent example of interdependence of a multitude of factors that have to be reconciled and integrated into a final composition.

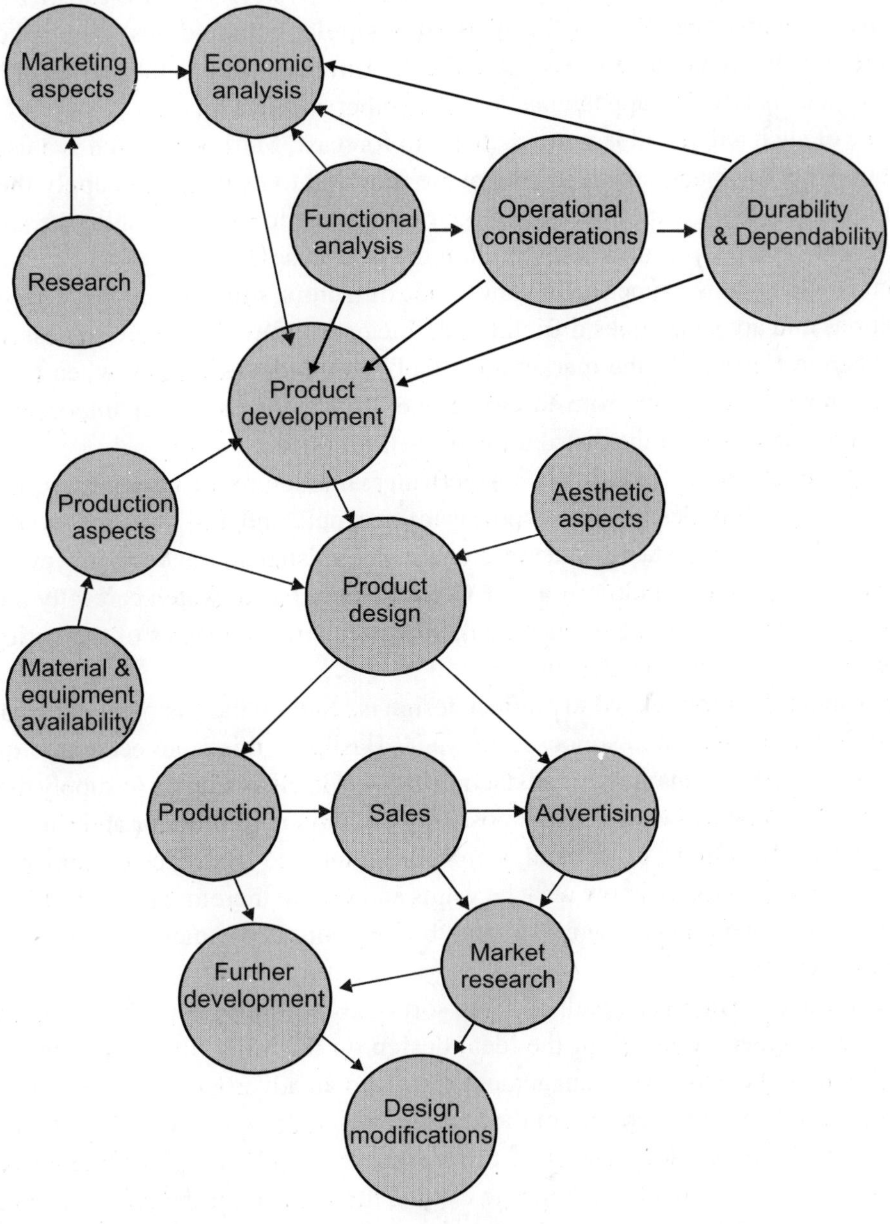

Fig. 6.1 Some interrelations involved in product design

6.3.1 Marketing Aspect

First, it is necessary to establish that the proposed product will satisfy a demand in the market, that what it is supposed to do and the services it can offer are both desirable and acceptable. If no consumption is envisaged, there is no point in proceeding with product design.

The demand for the product in the market may already exist, and its volume can then be assessed by consumer research and sales figures for identical or similar commodities. Demand can also be created with the introduction of a new product, either by filling in a gap in the market or by offering new properties, such as novelty, appearance, or some other specific merits.

The volume of such a demand is more difficult to forecast. Market research is a useful tool in these cases, but experience and sound judgment are required to evaluate and apply the results of such research, and in some cases a certain amount of speculation is inevitable. We shall discuss some problems connected with market research in the next chapter.

The volume of demand is a function of a multitude of factors, some of which are closely related to local conditions and are sometimes difficult to define or measure. It is therefore essential for an enterprise to keep in touch with the market and "feel" its trends, especially when this market is remote and different in character from the local one. This is of particular importance to firms depending on export markets for the distribution of their products.

If we analyze, for example, the case of an American manufacturer of automobiles, we shall find that the percentage of output destined for export is rather small, and design policy would therefore be mainly dictated by American tastes and preferences. A British manufacturer, however, who sells a substantial proportion of automobiles outside Great Britain, has to watch carefully the trends in export markets in order to try and amalgamate the requirements and tastes of the various foreign and home markets in an acceptable design.

Another pertinent question related to product design is : Should the customer get what he wants or should he be offered what he is supposed to want? Basically this is an economic question. If management wants to achieve maximum satisfaction and sets itself as a target to supply the customer with what he wants, it may be faced with the possibility of having to produce an infinite variety of models to suit every taste. On the other hand, were management to ignore the customer's wishes or to maintain that he does not really know what he wants and should therefore be told what is good for him, the designer's task would become far simpler, but the sales department would have to face an unpredictable market.

In practice, product design is a result of some sort of compromise between infinite variety on one hand and the designer's concept of the ideal design on the other. In order to try selling this compromise to potential customers, management resorts to an advertising campaign the policy of which is dependent on the characteristics of the "compromised design" and on how far it conforms to, or differs from, the expressed desires of the market to which such a campaign is directed. Generally, the main objective of advertising is to expand the market, this being achieved by:

- Providing general information about the existence of the product.
- Providing technical information about its functional characteristics or utilitarian purposes.
- Drawing the customer's attention to those attributes of the product which he wants.
- Winning undecided customers by exhibiting possible attractions (such as colour, design, novelty, and price) that may persuade him to prefer the product to one offered by competitors.
- Creating demand among a passive population of customers.
- Educating the customer, or telling him what he should want.

Apart from these direct techniques, management may have some additional aims, such as increasing the prestige of the firm as a whole, banking on the popularity of one product to strengthen or introduce another or to publicize one aspect of the firm's activity for the purpose of raising money or deviating attention from other activities, and so on. Once the design features of a product have been ascertained, appropriate advertising methods can be selected.

6.3.2 The Product Characteristics

Functional Aspect

When the marketing possibilities have been explored, the functional scope of the product has to be carefully analyzed and properly defined. The definition of the objective itself rarely tells us very much about the functional scope envisaged. A washing machine, for example, has a clearly defined objective: to wash clothing. This does not state, however, how the washing should be carried out, whether the machine should be capable of heating the water prior to washing, whether rinsing or drying, or both, are to be done by the machine, and if so by what method, and what should the proportion be between automatic functioning and manual supervision. A functional analysis of this kind obviously affects the design of the machine, its complexity, its appearance, and its price.

Sometimes functional aspects are detachable, and usage can be left to the customer's decision. A steam iron is a case in point. The additional function of dampening the cloth when required, prior to or during ironing, is incorporated in the steam iron, the main duty of which is to iron the cloth. The customer can decide whether and when to exploit this characteristic of the apparatus.

There is a trend to offer functional versatility of the product, thereby increasing the range of applications and sometimes combining several tools in one. A food mixer, for example, allows for a large number of attachments to be added for a variety of duties. Basically the mixer housing contains a power unit and a speed regulator, but it has to be designed so as to serve all the attachments, and the customer has to decide and define for himself the functional scope to be compatible with his needs, his taste, and his pocket. Household power-tool sets are designed on very much the same principle: The hand drill is the basic unit, and with attachments it can become a table drill, a lathe, a polisher, a hedge cutter, etc. Versatility of production machinery may quite often result in substantial savings in floor space and capital expenditure, and this may become one of the fundamental factors affecting design policy. Another example of versatility in design is shown in Figure 6.2.

Operational Aspect

After determining the functional aspect, the operational aspect has then to be considered. Not only must the product function properly, it must be easy to handle and simple to operate. Sometimes it has to be adaptable to various operational conditions, and very often it is subjected to varying degrees of skill of potential operators. The designer's problem becomes all the more critical with the trend for increased versatility because this characteristic implies using basic attachments as elements for building suitable combinations for specific purposes. This requires a certain amount of operator intelligence and skill, which increases with the complexity of the machine. The scarcity of skill is a prohibitive limitation in this respect on the product designer.

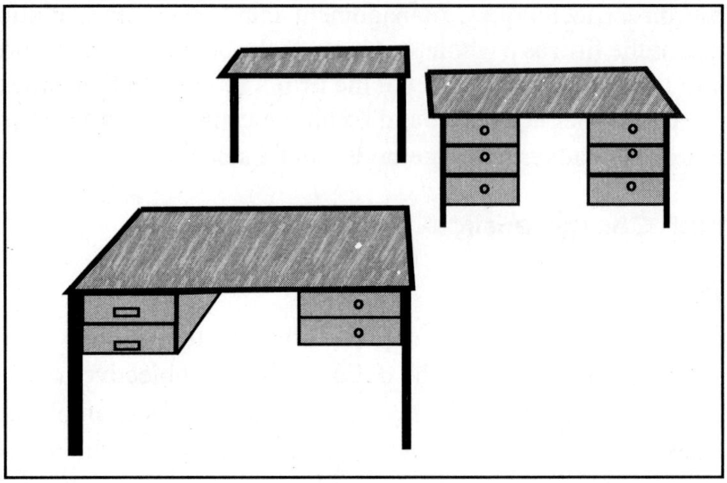

Fig. 6.2 Desk combinations (simplification of design). Variety achieved through standardization: With a limited number of components (one piece table to without joined corners or seams, legs made of seamless steel tubes, and interchangeable drawers) the designer managed to offer 36 possible combinations while exhibiting a pleasant style and functional simplicity

(*Courtesy*: N.V. Wed. J. Ahrend & Zoon—N.V. "Oda" Stallwerk–Amsterdam, Holland. Designer: Friso Kramer, 1958).

The 'get ready' stage before the operation proper and the 'put away' time (including cleaning) should be carefully analyzed with respect to the excepted skill of the operator. Too often one finds ingenious gadgets (for example, in the field of household equipment) that are capable of performing an operation in a fraction of the time normally required but which involve such complicated preparations or such lengthy cleaning and 'put away' subsequent operations, that the ratio of net machine time to overall machine time becomes absurdly small. The beneficial features attributed to the gadget in such cases are rather questionable.

Versatility of equipment should also be analyzed in this light. Especially when subsequent operations are to be carried out with the aid of different attachments, the designer should always bear in mind the time required for an operator to perform the change over and should make certain that this time is in reasonable proportion to the operation time.

DURABILITY AND DEPENDABILITY

These are two factors closely related to the selection of materials and class of workmanship and hence to the design of the product and the economical analysis of its cost. Quality is not always a simple characteristic to define, but durability and dependability are two factors that often determine quality and have to be carefully considered by the designer. Durability is defined mainly by the length of the active life, or endurance, of the product under given working conditions, but a measure of the product capability to idle or withstand storage is also often considered in assessing durability. Durability need not always be associated with selection of good materials. The actual working life of a match or a rocket motor may be rather limited, but that does not mean that materials for these articles may be of low quality. An additional criterion, therefore, has to be considered, that of dependability, or the capability of the product to function when called upon to do its job. Returning to our matches, dependability may be related to the number of duds in a box, and while the manufacturer is eager to reduce this number to a minimum, he need not choose the very best raw materials to ensure that not even one match will fail. Dependability of rocket motors, however, may be more rigidly defined, and first class materials are chosen in spite of the short active life that is envisaged for them in some applications.

Another aspect of durability is that of maintenance and repair. The amount of repair and preventative maintenance required for some products is closely related to quality and design policy. This is of particular importance when the equipment is supposed to operate continuously and when any repair involves a loss of running time.

Problems of convenience and accessibility in operating the equipment have already been discussed, and the same remarks are valid for maintenance and repair. Easy accessibility is a fundamental principle in a sound design, and thorough knowledge on the part of the operational durability, dependability, and maintenance requirements of the product are absolutely essential to ensure a well- balanced design within the policy outlined by higher management.

Aesthetic Aspect

In what way does the appearance of a product affect its design? In most cases, where the functional scope, durability, and dependability have already been defined, the aesthetics are mainly concerned with molding the final shape around the basic skeleton. This molding of shape may very often be severely limited in scope, and what finally emerges is sometimes termed a 'functional shape'. The view that functional shape is necessarily divorced from aesthetics, especially where engineering structures or equipment are concerned, is well-exemplified by bridges, locomotives, or machines of the late nineteenth or early twentieth century (see, for example, Fig. 6.1. However, a study of the gradual changes in shape of these objects in the past few decades would convince us that there has been an increasing recognition of the role of aesthetics in design. This is perhaps partly due to man's aesthetic taste being reconciled to accepting these objects as an integral part of the landscape or everyday life, thereby leading to a modification of the original attitude that these "Monstrosities" are hopelessly ugly and should be left alone.

Functional shape is a concept in its own right among designers. Those who believe in functional shape argue that compatibility of function with shape is logical and should therefore be accentuated and exploited, rather than covered up. A standard lamp is first and foremost a lamp and not a flying saucer, and there is nothing wrong with its looking like a lamp. This approach is referred to in Fig. 6.2, where the aesthetic aspects are dealt with at the design stage, after all the other aspects of the proposed product have been analyzed.

In some cases, however, molding of shape may have financial implications; for instance, when special materials have to be used or added to those basically required from the functional point of view or when additional processes are involved. Such cases will call for a careful cost analysis of the aesthetic aspects.

In extreme cases, aesthetics are the governing factor in design and completely dominate it. This is especially true for many consumer goods, such as automobiles and household equipment, or fashion goods. The functional scope, though more or less defined and accepted, may also be widened to accentuate the novelty of the new model. But the idea of the new design starts with the concept of its shape, from which the idea evolves and grows. The technical considerations have to be somehow fitted in at a later stage, this being in complete contrast to the conventional sequence shown in Fig. 6.1.

When styling is a dominant factor in product design, it is often used as a means to create demand. Changes in fashion and taste, evolution of form, and the introduction of new ideas quickly outdate previous designs. If the market is psychologically receptive and eager to discard former designs in favour of new ones, styling becomes a race against time, a race that determines the salability of the product.

Many tools can be utilized by the designer to bring out aesthetic characteristics. Some of these are:

1. Use of the special materials, either for the parts of the housing or as additional decorations. Notable is the use of chromium strips, plastics, wood, glass, and fabrics for the purpose.
2. Use of colour, either natural colour of the material concerned or by use of paints, plating, spraying, or even lighting. Composition and contrast of colours is of great importance to the industrial designer in facilitating convenient operation and attractive appearance.
3. Texture supplements colour, either by appropriate treatment of the given surfaces or coatings. Surface finish and requirements of brightness as determined by styling may in turn affect the production processes in the finishing stages.
4. Shape denoted by outer contours and similarity to familiar objects. Shape can be exploited to accentuate particular features, to create a sense of spaciousness or illusions of size, richness and dependability.
5. Line is used to break the form, also for the purpose of emphasizing parts of it, or to give a sense of continuity, graciousness, and stability.
6. Scaling the product, either to a blown-up size or to a small size (modeling). This creates novelty and a sense of completeness. The success of styling of some popular small automobiles in Europe may be partly due to the designer's talent in creating a feeling of still having the full-size version, with all its features.
7. Packaging, especially for small items. Novelty and attractiveness of packaging is often transferred in the mind of the customer, attributing perhaps non-existent values to the contents. In extreme cases packaging may assume an appreciable portion of the total production costs and become the center of the design project.

Aesthetic molding, especially when governed by the selection of material, colour, texture, and sometimes even line, has great economic advantages, since great variety can be achieved at a comparatively low cost. The basic product remains the same, and variety is obtained by finishing processes alone. Henry Ford's maxim that the customer may choose any colour he likes, provided it is black, is no longer valid. Modern production control techniques allow for a vast number of combinations of colours and textures to be offered with little difficulty.

Aesthetics have been fully recognized as an integral part of design, and no designer worth his mettle can afford to ignore their implications, their tools, and their benefits.

6.3.3 Economic Analysis

As shown in Figure 6.1, an economic analysis is the key to management decision in product design policy. Having obtained sufficient information about customers' requirements and market potentialities on the one hand and a detailed study about the functional, operational, and quality aspects of the proposed product on the other, the economic analysis can proceed by seeking an answer to the following questions:

- What capital expenditure is required for manufacturing the new product?
- What total production costs per piece are envisaged?
- What is the reasonable margin of profit that can be expected?
- Do the price (= total costs + profit) and the features of the product render it competitive in the market?
- In what numbers is the product expected to be sold?

Here, again, the interdependence of variables should be strongly emphasized. Not one single question in this list can be isolated and solved independently of the others. The economic analysis is in fact a cyclic and repetitive procedure. Each question is weighted in the light of the answer and the data provided by the previous question, and all the answers are checked when their turn comes again to be re-evaluated in the following cycles, until a state of equilibrium is reached and no further modifications to these answers are required.

PROFIT AND COMPETITIVENESS

The measure of competitiveness of the product corresponds to the portion of the market it succeeds in capturing. This is largely dependent on the value the customer is prepared to put on the product, and on the ratio of this value to the price. As customer assessment of value is not universally uniform but subject to preference of features, performance, or taste, ratios of values to prices vary with customers. A state of equilibrium is formed in which the market is divided between different preferences. This equilibrium may change: If the ratio of value to price of the product becomes more favourable, when compared with other products, the product increases its portion of the market and becomes more competitive.

Such an equilibrium is shown in Fig. 6.3 where the total costs include set-up, materials, overheads, storage, and distribution. The total profit is determined by the margin of profit per unit and by the sales volume. If the organization seeks to increase its profit, it can try one of the following methods 6.3:

(*a*) *Increase the margin of profit per unit*, hence the sales price, but leave the total production to costs unchanged. If such a course would not affect the sales volume, the total profit would be proportional to the increase in the margin of profit per unit. Such an increase, however, can upset the market equilibrium unfavourably, in that both the ratio of customers' value of the product to its price will deteriorate and the products of competitors will become more attractive. The market may shrink, and the total profit, far from attaining the expected value, may in extreme cases fall below its original level.

(*b*) *Leave the total costs unchanged*, but try to improve the ratio of value to price and thus widen the market. This can be done (1) by producing a better or more attractive product at the same cost, (2) by launching an intense advertising campaign in order to boost the customer's assessment of the product value, or (3) by reducing the sales price at the expense of the margin of profit per unit, in the hope that the market will expand enough to increase total profit. Too marginal a profit per unit is, however, undesirable, as it allows little protection from possible fluctuations in the market, and even slight instabilities may turn a small profit into a sizeable loss.

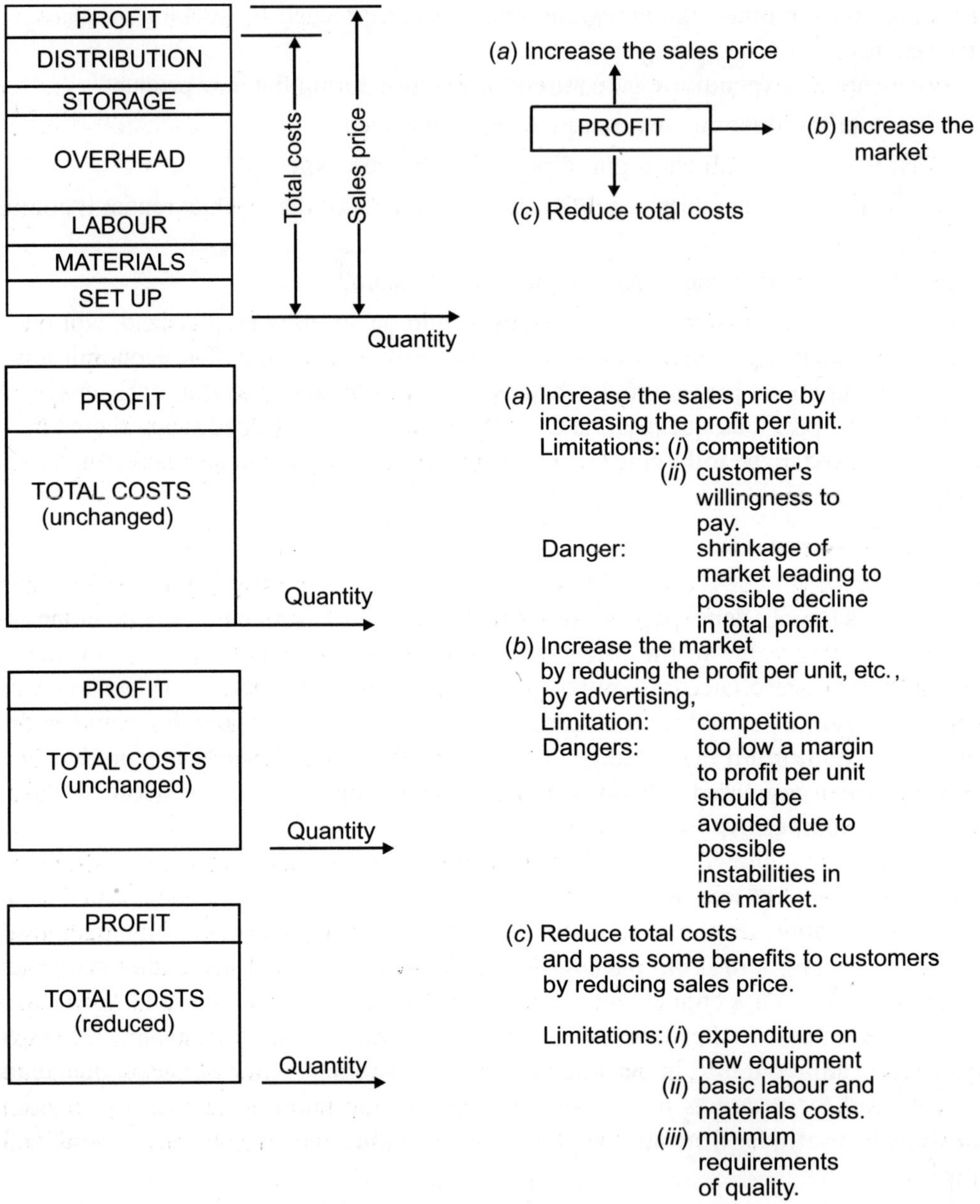

Fig. 6.3 Methods for increasing total profit

(*c*) *Reduce the total production costs* and pass some of the benefit to customers in the form of reduced sales prices. If both the profit per piece and the size of the market increase, a substantial improvement in total profits will be achieved. This course calls for a continuous search after better methods, better processes, better materials and their utilization, and better management to reduce overheads. There are, however, some limitations to the rate of improvement one can attain, such as basic labour and material costs and limited resources or credit hampering expenditure on new equipment and machines. Minimum requirements of quality should also be studied and met, as a reduction in price at the expense of quality is easy enough; customer's assessment of the product value, however, deteriorates accordingly. But reducing production costs and thereby expanding the market, while sustaining accepted quality standards, offers a challenge to the production engineer. Probably the most characteristic feature of this process is that it is both dynamic and continuous, that each success is a further advance along the spiral of increasing productivity and standard of living (see Figure 6.4).

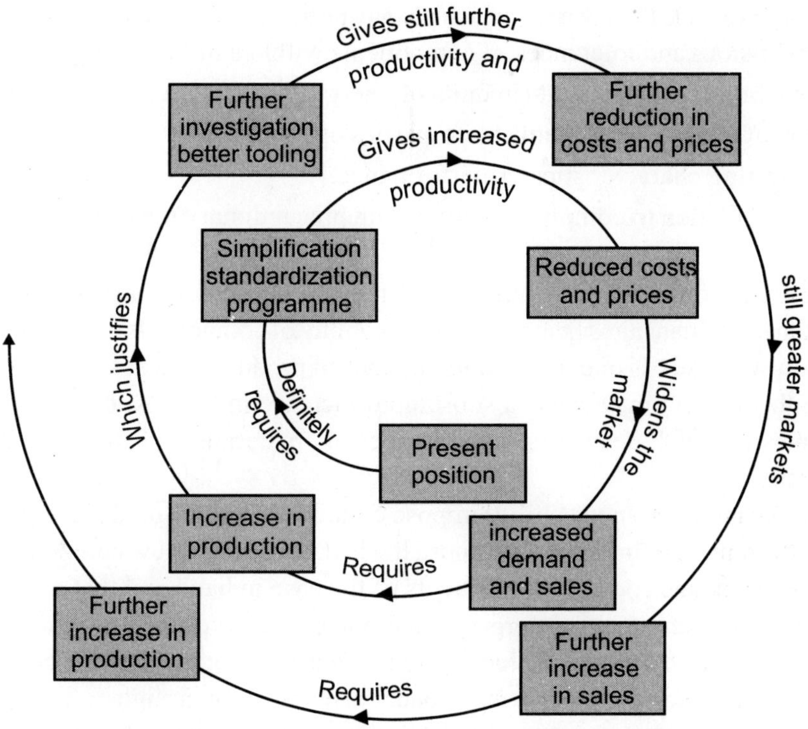

Fig.6.4 Spiral of increasing productivity and standard of living
(*Courtesy*: The British Productivity Council, Report on Metulworking Machine Tools, 1953).

The Three S's

The three S's refer to standardization, simplification and specialization—three related subjects that are at the root of any economic analysis of product design. The three S's can be defined as follows:

Standardization is the process of defining and applying the "conditions" necessary to ensure that a given range of requirements can normally be met with a minimum of variety and in a reproducible and economic manner on the basis of the best current technique.

Simplification is the process of reducing the number of types of products within a definite range.

Specialization is the process whereby particular firms concentrate on the manufacture of a limited number of products or types of products.

The three processes are usually linked together and develop as a logical sequence. From a wide range of requirements it is first necessary to sort out the essential features, define them, and then work out in a scientific manner, the minimum variety required to meet these essentials. This is a process of standardization, and it is mainly an engineering process. Within a given range, whether covered by standards or not, a process of simplification can be carried out with the view of reducing the variety of products or materials that are produced or purchased. This is both an economic and an engineering process, and specialization is one of its natural outcomes.

STANDARDIZATION

Standardization covers a wide field of activity, which may be described by the following main categories:

- Physical dimensions and tolerances of components within a defined range.
- Rating of machines or equipment (in units of energy, temperature, current, speed, etc.).
- Specification of physical and chemical properties of materials.
- Methods of testing characteristics or performance.
- Methods of installation to comply with minimum precautionary measures and convenience of use.

The first three categories relate to limitation of the number of sizes or grades and some aspects of quality, one of the important aims being interchangeability of components or assemblies. Adherence to standards of raw materials is one of the fundamentals of product design, since any deviation from the standards in this respect may cause a substantial increase in the cost of materials. Industry is rich with examples in which designers specify "special" materials wheareas the standard grades can do just as well.

Standardization and interchangeability impose certain limitations on the designer and demand higher skill and effort in planning. It is easy enough when designing a new component to decide that no standard really meets the special requirements of the case in hand and that a special part has to be specified. What designers seem to forget is that one of the purposes of standards is to provide solutions to relieve them of the task of having to solve afresh some basic problems, and thereby allow them more time to concentrate on the broader aspects of the design.

Another prerequisite of interchangeability is the precision required of the manufacturing process in order to obtain production within the specified tolerances. This implies that production control has to be tightened so that any deviations from the given standards will be immediately noticed and appropriate action can be taken to avoid the process getting out of control.

Standardization has, however, many advantages, some of which may be briefly listed below:

- Reduction of material waste and obsolescence.
- Concentration of effort in manufacturing; hence, simplification and specialization.
- Reduction in inventories, both of materials, semifinished, and finished products.
- Reduction in bookkeeping and other paper work.
- Lowering the grades of skill required in manufacture and assembly.
- Reduction in price; hence expansion of the market.
- Reduction of repair and maintenance costs.

SIMPLIFICATION

Simplification is a constant source of disagreement between the sales department and the production personnel. A production engineer prefers little variety, minimum set ups, and long runs (Figure 6.5). Simplification enables the production department to improve planning, achieve higher

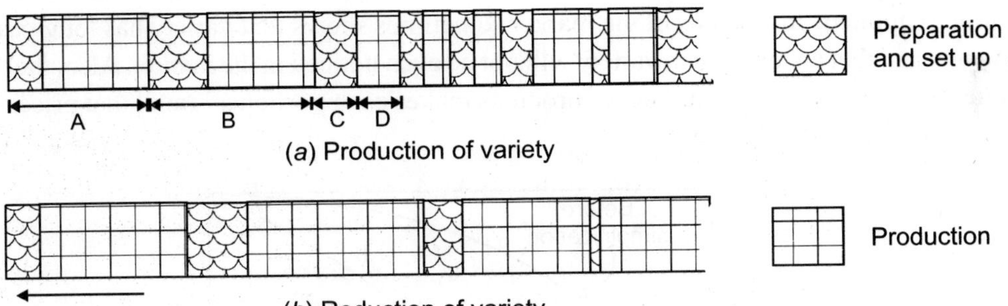

(a) Production of variety

(b) Reduction of variety

Fig. 6.5 Effect of variety on scheduling

rates of production and machine utilization, and simplify control procedures. The salesman, on the other hand, strives to satisfy the customer by giving him a choice or by offering him the nearest to what he wants. The pro's and con's simplification are given in the accompanying listing.

Pro simplification	Pro variety
Reduce inventories of materials and finished products.	Satisfy a wide range of demand.
Reduce investment in plant and equipment.	Enable better contact with the market to study its tastes and requirements.
Save storage space.	Avoid losing orders for more salable products because the customer directs all his orders to other vendors.
Simplify planning and production methods. Simplify inspection and control. Reduce required technical personnel. Reduce sales price (through production simplification. and reduction of distribution costs); hence expand. the market and the plant. Shorten or eliminate order queues.	Create demand.

The last point in favour of variety deserves, perhaps, some further clarification. Some sales people claim that variety encourages consumption and that, especially where consumer goods are concerned, the psychological effect of plenty creates demand. Furthermore, market research by some firms seems to suggest that in some cases similar products tend to capture roughly the same portion of a given market. The prospects of increasing total demand on the one hand and the firm's portion of the market on the other, may have been the main causes for boosting variety to the extent found nowadays in industry. From the customer's point of view this is a very unsatisfactory state of affairs. A flood of variety confuses the customer, who ceases in many cases to appreciate the fine differences between similar products and has either to make a haphazard choice or to invest effort, time, and study (and quite often money) to enable him to make an intelligent choice.

This is undesirable for the firm as well. Apart from missing all the advantages listed above when simplification is applied, an analysis of the market sometimes shows that variety has long passed the saturation point and that an increase in variety will not be even noticed in the market. Also, the division of the market between too large a number of products makes each portion so small that prices have to be kept at high levels to avoid losses.

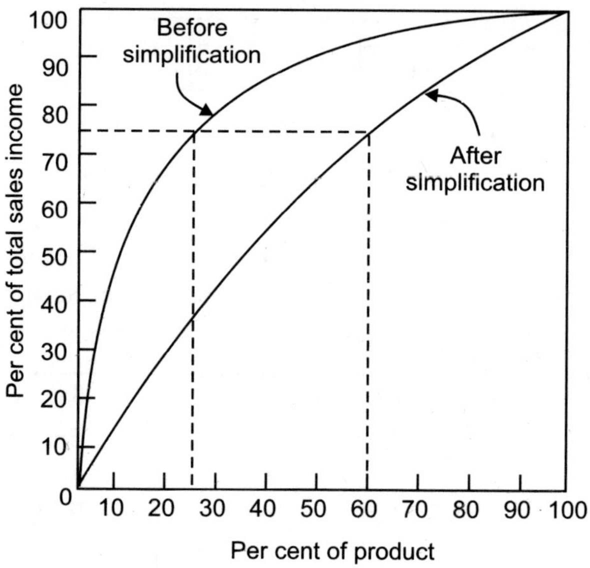

Fig. 6.6 Analysis of sales by products

When a great variety exists, a sales analysis can be made to establish the salability of the products. When the accumulative sales income is plotted against the number of products offered for sale, it is very often revealed that a comparatively small number of products contributes very little in this respect (Figure 6.5). This is sometimes referred to in industry as the "25% to 75%" relationship because in many cases it was found that 25 per cent of the products brought in 75 per cent of the income, although in some extreme cases studies revealed as small as 10 to 90 per cent relationships. This leads to unnecessary drain of the firm's efforts, which should be directed to promoting the more profitable products. A more desirable situation is when responsibility for income is more evenly distributed between products (*i.e.*, when the curve is "flat" as is the lower one in (Figure 6.6), which is achieved through reduction of variety.

The effect of quantity on the profit contribution of the product is illustrated in Figure. 6.6, where the sales income is represented by the straight line bQ, in which Q is the quantity sold and b is the income per unit. The costs to the firm consist of:

- Fixed costs F, which are independent of the quantity produced and include executive salaries, depreciation of plant and equipment, etc.

- Variable costs aQ, where a respresents the constant total costs per unit, including materials, labour, and other direct costs that vary with the plant activity. The variable costs are shown in Figure 6.7 by the straight line aQ.

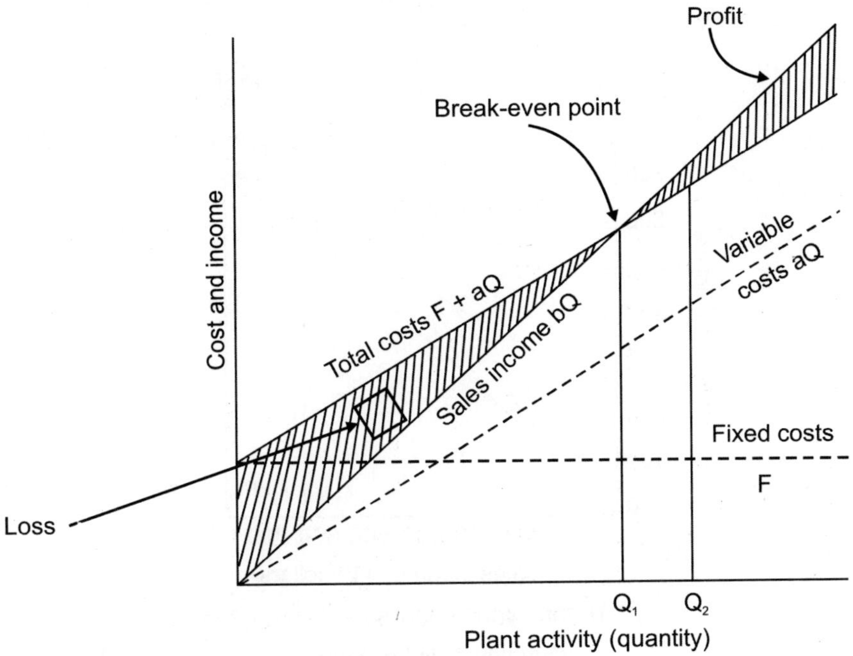

Fig. 6.7 A break-even chart

The division into fixed and variable costs represents only an approximate interpretation of the total costs function and may not be valid for a very wide range of Q.

The total costs are given by the summation of fixed and variable costs ($F + aQ$), and the point of intersection of this line with that of sales income is the break-even point (BEP) corresponding to a sales volume Q_1 gives profit. At the point of intersection,

$$F = aQ_1 = bQ_1$$

hence

$$Q_1 = \frac{F}{b-a} \tag{6.1}$$

If a plant is operating at point Q_2, it is working with a margin of safety (denoted by Δ), which can be defined as follows:

$$\Delta = \frac{Q_2 - Q_1}{Q_1} = \frac{Q_2}{Q_1} - 1 \tag{6.2 a}$$

and it can be shown that

$$\Delta = \frac{Z}{F} \tag{6.2 b}$$

where Z is the profit of the plant. The desirable level of the plant activity can be expressed in terms of the safety margin or the profit as

$$Q_2 = Q_1(1+\Delta) = Q_1\left(1+\frac{Z}{F}\right) \tag{6.3}$$

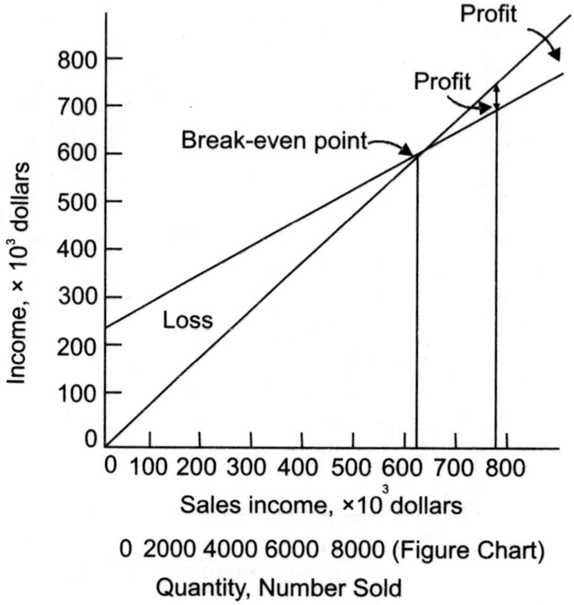

Fig. 6.8 An annual break-even chart

The break-even chart may be either on a monthly (Figure 6.8) or yearly (Figure 6.8) basis. A low BEP is hightly desirable because it increases the safety margin of the product. From Eqn.(6.1) it is obvious that the BEP can be lowered by three methods (see also Figure 6.9) as follows:

Reduce the fixed costs from F to F', thus lowering the BEP to

$$Q_1' = Q_1\frac{F'}{F}$$

Reduce the variable costs coefficient a to a'; hence

$$Q_1' = Q_1\frac{b-a}{b-a'}$$

Increase the slope of the income line from b to b', the new BEP being

$$Q_1' = Q_1\frac{b-a}{b'-a}$$

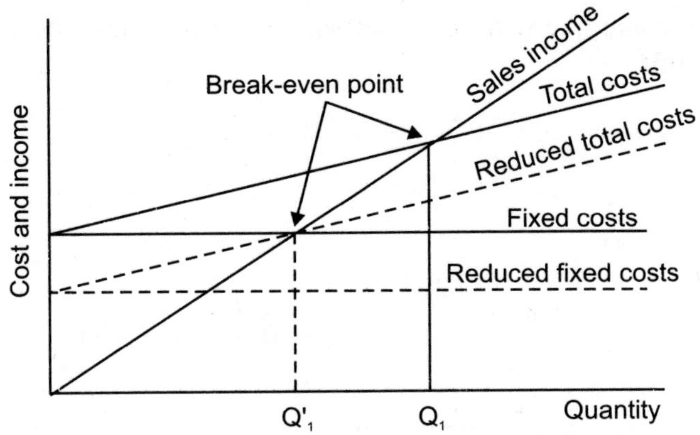

(*a*) Reduce the fixed costs

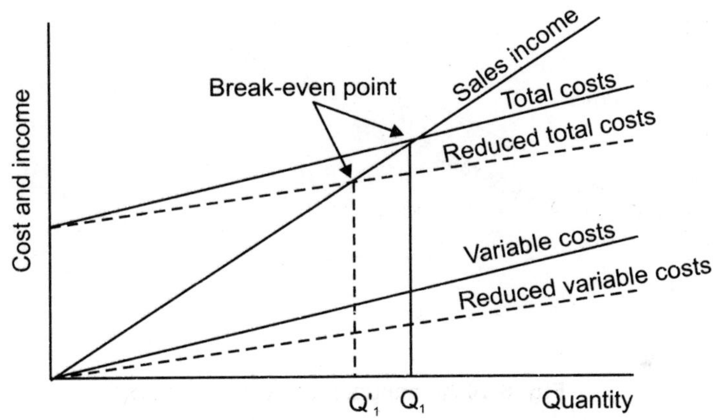

(*b*) Reduce the variable costs

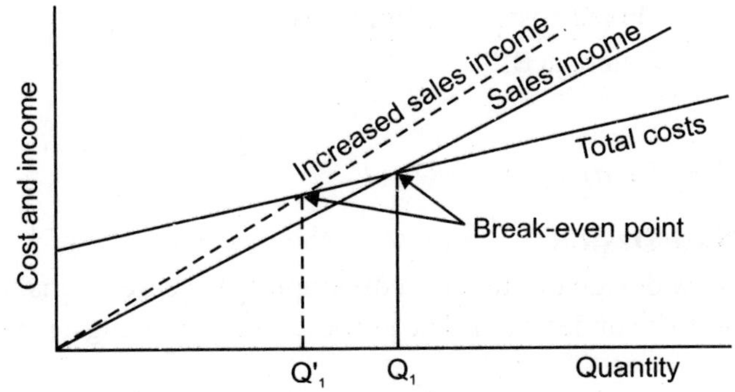

(*c*) Increase the sales income

Fig. 6.9 Methods for lowering the break-even point

A similar diagram to the break-even chart, called the *profit-volume chart* is shown in Figure 6.10, where the fixed costs are marked as a negative quantity on the ordinate. The BEP is given by the intersection of the income line with the abscissa. Operation below the abscissa incurs a loss; operations above it, a profit.

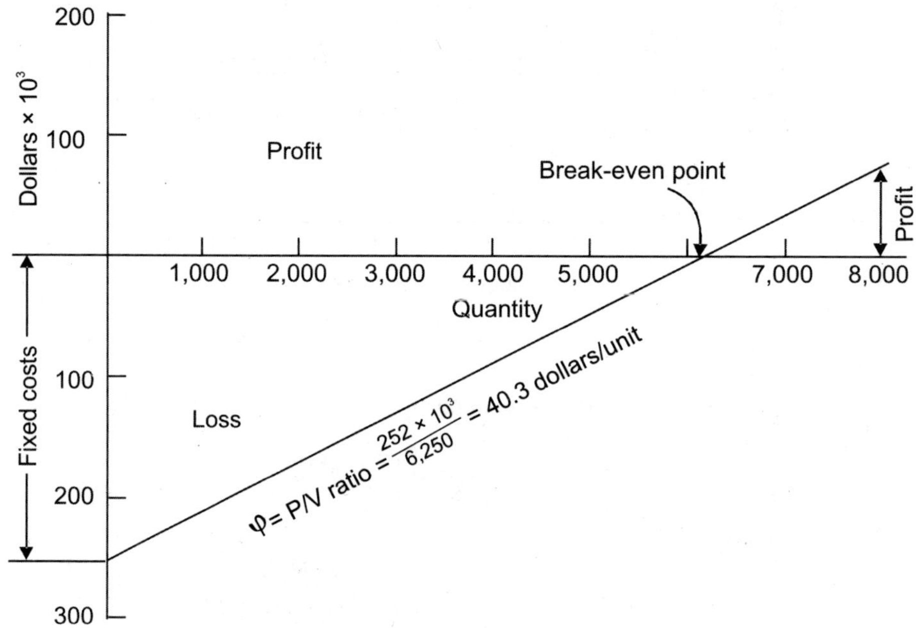

Fig. 6.10 An annual profit-volume chart

The profitability of the product is indicated by the slope of the income line, called the *P/V* (Profit-Volume) ratio and denoted by φ:

$$\varphi = \frac{\text{Fixed costs}}{\text{Volume at BEP}} = \frac{(\text{Profit}) + (\text{Fixed costs})}{\text{Volume}} = \frac{F}{Q_1} = b - a$$

and the profit

$$Z = (b - a)\ Q - F = \varphi Q - F \tag{6.4}$$

The Economics of a New Design

When the launching of a new design or model is contemplated, a careful analysis of the economics of the proposed project has to be undertaken. The purpose of introducing a new model to the market may be two fold:

1. To increase the profit of the organization.
2. To avoid decline in sales of an existing model due to serve competition. Such a situation calls for incorporating novelty and new features in the company's products; even when no immediate increase in the profit is envisaged, it is aimed to achieve such an increase on a long-term basis.

The profit of an existing product is computed, using Eqn. 6.5, as

$$Z_1 = \varphi_1 Q_1 - F \tag{6.5a}$$

where Q_1 is the number of pieces sold. If a new design is to be put into production, preparation costs incurred will include:

- Design and engineering.
- Production planning.
- Tooling, jigs, and fixtures; resetting of machines, etc.
- Purchase of special machines or equipment.
- Changes in layout.

These preparation and "changeover" costs (symbolized as s) will have to be returned by the new design, so that the new profit should be

$$Z_2 = j_2 Q_2 - F - s \tag{6.6}$$

It has been assumed here that the fixed costs are mainly dependent on the existing machinery of the organization and are therefore not likely to change very much. It is desirable that the new profit will be larger than, or at least equal to, the existing one or

$$Z_2 \geq Z_1$$

hence,

$$Z_2 - Z_1 = \varphi_2 Q_2 - \varphi_1 Q_1 - s \geq 0.$$

This condition tells us how many units of the new design ought to be sold in order to ensure that total profit does not decline:

$$Q_2 \geq \frac{s}{\varphi_2} + \frac{\varphi_1}{\varphi_2} Q_1$$

or

$$\frac{\varphi_2}{\varphi_1} \geq \left(1 + \frac{s}{Z_1 + F}\right) D \tag{6.7}$$

where D stands for the ratio

$$D = \frac{\varphi_1}{\varphi_2} = \frac{\text{P/V ratio of old design}}{\text{P/V ratio of new design}} \tag{6.8}$$

It is clear that unless the *P/V* ratio of the product can be greatly improved, the organization will have to sell more in order to justify the capital investment required for the introduction of the new design. If, for example, the *P/V* ratio of the new design remains at the same level as that of the old one,

$$D = 1$$

hence,

$$\frac{Q_2}{Q_1} \geq \frac{s}{Z_1 + F} + 1$$

or

$$Q_2 > Q_1$$

This fact is illustrated in the profit-volume chart shown in Figure 6.11. Line circle represents the existing product, yielding profit Z_1 when Q_1 units are sold.

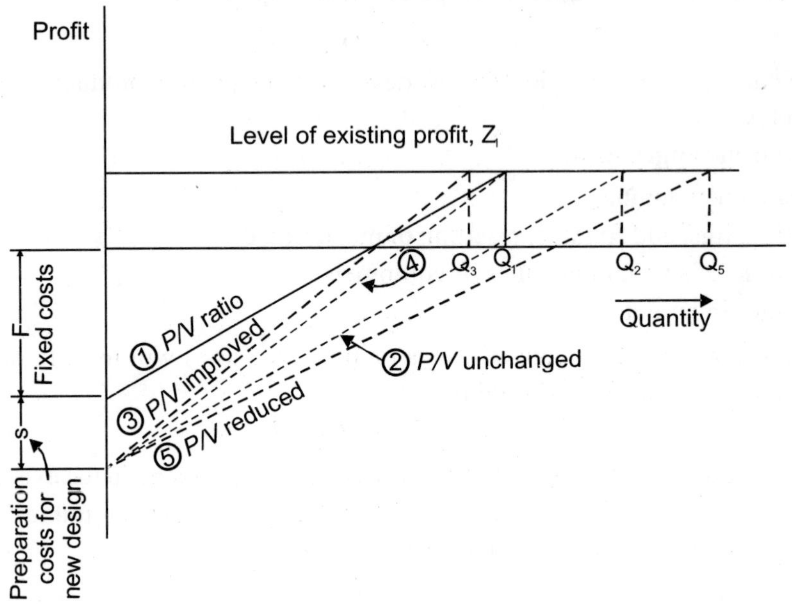

Fig. 6.11 Effect of P/V ratio on the required market size of a new design

For a new design, the preparation costs are added to the fixed costs *F*. If the *P/V* ratio is 2 unchanged (line ②), it is necessary to sell Q_2 units to obtain the same profit. From the similarity of triangles it is easy to see that in this case

$$\frac{Q_2}{Q_1} = \frac{s + Z_1 + F}{Z_1 + F} + 1$$

which is what we obtain from Eqn. 6.7 when $D = 1$. If an increase in the market is not envisaged, the *P/V* ratio must be increased (line ③). It is possible to achieve the original profit at Q3 < Q1 if the *P/V* ratio is steep enough (line ③). However, even when the number of pieces sold is to remain unchanged ($Q_4 = Q_1$), it is necessary to have a higher *P/V* ratio than the existing one (line ④), while a decrease in the *P/V* ratio will increase appreciably the required sales volume (line ⑤).

Example

The annual fixed costs of a product are known to be \$200,000 and the annual net profit \$40,000 the average monthly sale being 820 units. A new design is contemplated, involving an expenditure for preparations amounting to \$ 80,000, to be returned in two years. It is expected that with new production methods the *P/V* ratio may be increased by 5 per cent. What should the annual sales figure for the new design be

(*i*) so that the same net profit will be realized;

(*ii*) so that in addition to this profit a yield of 10 per cent on the capital invested will be obtained?

SOLUTION

(*i*) The ratio $D = 1.00/1.05 = 0.95$. The additional expenditure per year $s = 80{,}000/2 = \$40{,}000$.

$$\frac{Q_2}{Q_1} \geq \left(1+\frac{s}{Z_1+F}\right)D = \left(1+\frac{40,000}{40,000+200,000}\right)0.95 = 1.11$$

Annual Sales required:

$$Q \geq 1.11Q_1 = 1.11 \times 12 \times 820 = 10920 \text{ units.}$$

(*ii*) In the first year 10 per cent of the investment (*i.e.*, \$8,000) has to be added to the profit, or Z_2 = \$48,000. The following expression for Q_2/Q_1 can be obtained by use of Eqns.6.5*a* and 6.6.

$$\frac{Q_2}{Q_1} = \frac{S+Z_2+F}{Z_1+F} \times D$$

Hence, $$\frac{Q_2}{Q_1} = \frac{40.000+48.000+200.000}{40.000+200.000} 0.95 = 1.14$$

or $$Q_2 \geq 1.14 \times 12 \times 820 = 11,220 \text{ units.}$$

Similarly, in the second year,

$$Z_2 = 40,000 + 4,000 = \$44,000$$

and $$\frac{Q_2}{Q_1} = \frac{40,000+44,000+200,000}{40,000+200,000} 0.95 = 1.12$$

or $$Q_2 \geq 1.12 \times 12 \times 820 = 11,020 \text{ units.}$$

The case where the same profit should be realized by an unchanged volume of sales deserves special attention. It is often very difficult to forecast, let alone ascertain, an increased market for a new design, and considerations of "change-over" have to be based on the assumption that the sales volume will remain constant, i.e., $Q_1 = Q_2$. As already mentioned, this will require an improvement in the *P*/*V* ratio, which can be quantitatively determined by

$$\left(1+\frac{s}{Z_1+F}\right) D = 1$$

This relation is shown in Figure 6.12. Any point on the curve refers to a resultant profit equal to the existing one, while for any point below the curve, an increased profit is implied.

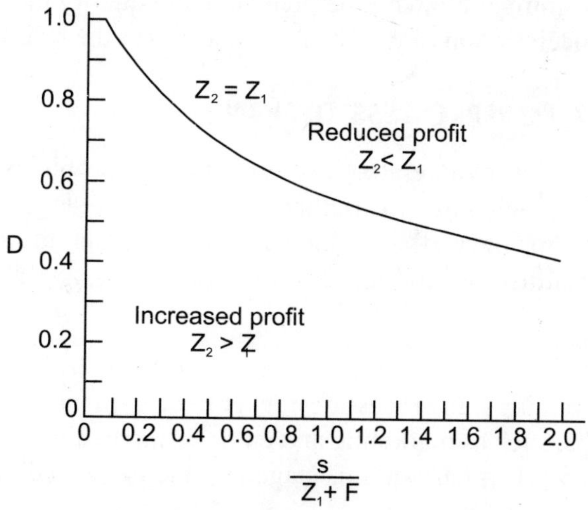

Fig. 6.12 Required improvement of the *P*/*V* ratio when $Q_1 - Q_2$ to yield a profit $Z_2 > Z_1$.

6.3.4 Production Aspect

Last but not least in the list of factors influencing design is the production aspect. The product need not only be well-planned on the drawing board, but its design must also be capable of being eventually translated into palpable fact. The designer must therefore face a multitude of practical production problems. "Design for production" has become a motto among designers. The following three aspects of production engineering have to be weighed:

1. Selection of processes that will be the most suitable and economical for the purpose. Such a selection will have to consider:

   (*i*) The production quantities involved. Some processes are very expensive to operate unless used for a suitable production run.

   (*ii*) Utilization of existing equipment. Such considerations may override acquisition of equipment for an ideally more suitable process.

   (*iii*) Selection of jigs and fixtures and other production aids, the use of which may affect the design of components.

   (*iv*) Sequence of operations and methods for subassembling and assembling.

   (*v*) Limitation of skill. The selection of a process must be compatible with available skill and sometimes may be solely governed by it. Mechanized and push button equipment is particularly suitable to non-skilled or semiskilled operators, but it is usually expensive to install and must be justified by long runs.

   (*vi*) Application of new production processes. The designer has to consider not only conventional techniques but also the latest developments and research into newer production methods.

2. Utilization of materials and components with the view of

   (*i*) Selection of materials having appropriate specifications.

   (*ii*) Selection of method or design to reduce waste and scrap.

   (*iii*) Using standard components and assemblies.

   (*iv*) Having interchangeability of components and assemblies with in the product.

3. Selection of appropriate workmanship and tolerances that satisfy quality requirements, but which are at the same time compatible with the precision and quality that can be attained through the available processes. Specification of quality may also affect the selection of processes.

6.4 A FRAMEWORK FOR PROCESS DESIGN

Process design can be viewed as an interative exercise. That is, problems are solved one at a time and sequentially; then after each stage, or perhaps after several stages, the previous stages are reexamined to see if later steps have affected the best way in which these steps should have been designed. This procedure is illustrated in Fig. 6.13.

6.4.1 Product Planning

Product planning serves as an input to process design. However, in most cases the responsibility for this phase rests with groups, such as marketing and engineering, which are generally found outside the domain of process design. It is early in this stage that the perceived needs of the consumer are identified. If the process is service-oriented, thesee needs will be reflected in the proposed quality, speed, cost, and réliability of the service. If, on the other hand, the process will be manufacturing-oriented, then these needs will be reflected in the product's proposed quality, cost, function, reliability and appearance. When these service or product parameters are transformed into a product, design, it is essential that a cross-functional alliance between product, planning and process design groups be established in order to ensure that the product objectives can indeed be profitably met. Otherwise only local goals may be pursued. For example, the marketing and engineering departments working alone may design a product which is very costly to manufacture and very difficult to service. In short, the transformation process should be considered well before the design is finalized. This can usually be accomplished in the following way:

Information from the *product development* stage can be directed to those responsible for *process R&D*. They in turn can determine if the process capability for this product now exists within the firm, whether it exists outside the firm or whether research and development effort would be necessary to meet the specified objectives. Rough cost estimates would also be made for each alternative identified. In large firms a special process R&D department may be organized just for this purpose. In smaller firms this function is less formalized and more reliance would be placed on outside suppliers of processing equipment and company engineers.

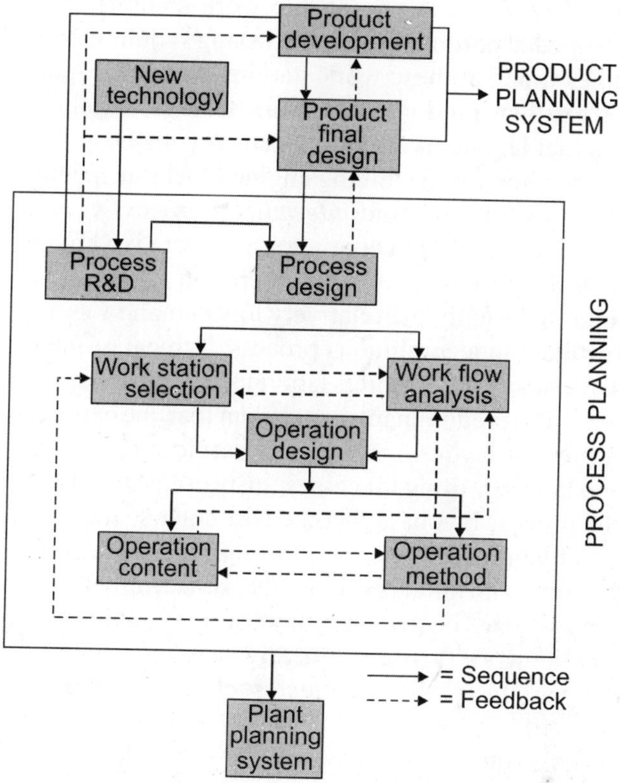

Fig. 6.13 The process planning task. (From Howard L. Timma and Michael F. Pohlen, The Production Function in Business, Richard D. Irwin, Inc., Homewood, (Il., 1970, p. 302.)

As the process R&D phase progresses, information is feedback to the product development group. If the R&D group will be able to comply with the product specifications, then the *product final design* stage can begin. If there are problems, however, in complying with product specifications, then modifications in the product development stage must occur.

Information from both product final design and process R&D are inputs to the *process design stage*. The purpose of this stage is to generate alternative ways of meeting the objectives formalized in the final design stage, determine the criteria by which they will be evaluated, and make the final selection.

6.4.2 Process Design : MACRO

Process design : macro is composed of two aspects: the choice of work station and the choice of work flow. Work station selection involves the choice of machines to be included in the process, whereas work flow analysis concerns the flow of work between these stations.

It is here that the decision is made as to whether the process will be continuous, intermittent, or some combination of both. In *continuous processing*, the process is in constant operation and usually involves a high capital-to-labour ratio. Typical of a continuous-process orientation are the automobile industry, chemical processing, plastics, some high-volume electronic manufacturers, and some utilities such as telephone, power and gas transmission. Also characteristic of continuous-process industries is a *product layout* where all the work stations are devoted exclusively to a single product and are grouped according to the processing requirements of that product. In more cases than not, the machines found at these work stations are special-purpose and costly and have little versatility outside their own product line. Work flow is largely specified by the physical characteristics that the product layout takes. Often a conveyor system is used. An example of this kind of process is an assembly line for machining engine blocks at an automotive plant.

At the other end of the spectrum we find *intermittent processing*. Here production or service for any one job is carried on intermently, not continuously. There is a high mix of products which use the facility, and portions of the process may be in operation several times during the day or only occasionally during the month. Usually the relatively low demand for each product or service does not warrant the high investment in a continuous process. Typical of intermittent processes are job shops, emergency rooms in hospitals, hospital laboratories, most office work, many educational processes, and most services. The predominant plant layout that one expects in intermittent processing is a *process layout*. In a process layout, machines or services of the same category are grouped together. We therefore find lathes, milling machines, inspection stations, and so on, in one location.

A characteristic of the process layout is that the particular sequence of operations that one job follows is seldom repeated by other jobs flowing through the process. For example, the sequence from admittance to discharge in a hospital is seldom the same from one patient to the next. A patient may or may not have X-rays, may or may not have surgery, may or may not undergo physical therapy, etc. Consequently the work flow is not nearly as predictable as in the continuous-process case, and we therefore find variable-path equipment, such as forklift trucks, employed in processes of this type.

The criteria used to make the choice between these two layouts include investment costs, material handling costs, direct labour costs, space requirements, equipment flexibility in meeting changes in output quantity, system reliability and maintenance costs. These economic and non-economic factors must, in turn, be weighed before making the final decision.

6.4.3 Process Design : MICRO

In the next stage attention shifts to the details that make up the work at each station. Concern is with the operational content and operational method of The task *Operational content* focuses on the appropriate combination of steps that should be assigned to a work station. *Operational method,* on the other hand, is concerned with the efficient execution of these steps.

PLANT-PLANNING SYSTEM

If a new plant will be built, then process planning proceeds in a relatively constraint-free setting. If, however, the process must be installed in existing plant, then a set of special constraints must be observed. Therefore, the *process planning system* must interact with the *plant-planning system* to ensure feasible layouts.

PROCESS DESIGN AS AN ONGOING ACTIVITY

Process design is not strictly limited to new design. Whenever the costs of inputs change by a substantial amount, or whenever output levels or quality objectives change, process review should be initiated. If the reason for the reexamination is a price change in an input factor, then a new input mix reflecting the different price ratio of the substitute inputs may be desirable. For example, if wage rates increase substantially as a result of a new labour contract, it might be possible that automated sequences in the production line which were inefficient uses of capital before might now be profitable.

Process design, then, should be a continuous activity—not one which is precipitated only when new products or services are introduced. Since it is continuous, the question of how much money to spend in its pursuit is of utmost importance. The amount which should be spend depends, of course, upon the benefits accured. At the limit, effort should continue as long as the *marginal* benefits from the improvement are greater than the marginal costs. Again we use the word *marginal*, since it is only those costs that change which are relevant. Fixed costs and some semivariable costs, to the extent that they are not affected by the redesign, are irrelevant.

For firms at the continuous-process end of the spectrum, considerable effort can be channeled in this direction. Small improvements made in the process are magnified when the volume going through each stage is large. Cost savings in the automotive industry, for example, are measured in fractions of a cent per unit. In the service industries, on the other hand, savings are usually measured in dollars, but the volume through each station is, of course, much less.

If redesign requires investment, it seems reasonable to subject the investment to the review of the capital-budgeting process. Therefore, this investment, along with all the other which the firm is considering, must face the final selection process in which only the most profitable survive.

6.5 DESIGN FOR MANUFACTURE (DFM)

Competing on time has much to do with the manufacturing/operations flow times. It is obvious that a proper planning of the production processes, their workload distribution, the scheduling decisions planning of the required materials and men, and removing bottlenecks would result in improved throughputs. However, what is not obvious is the fact that a good product design can help substantially towards the reduction in the manufacturing flow time.

A good product design would be such that it makes many or all of the manufacturing related functions to be done in less time, less effort, and with less cost. Such a product design would facilitate the manufacturing function. The manufacturing related operation include:

- **Material procurement,**
- Material handling,
- Product conversion (*e.g.* machining processes),
- Changeovers and set-ups, and
- Quality control procedures.

All of these, if not handled properly, could lead to increased lead times. A good product design takes the facts or realities of these operations into consideration, incorporates them into the design and thereby facilitated these operations.

WHAT IS DFM?

The idea behind a DFM effort is to modify the existing product's (and/or its components') design or have a new product designed in such a way that the processes to manufacture the same arc casier, quicker and or less expensive. Reducing the manufacturing time is a major consideration. This, of course, has to be achieved without compromising on quality.

DFM, as a concept, is not new although its huge importance has dawned on the manufacturers only lately because of the intensity of competition in the present times. It was Eli Whitney (and Le Blanc) in the Western part of the world, who developed system 200 years ago for manufacturing muskets that incorporated the concept of interchangeable parts. Earlier, all muskets were handmade. This was cumbersome in addition to being expensive. It was also terribly time consuming and made the immediate availability in large number a difficult task. Whitney redesigned each part to a specific dimension with a limited tolerance. This paved the way for mass manufacture of muskets. Thus, he designed the musket (and its components) for large scale manufacturability.

Henry Ford seemed to have grasped the concept of DFM about 90 years ago. The following statement by him, about Model T succinctly expresses the idea behind DFM.

"...It was up to me, the designer, to make the car so completely simple...The less complex the article, the easier it is to make, the cheaper it may be sold...We start with the consumer, work back through the design, and finally arrive at manufacturing."*

Product design influences the efficiency of manufacturing. Thereby it influences the flexibility of marketing strategies and the organisation's success in a competing business world.

Cultural barrier: It is indeed surprising that despite the emphasis during the last several decades on increasing efficiency in manufacturing, the importance of product design for manufacturing efficiency has not been appreciated. A majority of the organisations have had the design department and the manufacturing department hardly ever interacting. Product designers in some manufacturing industries have been sitting in ivory towers. They are highly respected, as their job is perceived to be creative like that of an accomplished artist, whereas, the manufacturing executive is seen as a rough-and-tough person who has risen from the ranks, and therefore lacking in such finer abilities. A cultural barrier seems to separate the designer of the product and the person manufacturing the product.

'Over the Wall' syndrome: Product designer believe that their job is over once they release their drawings. They, so to say, throw their designs 'over the wall', for the manufacturing person to do the next job of producing it. Manufacturing engineers then struggle to produce the product that is 'dumped into their laps'. At their best, design and development people have been more concerned with how a particular feature requested by marketing may be translated into a physical parameter. How it may be produced, what it may cost and in what time, have not been much of their concern.

As a result there are several engineering changes *after* the design has been released, because the design gives multitudinous problems when taken up for manufacture. The solution of these problems wastes precious time, and by the time the company has made the product it is too late as the market has shifted. It would have been so much better if the two departments—design and manufacturing—had sat together during the early stages of product design and exchanged notes.

With the heat of the global competition intensifying, companies have now started to seriously think as to how their products could remain competitive in a dynamic market. The Japanese companies such as Toyota, Honda, Mitsubishi and several others have been the forerunners in manufacturing products that were of high quality, yet inexpensive and available at short notice. They have done this consistently over the years, have been quite profitable all through and growing in the international markets, notably in the Western markets. They achieved this despite the fact that it was the West that had been the harbinger of computer technology and automation, While it was Whitney and Henry Ford who had initiated the concept, their message was lost because of the preoccupation with technological superiority. The Japanese have much automation in their factories too; however, they seem to have grasped the value of simplicity in the plants—fewer parts, same or similar parts and parts that are simpler to manufacture. Table 6.1 presents some DFM principles for assemblies.

Table 6.1 DFM Principles for Assemblies

I. Minimise the number of parts

(*i*) Reduce the absolute requirement of the variety of parts.
- Design the product in such a way that it consists of very few parts.
- Use a different technology, if necessary.

(*ii*) Combine parts where feasible

Parts can be combined with other parts when:
- They are of the same material.
- They do not move relative to other parts in the assembly.
- Their combination would not affect the assembly of other parts.
- After sales service does not require these to be separated.

II. Standardise designs

Standardise wherever possible:
- Parts, modules, sub-assemblies, manufacturing processes and systems may be standardised.
- Where the parts cannot be the same, see if they can be similar.
- Apply 'group technology' concept of 'families' of parts.
- Where possible use standard catalog components.

III. Minimise number of operations is the assembly

IV. Modify the part/s with simplification of assembling in mind

Even minor modifications yield greater Assembly simplification

- *Slight changes in a part's geometry can reduce the difficulty in grasping, positioning and inserting a part. The effort and time taken can reduce significantly. Human errors of putting a wrong part or of orienting it wrongly can be reduced.*

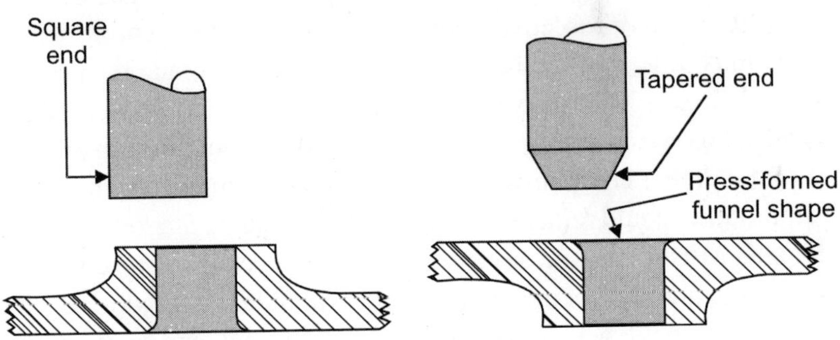

Fig. 6.14 Facilitation of insertion of parts by the use of funnel-shaped openings and tapered ends,
Source : Bralla, J.G., Design for Excellence, McGraw-Hill, New York, 1996.

V. Use modules

This allows for more standardisation and speeds up the assembly process.

VI. Minimise 'new'-ness

Minimise:

- new parts
- new processes
- new suppliers
- new machines

New things—particularly too many new things—introduce many imponderables and increase uncertainty and, consequently, errors resulting in unacceptable quality and time delays in assembling.

VII. Use 'Poka Yoke' or fool-proofing

Design in such a way that the parts cannot be assembled incorrectly.

6.6 DESIGN FOR EXCELLENCE

While designing for manufacturability, the product design team should keep in its consideration the entire product family. Unitary approach may only result in sub-optimiation. Moreover, by the same logic, the designer/team should look beyond its own organisation to other associated organisations in the value chain. Design being a strategic activity, the design effort should not only improve the present efficiencies but should also keep the future in view while making the design and other changes. Finally, customer service should be the motto that should drive the product design effort in any organisation. Hence product design should be an all-round exercise, contributing to the overall excellence of the organisation. DFM is only about one aspect amongst many. Truly, the efforts should be towards design for excellence or DFX (X ≡Excellence).

A key part of any product realization process is the robustness of the design. "Design for" initiatives such as Design for Assembly, Design for Cost, Design for Manufacturing, Design for Test, Design for Logistics, Design for Performance, and so on are now being referred to as Design for Excellence (DFX). It was found that Japanese design emphasizes two key areas; the overall development process and concurrent engineering. As shown in Figure 6.15 there is a strong customer focus at the product-planning phase and in the product evaluation phase of the product development process. The overall product development process is rooted in what Japanese firms call the "market-in". Market-in refers to having a clear set of customer-driven requirements as the basis for product development. This is a fundamental requirement for DFX. Concurrent engineering of product design and development activities provides the second main step in achieving DFX.

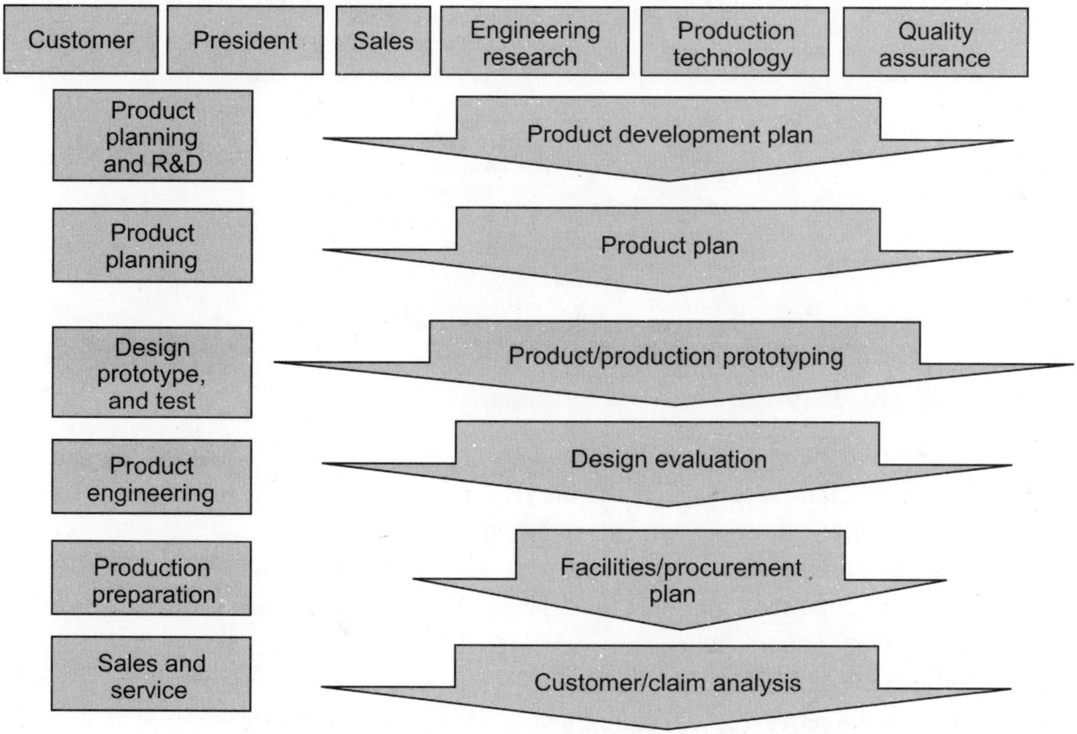

Fig. 6.15 Japan's product development activities (Toyoda Machine Tool Co.)

"In order to effectively deploy a timely design, thorough testing of the design and process training are considered a must. A successful DFX process requires carefully managed design of new products. As shown in Figure 6.16 there are numerous activities that must be coordinated in order to develop and implement a successful product realization effort. Information must be gathered and analyzed from regions of the globe in which products will be introduced, and products must be market-tested in those specific regions. An engine controller for use in an American version of a Japanese automobile, would, by necessity, receive its reliability testing in the United States.

Products that are targeted globally also get tested in Japan in order to carefully control the products' globalization. Technology development activities must operate in parallel with product technology planning and market development planning to assure timely development and introduction of new products.

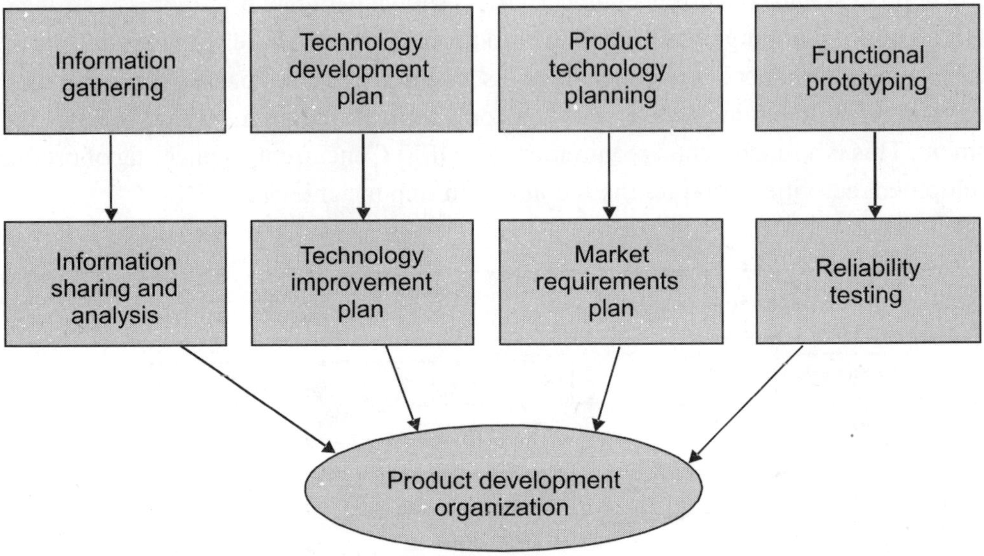

Fig. 6.16 Concurrent development requirements (Sony Corp.)

6.6.1 Concurrent Development Activities

Focus on concurrent engineering is prevalent in all the organizations. The primary objective is to get the overall design right at the lowest cost. This requires making critical decisions as to product features/functions, manufacturability, and most importantly, *cost.*

Firms use a variety of concurrent engineering schematics to depict product, process, and equipment development efforts. For a firm with a core material competence, the product is often a new material, and its schematic would show concurrent development of materials, process, and equipment. Concurrent engineering is a culture in Japan. New products and materials are developed simultaneously with the processes and equipment needed to produce them.

Japanese firms first attempted to break down functional barriers as part of the TQM (total quality management) activities initiated to incorporate quality into product design activities. This was the beginning of what is today referred to as concurrent engineering.

MITI described the first functional integration model based on teams, as shown in Figure 6.17. This approach is a minimum requirement for competitive success in product development and for facilitating rapid product introductions. MITI points out that close coordination between functions dramatically cuts time to market. The problem with this model is that anyone of the functions can still become a bottleneck to development activities because of shared resources.

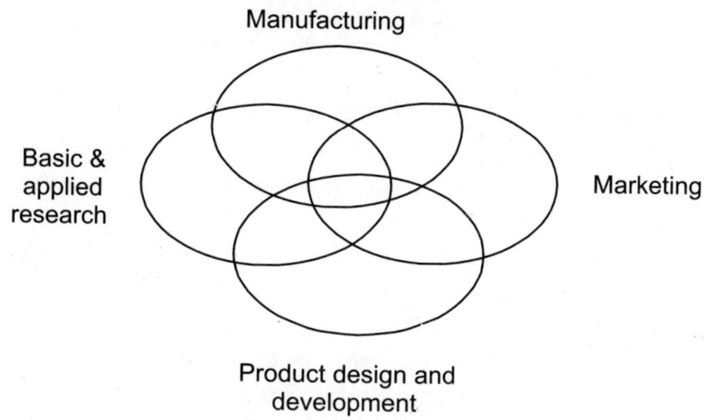

Fig. 6.17 Functional Integration required for technological innovations (MITI)

Going beyond team developments, the concept of concurrent engineering is being practiced in Japan under TQM systems. To shorten time to market for new technologies, firms are working simultaneously to develop component and insertion technologies to be introduced at the time the product is prototyped. As shown in Figure 6.18 concurrent engineering requires parallel implementation of all functional activities.

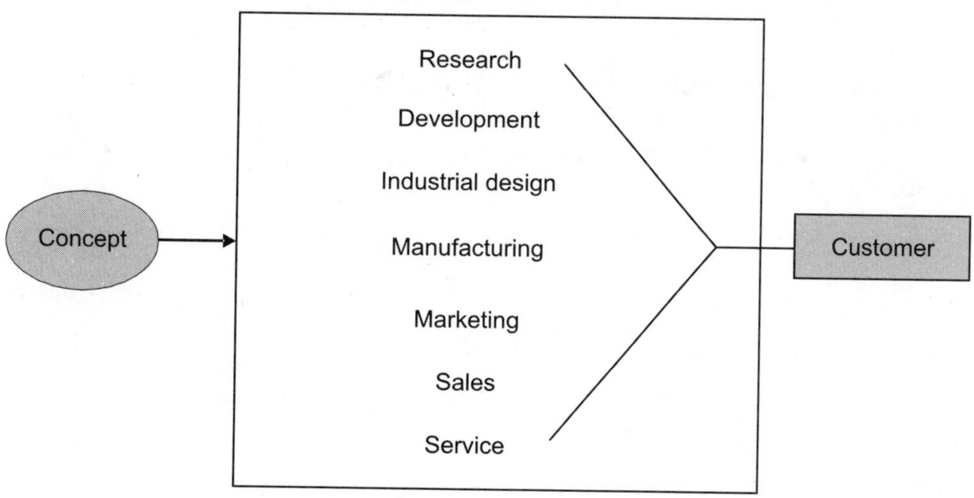

Fig. 6.18 Concurrent engineering for product innovation (MITI)

EXERCISE

1. How does a good product design increase Organisational efficiencies?
2. Should the product design concern itself with Organisational efficiencies? Discuss.
3. Why did, in your opinion, Henry fords message on product design get lost for so many decades? Discuss.
4. 'DFM is value engineering for manufacturing.' Do you agree with this statement? Explain.
5. Discuss the merits and demerits of using plastic parts in a product.
6. Would DFM suppress creativity in a firm? Discuss.
7. Several functions in the companies are getting to be strategic, product design being one of them. If that is the case, how should the organisation cope with this situation of multiple strategic functions?
8. "A Good Product Design Contributes To "TQM" in the Organisation." Explain how this may happen.
9. Wouldn't reliability concerns clash with DFM concerns? Discuss.
10. What is DFX? What all is included in DFX?
11. Time is money. How can a product design project bc hastened?
12. What are the problems, if any, with concurrent Engineering?
13. How will you incorporate environmental concerns into product design? Discuss.
14. Can there be a design for disassembling? Where could this concept be useful? Give your tips for such a design.

REFERENCES

1. S.N. Chary, *Production and Operation Management*, 3rd Edition, Tata McGraw-Hill Publishing Company Limited, 2004.
2. Eilon, Samuel, *Elements of Production Planning and Control*, Bombay Universal Book Co. 1985.
3. Barry Shore, *Operations Management*, McGraw-Hill Publication, 1973.

7

MATERIALS MANAGEMENT

CHAPTER OUTLINE

7.1 INTRODUCTION AND MEANING

Materials management is a function, which aims for integrated approach towards the management of materials in an industrial undertaking. Its main objective is cost reduction and efficient handling of materials at all stages and in all sections of the undertaking. Its function includes several important aspects connected with material, such as, purchasing, storage, inventory control, material handling, standardisation etc.

7.2 SCOPE OR FUNCTIONS OF MATERIALS MANAGEMENT

Materials management is defined as "*the function responsible for the coordination of planning, sourcing, purchasing, moving, storing and controlling materials in an optimum manner so as to provide a pre-decided service to the customer at a minimum cost*".

From the definition it is clear that the scope of materials management is vast. The functions of materials management can be categorized in the following ways: (as shown in Fig. 7.1.)

1. Material Planning and Control
2. Purchasing
3. Stores Management
4. Inventory Control or Management
5. Standardisation
6. Simplification
7. Value Analysis
8. Erogonomics
9. Just-in-Time (JIT)

All the above mentioned functions of materials management has been discussed in detail in this chapter.

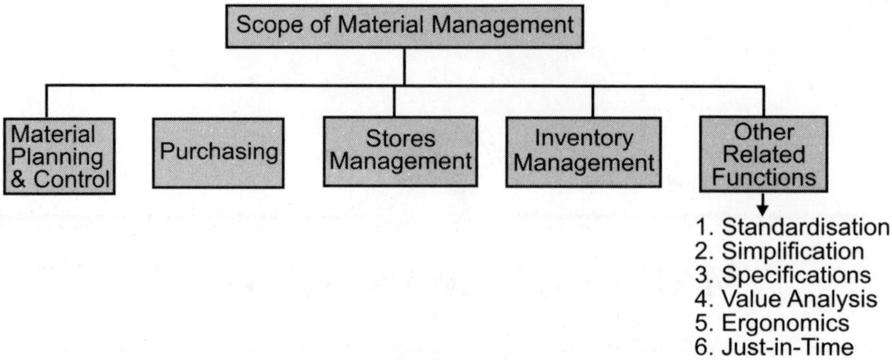

Fig. 7.1 Scope of materials management

1. **Materials planning and control:** Based on the sales forecast and production plans, the materials planning and control is done. This involves estimating the individual requirements of parts, preparing materials budget, forecasting the levels of inventories, scheduling the orders and monitoring the performance in relation to production and sales.

2. **Purchasing:** This includes selection of sources of supply finalization in terms of purchase, placement of purchase orders, follow-up, maintenance of smooth relations with suppliers, approval of payments to suppliers, evaluating and rating suppliers.

3. **Stores management or management:** This involves physical control of materials, preservation of stores, minimization of obsolescence and damage through timely disposal and efficient handling, maintenance of stores records, proper location and stocking. A store is also responsible for the physical verification of stocks and reconciling them with book figures. A store plays a vital role in the operations of a company.

4. **Inventory control or management:** Inventory generally refers to the materials in stock. It is also called the idle resource of an enterprise. Inventories represent those items, which are either stocked for sale or they are in the process of manufacturing or they are in the form of materials, which are yet to be utilized. The interval between receiving the purchased parts and transforming them into final products varies from industries to industries depending upon the cycle time of manufacture. It is, therefore, necessary to hold inventories of various kinds to act as a buffer between supply and demand for efficient operation of the system. Thus, an effective control on inventory is a must for smooth and efficient running of the production cycle with least interruptions.

5. **Other related activities**

(*a*) ***3S***

(*i*) *Standardization*: Standardization means producing maximum variety of products from the minimum variety of materials, parts, tools and processes. It is the process of establishing standards or units of measure by which extent, quality, quantity, value, performance etc. may be compared and measured.

(*ii*) *Simplification*: The concept of simplification is closely related to standardization. Simplification is the process of reducing the variety of products manufactured. Simplification is concerned with the reduction of product range, assemblies, parts, materials and design.

(*iii*) *Specifications*: It refers to a precise statement that formulizes the requirements of the customer. It may relate to a product, process or a service.

Example: Specifications of an axle block are Inside Dia. = 2 ± 0.1 cm, Outside Dia. = 4 ± 0.2 cm and Length = 10 ± 0.5 cm.

(*b*) ***Value analysis*:** Value analysis is concerned with the costs added due to inefficient or unnecessary specifications and features. It makes its contribution in the last stage of product cycle, namely, the maturity stage. At this stage research and development no longer make positive contributions in terms of improving the efficiency of the functions of the product or adding new functions to it.

(*c*) ***Ergonomics** (Human Engineering)***:** The human factors or human engineering is concerned with man-machine system. Ergonomics is "the design of human tasks, man-machine system, and effective accomplishment of the job, including displays for presenting information to human sensors, controls for human operations and complex man-machine systems." Each of the above functions are dealt in detail.

7.3 MATERIAL PLANNING AND CONTROL

Material planning is a scientific technique of determining in advance the requirements of raw materials, ancillary parts and components, spares etc. as directed by the production programme. It is a sub-system in the overall planning activity. There are many factors, which influence the activity of material planning. These factors can be classified as macro and micro systems.

1. *Macro factors*: Some of the micro factors which affect material planning, are price trends, business cycles Govt. import policy etc.
2. *Micro factors*: Some of the micro factors that affect material planning are plant capacity utilization, rejection rates, lead times, inventory levels, working capital, delegation of powers and communication.

7.3.1 Techniques of Material Planning

One of the techniques of material planning is bill of material explosion. Material planning through bill of material explosion is shown below in Fig. 7.2.

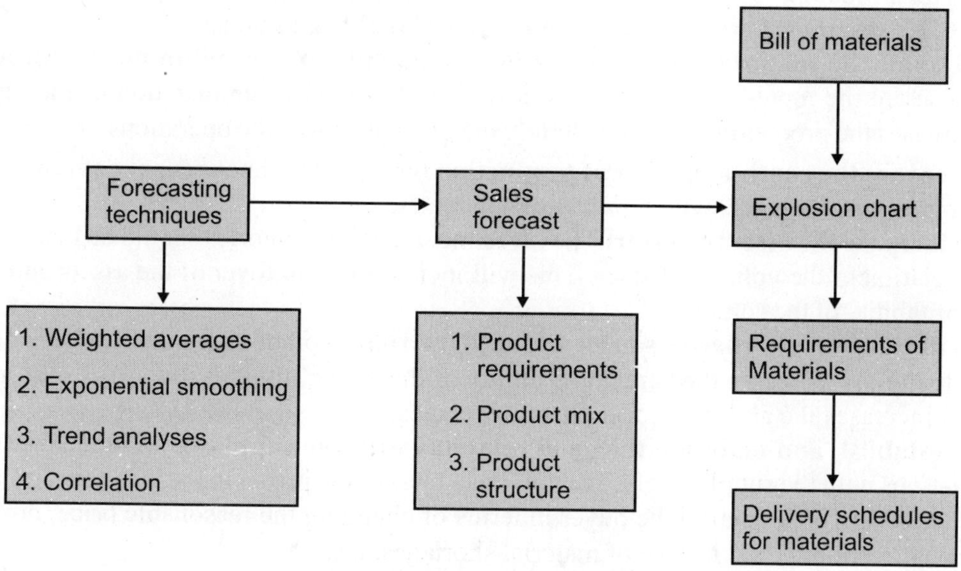

Fig. 7.2 Material planning

The basis for material planning is the forecast demand for the end products. Forecasting techniques such as weighted average method, exponential smoothening and time series models are used for the same. Once the demand forecast is made, it is possible to go through the excerse of material planning. Bill of materials is a document which shows list of materials required, unit consumption location code for a given product. An explosive chart is a series of bill of material grouped in a matrix form so that combined requirements for different components can be done requirements of various materials are arrives at from the demand forecast, using bill of materials, through explosion charts. Thus material requirement plan will lead to be the development of delivery schedule of the materials and purchasing of those material requirements.

7.4 PURCHASING

Purchasing is an important function of materials management. In any industry purchase means buying of equipments, materials, tools, parts etc. required for industry. The importance of the purchase function varies with nature and size of industry. In small industry, this function is performed by works manager and in large manufacturing concern; this function is done by a separate department. The moment a buyer places an order he commits a substantial portion of the finance of the corporation which affects the working capital and cash flow position. He is a highly responsible person who meets various salesmen and thus can be considered to have been contributing to the public relations efforts of the company. Thus, the buyer can make or mar the company's image by his excellent or poor relations with the vendors.

7.4.1 Objectives of Purchasing

The basic objective of the purchasing function is to ensure continuity of supply of raw materials, sub-contracted items and spare parts and to reduce the ultimate cost of the finished goods. In other words, the objective is not only to procure the raw materials at the lowest price but to reduce the cost of the final product.

The objectives of the purchasing department can be outlined as under:

- **To avail the materials, suppliers and equipments at the minimum possible costs:** These are the inputs in the manufacturing operations. The minimization of the input cost increases the productivity and resultantly the profitability of the operations.
- **To ensure the continuous flow of production** through continuous supply of raw materials, components, tools etc. with repair and maintenance service.
- **To increase the asset turnover:** The investment in the inventories should be kept minimum in relation to the volume of sales. This will increase the turnover of the assets and thus the profitability of the company.
- **To develop an alternative source of supply:** Exploration of alternative sources of supply of materials increases the bargaining ability of the buyer, minimisation of cost of materials and increases the ability to meet the emergencies.
- **To establish and maintain the good relations with the suppliers:** Maintenance of good relations with the supplier helps in evolving a favourable image in the business circles. Such relations are beneficial to the buyer in terms of changing the reasonable price, preferential allocation of material in case of material shortages, etc.

- **To achieve maximum integration with other department of the company:** The purchase function is related with **production department** for specifications and flow of material, **engineering department** for the purchase of tools, equipments and machines, **marketing department** for the forecasts of sales and its impact on procurement of materials, **financial department** for the purpose of maintaining levels of materials and estimating the working capital required, **personnel department** for the purpose of manning and developing the personnel of purchase department and maintaining good vendor relationship.
- **To train and develop the personnel:** Purchasing department is manned with varied types of personnel. The company should try to build the imaginative employee force through training and development.
- **Efficient record keeping and management reporting:** Paper processing is inherent in the purchase function. Such paper processing should be standardised so that record keeping can be facilitated. Periodic reporting to the management about the purchase activities justifies the independent existence of the department.

7.4.2 Parameters of Purchasing

The success of any manufacturing activity is largely dependent on the procurement of raw materials of right quality, in the right quantities, from right source, at the right time and at right price popularly known as **ten 'R's'** of the art of efficient purchasing. They are described as the basic principles of purchasing. There are other well known parameters such as right contractual terms, right material, right place, right mode of transportation and right attitude are also considered for purchasing.

1. **Right price:** It is the primary concern of any manufacturing organization to get an item at the right price. But right price need not be the lowest price. It is very difficult to determine the right price; general guidance can be had from the cost structure of the product. The 'tender system' of buying is normally used in public sector organizations but the objective should be to identify the lowest 'responsible' bidder and not the lowest bidder. The technique of 'learning curve' also helps the purchase agent to determine the price of items with high labour content. The price can be kept low by proper planning and not by rush buying. Price negotiation also helps to determine the right prices.

2. **Right quality:** Right quality implies that quality should be available, measurable and understandable as far as practicable. In order to determine the quality of a product sampling schemes will be useful. The right quality is determined by the cost of materials and the technical characteristics as suited to the specific requirements. The quality particulars are normally obtained from the indents. Since the objective of purchasing is to ensure continuity of supply to the user departments, the time at which the material is provided to the user department assumes great importance.

3. **Right time:** For determining the right time, the purchase manager should have lead time information for all products and analyse its components for reducing the same. Lead time is the total time elapsed between the recognition of the need of an item till the item arrives and is provided for use. This covers the entire duration of the materials cycle and consists of pre-contractual administrative lead time, manufacturing and transporting lead time and inspection lead time. Since the inventory increases with higher lead time, it is desirable to analyse each component of the lead time so as to reduce the first and third components which are controllable. While determining the purchases, the

buyer has to consider emergency situations like floods, strikes, etc. He should have 'contingency plans' when force major clauses become operative, for instance, the material is not available due to strike, lock-out, floods, and earthquakes.

4. **Right source:** The source from which the material is procured should be dependable and capable of supplying items of uniform quality. The buyer has to decide which item should be directly obtained from the manufacturer. Source selection, source development and vendor rating play an important role in buyer-seller relationships. In emergencies, open market purchases and bazaar purchases are restored to.

5. **Right quantity:** The right quantity is the most important parameter in buying. Concepts, such as, economic order quantity, economic purchase quantity, fixed period and fixed quantity systems, will serve as broad guidelines. But the buyer has to use his knowledge, experience and common sense to determine the quantity after considering factors such as price structure, discounts, availability of the item, favourable reciprocal relations, and make or buy consideration.

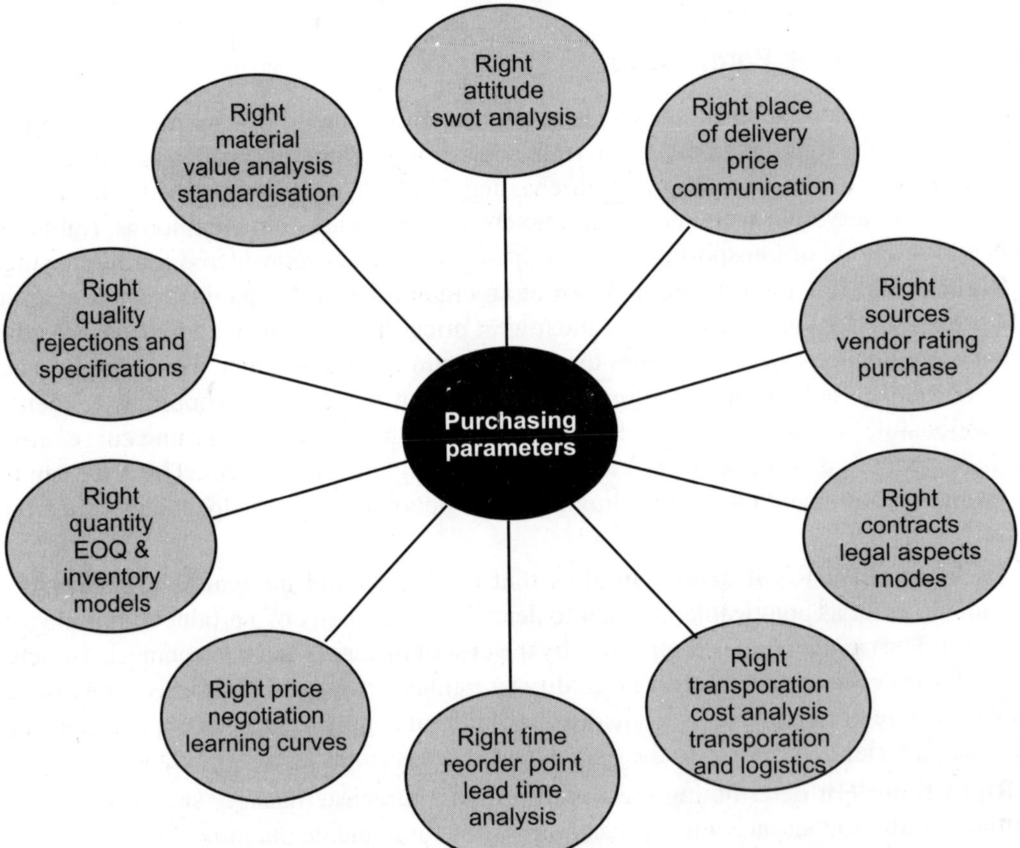

Fig. 7.3 Purchase parameters

6. **Right attitude:** Developing the right attitude too, is necessary as one often comes across such statement: 'Purchasing knows the price of everything and value of nothing'; 'We buy price and not cost'; 'When will our order placers become purchase managers?'; 'Purchasing acts like a post box'. Therefore, purchasing should keep 'progress' as its key activity and should be future-oriented.

The purchase manager should be innovative and his long-term objective should be to minimise the cost of the ultimate product. He will be able to achieve this if he aims himself with techniques, such as, value analysis, materials intelligence, purchases research, SWOT analysis, purchase budget lead time analysis, etc.

7. **Right contracts:** The buyer has to adopt separate policies and procedures for capital and consumer items. He should be able to distinguish between indigenous and international purchasing procedures. He should be aware of the legal and contractual aspects in international practices.

8. **Right material:** Right type of material required for the production is an important parameter in purchasing. Techniques, such as, value analysis will enable the buyer to locate the right material.

9. **Right transportation:** Right mode of transportation have to be identified as this forms a critical segment in the cost profile of an item. It is an established fact that the cost of the shipping of ore, gravel, sand, etc., is normally more than the cost of the item itself.

10. **Right place of delivery:** Specifying the right place of delivery, like head office or works, would often minimize the handling and transportation cost.

7.4.3 Purchasing Procedure

The procedure describes the sequence of steps leading to the completion of an identified specific task. The purchasing procedure comprises the following steps as indicated in Fig. 4.4.

1. **Recognition of the need:** The initiation of procedure starts with the recognition of the need by the needy section. The demand is lodged with the purchase department in the prescribed Purchase Requisition Form forwarded by the authorised person either directly or through the Stores Department. The purchase requisition clearly specifies the details, such as, specification of materials, quality and quantity, suggested supplier, etc. Generally, the low value sundries and items of common use are purchased for stock while costlier and special items are purchased according the production programmes. Generally, the corporate level executives are authorized signatories to such demands. Such purchases are approved by the Board of Directors. The reference of the approval is made on requisition and a copy of the requisition is sent to the secretary for the purpose of overall planning and budgeting.

2. **The Selection of the supplier:** The process of selection of supplier involves two basic aspects: searching for all possible sources and short listing out of the identified sources. The complete information about the supplier is available from various sources, such as, trade directories, advertisement in trade journals, direct mailing by the suppliers, interview with suppliers, salesmen, suggestions from business associates, visit to trade fair, participation in industries convention, etc. Identification of more and more sources helps in selecting better and economical supplier. It should be noted that the low bidder is not always the best bidder. When everything except price is equal, the low bidder will be selected. The important considerations in the selection are the price, ability to supply the required quantity, maintenance of quality standards, financial standing etc. It should be noted that it is not necessary to go for this process for all types of purchases. For the repetitive orders and for the purchases of low-value, small lot items, generally the previous suppliers with good records are preferred.

3. **Placing the order:** Once the supplier is selected the next step is to place the purchase order. Purchase order is a letter sent to the supplier asking to supply the said material. At least six copies of purchase order are prepared by the purchase section and each copy is separately signed

by the purchase officer. Out these copies, one copy each is sent to store-keeper, supplier, accounts section, inspection department and to the department placing the requisition and one copy is retained by the purchase department for record.

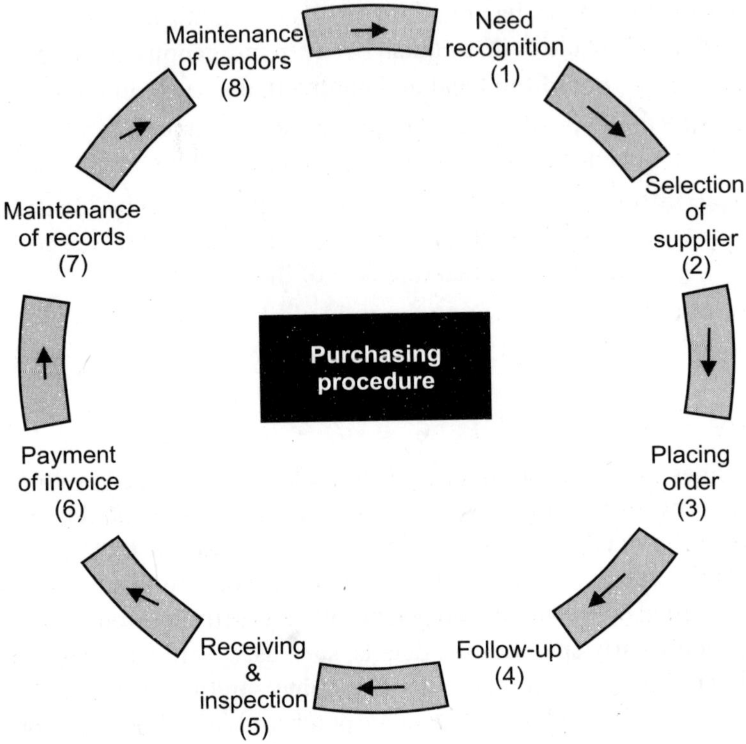

Fig. 7.4 Purchasing procedure

4. **Follow-up of the order:** Follow-up procedure should be employed wherever the costs and risks resulting from the delayed deliveries of materials are greater than the cost of follow-up procedure, the follow-up procedure tries to see that the purchase order is confirmed by the supplier and the delivery is promised. It is also necessary to review the outstanding orders at regular intervals and to communicate with the supplier in case of need. Generally, a routine urge is made to the supplier by sending a printed post card or a circular letter asking him to confirm that the delivery is on the way or will be made as per agreement. In absence of any reply or unsatisfactory reply, the supplier may be contact through personal letter, phone, telegram and/or even personal visit.

5. **Receiving and inspection of the materials:** The receiving department receives the materials supplied by the vendor. The quantity are verified and tallied with the purchase order. The receipt of the materials is recorded on the specially designed receiving slips or forms which also specify the name of the vendor and the purchase order number. It also records any discrepancy, damaged condition of the consignment or inferiority of the materials. The purchase department is informed immediately about the receipt of the materials. Usually a copy of the receiving slip is sent to the purchase department.

6. **Payment of the invoice:** When the goods are received in satisfactory condition, the invoice is checked before it is approved for the payment. The invoice is checked to see that the goods were duly authorised to purchase, they were properly ordered, they are priced as per the agreed terms, the quantity and quality confirm to the order, the calculations are arithmetically correct etc.

7. **Maintenance of the records:** Maintenance of the records is an important part and parcel of the efficient purchase function. In the industrial firms, most of the purchases are repeat orders and hence the past records serve as a good guide for the future action. They are very useful for deciding the timings of the purchases and in selecting the best source of the supply.

8. **Maintenance of vendor relations:** The quantum and frequency of the transactions with the same key suppliers provide a platform for the purchase department to establish and maintain good relations with them. Good relations develop mutual trust and confidence in the course of the time which is beneficial to both the parties. The efficiency of the purchase department can be measured by the amount of the goodwill it has with its suppliers.

7.4.4 Selection of Suppliers

Selection of the right supplier is the responsibility of the purchase department. It can contribute substantially to the fundamental objectives of the business enterprise. Different strategies are required for acquiring different types of materials. The selection of supplier for standardised products will differ from non-standardised products. Following factors are considered for the selection of suppliers:

A. Sources of Supplier

The best buying is possible only when the decision maker is familiar with all possible sources of supply and their respective terms and conditions. The purchase department should try to locate the appropriate sources of the supplier of various types of materials. This is known as 'survey stage'. A survey of the following will help in developing the possible sources of supply:

1. Specialised trade directories.
2. Assistance of professional bodies or consultants.
3. The buyer's guide or purchase handbook.
4. The manufacturer's or distributor's catalogue.
5. Advertisements in dailies.
6. Advertisement in specialised trade journals.
7. Trade fair exhibitions.

B. Development of Approved List of Suppliers

The survey stage highlights the existence of the source. A business inquiry is made with the appropriate supplier. It is known as 'Inquiry Stage'. Here a short listing is made out of the given sources of suppliers in terms of production facilities and capacity, financial standing, product quality, possibility of timely supply, technical competence, manufacturing efficiency, general business policies followed, standing in the industry, competitive attitude, and interest in buying orders etc.

C. Evaluation and Selection of the Supplier

The purchase policy and procedure differ according to the type of items to be purchased. Hence, evolution and selection of the supplier differ accordingly. In the 'purchasing handbook' edited by

Aljian, it has been described that the following variables to be considered while evaluating the quotations of the suppliers:

1. **Cost factors:** Price, transportation cost, installation cost if any, tooling and other operations cost, incidence of sales tax and excise duty, terms of payment and cash discount are considered in cost factor.

2. **Delivery:** Routing and F.O.B. terms are important in determining the point at which the title to the goods passes from vendor to the buyer and the responsibility for the payment of the payment charges.

3. **Design and specification factors:** Specification compliance, specification deviations, specification advantages, important dimensions and weights are considered in line with the demonstration of sample, experience of other users, after sale services etc.

4. **Legal factors:** Legal factors include warranty, cancellation provision, patent protection, public liability, federal laws and reputation compliance.

5. **Vendor rating:** The evaluation of supplier or vendor rating provides valuable information which help in improving the quality of the decision. In the vendor rating three basic aspects are considered namely quality, service and price. How much weight should be given to each of these factors is a matter of judgment and is decided according to the specific need of the organization. Quality would be the main consideration in the manufacturing of the electrical equipments while price would be the prime consideration in the product having a tense competitive market and for a company procuring its requirements under the blanket contract with agreed price, the supplier rating would be done on the basis of two variables namely quality and delivery.

The Development Project Committee of the National Association of Purchasing Agents (U.S.A.) has suggested following methods for evaluating the performance of past suppliers.

(*a*) **The categorical plan:** Under this method the members of the buying staff related with the supplier like receiving section, quality control department, manufacturing department etc., are required to assess the performance of each supplier. The rating sheets are provided with the record of the supplier, their product and the list of factors for the evaluation purposes. The members of the buying staff are required to assign the plus or minus notations against each factor. The periodic meetings, usually at the interval of one month, are held by senior man of the buying staff to consider the individual rating of each section. The consolidation of the individual rating is done on the basis of the net plus value and accordingly, the suppliers are assigned the categories such as 'preferred', 'neutral' or 'unsatisfactory'. Such ratings are used for the future guidance.

This is a very simple and inexpensive method. However, it is not precise. Its quality heavily depends on the experience and ability of the buyer to judge the situation. As compared to other methods, the degree of subjective judgment is very high as rating is based on personal whim and the vague impressions of the buyer. As the quantitative data supported by the profits do not exist, it is not possible to institute any corrective action with the vendor. The rating is done on the basis of memory, and thus it becomes only a routine exercise without any critical analysis.

(*b*) **The weighted-point method:** The weighted-point method provides the quantitative data for each factor of evaluation. The weights are assigned to each factor of evaluation according to the need of the organization, *e.g.*, a company decides the three factors to be considered—quality, price and timely delivery. It assigns the relative weight to each of these factors as under:

Quality	....	50 points
Price	....	30 points
Timely delivery	....	20 points

The evaluation of each supplier is made in accordance with the aforesaid factors and weights and the composite weighted-points are ascertained for each suppliers—A, B and C—are rated under this method. First of all the specific rating under each factor will be made and then the consolidation of all the factors will be made for the purpose of judgment.

(*c*) **Quality rating:** Percentage of quantity accepted among the total quantity is called quality rating. In other words, the quality of the materials is judged on the basis of the degree of acceptance and rejections. For the purpose of comparison, the percentage degree of acceptance will be calculated in relation to the total lots received. **Price rating** is done on the basis of net price charged by the supplier. **Timely delivery** rating will be done comparing with the average delivery schedule of the supplier.

(*d*) **The cost-ratio plan:** Under this method, the vendor rating is done on the basis of various costs incurred for procuring the materials from various suppliers. The cost-ratios are ascertained delivery etc. The cost-ratios are ascertained for the different rating variables such as quality, price, timely delivery etc. The cost-ratio is calculated in percentage on the basis of total individual cost and total value of purchases. At the end, all such cost-ratios will be adjusted with the quoted price per unit. The plus cost-ratio will increase the unit price while the minus cost-ratio will decrease the unit price. The net adjusted unit price will indicate the vendor rating. The vendor with the lowest net adjusted unit price will be the best supplier and so on. Certain quality costs can be inspection cost, cost of defectives, reworking costs and manufacturing losses on rejected items etc. Certain delivery costs can be postage and telegrams, telephones and extra cost for quick delivery etc.

VENDER RATING ILLUSTRATIONS

ILLUSTRATION 1: *The following information is available on 3 vendors: A, B and C. Using the data below, determine the best source of supply under weighed-point method and substantiate your solution.*

- *Vendor A: Delivered '56' lots, '3' were rejected, '2' were not according to the schedule.*
- *Vendor B: Supplied '38' lots, '2' were rejected, '3' were late.*
- *Vendor C: Finished '42' lots, '4' were defective, '5' were delayed deliveries.*
- *Give 40 for quality and 30 weightage for service.*

SOLUTION

$$\text{Quality performance (weightage 40\%)} = \frac{\text{Quality accepted}}{\text{Total quantity supplied}} \times 40$$

DELIVERY PERFORMANCE

X, Adherence to time schedule (weightage 30%)

$$= \frac{\text{No. of delivery made on the scheduled date}}{\text{Total no. of scheduled deliveries}} \times 30$$

Y, Adherence to quantity schedule (weightage 30%)

$$= \frac{\text{No. of correct lot size deliveries}}{\text{Total no. of scheduled deliveries}} \times 30$$

Total vendor rating $= X + Y$

$$\text{Vendor A} = \frac{53}{56} \times 40 + \frac{54}{56} \times 30 = 66.78$$

$$\text{Vendor B} = \frac{36}{38} \times 40 + \frac{35}{38} \times 30 = 65.52$$

$$\text{Vendor C} = \frac{38}{42} \times 40 + \frac{37}{42} \times 30 = 62.62$$

Vendor 'A' is selected with the best rating.

ILLUSTRATION 2: *The following information is available from the record of the incoming material department of ABC Co. Ltd.*

Vendor code	No. of lots submitted	No. of list accepted	Proportion defectives in lots	Unit price in Rs.	Fraction of delivery commitment
A	15	12	0.08	15.00	0.94
B	10	9	0.12	19.00	0.98
C	1	1	–	21.00	0.90

The factor weightage for quality, delivery and price are 40%, 35% and 25% as per the decision of the mar. Rank the performance of the vendors on the QDP basis and interpret the result.

SOLUTION

Formal mode:

$$= \frac{\text{No. of lots accepted}}{\text{No. of lots submitted}} \times (\text{weightage for quality})$$

$$+ \frac{\text{No. of accepted lots}}{\text{No.of lots submitted with time}} \times (\text{weightage for delivery})$$

$$+ \frac{\text{Lowest Price}}{\text{Price of lot}} \times (\text{weightage for price})$$

Total vendor rating = Quality performance + Delivery performance rating + Price rating

$$\text{Vendor A} = \frac{12}{15} \times 40 + 0.94 \times 35 + \frac{15}{15} \times 25 = 89.90$$

$$\text{Vendor B} = \frac{9}{10} \times 40 + 0.98 \times 35 + \frac{15}{19} \times 25 = 90.036$$

$$\text{Vendor C} = 1 \times 40 + 0.90 \times 35 + \frac{15}{21} \times 25 = 89.357$$

Vendor B is selected with higher rating.

7.4.5 Special Purchasing Systems

The following are some of the importnat purchasing systems:

1. **Forward buying:** Forward buying or committing an organization far into the future, usually for a year. Depending upon the availability of the item, the financial policies, the economic order quantity, the quantitative discounts, and the staggered delivery, the future commitment is decided. This type of forward buying is different from speculative buying where the motive is to make capital out of the price changes, by selling the purchased items. Manufacturing organizations normally do not indulge in such buying. However, a few organizations do 'Hedge', particularly in the commodity market by selling or buying contracts.

2. **Tender buying:** In public, all semblance of favouritism, personal preferences should be avoided. As such, it is common for government departments and public sector undertakings to purchase through tenders. Private sector organizations adopt tender buying if the value of purchases is more than the prescribed limits as Rs. 50000 or Rs. 100000. The steps involved are to establish a bidders' list, solicit bids by comparing quotations and place the order with the lowest bidder. However, care has to be taken that the lowest bidder is responsible party and is capable of meeting the delivery schedule and quality requirements. Open tender system or advertisement in newspapers is common in public sector organizations. As advertising bids is costly and time consuming, most private sector organizations solicit tenders only from the renowned suppliers capable of supplying the materials.

3. **Blanket order system:** This system minimizes the administrative expenses and is useful for 'C' type items. It is an agreement to provide a required quantity of specified items, over a period of time, usually for one year, at an agreed price. Deliveries are made depending upon the buyer's needs. The system relieves the buyers from routine work, giving him more time for focusing attention on high value items. It requires fewer purchase orders and thus reduces clerical work. It often achieves lower prices through quantity discounts by grouping the requirements. The supplier, under the system maintains adequate inventory to meet the blanket orders.

4. **Zero stock:** Some firms try to operate on the basis of zero stock and the supplier holds the stock for these firms. Usually, the firms of the buyer and seller are close to each other so that the raw materials of one is the finished products of another. Alternatively, the system could work well if the seller holds the inventory and if the two parties work in close coordination. However, the price per item in this system will be slightly higher as the supplier will include the inventory carrying cost

in the price. In this system, the buyer need not lock up the capital and so the purchasing routine is reduced. This is also significantly reduces obsolescence of inventory, lead time and clerical efforts in paper work. Thus, the seller can devote his marketing efforts to other customers and production scheduling becomes easy.

5. **Rate contract:** The system of rate contract is prevalent in public sector organizations and government departments. It is common for the suppliers to advertise that they are on 'rate contract' for the specific period. After negotiations, the seller and the buyer agree to the rates of items. Application of rate contract has helped many organizations to cut down the internal administrative lead time as individual firms need to go through the central purchasing departments and can place orders directly with the suppliers. However, suppliers always demand higher prices for prompt delivery, as rate difficulty has been avoided by ensuring the delivery of a minimum quantity at the agreed rates. This procedure of fixing a minimum quantity is called the running contract and is being practised by the railways. The buyer also has an option of increasing the quantity by 25% more than the agreed quantity under this procedure.

6. **Reciprocity:** Reciprocal buying means purchasing from one's customers in preference to others. It is based on the principle "if you kill my cat, I will kill your dog", and "Do unto your customers as you would have them do unto you". Other things, like soundness from the ethics and economics point of view being equal, the principles of reciprocity can be practiced. However, a purchasing executive should not indulge in reciprocity on his initiative when the terms and conditions are not equal with other suppliers. It is often sound that less efficient manufacturers and distributors gain by reciprocity what they are unable to gain by price and quality. Since this tends to discourage competition and might lead to higher process and fewer suppliers, reciprocity should be practised on a selective basis.

7. **Systems contract:** This is a procedure intender to help the buyer and the sellers to reduce administrative expenses and at the same time ensure suitable controls. In this system, the original indent, duly approved by competent authorities, is shipped back with the items and avoids the usual documents like purchase orders, materials requisitions, expediting letters and acknowledgements, delivery period price and invoicing procedure, Carborandum company in the US claims drastic reduction in inventory and elimination of 40000 purchase orders by adopting the system contracting procedure. It is suitable for low unit price items with high consumption.

7.5 STORES MANAGEMENT

Stores play a vital role in the operations of company. It is in direct touch with the user departments in its day-to-day activities. The most important purpose served by the stores is to provide uninterrupted service to the manufacturing divisions. Further, stores are often equated directly with money, as money is locked up in the stores.

Functions of Stores

The functions of stores can be classified as follows:

1. To receive raw materials, components, tools, equipment's and other items and account for them.
2. To provide adequate and proper storage and preservation to the various items.

3. To meet the demands of the consuming departments by proper issues and account for the consumption.
4. To minimise obsolescence, surplus and scrap through proper codification, preservation and handling.
5. To highlight stock accumulation, discrepancies and abnormal consumption and effect control measures.
6. To ensure good house keeping so that material handling, material preservation, stocking, receipt and issue can be done adequately.
7. To assist in verification and provide supporting information for effective purchase action.

7.5.1 Codification

It is one of the functions of stores management. Codification is a process of representing each item by a number, the digit of which indicates the group, the sub-group, the type and the dimension of the item. Many organizations in the public and private sectors, railways have their own system of codification, varying from eight to thirteen digits. The first two digits represents the major groups, such as raw materials, spare parts, sub-contracted items, hardware items, packing material, tools, oil, stationery etc. The next two digits indicate the sub-groups, such as, ferrous, non-ferrous etc. Dimensional characteristics of length, width, head diameter etc. constitute further three digits and the last digit is reserved for minor variations.

Whatever may be the basis, each code should uniquely represent one item. It should be simple and capable of being understood by all. Codification should be compact, concise, consistent and flexible enough to accommodate new items. The groupings should be logical, holding similar parts near to one another. Each digit must be significant enough to represent some characteristic of the item.

Objectives of Codification

The objectives of a rationalized material coding system are:

1. Bringing all items together.
2. To enable putting up of any future item in its proper place.
3. To classify an item according to its characteristics.
4. To give an unique code number to each item to avoid duplication and ambiguity.
5. To reveal excessive variety and promote standardization and variety reduction.
6. To establish a common language for the identification of an item.
7. To fix essential parameters for specifying an item.
8. To specify item as per national and international standards.
9. To enable data processing and analysis.

Advantages of Codification

As a result of rationalized codification, many firms have reduced the number of items. It enables systematic grouping of similar items and avoids confusion caused by long description of items since standardization of names is achieved through codification, it serves as the starting point of simplification and standardization. It helps in avoiding duplication of items and results in the minimisation of the number of items, leading to accurate record. Codification enables easy recognition of an item in stores, thereby reducing clerical efforts to the minimum. If items are coded according to the sources, it is possible to bulk the items while ordering. To maximise the aforesaid advantages, it is necessary to develop the codes as concerned, namely, personnel from design, production, engineering, inspection, maintenance and materials.

7.6 INVENTORY CONTROL OR MANAGEMENT

7.6.1 Meaning of Inventory

Inventory generally refers to the materials in stock. It is also called the idle resource of an enterprise. Inventories represent those items which are either stocked for sale or they are in the process of manufacturing or they are in the form of materials, which are yet to be utilised. The interval between receiving the purchased parts and transforming them into final products varies from industries to industries depending upon the cycle time of manufacture. It is, therefore, necessary to hold inventories of various kinds to act as a buffer between supply and demand for efficient operation of the system. Thus, an effective control on inventory is a must for smooth and efficient running of the production cycle with least interruptions.

7.6.2 Reasons for Keeping Inventories

1. **To stabilise production:** The demand for an item fluctuates because of the number of factors, *e.g.,* seasonality, production schedule etc. The inventories (raw materials and components) should be made available to the production as per the demand failing which results in stock out and the production stoppage takes place for want of materials. Hence, the inventory is kept to take care of this fluctuation so that the production is smooth.
2. **To take advantage of price discounts:** Usually the manufacturers offer discount for bulk buying and to gain this price advantage the materials are bought in bulk even though it is not required immediately. Thus, inventory is maintained to gain economy in purchasing.
3. **To meet the demand during the replenishment period:** The lead time for procurement of materials depends upon many factors like location of the source, demand supply condition, etc. So inventory is maintained to meet the demand during the procurement (replenishment) period.
4. **To prevent loss of orders (sales):** In this competitive scenario, one has to meet the delivery schedules at 100 per cent service level, means they cannot afford to miss the delivery schedule which may result in loss of sales. To avoid the organizations have to maintain inventory.
5. **To keep pace with changing market conditions:** The organizations have to anticipate the changing market sentiments and they have to stock materials in anticipation of non-availability of materials or sudden increase in prices.

Sometimes the organizations have to stock materials due to other reasons like suppliers minimum quantity condition, seasonal availability of materials or sudden increase in prices.

7.6.3 Meaning of Inventory Control

Inventory control is a planned approach of determining what to order, when to order and how much to order and how much to stock so that costs associated with buying and storing are optimal without interrupting production and sales. Inventory control basically deals with two problems: (*i*) When should an order be placed? (Order level), and (*ii*) How much should be ordered? (Order quantity).

These questions are answered by the use of inventory models. The scientific inventory control system strikes the balance between the loss due to non-availability of an item and cost of carrying the stock of an item. Scientific inventory control aims at maintaining optimum level of stock of goods required by the company at minimum cost to the company.

7.6.4 Objectives of Inventory Control

1. To ensure adequate supply of products to customer and avoid shortages as far as possible.
2. To make sure that the financial investment in inventories is minimum (*i.e.,* to see that the working capital is blocked to the minimum possible extent).
3. Efficient purchasing, storing, consumption and accounting for materials is an important objective.
4. To maintain timely record of inventories of all the items and to maintain the stock within the desired limits
5. To ensure timely action for replenishment.
6. To provide a reserve stock for variations in lead times of delivery of materials.
7. To provide a scientific base for both short-term and long-term planning of materials.

7.6.5 Benefits of Inventory Control

It is an established fact that through the practice of scientific inventory control, following are the benefits of inventory control:

1. Improvement in customer's relationship because of the timely delivery of goods and service.
2. Smooth and uninterrupted production and, hence, no stock out.
3. Efficient utilisation of working capital. Helps in minimising loss due to deterioration, obsolescence damage and pilferage.
4. Economy in purchasing.
5. Eliminates the possibility of duplicate ordering.

7.6.6 Techniques of Inventory Control

In any organization, depending on the type of business, inventory is maintained. When the number of items in inventory is large and then large amount of money is needed to create such inventory, it becomes the concern of the management to have a proper control over its ordering, procurement, maintenance and consumption. The control can be for order quality and order frequency.

The different techniques of inventory control are: (1) ABC analysis, (2) HML analysis, (3) VED analysis, (4) FSN analysis, (5) SDE analysis, (6) GOLF analysis and (7) SOS analysis. The most widely used method of inventory control is known as ABC analysis. In this technique, the total inventory is categorised into three sub-heads and then proper exercise is exercised for each sub-heads.

1. **ABC analysis:** In this analysis, the classification of existing inventory is based on annual consumption and the annual value of the items. Hence we obtain the quantity of inventory item consumed during the year and multiply it by unit cost to obtain annual usage cost. The items are then arranged in the descending order of such annual usage cost. The analysis is carried out by drawing a graph based on the cumulative number of items and cumulative usage of consumption cost. Classification is done as follows:

Table 7.1

Category	Percentage of items	Percentage of annual consumption value
A	10–20	70–80
B	20–30	10–25
C	60–70	5–15

The classification of ABC analysis is shown by the graph given as follows (Fig. 7.5).

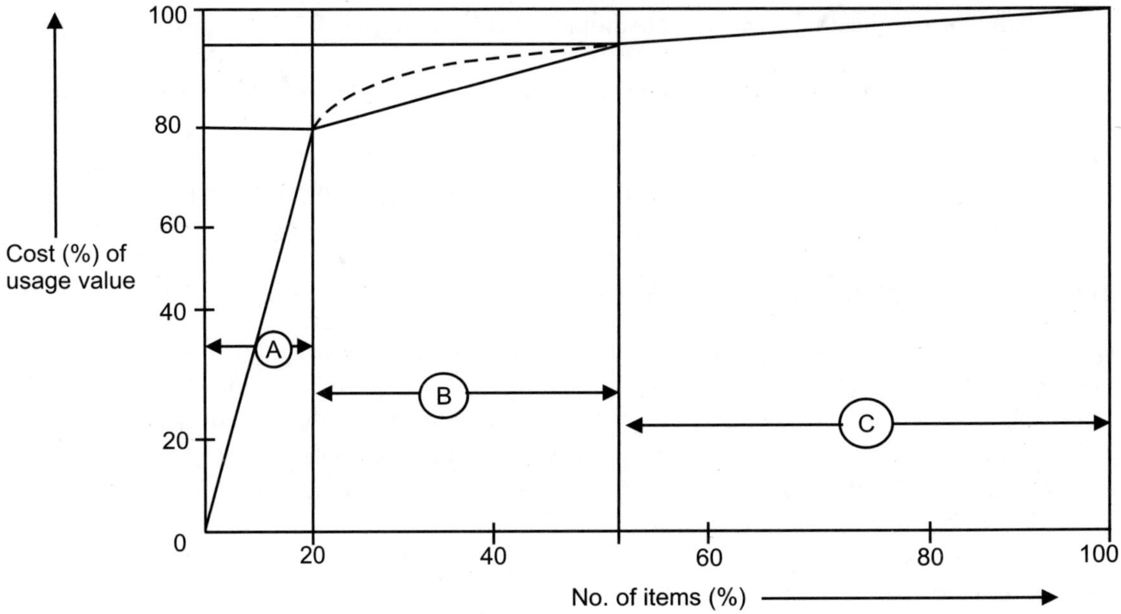

Fig. 7.5 ABC classification

Once ABC classification has been achieved, the policy control can be formulated as follows:

(*a*) ***A-Item:*** Very tight control, the items being of high value. The control need be exercised at higher level of authority.

(*b*) ***B-Item:*** Moderate control, the items being of moderate value. The control need be exercised at middle level of authority.

(*c*) ***C-Item:*** The items being of low value, the control can be exercised at gross root level of authority, *i.e.*, by respective user department managers.

2. **HML analysis:** In this analysis, the classification of existing inventory is based on unit price of the items. They are classified as high price, medium price and low cost items.

3. **VED analysis:** In this analysis, the classification of existing inventory is based on criticality of the items. They are classified as vital, essential and desirable items. It is mainly used in spare parts inventory.

4. **FSN analysis:** In this analysis, the classification of existing inventory is based consumption of the items. They are classified as fast moving, slow moving and non-moving items.

5. **SDE analysis:** In this analysis, the classification of existing inventory is based on the items.

6. **GOLF analysis:** In this analysis, the classification of existing inventory is based sources of the items. They are classified as Government supply, ordinarily available, local availability and foreign source of supply items.

7. **SOS analysis:** In this analysis, the classification of existing inventory is based nature of supply of items. They are classified as seasonal and off-seasonal items.

For effective inventory control, combination of the techniques of ABC with VED or ABC with HML or VED with HML analysis is practically used.

7.6.7 Inventory Model

Economic Order Quantity (EOQ)

Inventory models deal with idle resources like men, machines, money and materials. These models are concerned with two decisions: how much to order (purchase or produce) and when to order so as to minimize the total cost.

For the first decision—how much to order, there are two basic costs are considered namely, inventory carrying costs and the ordering or acquisition costs. As the quantity ordered is increased, the inventory carrying cost increases while the ordering cost decreases. The 'order quantity' means the quantity produced or procured during one production cycle. Economic order quantity is calculated by balancing the two costs. Economic Order Quantity (EOQ) is that size of order which minimizes total costs of carrying and cost of ordering. *i.e.,* Minimum Total Cost occurs when Inventory Carrying Cost = Ordering Cost.

Economic order quantity can be determined by two methods:

1. Tabulation method. 2. Algebraic method.

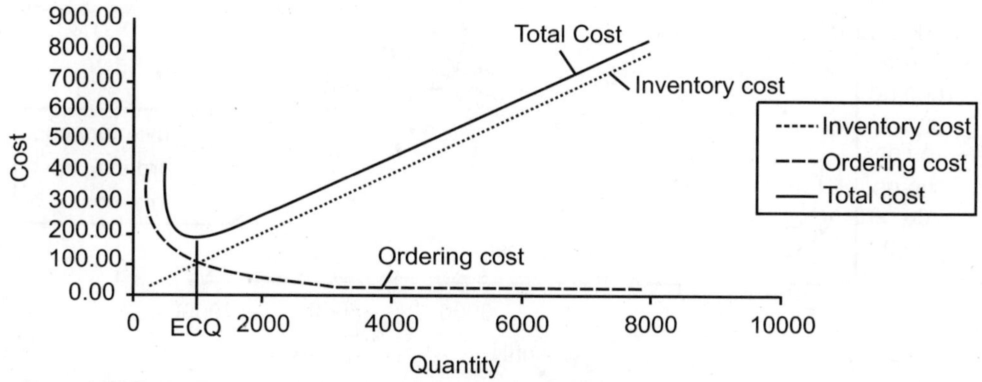

Fig. 7.6 Inventory cost curve

1. **Determination of EOQ by tabulation (Trial & Error) method**

This method involves the following steps:

- Select the number of possible lot sizes to purchase.
- Determine average inventory carrying cost for the lot purchased.

(*a*) Determine the total ordering cost for the orders placed.

(*b*) Determine the total cost for each lot size chosen which is the summation of inventory carrying cost and ordering cost.

(*c*) Select the ordering quantity, which minimizes the total cost.

The data calculated in a tabular column can plotted showing the nature of total cost, inventory cost and ordering cost curve against the quantity ordered as in Fig. 7.6.

ILLUSTRATION 3: *The XYZ Ltd. carries a wide assortment of items for its customers. One of its popular items has annual demand of 8000 units. Ordering cost per order is found to be Rs. 12.5. The carrying cost of average inventory is 20% per year and the cost per unit is Re. 1.00. Determine the optimal economic quantity and make your recommendations.*

SOLUTION

No. of orders/ year (1)	Lot size (2)	Average inventory (3)	Carrying cost (4)	Ordering cost (5)	Total cost/ year (6) =(4) + (5)
1	8000	4000	800.00	12.5	812.50
2	4000	2000	400.00	25	425.00
4	2000	1000	200.00	50	250.00
8	1000	500	100.00	100	200.00
12	666.667	333.333	66.67	150	216.67
16	500	250	50.00	200	250.00

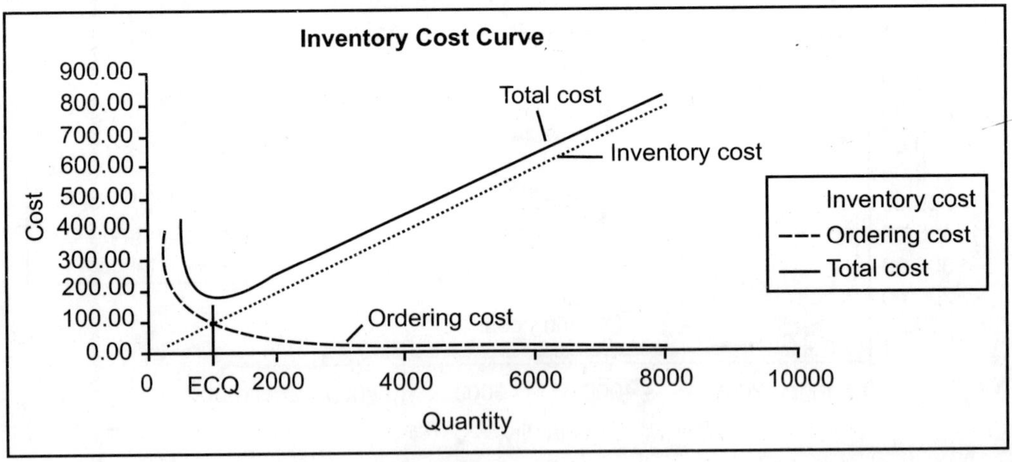

The table and the graph indicates that an order size of 1000 units will gives the lowest total cost among the different alternatives. It also shows that minimum total cost occurs when carrying cost is equal to ordering cost.

2. Determination of EOQ by analytical method

In order to derive an economic lot size formula following assumptions are made:

(*a*) Demand is known and uniform.

(*b*) Let D denotes the total number of units purchase/produced and Q denotes the lot size in each production run.

(*c*) Shortages are not permitted, *i.e.*, as soon as the level of the inventory reaches zero, the inventory is replenished.

(*d*) Production or supply of commodity is instantaneous.

(*e*) Lead-time is zero.

(*f*) Set-up cost per production run or procurement cost is C_3.

(*g*) Inventory carrying cost is $C_1 = CI$, where C is the unit cost and I is called inventory carrying cost expressed as a percentage of the value of the average inventory.

This fundamental situation can be shown on an inventory-time diagram, (Fig. 7.7) with Q on the vertical axis and the time on the horizontal axis. The total time period (one year) is divided into *n* parts.

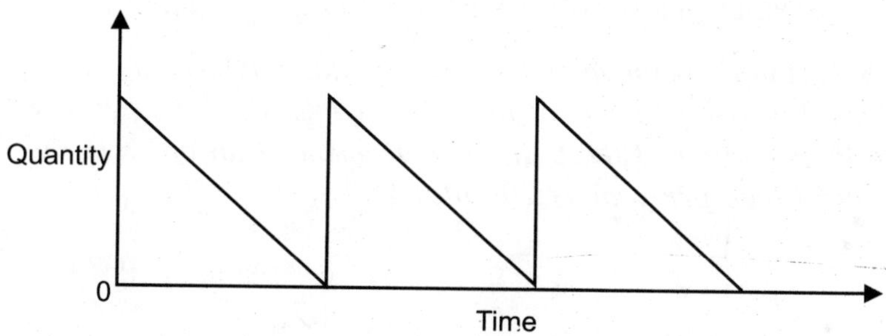

Fig. 7.7

The most economic point in terms of total inventory cost exists where,

Inventory carrying cost = Annual ordering cost (set-up cost)

Average inventory = 1/2 (maximum level + minimum level)

$= (Q + 0)/2 = Q/2$

Total inventory carrying cost = Average inventory× Inventory carrying cost per unit

i.e., Total inventory carrying cost $= Q/2 \times C_i = QC_1/2$ ...(1)

Total annual ordering costs = Number of orders per year × Ordering cost per order

i.e., Total annual ordering costs $= (D/Q) \times C_3 = (D/Q)C_3$ ...(2)

Now, summing up the total inventory cost and the total ordering cost, we get the total inventory cost C(Q).

i.e., Total cost of production run = Total inventory carrying cost + Total annual ordering costs

$$C(Q) = QC_1/2 + (D/Q)C_3 \quad \text{(cost equation)} \qquad ...(3)$$

But, the total cost is minimum when the inventory carrying costs becomes equal to the total annual ordering costs. Therefore,

$$QC_1/2 = (D/Q)C_3$$

or
$$QC_1 = (2D/Q)C_3$$

or
$$Q^2 = 2C_3D/C_1$$

or
$$Q = \sqrt{\frac{2C_3D}{C_1}}$$

i.e.,
$$\text{Optimal quantity (EOQ), } Q_0 = \sqrt{\frac{2C_3D}{C_1}} \quad \text{...(4)}$$

$$\text{Optimum number of orders, } (N_0) = \frac{D}{Q_0} \quad \text{...(5)}$$

$$\text{Optimum order interval, } (t_0) = \frac{365}{N_0} \text{ in days} = \frac{1}{N_0} \text{ in years or } (t_0) = \frac{Q_0}{D} \quad \text{...(6)}$$

$$\text{Average yearly cost (TC)} = \sqrt{2C_3DC_1} \quad \text{...(7)}$$

ILLUSTRATION 4: *An oil engine manufacturer purchases lubricants at the rate of Rs. 42 per piece from a vendor. The requirements of these lubricants are 1800 per year. What should be the ordering quantity per order, if the cost per placement of an order is Rs. 16 and inventory carrying charges per rupee per year is 20 paise.*

SOLUTION

Given data are:

Number of lubricants to be purchased, D = 1800 per year

Procurement cost, C_3 = Rs. 16 per order

Inventory carrying cost, $CI = C_1$ = Rs. 42 × Re. 0.20 = Rs. 8.40 per year

$$\text{Then, optimal quantity (EOQ), } Q_0 = \sqrt{\frac{2C_3D}{C_1}}$$

$$Q_0 = \sqrt{\frac{2 \times 16 \times 1800}{8.4}} = 82.8 \text{ or } 83 \text{ lubricants (approx).}$$

ILLUSTRATION 5: *A manufacturing company purchase 9000 parts of a machine for its annual requirements ordering for month usage at a time, each part costs Rs. 20. The ordering cost per order is Rs. 15 and carrying charges are 15% of the average inventory per year. You have been assigned to suggest a more economical purchase policy for the company. What advice you offer and how much would it save the company per year?*

SOLUTION

Given data are:

Number of lubricants to be purchased, D = 9000 parts per year

Cost of part, C_s = Rs. 20

Procurement cost, C_3 = Rs. 15 per order

Inventory carrying cost, CI = C_1 = 15% of average inventory per year

= Rs. 20 × 0.15 = Rs. 3 per each part per year

$$\text{Then, optimal quantity (EOQ), } Q_0 = \sqrt{\frac{2C_3D}{C_1}}$$

$$Q_0 = \sqrt{\frac{2 \times 15 \times 9000}{3}} = 300 \text{ units}$$

and

$$\text{Optimum order interval, } (t_0) = \frac{Q_0}{D} \text{ in years} = \frac{300}{9000} = \frac{1}{30} \text{ years}$$

$$= \frac{1}{30} \times 365 \text{ days} = 122 \text{ Days}$$

$$\text{Minimum average cost} = \sqrt{2C_3DC_1} = \sqrt{2 \times 3 \times 15 \times 9000} = \text{Rs. } 900$$

If the company follows the policy of ordering every month, then the annual ordering cost is

= Rs 12 × 15 = Rs. 180

Lot size of inventory each month = 9000/12 = 750

$$\text{Average inventory at any time} = \frac{Q}{2} = 750/2 = 375$$

Therefore, storage cost at any time = 375 × C_1 = 375 × 3 = Rs. 1125

Total annual cost = 1125 + 180 = Rs. 1305

Hence, the company should purchase 300 parts at time interval of 1/30 year instead of ordering 750 parts each month. The net saving of the company will be

= Rs. 1305 – Rs. 900 = Rs. 405 per year.

7.7 STANDARDIZATION

Standardization means producing maximum variety of products from the minimum variety of materials, parts, tools and processes. It is the process of establishing standards or units of measure by which extent, quality, quantity, value, performance etc., may be compared and measured.

7.7.1 Advantages of Standardization

All the sections of company will be benefited from standardization as mentioned below.

1. **Benefits to Design Department**

   (*a*) Fewer specifications, drawings and part list have to prepared and issued.

(*b*) More time is available to develop new design or to improve established design.

(*c*) Better resource allocation.

(*d*) Less qualified personnel can handle routine design work.

2. **Benefits to Manufacturing Department**

(*a*) Lower unit cost.

(*b*) Better quality products.

(*c*) Better methods and tooling.

(*d*) Increased interchangeability of parts.

(*e*) Better utilization of manpower and equipment.

(*f*) Accurate delivery dates.

(*g*) Better services of production control, stock control, purchasing, etc.

(*h*) More effective training.

3. **Benefits to Marketing Department**

(*a*) Better quality products of proven design at reasonable cost leads to greater sales volume.

(*b*) Increased margin of profit.

(*c*) Better product delivery.

(*d*) Easy availability of sales part.

(*e*) Less sales pressure of after-sales services.

4. **Benefits to Production Planning Department**

(*a*) Scope for improved methods, processes and layouts.

(*b*) Opportunities for more efficient tool design.

(*c*) Better resource allocation.

(*d*) Reduction in pre-production activities.

5. **Benefits to Production Control Department**

(*a*) Well proven design and methods improve planning and control.

(*b*) Accurate delivery promises.

(*c*) Fewer delays arise from waiting for materials, tools, etc.

(*d*) Follow-up of small batches consumes less time.

6. **Benefits to Purchase and Stock Control Department**

(*a*) Holding of stock of standard items leads to less paper work and fewer requisitions and orders.

(*b*) Storage and part location can be improved.

(*c*) Newer techniques can be used for better control of stocks.

(*d*) Because of large purchase quantities involved, favourable purchase contracts can be made.

7. **Benefits to Quality Control Department**

(*a*) Better inspection and quality control is possible.

(*b*) Quality standards can be defined more clearly.

(*c*) Operators become familiar with the work and produce jobs of consistent quality.

8. Other Benefits

(*a*) Work study section is benefited with efficient break down of operations and effective work measurement.

(*b*) Costing can obtain better control by installing standard costing.

(*c*) More time is available to the supervisors to make useful records and preserve statistics.

(*d*) Reduced reductions and scrap.

(*e*) Helps supervisors to run his department efficiently and effectively.

7.7.2 Disadvantages of Standardization

Following are the disadvantages of standardization:

1. Reduction in choice because of reduced variety and consequently loss of business or customer.
2. Standard once set, resist change and thus standardization may become an obstacle to progress.
3. It tends to favour only large companies.
4. It becomes very difficult to introduce new models because of less flexible production facilities and due to high cost of specialised production equipment.

7.8 SIMPLIFICATION

The concept of simplification is closely related to standardization. Simplification is the process of reducing the variety of products manufactured. Simplification is concerned with the reduction of product range, assemblies, parts, materials and design.

7.8.1 Advantages of Simplification

Following are the advantages of simplification:

1. Simplification involves fewer, parts, varieties and changes in products; this reduces manufacturing operations and risk of obsolescence.
2. Simplification reduces variety, volume of remaining products may be increased.
3. Simplification provides quick delivery and better after-sales services.
4. Simplification reduces inventory and thus results in better inventory control.
5. Simplification lowers the production costs.
6. Simplification reduces price of a product.
7. Simplification improves product quality.

7.9 VALUE ANALYSIS

Value engineering or value analysis had its birth during the World War II Lawrence D. Miles was responsible for developing the technique and naming it. Value analysis is defined as "an organized creative approach which has its objective, the efficient identification of unnecessary cost-cost which provides neither quality nor use nor life nor appearance nor customer features." Value analysis focuses engineering, manufacturing and purchasing attention to one objective-equivalent performance at a lower cost.

Value analysis is concerned with the costs added due to inefficient or unnecessary specifications and features. It makes its contribution in the last stage of product cycle, namely, the maturity stage. At this stage, research and development no longer make positive contributions in terms of improving the efficiency of the functions of the product or adding new functions to it.

Value is not inherent in a product, it is a relative term, and value can change with time and place. It can be measured only by comparison with other products which perform the same function. Value is the relationship between what someone wants and what he is willing to pay for it. In fact, the heart of value analysis technique is the functional approach. It relates to cost of function whereas others relate cost to product. It is denoted by the ratio between function and cost.

$$\text{Value} = \frac{\text{Function}}{\text{Cost}}.$$

7.9.1 Value Analysis Framework

The basic framework for value analysis approach is formed by the following questions, as given by Lawrence D. Miles:

1. What is the item?
2. What does it do?
3. What does it cost?
4. What else would do the job?
5. What would the alternative cost be?

Value analysis requires these questions to be answered for the successful implementation of the technique.

7.9.2 Steps in Value Analysis

In order to answer the above questions, three **basic steps** are necessary:

1. **Identifying the function:** Any useful product has some primary function which must be identified—a bulb to give light, a refrigerator to preserve food, etc. In addition it may have secondary functions such as withstanding shock, etc. These two must be identified.

2. **Evaluation of the function by comparison:** Value being a relative term, the comparison approach must be used to evaluate functions. The basic question is, 'Does the function accomplish reliability at the best cost' and can be answered only comparison.

3. **Develop alternatives:** Realistic situations must be faced, objections should overcome and effective engineering manufacturing and other alternatives must be developed. In order to develop effective alternatives and identify unnecessary cost the following thirteen value analysis principles must be used:

- Avoid generalities.
- Get all available costs.

- Use information only from the best source.
- Brain-storming sessions.
- Blast, create and refine: In the blast stage, alternative productive products, materials, processes or ideas are generated. In the 'create' stage the ideas generated in the blast stage are used to generate alternatives which accomplish the function almost totally. In the refining stage the alternatives generated are sifted and refined so as to arrive at the final alternative to be implemented.
- Identify and overcome road blocks.
- Use industry specialists to extend specialised knowledge.
- Key tolerance not to be too light.
- Utilise the pay for vendors' skills techniques.
- Utilise vendors' available functional products.
- Utilise speciality processes.
- Utilise applicable standards.
- Use the criterion 'Would I spend my money this way?'

7.10 ERGONOMICS (HUMAN ENGINEERING)

The word 'Ergonomics' has its origin in two Greek words *Ergon* meaning laws. So it is the study of the man in relation to his work. In USA and other countries it is called by the name 'human engineering or human factors engineering". ILO defines human engineering as, "The application of human biological sciences along with engineering sciences to achieve optimum mutual adjustment of men and his work, the benefits being measured in terms of human efficiency and well-being."

The human factors or human engineering is concerned with man-machine system. Thus another definition which highlights the man-machine system is: "The design of human tasks, man-machine system, and effective accomplishment of the job, including displays for presenting information to human sensors, controls for human operations and complex man-machine systems."

Human engineering focuses on human beings and their interaction with products, equipment facilities and environments used in the work. Human engineering seeks to change the things people use and the environment in which they use the things to match in a better way the capabilities, limitations and needs of people.

7.10.1 Objectives of Human Engineering

Human engineering (ergonomics) has two broader objectives:

1. To enhance the efficiency and effectiveness with which the activities (work) is carried out so as to increase the convenience of use, reduced errors and increase in productivity.
2. To enhance certain desirable human values including safety reduced stress and fatigue and improved quality of life.

Thus, in general the scope and objective of ergonomics is "designing for human use and optimising working and living conditions". Thus human factors (ergonomics) discover and apply information about human behaviour. Abilities and limitations and other characteristics to the design of tools, machines, systems, tasks, jobs and environment for productive, safe, comfortable and effective human use. Ergonomics aims at providing comfort and improved working conditions so as to channelise the energy, skills of the workers into constructive productive work. This accounts for increased productivity, safety and reduces the fatigue. This helps to increase the plant utilisation.

7.11 JUST-IN-TIME (JIT) MANUFACTURING

Introduction

Just-in-Time (JIT) Manufacturing is a philosophy rather than a technique. By eliminating all waste and seeking continuous improvement, it aims at creating manufacturing system that is response to the market needs.

The phase just in time is used to because this system operates with low WIP (Work-In- Process) inventory and often with very low finished goods inventory. Products are assembled just before they are sold, subassemblies are made just before they are assembled and components are made and fabricated just before subassemblies are made. This leads to lower WIP and reduced lead times. To achieve this organizations have to be excellent in other areas *e.g.* quality.

According to Voss, JIT is viewed as a "*Production methodology which aims to improve overall productivity through elimination of waste and which leads to improved quality*". JIT provides an efficient production in an organization and delivery of only the necessary parts in the right quantity, at the right time and place while using the minimum facilities".

7.11.1 Seven Wastes

Shiego Shingo, a Japanese JIT authority and engineer at the Toyota Motor Company identifies seven wastes as being the targets of continuous improvement in production process. By attending to these wastes, the improvement is achieved.

1. Waste of over production eliminate by reducing set-up times, synchronizing quantities and timing between processes, layout problems. Make only what is needed now.
2. Waste of waiting eliminate bottlenecks and balance uneven loads by flexible work force and equipment.
3. Waste of transportation establish layouts and locations to make handling and transport unnecessary if possible. Minimise transportation and handling if not possible to eliminate.
4. Waste of processing itself question regarding the reasons for existence of the product and then why each process is necessary.
5. Waste of stocks reducing all other wastes reduces stocks.
6. Waste of motion study for economy and consistency. Economy improves productivity and consistency improves quality. First improve the motions, then mechanise or automate otherwise. There is danger of automating the waste.

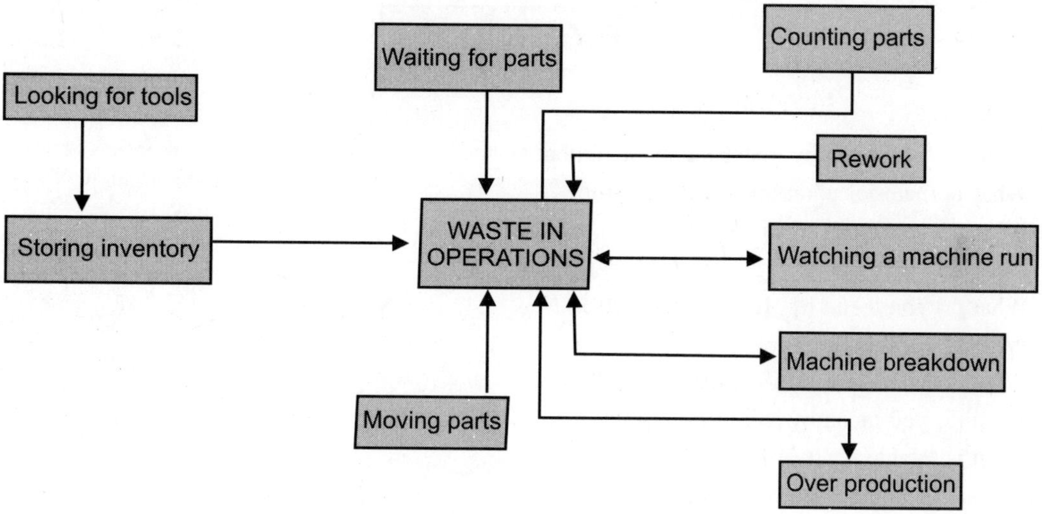

Fig. 7.8 Wastes in operations

7. Waste of making defective products develop the production process to prevent defects from being produced, so as to eliminate inspection. At each process, do not accept defects and makes no defects. Make the process fail-safe. A quantify process always yield quality product.

7.11.2 Benefits of JIT

The most significant benefit is to improve the responsiveness of the firm to the changes in the market place thus providing an advantage in competition. Following are the benefits of JIT:

1. *Product cost*—is greatly reduced due to reduction of manufacturing cycle time, reduction of waste and inventories and elimination of non-value added operation.
2. *Quality*—is improved because of continuous quality improvement programmes.
3. *Design*—Due to fast response to engineering change, alternative designs can be quickly brought on the shop floor.
4. Productivity improvement.
5. Higher production system flexibility.
6. Administrative and ease and simplicity.

EXERCISE

Section A

1. What do you mean by materials management?
2. What is material planning and budgeting?
3. What do you mean by purchasing?
4. What do you mean by 'Inventory Management'?
5. What do you mean by 'Inventory Control'?
6. What is codification?
7. What do you mean by 'Standardisation'?
8. What do you mean by 'Simplification'?
9. What is 'Value Analysis'?
10. What do you mean by 'Ergonomics'?
11. What is EOQ?

Section B

1. Explain the objectives of materials management.
2. What are the functions of stores?
3. Explain the reasons for keeping inventories.
4. What are the objectives of inventory control?
5. What are the benefits of inventory control?
6. What are the objectives of codification?
7. What are the advantages of simplification?
8. Explain the basic steps in value analysis.
9. Explain the objective of 'Ergonomics'.

Section C

1. Discuss the scope of materials management.
2. Discuss the parameters of purchasing.
3. Discuss the ten 'R's' of purchasing.
4. Discuss the purchasing procedure.
5. Discuss the selection of suppliers.
6. Discuss the benefits of standardisation.

8

AGGREGATE PLANNING AND MASTER SCHEDULING

CHAPTER OUTLINE

8.1 INTRODUCTION

Aggregate planning is the process of planning the *quantity* and *timing* of output over the intermediate range (often 3 to 18 months) by adjusting the production rate, employment, inventory, and other controllable variables. Aggregate planning links long-range and short-range planning activities. It is "aggregate" in the sense that the planning activities at this early stage are concerned with homogeneous categories (families) such as gross volumes of products or number of customers served.

Master scheduling follows aggregate planning and expresses the overall plan in terms of the amounts of specific end items to produce and dates to produce them. It uses information from both forecasts and orders on hand, and it is the major control (driver) of all production activities. Figure 8.1 illustrates a simplified aggregate plan and master schedule.

Table 8.1 Aggregate plan and master schedule for electric motors

Aggregate Plan

Month	**J**	**F**	**M**	**A**	**M**	**J**	**J**	**A**	**S**
Number of motors	40	25	55	30	30	50	30	60	40

Master Schedule

Month	**J**	**F**	**M**	**A**	**M**	**J**	**J**	**A**	**S**
AC motors									
5hp	15	–	30	–	–	30	–	–	10
25hp	20	25	25	15	15	15	20	30	20
DC motors									
20hp	–	–	–	–	–	–	10	10	–
WR motors									
10hp	5	–	–	15	15	5	–	20	10

8.2 VARIABLES USED IN AGGREGATE PLANNING

Aggregate planning is a complex problem largely because of the need to coordinate interacting variables in order for the firm to respond to the (uncertain) demand in an effective way. Table 8.2 identifies some of the key variables available to planners and the costs associated with them.

Table. 8.2

	Decision variable		Associated cost
1.	Varying size of work force	1.	Hiring, training, and layoff costs
2.	Using overtime or accepting idle time	2.	Wage premiums and non-productive timecosts
3.	Varying inventory levels	3.	Carrying and storage costs
4.	Accepting back orders	4.	Stockout costs of lost orders
5.	Subcontracting work to others	5.	Higher labour and material costs
6.	Changing the use of existing capacity	6.	Delayed response and higher fixed costs

To best understand the effect of changes in these variables, it is useful to first focus upon the impact of a change in only one variable at a time, with other variables held constant. The examples that follow show the effect on production costs of (isolated) changes in the decision variables. They are presented in a simplified format in order to best convey the underlying concept; more realistic examples follow in later sections.

ILLUSTRATION 1: *Paris Candy Company has estimated its quarterly demand (cases) as shown in Table 8.3 and Figure 8.1. It expects the next demand cycle to be similar to this one and wishes to restore ending inventory, employment, etc., to beginning levels accordingly.*

Table 8.3

Demand	
Quarter	**Units**
1st	500
2nd	900
3rd	700
4th	300

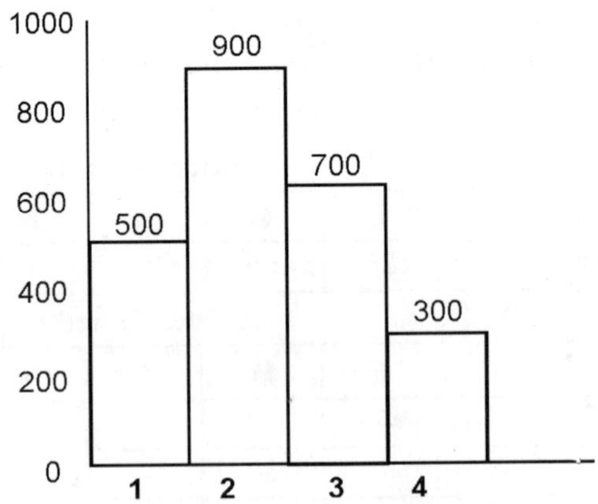

Fig. 8.1 Histogram of demand

Each quarterly change of 200 units output has an incremental labour cost of Rs. 2,000 and ending levels must be restored to initial levels. What is the cost associated with changing the work force size?

SOLUTION

Table 8.4

Period	Demand	Work force required	Change of work	Cost
1	500	3	1	2000
2	900	5	2	4000
3	700	4	1	2000
4	300	2	2	4000

Six changes of work force have to be made. Employment change cost = 6 (Rs.2,000) = Rs.12,000.

ILLUSTRATION 2: *(Overtime and idle time) Maintain a stable work force capable of producing 600 units per quarter, and use OT (at Rs. 5 per unit) and IT (at Rs. 20 per unit).*

SOLUTION

Table 8.5

Period	Demand	OT production (units)	Idle Time (IT) capacity (units)	Cost in Rs.
1	500	-	100	2000
2	900	300	-	1500
3	700	100	-	500
4	300	-	300	6000
		Total cost		10000

As shown in Table 8.5, 400 units will be produced on overtime, and workers will be idle when 400 units could have been produced. Total cost is Rs.10000.

ILLUSTRATION 3: *Vary inventories: Vary inventory levels, but maintain a stable work force producing at an average requirement rate (of 2,400 units + 4 quarters = 600 units per quarter) with no OT or IT. The carrying cost (based on average inventory) is Rs. 32 per unit per year, and the firm can arrange to have whatever inventory level is required before period I at no additional cost. Annual storage cost (based on maximum inventory) is Rs. 5 per unit.*

SOLUTION

Table 8.6

Quarter	Forecast	Rate of production	Change in inventory	Cls. balance	End balance
1	500	600	100	100	400
2	900	600	–300	–200	100
3	700	600	–100	–300	0
4	300	600	300	0	300
Total	2400				800

As shown in Table 8.6, inventory is accumulated during quarters 1 and 4, and depleted in quarters 2 and 3. The preliminary inventory balance column shows a negative inventory of 300 in quarter 3, so 300 must be on hand at the beginning of quarter 1 to prevent any shortage. The average inventory on hand is the ending balance total of 800 units divided by 4 quarters = 200 units.

Carrying cost, *Cc* (on avg. inventory) = (Rs. 32 per unit-yr) (200 units) = Rs. 6,400

Storage cost, *Cs* (on max. inventory) = (Rs. 5 per unit) (400 units) = Rs. 2,000

Total inventory cost (*Cc* + *Cs*) = Rs. 8,400

ILLUSTRATION 4: *Back orders: Produce at a steady rate of 500 units per period, and accept a limited number of back orders when demand exceeds 500. The Stockout cost of lost sales is Rs. 20 per unit.*

SOLUTION: A back order is an arrangement to fill a current order during a later period. Stockout costs occur when some sales (or customers) are lost because products are not immediately available. In this example, 200 units of the excess demand in period 2 are placed on back order for delivery in period 4. The other 200 units demanded in period 2 are lost, alongwith the 200 in period 3.

Stockout cost = (200 + 200) (Rs.20 per unit) = Rs. 8,000

ILLUSTRATION 5: *Subcontract: Produce at a steady rate of 300 units per period, and subcontract for excess requirements at a marginal cost of Rs. 8 per unit.*

SOLUTION: The firm must subcontract 200 units in period 1, 600 in period 2, and 400 in period 3, as shown in table.

Subcontract cost = (1200)(Rs. 8 per unit) = Rs.9,600

of the five decision variables considered above, accepting back orders results in the least cost (Rs. 8,000).

Qt.	Demand unit	Rs.	Subcontract
1	500	300	200
2	900	300	600
3	700	300	400
4	300	300	400
		Total	1200

8.3 AGGREGATE PLANNING STRATEGIES

Several different strategies have been employed to assist in aggregate planning. Three "pure" strategies are recognized. The pure strategies stem from early models that depicted production results when only one of the decision variables was permitted to vary all others being held constant.

Three focussed strategies are:

1. **Vary production to match demand by changes in employment (Chase demand strategy):** This strategy permits hiring and layoff of workers, use of overtime, and subcontracting as required in each period. However, inventory build-up is not used.

2. **Produce at a constant rate and use inventories. (Level production strategy):** This strategy retains a stable work force producing at a constant output rate. Inventory can be accumulated to satisfy peak demands. In addition, subcontracting is allowed and back orders can be accepted. Promotional programmes may also be used to shift demand.

3. **Produce with stable workforce but vary the utilization rate (Stable work-force strategy):** This strategy retains a stable work force but permits overtime, part-time, and idle time. Some versions of this strategy permit back orders, subcontracting, and use of inventories. Although this strategy uses overtime, it avoids the detrimental effects of layoff.

We can use the following data in Figs. 8.2 and 8.3 to illustrate the three focussed strategies described above. These figures display a histogram of a 9-month forecast for motors. The total requirement for the 9 months is 360 motors. This works out to an average (mean) of 40 motors per month, which is shown as a dotted line in Figure 8.2.

Table 8.7

Month	Jan.	Feb.	Mar.	April	May	June	July	Aug.	Sept.	Total
Forecast	40	25	55	30	30	50	30	60	40	360
Cumulative Demand	40	65	120	150	180	230	260	320	360	

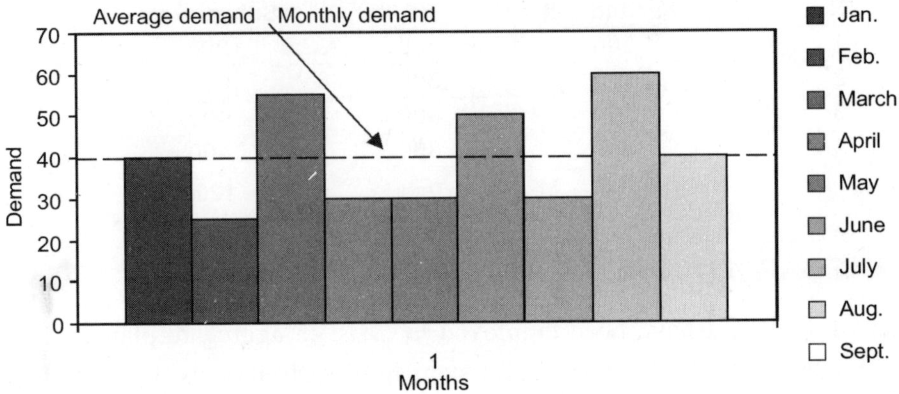

Fig. 8.2

1. **Chase Strategy:** If the production planner designed a plan to exactly match the forecast of demand shown in Figure 8.2, by adding or laying off employees to change the level of production, the planner would be using a *chase strategy.* Some overtime or subcontracting might also be used, but no inventories would be accumulated.

2. **Level Production Strategy:** The graph in Figure 8.2 shows (visually) that the demand exceeds the average requirement in some months and is below average in others. A production plan could be developed to produce at the constant rate of 40 motors per month, accumulating inventory in months 2, 4, 5, and 7, and using that inventory to meet the above average demands in months 3, 6, and 8. Table shows that the cumulative demand (forecast) never exceeds the cumulative averages (production), so no initial inventory is needed to prevent shortages. However, if there were shortages, some back orders could be allowed under a *level production, or inventory strategy.*

3. **Stable Work-Force Strategy**: Referring to Figure 8.2, suppose the firm has a stable work force capable of producing 36 motors per month on regular time. Production might go as high as 60 motors per month by using overtime, but if demand falls to less than 36 motors per month, some workers would be idle. Using overtime and idle time to meet demand would be employing a *stable work-force strategy.* As part of this strategy, however, it seems likely that planners would build up some inventory during what might otherwise be idle time periods.

ILLUSTRATION 6: *An aggregate plan is to be developed for the forecast of demand covering nine periods shown in Table 8.8. Other relevant production and cost information is also provided. Find the cost associated with an aggregate plan that involves varying the size of the work force in order to have a production rate that matches demand.*

Note: *Since this plan does not allow for any inventory build up, a decision has been made to carry 10 units of safety stock, but no overtime or subcontract labour is used.*

Table 8.8 Demand, production, and cost information

Month	Jan.	Feb.	Mar.	April	May	June	July	Aug.	Sept.	Total
Forecast	40	25	55	30	30	50	30	60	40	360

Production information		Cost information	
Current number workers	10	Hiring cost	Rs.600/employee
Worker time/month	160 hr	Layoff cost	Rs.500/employee
Time to produce one unit	40 hr	Regular-time cost	Rs. 30/hr
Individual worker output:		Overtime cost	Rs. 45/hr
(160 hr/mo/40 hr/unit)	4 units	Subcontract labor cost	Rs. 50/hr
Safety stock of inventory required	10 units	Inventory carrying cost	Rs. 35/period

SOLUTION: The cost associated with changing the employment level is calculated in Table 8.9. The number of workers required is first determined by dividing the forecast amount by the worker output of 4 units per month. Fractional values have been rounded up. Beginning with the current level of 10 workers, the number that must be hired, or laid off, is then determined. Costs are then computed for (1) regular-time hours, (2) hiring and layoff, and (3) carrying safety stock. These are added to get the total plan cost of Rs. 470,450.

Table 8.9 Cost calculations for varying work force to match demand

PERIOD	**1**	**2**	**3**	**4**	**5**	**6**	**7**	**8**	**9**
Production forecast (units/mo)	40	25	55	30	30	50	30	60	40
WORK-FORCE SIZE DATA									
No. Workers required (fost./o/p of 4 units/wk-mo)	10	7	14	8	8	13	8	15	10
(a) No. hired @ beg. of mo	0	0	7	0	0	5	0	7	0
(b)No. laid off @ beg. of mo	0	3	0	6	0	0	5	0	5
COSTS									
Regular time cost, Rs. (No. Wkr)(Rs.30/wkr-hr) (l60 hr/wkr-mo)	48, 000	33,600	67,200	38,400		38,400	62,400	38,400	72,000
Hiring or layoff cost, Rs.: @(a) (Rs.600) or (b) (Rs.500)	0	1,500	4,200	3,00	0	3,000	2,500	4,200	2,500
Inventory carrying cost (10 units) (Rs.35/unit-period)	350	350	350	350	350	350	350	350	350
Total cost for plan = SRegular-time employment + SHiring and layoff + SInventory carrying cost = Rs. 446,400 + Rs. 20,900 + Rs. 3,150 = Rs. 470,450									

ILLUSTRATION 7: *Produce at a constant rate: Using the demand shown in Table 8.8 (plus 10 more units in periods 8 and 9), develop an aggregate plan based upon the use of the 10 regular-time production workers at a constant rate, with inventories used to satisfy peak demand. The inventory carrying cost is Rs. 35 per unit per period. Some subcontracting can be used at a labour cost of Rs. 50 per hour if necessary. Assume a constant output rate of 40 units per period. No safety stock is required, but total demand of 380 units must be met.*

The costs associated with producing at a constant rate and using—inventories to help meet non-uniform demands are shown in Table 8.10. Note that the constant production rate of 40 units per period yields 360 units, which is 20 units short of total demand. Insofar as the additional demand is in periods 8 and 9—when demand already consumes all production-the additional demand will be subcontracted out in these two periods. The labour cost for each subcontracted unit is (40 hours per unit) (Rs. 50 per hour) = Rs. 2,000 per unit, so for the 10 units in periods 8 and 9, the subcontracting costs are Rs. 20,000 in each period.

Table 8.10 Costs calculation for using inventories to meet demand

Period	1	2	3	4	5	6	7	8	9
Production forecast	40	25	55	30	30	50	30	70	50
PRODUCTION DATA									
Output: Regular time	40	40	40	40	40	40	40	40	40
Subcontract	–	–	–	–	–	–	–	10	10
Output-forecast	0	15	–15	10	10	–10	10	–20	0
Inventory:									
Beginning-of-period	0	0	15	0	10	20	10	20	0
End-of-period	0	15	0	10	20	10	20	0	0
Average inventory	0	7.5	7.5	5	15	15	15	10	0
COSTS									
Regular-time cost, Rs. (L0)(Rs.30/hr)(L60 hr)	48,000	48,000	48,000	48,000	48,000	48,000	48,000	48,000	48,000
Subcontract (@ Rs. 2,000/per unit)	–	–	–	–	–	–	–	20,000	20,000
Inventory carrying cost (avg. inv.) (Rs.35/period)	0	263	263	175	525	525	525	350	0

Total cost for plan = SRegular-time employment + SSubcontract cost + SInventory carrying cost

= Rs. 432,000 + Rs. 40,000 + Rs. 2,826

= Rs. 474,826

Inventory costs under this format are computed by first determining how many units go into (or out of) inventory. This amount (*i.e.*, the output minus production forecast) is shown in the table. For period 1, where forecast and output are both 40 units, it is zero. For period 2, when 40 units are produced and only 25 are needed, 15 go into inventory. The beginning- and end-of-period inventory rows in the table show how the inventory balance fluctuates. Average inventory is the sum of beginning- plus end-of-period inventory divided by two. The inventory carrying cost is the average amount multiplied by the Rs. 35 per period carrying charge.

8.4 MIXED STRATEGIES

The number of mixed strategy alternative production plans is almost limitless. However, the realities of the situation will most likely limit the number of practical solutions. These can be evaluated on a trial-and-error basis to find which plan best satisfies the requirements, taking cost, employment policies, etc., into account.

ILLUSTRATION 8: *Custom Furniture Co. currently has 100 employees and has forecast quarterly demand as shown in Table 8.11. The historical average production rate is 40 units per employee per quarter, and the firm has a beginning (safety stock) inventory of 1,000 units. The hiring and training cost is Rs. 400 per employee, and the layoff cost is Rs. 600 per employee. Inventory is carried at a cost of Rs. 8 per unit per quarter. Use the data to develop an aggregate plan that uses variable employment and inventory to meet demand.*

Table 8.11 Quarterly demand forecast for furniture manufacture

Quarter	1	2	3	4	Total
Demand	3,500	5,000	4,000	3,450	15,950

SOLUTION: One alternative plan is shown in Table 8.12. (Many others, including better ones, are possible.) The planner has chosen to build some extra inventory in quarter 1 with the workers already on the payroll. Producing at a rate of 40 units per employee, the first quarter production of 4,000 units is 500 more than demand (3,500), so the ending inventory equals the beginning 1,000 plus 500, or 1,500 units. This results in a carrying cost of Rs.8 (1,500) = Rs.12,000. Twenty employees are hired at the beginning of quarter 2 to help meet the larger demand during the quarter. This results in a hiring cost of Rs.400 (20) = Rs.8,000. Employment is cut back again at the beginning of quarter 3, as the firm dips into safety stock, and employment is restored to its original level at the beginning of quarter 4. *(Note:* This firm bases inventory cost on ending inventory balance.)

Table 8.12 Aggregate plan for varying work force and inventory levels

(1) Qtr.	(2) Fcst. or demand	(3) No. of empl.	(4) Change in empl.	(5) Total prodn.	(6) Cum. prodn.	(7) Cum. demand	(8) Ending inv.	(9) Inv. cost @Rs.8	(10) Empl. chg cost @Rs.400 or Rs. 600
1	3,500	100	–	4,000	4,000	3,500	1,500	12,000	–
2	5,000	120	+ 20	4,800	8,800	8,500	– 1,300	10,400.	8,000
3	4,000	80	– 40	3,200	12,000	12,500	500	. 4,000	24,000
4	3,450	100	+20	4,000	16,000	15,950	1,050	8,400	8,000
							Totals	34,800	40,000

The total (comparative) cost for this is Rs. 34,800 + Rs. 40,000 = Rs. 74,800. Note that inventory and employment costs are not well balanced, and employment is the lowest during quarter 3 when demand is relatively high. With some additional trials, the planner could undoubtedly develop a plan that would result in a lower total cost. Large fluctuations in production often result in more problems (and higher costs) than more steady-state operations.

8.5 MATHEMATICAL PLANNING MODELS

Mathematical models attempt to refine or improve upon the trial-and-error approaches. Table 8.13 identifies four mathematical approaches. The value from some of these models is more theoretical than practical. The LDR is not easily understood, nor are the outputs always realistic. The management coefficients model is non-optimal and not easily transferable, whereas the computer search models do not necessarily yield a "global" minimum cost.

Table 8.13 A summary of some mathematical aggregate planning models

Approach	Linear programming	Linear decision rule (LDR)	Management coefficients	Computer search models
Application	Minimizesx cost of employment, over-time, and inventories subject to meeting demand.	Uses quadratic cost functions to derive rules for workforce size and number of units.	Develops regression model that incorporate managers' past decisions to predict capacity needs.	Computer routine searches numerous combinations of capacity and selects the one of least cost.

A useful version of the linear-programming model (the transportation algorithm) views the aggregate planning problem as one of allocating capacity (supply) to meet forecast requirements (demand) where supply consists of the inventory on hand and units that can be produced using regular time (RT), overtime (OT), and subcontracting (SC), etc. Demand consists of individual-period requirements plus any desired ending inventory. Costs associated with producing units in the given period or producing them and carrying them in inventory until a later period are entered in the small boxes inside the cells in the matrix, as is done in the standard transportation linear-programming format.

ILLUSTRATION 9: *Given the accompanying supply, demand, cost, and inventory data (Tables 8.14, and 8.15) for a firm that has a constant work force and wishes to meet all demand (that is, with no back orders), allocate production capacity to satisfy demand at minimum cost.*

Table 8.14 Supply capacity (units)

Period	Regular time (Rs. 100/unit)	Overtime (Rs. 125/unit)	Subcontract (Rs. 130/unit)
1	60	18	1,000
2	50	15	1,000
3	60	18	1,000
4	65	20	1,000

*50 per cent of cost is labour.

Table 8.15 Demand and inventory

Demand:				
Period	1	2	3	4
Units	100	50	70	80
Initial = 20, Final = 25			Carrying cost = Rs. 2 per unit-period	

The initial linear-programming matrix in units of capacity is shown in table 8.16, with entries determined as explained below. Because total capacity exceeds demand, a *slack* demand of unused capacity is added to achieve the required balance in supply versus demand.

Table 8.16 Linear programming format for scheduling

Supply units from		Demand, Units for Period 1	Period 2	Period 3	Period 4	Capacity Unused	Total available
Initial inventory		0	2	4	6	8	20
Period 1	Regular	100	102	104	106	50	16
	Overtime	125	127	129	131	0	18
	Subcontract	130				0	1000
Period 2	Regular		100	102	104	50	50
	Overtime		125	127	129	0	15
	Subcontract		130			0	1000
Period 3	Regular			100	102	50	60
	Overtime			125	127	0	18
	Subcontract			130		0	1000
Period 4	Regular				100	50	65
	Overtime				125	0	20
	Subcontract				130	0	1000
Demand		100	5	70	105	4001	4326

Initial inventory: There are 20 units available at no additional cost if used in period 1. Carrying cost is Rs. 2 per unit per period if units are retained until period 2, Rs. 4 per unit until period 3, and so on. If the units are unused during any of the four periods, the result is Rs.6 per-unit cost, plus Rs. 2 per unit to carry it forward to the next planning horizon, for Rs. 8 total if unused.

Regular time: Cost per unit-month is Rs.100 if units are used in the month produced; otherwise, a carrying cost of Rs. 2 per unit-month is added on for each month the units are retained. Unused regular time costs the firm 50 per cent of Rs. 100 = Rs. 50.

Overtime: Cost per unit is Rs. 125 if the units are used in the month produced; otherwise, a carrying cost of Rs. 2 per unit-month is incurred, as in the regular-time situation. Unused overtime has zero cost.

Subcontracting: Cost per unit is Rs.130 plus any costs for units carried forward. This latter situation is unlikely, however, because any reasonable demand can be obtained when needed, as indicated by the arbitrarily high number (1,000) assigned to subcontracting capacity. There is no cost for unused capacity here.

Note: If the initial allocations are made so as to use regular time as fully as possible, the solution procedure is often simplified. Overtime and subcontracting amounts can also be allocated on a minimum-cost basis.

Final inventory: The final-inventory requirement (25 units) must be available at the end of period 4 and has been added to the period 4, demand of 80 units to obtain a total of 105 units.

Since no back orders are permitted, production in subsequent months to fill demand in a current month is not allowed. These unavailable cells, along with the cells associated with carrying forward any subcontracted units, may therefore be blanked out, since they are infeasible. The final solution, following normal methods of distribution linear programming, is shown in table. 8.17. This result flows from a least-cost allocation.

Table 8.17 Master Schedule for Furniture Company

Supply units from		Demand, Units for Period 1	Period 2	Period 3	Period 4	Capacity Unused	Total available
	Initial inventory	0 20	2	4	6	8	20
Period 1	Regular	100 60	102	104	106	50	16
	Overtime	125 18	127	129	131	0	18
	Subcontract	130 2				0	1000
Period 2	Regular		100 50	102	104	50	50
	Overtime		125	127	129 12	0 3	15
	Subcontract		130			0 100	1000
Period 3	Regular			100 60	102	50	60
	Overtime			125 10	127 8	0	18
	Subcontract			130		0 1000	1000
Period 4	Regular				100 65	50	65
	Overtime				125 20	0	20
	Subcontract				130 0	0 100	1000
Demand		100	5	70	105	4001	4326

The optimal solution values can be taken directly from the cells. Thus in period 2, the planners will schedule the full 50 units to be produced on regular time plus 12 units on overtime to be carried forward to period 4. This leaves 3 units of unused overtime capacity and no subcontracting during that period. Because of the similar carrying cost for units produced on regular time or overtime, it does not matter which physical units are carried forward, once overtime production is required. Thus, different optimal solutions (but with identical costs) may be obtained.

8.6 MASTER SCHEDULING

The Master Production Schedule (MPS) formalizes the production plan and translates it into specific end-item requirements over a short to intermediate planning horizon. The end items are then exploded into specific material and capacity requirements by the Material Requirements Planning (MRP) and Capacity Requirements Planning (CRP) systems. Thus, the MPS essentially drives the entire production and inventory system.

The major inputs to the master production schedule are:

1. Forecasts of demand, *e.g.*, of end items and service parts.
2. Customer orders, *i.e.*, including any warehouse and interplant needs.
3. Inventory on-hand from the previous period.

Forecasts of demand are the major input for make-to-stock items. However, to be competitive, many make-to-order firms must anticipate orders by using forecasts for long lead-time items and by matching the forecasts with customer orders as the orders become available.

8.6.1 Master Scheduling Planning Horizon

The time horizon of master scheduling depends upon the type of product, volume of production, and component lead times. It can be weeks, months, or some combination, but the schedule must normally extend far enough into the future so that the lead times for all purchased and assembled components are adequately encompassed.

Master schedules frequently have both firm and flexible (or tentative) portions. Table 8.18 illustrates an MPS for a furniture company that has one such schedule-where the firm and flexible portions have been marked. The firm portion encompasses the minimum lead-time necessary and is not open to change.

Table 8.18 Master schedule for furniture company

	Week																	
Item	1	2	3	4	5	6	7	8	9	10	11	12	13	14	15	16	17	18
R28 table	50		50	50		40			40	40		40	40			40		
R30 table		80		20	60		80	80			60				80			
L7 lamp	20		20		10	20			20	20	10	20	20	20				
	(Firm)					(Flexible)									(Open)			
	(Emergency changes only)					(Capacity firm and material ordered)									(Additions and changes OK)			

Two-time fence can be identified in MPS: A demand and a planning time fence.

(*a*) **A demand time fence is** the firm or 'frozen' portion of the master schedule (beginning with the current period) during which no changes can be made to the schedule without management approval.

(*b*) **A planning time fence** is the portion of the master schedule (also beginning with the current period) during which changes will not automatically be made (*i.e.*, via computer) to accommodate demand. This gives the master scheduler a manageable base to work from and still allows some discretion in overriding the constraint.

Question: How does master scheduling differ under manufacturing strategies of (*a*) make-to-stock, (*b*) assemble-to-order, and (*c*) make-to-order?

See Figure 8.3 where the shorter line segments represent fewer items. In (*a*) make-to-stock operations, the (fewer) end items are stocked, to support customer service, and the master production schedule (MPS) is structured around those end items. In (*b*) assemble-to-order plants, such as in automobile manufacturing, the master scheduling is done for the major sub-assembly-level items. In (*c*) make-to-order products, such as customized furniture, there are fewer raw materials than end items; the end items may even be one of a kind. Here, the master schedule is typically structured around the raw material usage.

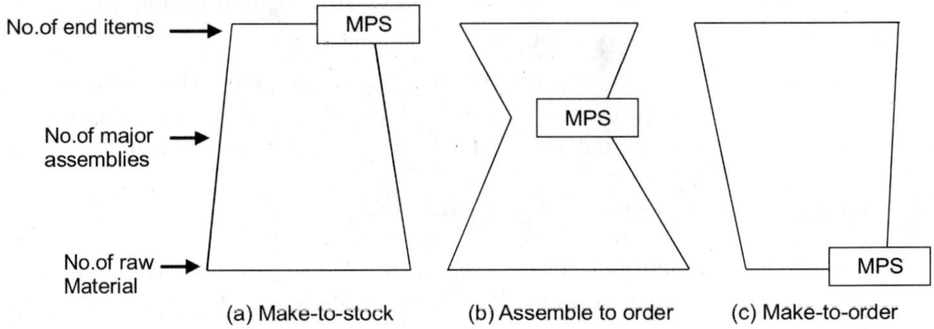

Fig. 8.3 Location of master scheduling activities

8.6.2 Master Scheduling Format

Planning production that integrates a forecast of demand, incoming customer orders, and current inventory levels is difficult–especially when it must be done over a multi week period. These difficulties are amplified as hundreds or thousands of items become involved. Numerous computer programmes have been designed to assist in the scheduling and to provide detailed reports and graphs for analyzing and testing proposed master schedules. Although the extras differ from one programme to another, much of the logic is similar. It consists of (1) incorporating the forecast and customer orders, (2) determining whether the inventory balance is sufficient to satisfy the larger of either the forecast or the orders on hand for the period, and (3) scheduling the production of a predetermined lot size in periods whenever the inventory balance is inadequate.

ILLUSTRATION 10: *Use the master schedule shown in Table 8.19 to answer the following:*

(*a*) Does this product appear to be made primarily for stock, or is it made-to-order?

(*b*) How long is the planning period, and how many production runs will be scheduled in response to demand?

(*c*) Why is no production run scheduled for week 1, and how is the projected available balance determined?

(*d*) How many end items will be "exploded" into component parts in the MRP system as a result of the MPS requirements during week 3?

(*e*) Does the capacity appear to be fully utilized during the 6-week planning period?

Table 8.19 Master schedule for TR28 blood analyzer unit

Lead time 0	**Lot size 25**			**Demand time fence 0**					
On-hand 30	**Safety stock 0**			**Planning time fence 6**					
Period	1	2	3	4	5	6	7	8	9
Forecast		20	20	20	20	20	20		
Customer orders (booked)									
Projected available balance	10	15	20	0	5	10			
Master production schedule		25	25		25	25			

SOLUTION

(*a*) Product appears to be made for stock in response to a forecast; no customer orders are shown.

(*b*) The planning time fence is 6 weeks, and the schedule calls for four production runs (*i.e.*, of 25 units each in weeks 2, 3, 5, and 6).

(*c*) No production is needed in week 1 because the beginning inventory of 30 is more than enough to meet the forecast demand of 20 needed in week 1.

Projected Available Balance = Previous available balance + MPS – Current period requirements (@ end of period) = 30 + 0 – 20 = 10 units.

(*Note:* No changes are normally accepted up to the Demand Time Fence (DTF). Prior to the DTF the Projected Available Balance is based upon customer orders only, and disregards the forecast.)

(*d*) The MPS amount in week 3 (25 units). All MPS items become projected requirements in the MRP system.

(*e*) We cannot tell the extent to which capacity is utilized without additional information from the capacity planning system. One of the uses of the MPS is to provide the information to drive rough-cut capacity planning. However, no production of blood analyzer units is scheduled for weeks 1 and 4, so the production facilities might be idle at that time-unless they are being used for another product.

8.6.3 Available-to-Promise Quantities

In make-to-order operations, as actual customer orders are received, they essentially take the place of an equivalent amount in the forecast, or consume the forecast. For this reason, the scheduled production of a lot is initiated by the larger demand of either the forecast amount or the actual (booked) customer orders.

As new orders are evaluated (and received), it is important to provide marketing with realistic promises of when shipments can be made. In well-designed master scheduling systems, this information is provided by a simple calculation that yields an available-at-promise inventory.

Available-to-Promise (ATP) inventory is that portion of the on-hand inventory plus scheduled production that is not already committed to customer orders. For the first (current) period, the ATP includes the beginning inventory plus any MPS amount in that period, minus the total of booked orders up to the time when the next MPS amount is available. In subsequent periods, the ATP inventory consists of the MPS amount in that period, minus the actual customer orders already received for that period and all other periods until the next MPS amount is available.

ILLUSTRATION 11: *Find the ATP inventory values for the master schedule shown in Table 8.20.*

Table 8.20 Master schedule for tractor levellers

On-hand 23	Lot size 25			Planning time fence 6					
Period	1	2	3	4	5	6	7	8	9
Forecast	10	10	10	10	20	20			
Customer orders (booked)	13	5	3	1					
Projected available balance	10	0	15	5	10	15			
Master production schedule			25		25	25			
Available-to-promise									

Available-to-Promise values are computed for the current period (1) and for other periods when the MPS shows that a lot will be produced.

For period

1. ATP1 = (On-hand Inv.) – (orders in periods 1 and 2) = 23 – (13 + 5) = 5
2. ATP3 = (MPS amount in 3) – (orders in periods 3 and 4) = 25 – (3 + 1) = 21
3. ATP5 = (MPS amount in 5) – (orders in period 5) = 25 – 0 = 25
4. ATP6 = (MPS amount in 6) – (orders in period 6) = 25 – 0 = 25

The last row should have values of 5, 21, 25 and 25 in the columns for periods 1, 3, 5 and 6 respectively.

Additional Illustrations

ILLUSTRATION 12: *From the following forecast determine the monthly inventory balances required to follow a plan of letting the inventory absorb all fluctuations in demand. In this case, we have a constant work force, no idle time or overtime, no back orders, no use of subcontractors, and no capacity adjustment. Assume that the firm does not use safety stock or cushion inventory to meet the demand.*

Table 8.21

Month	Jan.	Feb.	Mar.	Apr.	May	June	July	Aug.	Sept.	Oct.	Nov.	Dec.
Forecast demand	220	90	210	396	616	700	378	220	200	115	95	260
Production days	22	18	21	22	22	20	21	22	20	23	19	20

SOLUTION

$$\text{Average requirements} = \left[\frac{\text{total demand}}{\text{total production days}}\right] = \frac{3500}{250} = 14 \text{ units per day.}$$

The firm can satisfy demand by producing at an average requirement (14 units per day) and by accumulating inventory during periods of slack demand and depleting it during periods of strong demand. Disregarding any safety stock, the inventory balance is:

Inventory balance = Σ (production – demand).

See Table 8.22 for the solution. The pattern of demand is such that column 4 reveals a maximum negative balance of 566 units at the end of July, so 566 additional units must be carried in stock initially if demand is to be met. Column 5 shows the resulting inventory balances required.

Table 8.22

Month	(1) Production at 14 units/day	(2) Forecast demand	(3) Inventory change	(4) Ending inventory balance	(5) Ending balance with 566 as on Jan. 1st
January	308	220	+88	88	654
February	252	90	+162	250	816
March	294	210	+84	334	900
April	308	396	-88	246	812
May	308	616	-308	-62	504
June	280	700	-420	-482	84
July	294	378	-84	-566	0
August	308	220	+88	-478	88
September	280	200	+80	-398	168
October	322	115	+207	-191	375
November	266	95	+171	-20	546
December	280		+20	0	566
		3,500			

ILLUSTRATION 13: *Given the data of Illustration 12, suppose the firm has determined that to follow a plan of meeting demand by varying the size of the work force would result in hiring and layoff costs estimated at Rs.12,000. If the units cost Rs.100 each to produce, the carrying costs per year are 20 per cent of the average inventory value, and the storage costs (based on maximum inventory) are Rs. 90 per unit, which plan results in the lower cost: varying inventory, or varying employment?*

SOLUTION: From Illustration 12

Maximum inventory requiring storage = 900 units (from Table 8.22, column 5)

$$\text{Average inventory balance} = \cong \frac{654+816+900+......+566}{12} \cong 460 \text{ units}$$

Plan 1 (varying inventory): Inventory cost = carrying cost + storage cost

$$= (0.20)(460)(\text{Rs.}100) + (\text{Rs.}0.90)(900) = \text{Rs.}10{,}010$$

Plan 2 (varying employment): Rs.12,000

Therefore, varying inventory is the strategy with the lower cost.

ILLUSTRATION 14: *Michigan manufacturing produces a product that has a 6-month demand cycle, as shown in Table 8.23. Each unit requires 10 worker-hours to produce, at a labour cost of Rs. 6 per hour regular rate (or Rs. 9 per hour overtime). The total cost per unit is estimated at Rs. 200, but units can be subcontracted at a cost of Rs. 208 per unit. There are currently 20 workers employed in the subject department, and hiring and training costs for additional workers are Rs. 300 per person, whereas layoff costs are Rs. 400 per person. Company policy is to retain a safety stock equal to 20 per cent of the monthly forecast, and each month's safety stock becomes the beginning inventory for the next month. There are currently 50 units in stock carried at a cost of Rs. 2 per unit-month. Unit shortage, or stockouts, has been assigned a cost of Rs. 20 per unit month.*

Table 8.23

	January	February	March	April	May	June
Forecast demand	300	500	400	100	200	300
Workdays	22	19	21	21	22	20
Work hr at 8 per day	176	152	168	168	176	160

Three aggregate plans are proposed.

Plan 1: Vary work force size to accommodate demand.

Plan 2: Maintain constant work force of 20, and use overtime and idle time to meet demand.

Plan 3: Maintain constant work force of 20, and build inventory or incur Stockout cost. The firm must begin January with the 50-unit inventory on hand.

Compare the costs of the three plans in table form.

SOLUTION: We must first determine what the production requirements are, as adjusted to include a safety stock of 20 per cent of next month's forecast. Beginning with a January inventory of 50, each subsequent month's inventory reflects the difference between the forecast demand and the production requirement of the previous month. See Table 8.24. The costs of the three plans are shown in Tables 8.25, 8.26, and 8.27.

Table 8.24

	Forecast demand	Cumulative demand	Safety stock @20 per cent forecast	Beginning inventory	Production requirement (fest. + SS – beg. inv.)
January	300	300	60	50	300 + 60 – 50 = 310
February	500	800	100	60	500 + 100 – 60 = 540
March	400	1,200	80	100	400 + 80 – 100 = 380
April	100	1,300	20	80	100 + 20 – 80 = 40
May	200	1,500	40	20	200 + 40 – 20 = 220
June	300	1,800	60	40	300 + 60 – 40 = 320

Table 8.25 Plan 1(Vary Work-force Size)

January	February	March	April	May	June	Total
1. Production required	310	540	380	40	220	320
2. Production hours Required (1 × 10)	3,100	5,400	3,800	400	2,200	3,200
3. Hours available per Worker at 8/day	176	152	168	168	176	160
4. Number of workers Required (2/3)	18	36	23	3	13	20
5. Number of workers Hired		18			10	7
6. Hiring cost (S × Rs. 300)		Rs. 5,400		Rs. 3,000	Rs. 2,100	Rs. 10,500
7. Number of workers Laid off	2		13	20		
8. Layoff cost (7 × Rs. 400)	Rs. 800		Rs. 5,200	Rs. 8,000		Rs. 14,000

Table 8.26 Plan 2 (Use Overtime and Idle Time)

	January	February	March	April	May	June	Total
1. Production required	310	540	380	40	220	320	
2. Production hours Required (1 × 10)	3,100	5,400	3,800	400	2,200	3,200	
3. Hours available. per Worker at 8/ day	176	152	168	168	176	160	
4. Total hours available (3 × 20)	3,520	3,040	3,360	3,360	3,520	3,200	
5. Number of OT hours Required (2 – 4)	2,360	440			0		
6. OT prem.* (5 × Rs. 3)	Rs. 7,080	Rs. 1,320			0	Rs. 8,400	
7. Number IT hours (4–2)	420			2,960	1,320		
8. IT cost (7 × Rs.6)	Rs. –2,520	Rs. 17,760	Rs. 7,920		Rs.28,200		

*Incremental cost of OT = overtime cost – regular time cost = Rs. 9 – Rs. 6 = Rs. 3.

Table 8.27 Plan 3 (Use Inventory and Stockout Based on Constant 20-Worker Force)

	January	February	March	April	May	June	Total
1. Production required	310	540	380	40	220	320	
2. Cumulative production Required	310	850	1,230	1,270	1,490	1,810	
3. Total hours available at 20 workers	3,520	3,040	3,360	3,360	3,520	3,200	
4. Units produced (3/10)	352	304	336	336	352	320	
5. Cumulative production	352	656	992	1,328	1,680	2,000	
6. Units short (2 – 5)		194	238				
7. Shortage cost (6 × Rs. 20)		Rs. 3,880	Rs. 4,760				Rs. 8,640
8. Excess units (5 – 2)	42			58	190	190	
9. Inventory cost (8 × Rs. 2)	Rs. 84			Rs. 116	Rs. 380	Rs. 380	Rs. 960

Note that plan 3 assumes that a Stockout cost is incurred if safety stock is not maintained at prescribed levels of 20 per cent of forecast. The firm is in effect managing the safety-stock level to yield a specific degree of protection by absorbing the cost of carrying the safety stock as a policy decision.

Summary

Plan 1: Rs. 10,500 hiring + Rs. 14,000 layoff = Rs. 24,500

Plan 2: Rs. 8,400 overtime + Rs. 28, 200 idle time = Rs. 36,600

Plan 3: Rs. 8,640 Stockout + Rs. 960 inventory = Rs. 9,600 **(least-cost plan)**

ILLUSTRATION 15: *Use the data from Illustration 14 except modify as follows: Monthly demand and number of workdays per month are as shown below, employees work 8 hours per day, and time to produce one unit is 40 hours. Regular-time cost is (Rs.30 per hour) (40 hours per unit) = Rs.1,200 per unit, and subcontract time cost is (Rs.50 per hour) (40 hours per unit) = Rs.2,000 per unit. Produce with a (minimal) constant work force of six workers on regular time and subcontract to meet additional requirements.*

SOLUTION

Table 8.28

(1) Month	Jan.	Feb.	Mar.	April	May	June	July	Aug.	Sept.	Total
(2) Forecast	40	25	55	30	30	50	30	60	40	360
(3) Workdays/mo	22	18	21	22	22	20	21	22	20	
(4) Prod. hr avail. =[3](6 wkrs) (8 hr)	1056	864	1008	1056	1056	960	1008	1056	960	

contd.

(5) Reg.-time prod. [4] 740 hr/unit	26.4	21.6	25.2	26.4	26.4	24.0	25.2	26.4	24.0	
(6) Units subcon't (2)-(3)	13.6	3.4	29.8	3.6	3.6	26.0	4.8	33.6	16.0	
(7) Subcon't cost (6) (Rs.2,000)	27,200	6,800	59,600	7,200	7,200	52,000	9,600	67,200	32.000	268,800
(8) Reg.-time cost(5) (Rs.1,200)	31,680	25,920	30,240	31,680	31,680	28,800	30,240	31,680	28,800	270,720

The total cost of this plan is Rs. 268,800 + Rs. 270,720 = Rs. 539,520.

ILLUSTRATION 16: *Idaho Instrument Co. produces calculators in its Lewiston plant and has forecast demand over the next 12 periods, as shown in Table 8.29. Each period is 20 working days (approximately 1 month). The company maintains a constant work force of 40 employees, and there are no subcontractors available who can meet its quality standards. The company can, however, go on overtime if necessary and encourage customers to back-order calculators. Production and cost data follow.*

Table 8.29

Period	Units	Period	Units	Period	Units
1	800	5	400	9	1,000
2	500	6	300	10	700
3	700	7	400	11	900
4	900	8	600	12	1,200

Production capacity:

Initial inventory: 100 units (final included in period 12 demand)

RT hours: (40 employees)(20 days/period)(8 hr/day) = 6,400 hr/period OT hours: (40 employees) (20 days/period) (4 hr/day) = 3,200 hr/period Standard labor *hours* per unit: 10 hr

Costs:

Labor: RT = Rs. 6/hr OT = Rs. 9/hr

Material and overhead: Rs. 100/unit produced

Back-order costs: apportioned at Rs. 5/unit-period (and increasing in reverse) Inventory carrying cost: Rs. 2/unit-period

Assume that five periods constitute a full demand cycle, and use the transportation linear programming approach to develop an aggregate plan based on the first five periods only. (*Note*: A planning length of five periods is useful for purposes of methodology, but in reality the planning horizon should cover a complete cycle, or else the plan should make inventory, personnel, and other such allowances for the whole cycle.)

SOLUTION

RT capacity, avail. /period = 6,400 hr/10 hr/unit = 640 units

OT capacity, avail./period = 3,200 hr/10 hr /unit = 320 units

RT cost = (10 hr/unit)(Rs. 6/hr) + Rs. 100 mat's. And OH = Rs. 160/unit

OT cost =(10 hr/unit)(Rs. 9/hr)+Rs. 100 mat' I. And OH=Rs. 190/unit

Table 8.30

	Supply	Demand, Units for						Capacity
	units from	**Period 1**	**Period 2**	**Period 3**	**Period 4**	**Period 5**	**Unused**	**Total available**
	Initial inventory	0 100	2	4	6	8	10	100
Period 1	Regular	160 640	162	164	166	168	60	640
	Overtime	190	192	194	196	198	0 320	320
Period 2	Regular	165 60	160 500	162 60	164 20	166	60	640
	Overtime	195	190	192	194	196	0 320	320
Period 3	Regular	170	165	160 640	162	164	80	640
	Overtime	200	195	190	192	194	0 320	320
Period 4	Regular	175	170	165	160 640	162	60	640
	Overtime	205	200	195	190	192	0 320	320
Period 5	Regular	180	175	170	165	160 400	60	640
	Regular	210	205	200	195	190	0 320	320
	Demand	800	500	700	900	400	1600	4900

ILLUSTRATION 17: *Taiwan Shoe Company schedules running shoe production in lot sizes of 40 units (each of which consists of a carton of pairs). They have a beginning inventory of 45 units and have developed a forecast of demand as shown in Table 8.31. The company has received orders for 22 units in week 1, 9 units in week 2, 4 units in week 3, 15 units in week 4, and 5 units in week 5. Set up a master production schedule, and find the ATP inventory values for weeks 1 through 8.*

Table 8.31 Master Schedule for Running Shoe Production

On-hand 45	**Lot size 40**			**Planning time fence 8**				
Period	1	2	3	4	5	6	7	8
Forecast	20	20	30	20	20	13	15	20
Customer orders (booked)	22	9	4	15	5			
Projected available balance	23	3	13	33	13	0	25	5
Master production schedule			40	40			40	
Available-to-promise								

SOLUTION

Period	1	2	3	4	5	6	7	8
Available-to-promise	14		36	20			40	

See Table 8.31. The period 1 balance is 45–22 (*i.e.*, 22, because orders are *larger* than forecast) = 23, and period 2 balance is 23 – 20 = 3. Period 3 balance would be a negative (3 – 30), so a lot size of 40 goes into the MPS in week 3, resulting in a balance of (3 + 40) – 30 = 13.

For period 1, ATP = (On-hand Inv.) – (Orders in periods 1 and 2) = 45 – (22 + 9) = 14; and ATP3 = (MPS amount in 3) – (Orders for period 3) = 40 – (4) = 36. For week 4, ATP4 = (MPS amount in 4) – (Orders for periods 4, 5 and 6) = 40 – (15 + 5) = 20.

EXERCISE

1. What is aggregate planning?
2. What is scheduling, and does it differ from aggregate planning?
3. What focused strategies are employed by production planners to meet nonuniform demands?
4. What are the major inputs to master production schedule?
5. What determines the planning horizon length (time span) of a master schedule?
6. How do firms accommodate changes in their master schedule?
7. What is meant by the terms (*a*) demand time fence and (*b*) planning time fence?
8. How does master scheduling differ under manufacturing strategies of (*a*) make-to-stock, (*b*) assemble-to-order, and (*c*) make-to-order?
9. What is available-to-promise inventory, and it is determined?
10. Rainwear Manufacturing, Inc., produces outdoor apparel that has a demand projected to be as shown in Table 8.32. The plant has a 2-week vacation shutdown in July, so the available production days per month are 22, 19, 21, 21, 22, 20, 12, 22, 20, 23, 19, and 21, respectively.

Table 8.32

January	4,400	April	6,300	July	1,200	October	9,200
February	4,750	May	4,400	August	3,300	November	7,600
March	6,300	June	2,000	September	5,000	December	7,350

(*a*) Prepare a chart showing the daily production requirements. (*b*) Plot the demand as a histogram and as a cumulative requirement over time. (*c*) Determine the production rate required meeting average demand, and plotting this as a dotted line on your graph.

Ans. (*a*) Chart should show January through December daily demands of 200, 250, 300, 300, 200, 100, 100, 150, 250, 400, 400 and 350.

(*b*) Histogram should show cumulative production days on *x*-axis, production rate (units per day) on *y*-axis. Cumulative requirement should show cumulative production days on *x*-axis and cumulative demand (units) on *y*-axis.

(*c*) 255.4 units

11. The Speedee Bicycle Co. makes 3-speed bikes that sell for Rs. 100 each. This year's demand forecast is shown in Table 8.33. Units not sold are carried in stock at a cost of 20 per cent of the average inventory value per year, and storage costs are Rs. 2 per bike per year, based upon maximum inventory.

Table 8.33 Bike demand forecast

Quarter	First	Second	Third	Fourth
Units	30	120	60	70

(*a*) Plot the demand as a histogram on a quarterly basis, and show the average requirement as a dotted line on your graph. (*b*) Assume Speedee wishes to maintain a steady work force and to produce at a uniform rate (that is, with no overtime, back orders, subcontracting, or capacity changes) by letting inventories absorb all fluctuations. How many bikes must they have on hand on January 1 in order to meet the forecast demand throughout the year? (*c*) For an incremental amount of Rs. 400 in labor costs (total), Speedee can vary its work-force size so as to produce exactly to demand. Compare the costs of producing at a uniform versus variable rate, indicate which plan is less costly, and show the net difference in cost.

Ans. (*a*) Histogram should show quarters on *x*-axis and production rate (units per quarter) on *y*-axis. (*b*) 10 (*c*) Variable rate is Rs.50 per year less costly

12. An aggregate planner at Duotronix has estimated the demand requirements (Table 8.34) for forthcoming work periods, which represent one complete demand cycle for them. The company is a "going concern" and expects the next demand cycle to be similar to this one. Five plans are being considered.

Table 8.34

Period	Forecast	Period	Forecast
1	400	6	1,200
2	400	7	600
3	600	8	200
4	800	9	200
5	1,200	10	400

Plan 1: Vary the labour force from an initial capability of 400 units to whatever is required to meet demand. See Table 8.35.

Table 8.35

Amountof of change	Incremental cost to change labour force	
	Increase	Decrease
200 units	Rs. 9,000	Rs. 9,000
400 units	15,000	18,000
600 units	18,000	30,000

Plan 2: Maintain a stable work force capable of producing 600 units per period, and meet demand by overtime at a premium of Rs. 40 per unit. Idle-time costs are equivalent to Rs. 60 per unit.

Plan 3: Vary inventory levels, but maintain a stable work force producing at an average requirement rate with no overtime or idle time. The carrying cost per unit per period is Rs. 20.

Plan 4: Produce at a steady rate of 400 units per period and accept a limited number of back orders during periods when demand exceeds 400 units. The Stockout cost of lost sales is Rs.110 per unit.

Plan 5: Produce at a steady rate of 200 units per period, and subcontract for excess requirements at a marginal cost of Rs.40 per unit.

Graph the forecast in the form of a histogram, and analyze and relevant costs of the various plans. You may assume the initial (period 1) work force can be set at a desired level without incurring additional cost. Summarize your answer in the form of a table showing the comparative costs of each plan.

Ans. Graph shows period on x-axis and demand level on y-axis. Plan costs are as follows: plan 1 = Rs. 90,000, plan 2 = Rs. 140,000, plan 3 = Rs. 160,000, plan 4 = Rs. 220,000, plan 5 = Rs. 160,000.

5 shown in Table 8.36 is the expected demand for an end item X, which has a beginning inventory of 30 units. The production lot size is 70 units, and the firm maintains a safety stock of 5 units.

Table 8.36

	Week number							
	1	2	3	4	5	6	7	8
Customer forecast	5	5	5	30	15	5	25	25
Service forecast	–	–	20	–	–	20	–	–
International orders	–	–	–	30	–	25	–	40
Warehouse orders	–	5	–	10	20	–	30	–

Complete a master schedule by determining the projected inventory balance, MPS entries, and the ATP amounts.

REFERENCES

1. Joseph G. Monks, *Theory and Problems of Operations Management*, Tata McGraw-Hill Publishing Company Limited, 2nd Edition, 2004.
2. Joseph G. Monks, *Operations Management*, McGraw-Hill International Edition, 3rd Edition.
3. S. Anil Kumar, N. Suresh, *Production and Operations Management*, New Age International Publishers, 2nd Edition, 2008.

9

MATERIAL AND CAPACITY REQUIREMENTS PLANNING (MRP AND CRP)

CHAPTER OUTLINE

9.1 MRP AND CRP OBJECTIVES

The demand for a finished good tends to be independent and relatively stable. However, firms typically make more than one product on the same facilities, so production is generally done in lots, e.g., of different end items or models. The quantities and delivery times for the materials needed to make those end items are determined by the production schedule.

Material Requirements Planning (MRP) is a computer-based technique for determining the quantity and timing for the acquisition of dependent demand items needed to satisfy the master schedule requirements.

By identifying precisely what, how many, and when components are needed, MRP systems are able to reduce inventory costs improve scheduling effectiveness, and respond quickly to market changes.

Capacity Requirements Planning (CRP) is the process of determining what personnel and equipment capacities (times) are needed to meet the production objectives embodied in the master schedule and the material requirements plan.

MRP focuses upon the priorities of materials, whereas CRP focuses primarily upon *time.* Although both MRP and CRP can be done manually and in isolation, they are typically integrated within a computerized system, and CRP (as well as production activity control) functions are often assumed to be included within the concept of "an MRP system." Computerized MRP systems can effectively manage the flow of thousands of components throughout a manufacturing facility.

Following are some of the terminology used to describe the functioning of MRP systems.

- **MRP:** A technique for determining the quantity and timing dependent demand items.

- **Dependent demand:** Demand for a component that is derived from the demand for other items.
- **Parent and component items:** A parent is an assembly made up of basic parts, or *components.* The parent of one subgroup may be a component of a higher-level parent.
- **Bill of materials:** A listing of all components (subassemblies and materials) that go into an assembled item. It frequently includes the part numbers and quantity required per assembly.
- **Level code:** The level on which an item occurs in the structure, or bill-of-materials format.
- **Requirements explosion:** The breaking down (exploding) of parent items into component parts that can be individually planned and scheduled.
- **Time phasing:** Scheduling to produce or receive an appropriate amount (lot) of material so that it will be available in the time periods when needed-not before or after.
- **Time bucket:** The time period used for planning purposes in MRP-usually a week.
- **Lot size**. The quantity of items required for an order. The order may be either purchased from a vendor or produced in-house. *Lot sizing* is the process of specifying the order size.
- **Lead-time offset:** The supply time, or number of time buckets between releasing an order and receiving the materials.

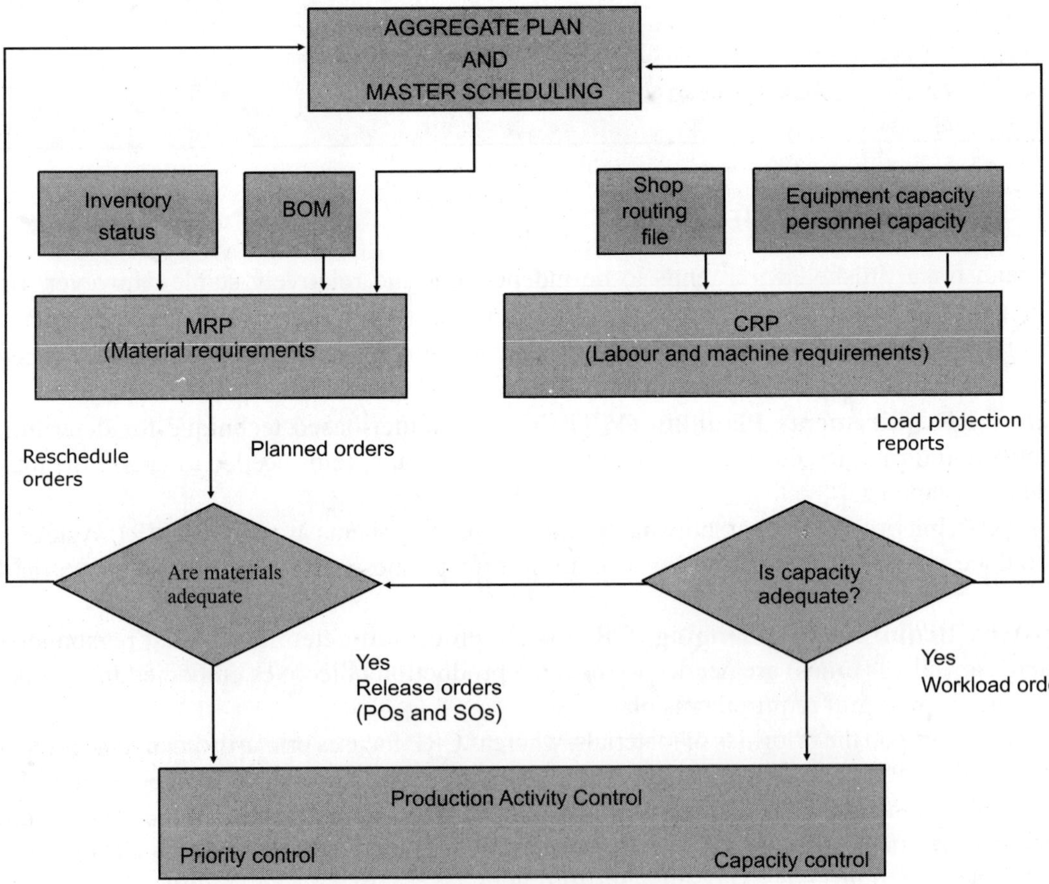

Fig. 9.1 Material and capacity planning flowchart

Figure 9.1 describes MRP and CRP activities in schematic form. Forecasts and orders are combined in the production plan, which is formalized in the master production schedule (MPS). The MPS, along with a bill-of-material (BOM) file and inventory status information, is used to formulate the material-requirements plan. The MRP determines what components are needed and when they should be ordered from an outside vendor or produced in-house. The CRP function translates the MRP decisions into hours of capacity (time) needed. If materials, equipment, and personnel are adequate, orders are released and the workload is assigned to the various work centers.

End items, such as TV sets, have an *independent demand* that is closely linked to the ongoing needs of consumers. It is random but relatively constant. *Dependent* demand is linked more closely to the production process itself. Many firms use the same facilities to produce different end items because it is economical to produce large lots once the set-up cost is incurred. The components that go into a TV set, such as 24-inch picture tubes, have a dependent demand that is governed by the lot size. Dependent demand is predictable.

MRP systems compute material requirements and specify when orders should be released so that materials arrive exactly when needed. The process of scheduling the receipt of inventory as needed over time is *time phasing.*

9.2 MRP INPUTS AND OUTPUTS

The essential inputs and outputs in an MRP system are listed below:

Table 9.1

Inputs	Outputs
• MPS of end items required. • Inventory status file of on-hand and on-order items, lot sizes, lead times, etc. • Product structure (BOM) file of what components and subassemblies go into each end product.	• Order release data to CRP for load profiles • Orders to purchasing and in-house production shops. • Rescheduling data to MPS. • Management reports and inventory updates.

9.2.1 Bill of Materials

A *bill of materials* (BOM) is a listing of all the materials, components, and subassemblies needed to assemble one unit of an end item. Major function of the bill of materials is to provide the product structure hierarchy that guides the explosion process.

Different methods of describing a BOM are in use. Figure 9.2 shows *(a)* a product structure tree, and *(b)* an indented BOM. Both are common ways of depicting the *parent-component* relationships on a hierarchical basis. Knowledge of this dependency structure reveals clearly and immediately what components are needed for each higher-level assembly. A third method *(c)* is to use single-level bills of material.

9.2.2 Low-level Coding

Figure 9.2 also includes *level coding* information. Level 0 is the highest (*e.g.*, the end-item code) and level 3 the lowest for this particular BOM. Note that the four clamps

(C 20) constitute a subassembly that is combined with base (A 10) and two springs (B 11) to complete the end-item bracket (Z 100). However, the same clamp (C 20) is also a component of the base (A 10). To facilitate the calculation of net requirements, the product tree has been restructured from where the clamp components might have been (shown dashed) to the lower level consistent with the other (identical) clamp. This *low-level coding* enables the computer to scan the product structure *level-by-level,* starting at the top, and obtain an accurate and complete count of all components needed at one level before moving on to the next.

Bill of materials for Z 100 bracket is shown below:

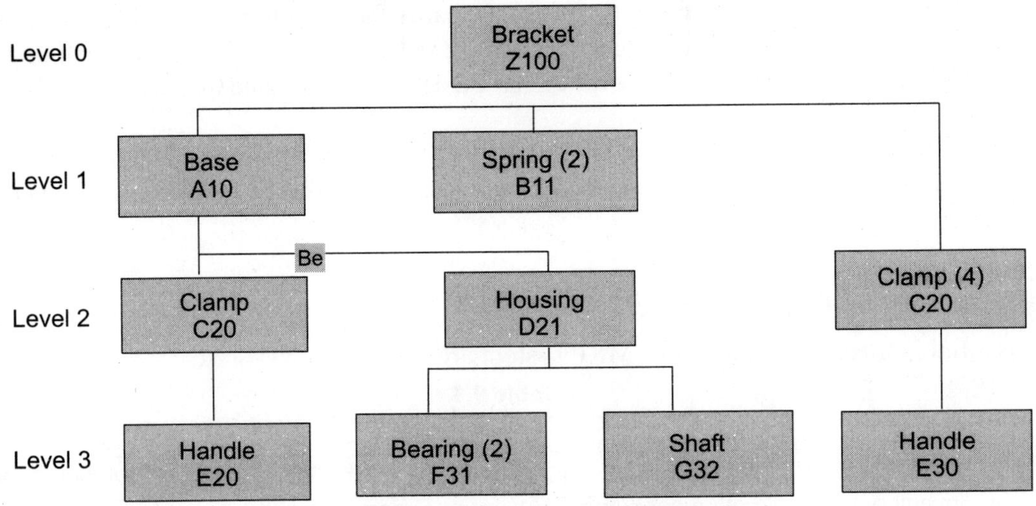

Fig. 9.2 Product structure tree

Table 9.1(*a*) Indented bill of materials

Bill of Materials					
Item: Z 100 Bracket					**Level 0**
Part No.			**Description**	**NO.**	**Level**
	C20		Clamp	4	2
		E30	Handle	1	3
A10			Base	1	1
	C20		Clamp	1	2
		E30	Handle	1	3
	D21		Housing	2	2
		F31	Bearing	2	3
		G32	Shaft	1	3
B11			Spring	2	1

SINGLE-LEVEL BOM

Table 9.1 (*a*) depicts a single-level bill of materials for Z 100 bracket. It is a less intuitive but more efficient means of storing the information on computer. In the single-level bill each entry (on the left) contains only an item or part number followed by a list of the part numbers and quantities of components needed to make up the parent item only. This type of listing avoids the searches for duplicate items down through several levels of a tree. On the other hand, it necessitates that the computer search through many single-level bills to find all the components that are included in a product that has several levels of code. Single-level bills frequently contain "pointers" to link the records of components with their parents and accommodate the retrieval of a complete bill of materials for an item.

Table 9.1 (*b*) Single-level BOM

	Number	Description
Zl00		Bracket
	A10 (1)	Base
	B 11 (2)	Spring
	C20 (4)	Clamp
Al0		Base
	C20(1)	Clamp
	D21 (2)	Housing
C20		Clamp
	E30 (1)	Handle
D21		Housing
	F31 (2)	Bearing
	G32(1)	Shaft

ILLUSTRATION 1: *Determine the quantities of A10, B11, C20, D2l, E30, F3l, and G32 needed to complete 50 of the Z100 brackets depicted in Fig. 9.2.*

SOLUTION

Table 9.2 Determining BOM requirements

Component	Dependency Effect	Requirements
A (base)	1A per Z	1
B (spring)	2B's per Z	2
C (clamp)	(IC per A)' (IA per Z) + (4C's per Z)	5
D (housing)	(2D's per A)' (IA per Z)	2
E (handle)	(IE per C) (IC per A)' (IA per Z) + (IE per C)' (4C's per Z)	5
F (bearing)	(2F's per D) . (2D's per A) . (IA per Z)	4
G (shaft)	(IG per D) . (2D's per A) . (IA per Z)	2

First determine the requirements for one bracket as shown in Table 9.2, and then multiply by 50. Note that parts C and E are used in two different subassemblies, so their separate amounts must be summed. For 50 brackets, each of the requirements column amounts must be multiplied by 50 to obtain the gross requirements.

ILLUSTRATION 2: 1. *Given the product structure tree shown in Figure 9.3 for wheelbarrow W099, develop an indented bill of materials.*

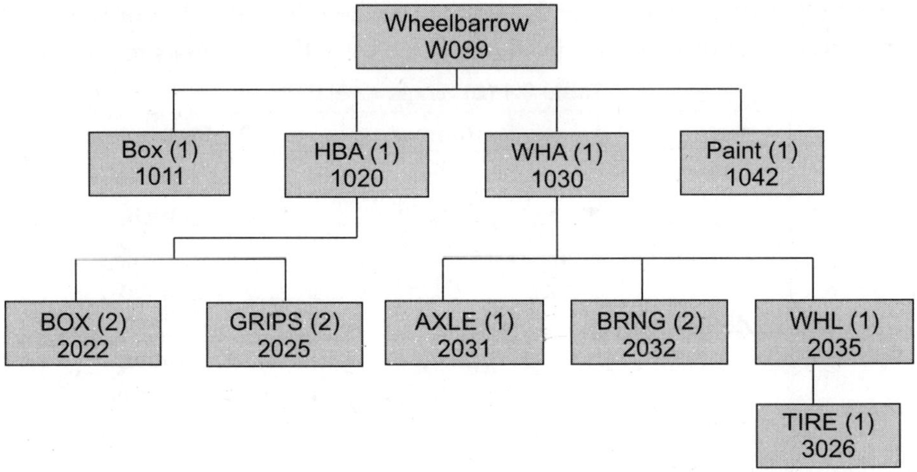

Fig. 9.3

Table 9.3

Part No. W099: Wheelbarrow					**Level: 0**
Part No.		**Description**	**Quantity/Assembly**	**Units**	**Level**
1011		Box: deep size, aluminum	1	Each	1
1020		Handlebar assembly	1	Each	1
	2022	Aluminum bars	2	Each	2
	2025	Grips: neoprene	2	Each	2
1030		Wheel assembly	1	Each	1
	2031	Axle	1	Each	2
	2032	Bearing: normal-duty	2	Each	2
	2035	Wheel	1	Each	2
	3026	Tire: size A	1	Each	3
1042		Paint: blue	1	Pint	1

ILLUSTRATION 3: *Design an indented bill of materials for the flashlight in Illustration 3. (Note: Assign appropriate four-digit part numbers to the components.)*

Table 9.4

Bill of Materials						
Item:0010 flashlight						**Level: 0**
Part No.				**Description**	**No.**	**Level**
1001				Head assembly	1	1
	2001			Plastic head	1	2
		4001		Plastic powder	1	4
	2002			Lens	1	2
	2003			Bulb assembly	1	2
		3001		Bulb	1	3
		3002		Bulb holder	1	3
	2004			Reflector	1	2
1002				Batteries	2	1
						I
1003				Body assembly	1	1'
	2005			Shell assembly	1	2'
		3903		On-off switch	1	3
			4002	Knob	1	4
			4003	Metal slides	2	4
		3004		Connector bars	2	3
		3005		Plastic shell	1	3
			4001	Plastic powder	3	4
	2006			Spring	1	2

Gross requirements are the total quantities needed to produce the 200 flashlights, whereas *net* requirements are the quantities needed in addition to existing inventory levels (or scheduled receipts). The net requirements must therefore take into account the components already assembled (or hidden) in completed assemblies.

We shall first determine the gross requirements by taking account of all dependencies. For example the gross requirements of connector bars (No. 3004) are (2 connector bars per shell assembly) times (1 shell assembly per body assembly) times (1 body assembly per flashlight) times (200 flashlights), or $2 \times 1 \times 1 \times 200 = 400$. See Table 9.5.

Then we complete the on-hand inventory by totaling both the individual stock items on hand plus any units of the same item that are already in subassemblies or assemblies. For example, the on-hand inventory of lenses consists of 12 lenses in stock plus 10 lenses already installed in the head assemblies. Requirements will be computed on a level-by-level basis so that components used in more than one subassembly (such as the plastic powder, no. 4001) can be combined.

Table 9.5

PartNo.	Description	Gross requirements	On hand	Net requirements
0010	Flashlight	200	0	200
1001	Head assembly	1 × 200 = 200	10	190
1002	Batteries	2×200 = 400	0	400
1003	Body assembly	1 × 200 = 200	0	200
2001	Plastic head	(1 × 1 × 200) = 200	10	190
2002	Lens	1 × 1 × 200 = 200	22	178
2003	Bulb assembly	1 × 1 × 200 = 200	10	190
2004	Reflector	1 × 1 × 200 = 200	10	190
2005	Shell assembly	1 × 1 × 200 = 200	0	200
2006	Spring	1 × 1 × 200 = 200	50	150
3001	Bulb	1 × 1 × 1 × 200 = 200	10	190
3002	Bulb holder	1 × 1 × 1 × 200 = 200	10	190
3003	On-off switch	1 × 1 × 1 × 200 = 200	15	185
3004	Connector bars	2 × 1 × I × 200 = 400	0	400
3005	Plastic shell	1 × 1 × 1 × 200 = 200	0	200
4001	Plastic powder	(1 × 1 × 1 × 200) +	10	790
		(3 " × 1 × 1 × 1 × 200) = 800		
4002	Knob	1 × 1 × 1 × 1 × 200 = 200	15	185
4003	Metal slides	2 × I × I × I × 200 = 400	30	370

9.3 MRP LOGIC

Following are some of the terms frequently used on (computerized) MRP planning forms. Note, however, that not all programs use the same terms or provide the same detail of information.

1. **Gross requirements:** Projected needs for raw materials, components, subassemblies, or finished goods by the end of the period shown. Gross requirements come from the master schedule (for end items) or from the combined needs of other items.
2. **Scheduled receipts:** Materials *already on order* from a vendor or in-house shop due to be received *at the beginning* of the period. MRP form shows quantity and projected time of receipt. (***Note:*** Some MRP forms include planned receipts here too.)
3. **On hand/available:** The quantity of an item exected to be available *at the end* of the time period in which it is shown. This includes amount available from previous period plus planned-order receipts and scheduled receipts less gross requirements.
4. **Net requirements***:* Net amount needed in the period. This equals the gross requirements less any projected inventory available from the previous period along with any scheduled receipts.
5. **Planned-order receipt***:* Materials that *will be ordered* from a vendor or in-house shop to be received at the beginning of the period. Otherwise similar to a scheduled receipt.

6. **Planned-order release:** The planned amount to be ordered in the time period adjusted by the lead-time offset so that materials will be received on schedule. Once the orders are actually released, the planned-order releases are deleted from the form and the planned-order receipts they generated are changed to scheduled receipts.

The master production schedule dictates *gross or projected requirements* for end items to the MRP system. Gross requirements do not take account of any inventory on hand or on order. The MRP computer program then "explodes" the end-item demands into requirements for components and materials by processing all relevant bills of materials on a level-by-level (or single-level) basis. Net requirements are then calculated by adjusting for existing inventory and items already on order as recorded in the inventory status file.

Net requirements = gross requirements – (on hand/available + scheduled receipts) ... 9.1

Order releases are planned for components in a time-phased manner (using lead-time data from the inventory file) so that materials will arrive precisely when needed. At this stage the material is referred to as a planned-order receipt. When the orders are actually issued to vendors or to in-house shops, the planned receipts become scheduled receipts. The inventory on hand at the end of a period is the sum of the previous period on-hand amount plus any receipts (planned or scheduled) less the gross requirements.

On hand/available = on hand at end of previous period + receipts – gross requirements ...9.2

ILLUSTRATION 4: *A firm producing wheelbarrows is expected to deliver 40 wheelbarrows in week 1, 60 in week 4, 60 in week 6, and 50 in week 8. Among the requirements for each wheelbarrow are two handlebars, a wheel assembly, and one tire for the wheel assembly. Orders quantities, lead times, and inventories on hand at the beginning of period 1 are shown in Table 9.6.*

Table 9.6 BOM and inventory data for wheelbarrow components

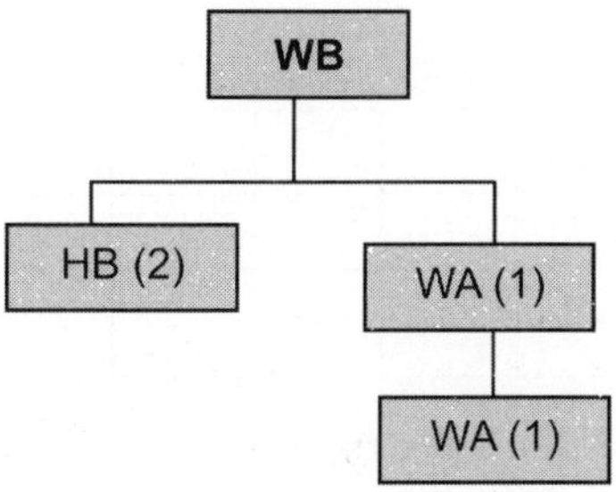

Part	Order quantity	Lead time	Inventory on hand
Handlebars	300	2 week	100
Wheel assemblies*	200	3 week	220
Tires	400	1 week	50

*90 wheel assemblies are also needed in period 5 for a garden tractor shipment.

A shipment of 300 handlebars is already scheduled to be received at the beginning of week 2 (*i.e.*, a scheduled receipt). Complete the MRP for the handlebars, wheel assemblies, and tires; and show what quantities or orders must be released and when they must be released to satisfy the master schedule.

SOLUTION: Table 9.7 depicts the master schedule and component part schedules. We shall assume that the customer completes the final assembly, so no time allowance is required there. Note that because each wheelbarrow requires two handlebars, the gross requirements for handlebars are double the number of end products. Thus the gross requirements in period 1 are 40 × 2 = 80 units.

Table 9.7 Master schedule and MRP component plans for wheelbarrows

Master schedule (wheelbarrow)	**Week number**	**1**	**2**	**3**	**4**	**5**	**6**	**7**	**8**
	Quantity	40			60		60		50
Item ID: HB	Gross requirements	80			120		120		100
Level code: 1	Scheduled receipts		300						
On hand: 100	On hand/Available	20	320	320	200	200	80	80	280
Lot size: 300	Net requirements								20
LT (wk): 2	Planned-order receipts								300
Safety stock: 0	Planned-order release						300		
Item ID: WA	Gross requirements	40			60	90*	60		50
Level code: 1	Scheduled receipts								
On hand: 220	On hand/Available	180	180	180	120	30	170	170	120
Lot size: 200	Net requirements						30		
LT (wk): 3	Planned-order receipts						200		
Safety stock: 0	Planned-order releases			200					
Item ID: Tire	Gross requirements			200					
Level code: 2	Scheduled receipts								
On hand: 50	On hand/Available	50	50	250	250	250	250	250	250
Lot size: 400	Net requirements			150					
LT (wk): 1	Planned-order receipts			400					
Safety stock: 0	Planned-order releases		400						

* Requirements from another product (garden tractor) that uses the same wheel assembly.

The 100 handlebars on hand at the beginning of period 1 are adequate to supply the gross requirement of 80 handlebars, leaving 20 on hand at the end of period 1. With the (scheduled) receipt of 300 handlebars in period 2, the on-hand inventory remains adequate until the end of week 8, when 80 units are on hand. However, the gross requirement for 100 units in period 9 exceeds the on-hand inventory. This results in net requirements (using Eq. 9.1) of 100 – 80 = 20 units.

To satisfy this, a planned-order receipt for the standard order quantity (300) is scheduled for the beginning of period 8. In so far as the handlebars have a 2 week lead-time, the planned order for the handlebars must be released 2 weeks earlier (week 6). The planned order receipt will result in a projected end-of-period on-hand inventory (using Eq. 9.2) of 80 + 300 – 100 = 280 units.

9.4 SYSTEM REFINEMENTS

Key features of MRP systems are (1) the generation of lower-level requirements, (2) time phasing of those requirements, and (3) the planned-order releases that flow from them. Note particularly that planned-order releases of parent items generate gross requirements at the component level (*e.g.*, tires).

Additional features of many MRP systems are their capability to handle *(a)* simulations, *(b)* firm-planned orders, *(c)* pegging, and *(d)* the availability of planning bills of material.

Simulation: The *simulation capability* allows planners to "trial fit" a master schedule onto the MRP system before the schedule is actually accepted and released. With this feature, a planner can "try" a potential customer order on the system to see if materials and delivery dates can be met even before the order is accepted. If lead times, materials, and capacities are sufficient, the order can be accepted; otherwise, changes in quantities or delivery times may have to be negotiated, or the order may even have to be turned down.

Firm-Planned Orders: Sometimes the "normal" manufacturing times are not enough to meet an emergency, secure a special order, or service a valued customer. *Firm-planned order capability* enables planners to instruct the computer to accept certain requirements, even though normal MRP logic would automatically delay or reschedule such orders. By designating certain orders as "firm-planned orders," planners can ensure that the computer will not automatically change the release date, the planned-order receipt date, or the order quantity. In addition, the system can establish a "time fence" around the planned-order release date to preclude the scheduling of other orders near that time so as to ensure that resources are available to do the special job.

Pegging: *Pegging* refers to the ability to work backward from component requirements to identify the parent item, or items that generated those requirements. For example, suppose an automobile manufacturer learned that some of the brake materials (already used in production) were defective. The "where used" pegging file would allow production analysts to trace requirements upward in the product structure tree to determine what end-item models contained the defective components.

Modular and Planning Bills: *Modular bills of materials* describe the product structure for basic subassemblies of parts that are common to different end items. For example, several models of a manufacturer's automobiles may contain the same transmission, drive train, air-conditioning, and braking systems. By scheduling these items as (common) modules, production can sometimes be more effectively "smoothed" and inventory investment minimized.

9.5 SAFETY STOCK, LOT SIZING AND SYSTEM UPDATING

Safety stock: Note that the MRP component plan shown in Table 9.7 includes space for an entry of safety stock. Although one of the reasons for using MRP to manage dependent demand inventory items is to avoid the need for safety stock, in reality firms may elect to carry safety stock on some items for a variety of reasons: Safety stock amounts are sometimes deducted before showing the On hand/Available quantities.

Following are some of the reasons for carrying safety stock of components on an MRP format

1. Not all demand is dependent. Some items (*e.g.*, repair parts) may have a service requirement that has an independent demand component.

2. Variable lead times from suppliers are a common source of uncertainty to many firms.
3. Firms may experience machine breakdowns, scrap losses, and last-minute customer changes.

Lot sizing: Order quantities are not always specified in advance. Different lot-sizing methods are in use, they are (1) fixed-order quantity amounts, *e.g.*, 300 handlebars; (2) EOQ or ERL amounts; (3) lot for lot, which is ordering the exact amount of the net requirements for each period; (4) fixed-period requirements, *e.g.*, a 2-month supply; and (5) various least-cost approaches, *e.g.*, least-unit cost, least-total cost.

The part-period algorithm is a method that uses a ratio of ordering costs to carrying costs per period, which yields a part-period number. Then requirements for current and future periods are cumulated until the cumulative holding cost (in part-period terms) is as close as possible to this number.

System updating: MRP system designs typically use one of two methods to process data, update files, and ensure that the system information is valid and conforms with actual: (1) regenerative processing or (2) net change processing.

Regenerative MRP systems: use batch processing to replan the whole system (full explosion of all items) on a regular basis (*e.g.*, weekly).

Net change MRP systems: are online and react continuously to changes from the master schedule, inventory file, and other transactions.

Early MRP installations were largely of the regenerative type, but then as net change systems became perfected, more firms began installing them. However, being "activity driven," net change systems are sometimes "nervous" and tend to overreact to changes. The major disadvantage of regenerative systems is the time lag that exists until updated information is incorporated into the system.

System application: Although MRP systems are widely used, they are most beneficial in manufacturing environments where products are manufactured to order, or assembled to order or to stock. MRP does not provide as much advantage in low-volume, highly complex applications or in continuous flow processes, such as refineries. It does, however, enjoy wide application in metals, paper, food, chemical, and other processing applications.

ILLUSTRATION 4: *Clemson Industries produces products X and Y, which have demand, safety stock, and product structure levels as shown in Fig. 9.4. The on hand inventories are as follows: X = 100, Y = 30, A = 70, B = 0, C = 200, and D = 800. The lot size for A is 250, and the lot size for D is 1,000 (or multiples of these amounts); all the other items are specified on a lot-for-lot (LFL) basis (that is, the quantities are the same as the net requirements). The only scheduled receipts are 250 units of X due in period 2. Determine the order quantities and order release dates for all requirements using an MRP format. (Note: Assume safety stock amounts are to be included in the on hand/Available).*

Products		Demand in period							
		1	2	3	4	5	6	7	8
X	50			300			200		250
Y	30							400	

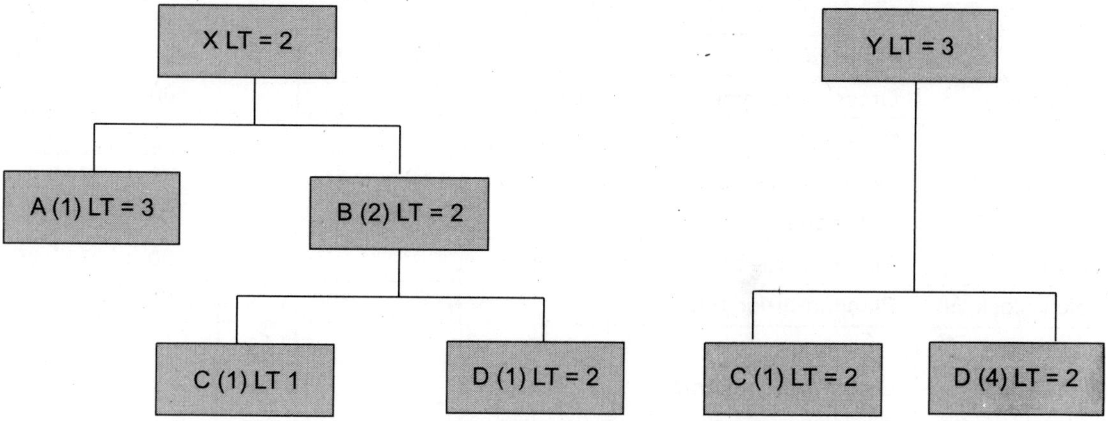

Fig. 9.4 Product structure with BOM

First, establish the codes (lowest level) applicable to each product as shown in Table 9.8. Items C and D appear both at level 1 in product Y and at level 2 in product X, so they are assigned to level 2. Thus their requirements are not netted out until all level 0 and 1 requirements have been netted out.

Table 9.8

Item	Low-Level Code
	0
Y	0
A	1
B	1
2	
D	2

Next, set up an MRP format for all items (see Table 9.9), and enter the end-item gross requirements for X and Y. They both have low-level codes of 0 and so can be netted out using order quantities that match their requirements (preserving safety stocks, of course). This results in planned-order releases of 200 and 250 units for X (periods 4 and 6) and 400 units of Y (period 4).

Next, explode the planned-order releases for X and Y (that is, multiply them by the quantities required of the level l items, A and B). (Note that C and D are not level l items.) Projected requirements for A (200 and 250 units) are direct results of the planned-order releases for X. Two units of B are required for each X, so item B's projected requirements in periods 4 and 6 are 400 and 500, respectively. Items A and B are then netted, and the order release dates and amounts are set.

Next, explode the level 2, planned-order releases to the level 3 items. The arrows in Table 9.9 show that requirements for C and D come from planned-order releases for both B and Y. End item Y requires 4 units of D, so the projected requirements in period 4 are 2,100 units, with 1,600 from Y (that is, 4 × 400) and 500 from B. Together, they generate a planned-order release for 2,000 units of D in period 2.

Table 9.9

	Week number	**1**	**2**	**3**	**4**	**5**	**6**	**7**	**8**
Item ID: X	Gross requirements	300					300		200
Level code: 0	Scheduled receipts								
On hand: 100	On hand/Available	50	50	50	50	50	50	50	50
Lot size: LFL	Net requirements						150		200
LT (wk): 2	Planned-order receipts						200		250
Safety stock: 50	Planned-order releases				300		250		
Item ID: Y	Gross requirements							400	
Level code: 0	Scheduled receipts								
On hand: 30	On hand/Available	30	30	30	30	30	30	30	30
Lot size: LFL	Net requirements							400	
LT (wk): 3	Planned-order receipts							400	
Safety stock: 30	Planned-order releases				400				
Item ID: A	Gross requirements				200		250		
Level code: 1	Scheduled receipts								
On hand: 30	On hand/Available	70	70	70	120	120	120	120	120
Lot size: 250	Net requirements				130		130		
LT (wk): 3	Planned-order receipts				250		250		
Safety stock:	Planned-order releases	250		250					
Item ID: B	Gross requirements				400		500		
Level code: 1	Scheduled receipts								
On hand: 0	On hand/Available	0	0	0	0	0	0	0	0
Lot size: LFL	Net requirements				400		500		
LT (wk): 2	Planned-order receipts				400		500		
Safety stock:	Planned-order releases		400		500				
Item ID: C	Gross requirements		400		900				
Level code: 2	Scheduled receipts								
On hand: 200	On hand/Available	200	0	0	0	0	0	0	0
Lot size: LFL	Net requirements		200		900				
LT (wk): 1	Planned-order receipts		200		900				
Safety stock:	Planned-order releases	200		900					

contd.

Item ID: D	Gross requirements		400		2100				
Level code: 2	Scheduled receipts								
On hand: 800	On hand/Available	800	400	400	300	300	300	300	300
Lot size: 1000	Net requirements				1700				
LT (wk): 2	Planned-order receipts				2000				
Safety stock:	Planned-order releases		2000						

9.6 CRP INPUTS AND OUTPUTS

Capacity is a measure of the productive capability of a facility per unit of time. In terms of the relevant time horizon, capacity management decisions are concerned with the following:

1. *Long range-resource* planning of capital facilities, equipment, and human resources.
2. *Medium range-requirements* planning of labor and equipment to meet MPS needs.
3. *Short range-control* of the flow (input-output) and sequencing of operations.

Capacity-requirements planning (CRP) applies primarily to medium-range activities. The CRP system receives planned and released orders from the material-requirements planning system and attempts to develop loads for the firm's work centers that are in good balance with the work-center capacities. Like MRP, CRP is an iterative process that involves planning, revision of capacity (or revision of the master schedule), and replanning until a reasonably good load profile is developed. Planned-order releases (in the MRP system) are converted to standard hours of load on key work centers in the CRP system.

Following are the essential inputs and outputs in a CRP system:

Inputs	Outputs
• Planned and released orders from the MRP system	• Verification reports to the MRP system
• Loading capacities from the work-center status file	• Load reports of planned and released orders on key work centers
• Routing data from the routing file	• Rescheduling data to the MPS
• Changes that modify capacity, give alternative routings, or alter planned orders	• Capacity modification data

9.7 LOADING

There are two basic techniques for planning the control of a production system. One of these is loading; the other is scheduling. Of the two loading is the easier to do. But scheduling can give more control and is more detailed, although it is usually done for a shorter time period. A **load** is the amount of work assigned to a facility work centre or operator, and loading is the assignment of work. Loading does not specify the sequence in which the work is done or when it is to be done. Loading is the aggregate assignment of jobs to specific entities. Inputs necessary for loading include:

- Routing
- Standard hours per operation or work centre
- Gross machine/man-hour available
- Efficiency factors
- Due date.

Loading is closely tied to capacity planning in the sense that loading is the first indication that capacity levels need adjusting.

9.7.1 Steps in the Loading

Typically, the loading process considered as a six step procedure. Step I through 4 is managerial decision steps that usually do not change week to week or month to month. The last two steps are required on a periodic basis as an input to scheduling.

1.	Choose load centers;	4.	Choose loading method
	• Department		• To infinite capacity
	• Group		• To finite capacity
	• Machine/Work-center		• Combination
2.	Develop efficiency factors by load centers	5.	Load schedule orders into load centers
3.	Determine capacity by centers	6.	Unload completed hours

***Step 1*:** The first step in machine loading is to choose the load centers. Some companies load by department only if all the machines are interchangeable. When different machine centers within the department have different capacities, the typical approach is to break the machines down into similar machine groups. For example, all 24 inch boring machines might be included in the same group, if jobs are interchangeable among the machines. The trend is to group as many machines together as possible since doing so will reduce the complexity of the loading problem and tend to stabilize the load.

***Step 2*:** The second step is to develop efficiency factors by load centers/work stations. A load center with two people is theoretically capable of 80 hours of production per week, but actual output might be considerably less than 80 hours of production per week, indirect activities, or other non-value adding activities. If they are working on incentives, they could be turning out more than 80 standard hours of production.

***Step 3*:** The third step is to determine the gross capacity by load centers. This capacity is either human or machine dependent. A center is machine dependent if all machines have at least one operator assigned. A center is human dependent if there are more workers than machines and machine stand idle while all workers are busy. With the number of people or machine as an input, the gross capacity is the gross number of hours that the resources are available per planning period. The center's capacity is then the gross capacity times of the efficiency factor.

***Step 4*:** The fourth step is to choose the loading method, which may be either to finite or to infinite capacity. Infinite capacity loading means showing the work for a work center in the time period required, regardless of the work center's capacity. Finite capacity loading means putting no more work into a work center than it can be expected to execute.

Step 5: The fifth step is to load the scheduled orders into the load centers while at the same time considering the capacity and other restrictions.

Step 6: The sixth step is to select the unloading technique. Unloading is the process of removing the planned work from the work center load as jobs are partially or totally completed. Manual systems may require shortcuts, such as considering a job to be completed when the first lot of pieces is reported. This saves posting many partial lots and recalculating load balances, but the load is always understated by the number of hours remaining on jobs unloaded. Another short-cut relieves the load only when the last lot is completed, giving a load constantly overstated by the hours completed but not removed. The number of hours to be unloaded must be equal to the number of hours loaded for each job.

A work center load, based on the actual work order released, is a good short-tenn technique for highlighting the under load or overloads on work centers and showing the need for overtime, temporary transfer, subcontracting or other short-range adjustments.

9.7.2 Loading Concepts

Why use loading? The major reason is that it can predict some future events. A chart tells of an overload, and it tells this in advance. 'This same chart can warn of excess capacity before the machine and workers are idle. Therefore, loading is most useful to dispatchers, supervisors, and production schedulers planning shop work. Loading can be used to smooth the workload from month to month or between the work centers. It is an aid in identifying the critical departments or machines and in judging the effect of break-downs, rush orders, and new products. It is also useful for documenting the requirements for more or less capacity.

Infinite Loading

Infinite capacity loading means showing the work for a work center in the time period required, regardless of the work center's capacity. When using infinite loading to create the schedule, it is necessary to check the load to determine whether there is sufficient capacity available in the time period in which the work is required.

Finite Loading

Finite capacity loading means putting no more work into a work center than it can be expected to execute. Loading to finite capacity by operation is more complex than infinite capacity. A facility activity that does not go according to schedule may require that the load be recalculated, and therefore, loads will fall in different time periods. Finite loading also requires that the company establish priority for loading the jobs. In practice, finite loading is unsatisfactory since it assumes that the present capacity is all that is available and does not show the time period in which overloads will occur if an attempt is made to meet desirable schedules.

Combination Loading

A good machine loading system involves a combination of both techniques. Orders are first scheduled and loaded to infinite capacity to see where overload will occur, then rescheduled to level the load based on available capacity after corrective actions have been taken wherever possible.

Companies have successfully used computer machine loads over longer planning periods to assist capacity planning. Forecasts of individual finished products to be manufactured during this period can be exploded into detailed requirements of production hours for each of major work centers. The machine hours based on these aggregate hours will give dependable data on the average capacity required to meet the forecasted demand on manufacturing facilities.

The work may be assigned by the nature of the job. If the work can be done by more than one center, it must be assigned to just one. If it can be done by only one work center, then there is no alternative, but to one work center. The work may be assigned on an individual job basis, but if the jobs are repetitive, they may be assigned on a standard basis by the use of routings. Standard routings shows all operations that must be done to make the part or assembly. If the standard routings are not available, someone must assign the individual jobs to the facilities and must estimate the work content of the assignments. The work contents must be in terms that are comparable between jobs. Measures that can be used are hours, pieces, batches, gallons and so on per hour, per shift, per day and so on.

Work assignments must be accumulated by the facility in order to calculate the load on each facility. One method is to use a ledger in which the job members and job loads are entered by each facility. When the job is completed, it is marked off. The jobs are then added periodically to obtain the load on the facility.

Another method is to accumulate the assignments in 'buckets' one bucket for each facility. The bucket may be box, a file, a peg and so on. A ticket is prepared for each job assigned to the facility and is placed in the bucket. A perpetual total of the facility load may be kept for each bucket. Job tickets, as added to the bucket are added to this total. When completed and removed from the bucket, they are deducted from the total. If a computer is available, bucket may be computer file. If standard routings are available, these can be kept as computer files.

EXERCISE

1. (*a*) What is meant by "time phasing" (*b*) What is a "time bucket"?
2. (*a*) Why is the BOM file sometimes called a product structure tree? (*b*) Suppose a 5-level BOM has one subassembly (AX205) on level 2 and another (BY407) on level 4. Which subassembly has a level code nearest the end item?
3. Why do MRP programs use single-level BOMs?
4. What is the advantage of low-level coding?
5. What are the three essential sources of data for an MRP program?
6. What must take place to change a planned-order release to a scheduled receipt?
7. By using a time-phased plan for component inventories, a firm can reduce average inventory levels from 105 units to 42.5 units. If the average component value is Rs.12 and the reduction applies to 4,000 components, how much of a saving would result? Use inventory-carrying costs of 30 per cent per year.
8. Determine the net requirements for the three items shown in table.

	Switches	Microprocessor	Keyboards
Gross requirements	55	14	28
On-hand Inventory	18	2	7
Inventory on order (scheduled receipt)	12	12	10

Ans: 25 Switches, 0 Microprocessors and 11 Keyboards

9. Given the product structure tree shown in table compute the net requirements for A, B, C, D, and E, to produce 50 units of X.

Components	A	B	C	D	E
Inventory on hand and on order	20	10	15	30	100

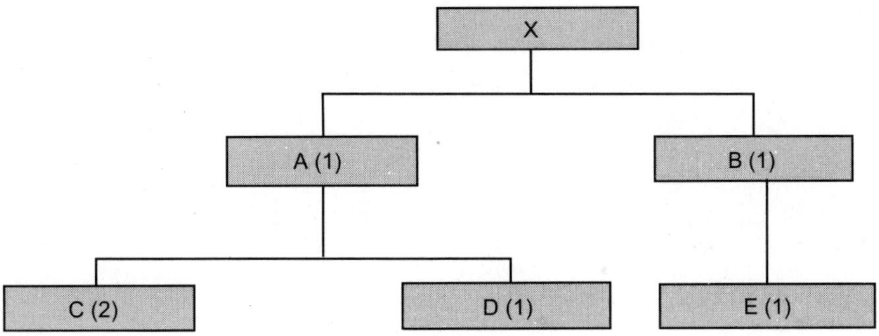

REFERENCES

1. Everett, E. Adam, Jr. Ronald J. Ebert, *Production and Operations Management*, Prentice-Hall of India Private Limited, 5th Edition, 1994.
2. R. Pannerselvam, *Production and Operations Management*, Prentice-Hall of India Private Limited, 9th print, 2004.
3. Joseph, G. Monks, *Theory and Problems of Operations Management*, Tata McGraw-Hill Publishing Company Limited, 2nd Edition, 2004.
4. Joseph G. Monks, *Operations Management*, McGraw-Hill International Edition, 3rd Edition.
5. S. Anil Kumar, N. Suresh, *Production and Operations Management*, New Age International Publishers, 2nd Edition, 2008.

10

SCHEDULING AND CONTROLLING PRODUCTION ACTIVITIES

CHAPTER OUTLINE

10.1 INTRODUCTION

Scheduling is the allocation of starts and finish time to each particular order. Therefore scheduling can bring productivity in shop floor by providing a calendar for processing a set of jobs.

The **single machine-scheduling problem** consists of *n* jobs with the same single operation on each of the jobs, while the **flow shop-scheduling problem** consists of *n* jobs with *m* operations on each of the jobs. In this problem, all the jobs will have the same process sequences. The **job shop-scheduling problem** contains *n* jobs with *m* operations on each of the jobs; but, in this case, the process sequences of the jobs will be different from each other.

10.2 CONCEPT OF SINGLE MACHINE SCHEDULING

The basic single machine scheduling problem is characterized by the following conditions:

1. A set of independent, single-operation jobs is available for processing at time zero.
2. Set-up time of each job is independent of its position in jobs sequence. So, the set-up time of each job can be included in its processing time.
3. Job descriptors are known in advance.
4. One machine is continuously available and is never kept idle when work is waiting.
5. Each job is processed till its completion without break.

Under these conditions, one can see one-to-one correspondence between a sequence of the n jobs and a permutation of the job indices 1, 2, ... n. The total number of sequences in the basic single machine problem is $n!$ which is the number of different permutation of n elements. The following three basic data are necessary to describe jobs in a deterministic single machine-scheduling problem.

Processing time **(t_j):** It is the time required to process job j. The processing time, tj will normally include both actual processing time and set-up time.

Ready time **(r_j):** It is the time at which job j is available for processing. The ready time of a job is the difference between the arrival time of that job and the time at which that job is taken for processing. In the basic model, as per condition I, $r_j = 0$ for all jobs.

Due date **(d_j):** It is the time at which the job j is to be completed.

Completion time **(C_j):** It is the time at which the job j is completed in a sequence. Performance measures for evaluating schedules are usually function of job completion time. Some, sample performance measures are Flow time, Lateness, Tardiness, etc.

Flow time **(F_j):** It is the amount of time job j spends in the system. Flow time is a measure, which indicates the waiting time of jobs in a system. This in turn gives some idea about in-process inventory due to a schedule. It is the difference between the completion time and the ready time of the job j. *i.e.* $F_j = C_j - r_j$.

Lateness **(L_j):** It is the amount of time by which the completion time of job j differs from the due date ($L_j = C_j - d$). Lateness is a measure which gives an idea about conformity of the jobs in a schedule to a given set of due dates of the jobs. Lateness can be either positive lateness or negative lateness. Positive lateness of a job means that the job is completed after its due date. Negative lateness of a job means that the job is completed before its due date. The positive lateness is a measure of poor service. The negative lateness is a measure of better service. In many situations, distinct penalties and other costs are associated with positive lateness, but generally, no benefits are associated with negative lateness. Therefore, it is often desirable to optimize only positive lateness.

Tardiness **(T_j):** Tardiness is the lateness of job j if it fails to meet its due date, or zero, otherwise

$$T_j = \max \{O, C_j - d_j\}$$
$$= \text{Max } \{O, L_j\}.$$

10.3 MEASURES OF PERFORMANCE

The different measures of performance which are used in the single machine scheduling are listed below with their formulas.

$$\text{Mean flow time: } \overline{F} = \frac{1}{n}\sum_{j=1}^{n} F_j$$

$$\text{Mean tardiness: } \overline{T} = \frac{1}{n}\sum_{j=1}^{n} T_j$$

$$\text{Maximum flow time: } F_{\max} = \underset{1 \le j \le n}{Max}\{F_j\}$$

$$\text{Maximum tardiness: } T_{\max} = \underset{1 \le j \le n}{Max}\{T_j\}$$

Number of tardy jobs: $N_T = \sum_{j=1}^{n} f(T_j)$

where

$$f(T_j) = I, \text{ if } T_j > 0, \text{ and } f(T_j) = 0, \text{ otherwise.}$$

10.4 SHORTEST PROCESSING TIME (SPT) RULE

In single machine scheduling problem, sequencing the jobs in increasing order of processing time is known as the shortest processing time (SPT) sequencing.

Sometimes we may be interested in minimizing the time spent by jobs in the system. This, in turn, will minimize the in-process inventory. Also, we may be interested in rapid turnaround/throughput times of the jobs.

The time spent by a job in the system is nothing but its flowtime, and the 'rapid turnaround time' is its mean flow time *(F)*. Shortest processing time (SPT) rule minimizes the mean flow time.

ILLUSTRATION 1: *Consider the following single machine-scheduling problem.*

Job (j)	1	2	3	4	5
Processing time (t) (hrs)	15	4	5	14	8

Find the optimal sequence, which will minimize the mean flow time and also obtain the minimum mean flow time.

SOLUTION

No. of jobs = 5

Arrange the jobs as per the SPT ordering

Job (j)	2	3	5	4	1
Processing time (t) (hrs)	4	5	8	14	15

Therefore, the job sequence, which will minimize the mean flow time, is 2-3-5-4-1.

Computation of F_{min}

Job (j)	2	3	5	4	1
Processing time (t) (hrs)	4	5	8	14	15
Completion time (Cj) (Fj)	4	9	17	31	46

Since, the ready time $r_j = 0$ for all *j*, the flow time (F_j) is equal to C_j for all *j*.

$$\bar{F} = \frac{1}{n}\sum_{j=1}^{n} F_j = \frac{1}{5}(4+9+17+31+46) = \frac{1}{5}(107) = 21.4 \text{ hours}$$

Therefore, the optimal mean flow time = 21.4 hours.

10.5 WSPT RULE

Sometimes, the jobs in a single machine-scheduling problem will not have equal importance. Under such situation, each job is assigned a weight, w_j. The mean flow time, which is computed after considering w_j is called, weighted mean flow time, which is shown below:

$$\bar{F}w = \frac{\sum_{j=1}^{n} w_j \cdot F_j}{\sum_{j=1}^{n} w_j}$$

In single machine scheduling problem, sequencing the jobs in increasing order of weighted processing time is known as Weighted Shortest Processing Time (WSPT) sequencing. The weighted processing time of a job is obtained by dividing its processing time by its weight.

ILLUSTRATION 2: *Consider the following single machine-scheduling problem with weights:*

Job (j)	1	2	3	4	6
Processing time (t_j)	15	4	5	14	8
Weight (w)	1	2	1	2	3

Determine the sequence, which will minimize the weighted mean flow time of the above problem. Also find the weighted mean flow time.

SOLUTION

Job (j)	1	2	3	4	5
Processing time (t) (hrs)	15	4	5	14	8
Weight (w_j)	1	2	1	2	3
T/w_j	15	2	5	7	2.67

Arrange the jobs in the increasing order of t_j / w_j (*i.e.* WSPT ordering). From the above table, we get the following relation.

$$t_2/w_2 \leq t_5/w_5 \leq t_3/w_3 \leq t_4/w_4 \leq t_1/w_1$$

Therefore optimal sequence, which will minimize the weighted mean flow time, is, 2 – 5 – 3 – 4 – 1.

$\bar{F}w$ Calculation:

Job (j)		2	3	5	4	1
T_j	4	5	8	14	15	
C_j (F_j)	4	9	17	31	46	
F_j* W_j	4	9	17	31	46	

$$\bar{F}w = \frac{\sum_{j=1}^{n} w_j . F_j}{\sum_{j=1}^{n} w_j} = \frac{(8+36+17+62+46)}{(2+3+1+2+1)} = \frac{169}{9} = 18.78 \text{ hours.}$$

10.6 EARLIEST DUE DATE (EDD) RULE

The lateness (L_j) of a job is defined as the difference between the completion time and the due date of that job. L_j can be either positive or negative values.

$$L_j = C_j - d_j$$

The maximum job lateness (L_{max}) and the maximum job tardiness (T_{max}) are minimized by Earliest Due Date sequencing. In a single machining scheduling problem, sequencing of jobs in increasing order of due date is known as 'Earliest Due Date Rule'.

ILLUSTRATION 3: *Consider the following single machining scheduling problem:*

Job (j)	1	2	3	4	5	6
Processing time (t_j)	10	8	8	7	12	15
Due date (d_j)	15	10	12	11	18	25

Determine the sequence which will minimize the maximum lateness (L_{max}). Also, determine L_{max} with respect to the optimal sequence.

SOLUTION: Arrange the jobs as per EDD rule (*i.e.* in the order of their due dates). The EDD sequence is 2-4-3-1-5-6.This sequence gives a minimum value for L_{max}.

Job (j) (EDD Sequence)	2	4	3	1	5	6
Processing time (t_j)	8	7	8	10	12	15
Completion Time (C_j)	8	15	23	33	45	60
Due Date (d_j)	10	11	12	15	18	25
Lateness (L_j)	–2	4	11	18	27	35

From the table, the maximum is 35. This is the optimal value for L_{max}. The L_{max} of any other non-EDD sequence will not be less than 35.

10.7 MINIMIZING THE NUMBER OF TARDY JOBS

If a job is completed beyond its due date, then it is called tardy job; otherwise it is called non-tardy job. In many organizations, the objective may be to minimize the total number of tardy jobs.

If the EDD sequence yields zero tardy, or it yields exactly one tardy job, then it is an optimal sequence for minimizing the total number of tardy jobs *(NT),* If it yields more than one tardy job, the EDD sequence may not yield the optimal solution. An exact algorithm for the general case is given below. The final sequence consists of two streams of jobs as given below:

(*a*) First, a set *(E)* of early jobs, in EDD order.

(*b*) Then, a set *(L)* of late jobs, in any order.

This algorithm gives optimal sequence, which will result in minimum number of tardy jobs *(NT).*

HODGSON'S ALGORITHM TO MINIMIZE NT

Step 1: Arrange the jobs in EDD order and assume this, as set *E*. Let set *L* be empty.

Step 2: If no jobs in *E* are late, then stop. Find the union of *E* and *L* (*Note:* The remaining jobs in *E* should be in EDD order. But the jobs in *L* can be in any order); otherwise, identify the first late job in *E*. Let it be job *K*.

Step 3: Identify the longest job, among the first *K* jobs in the sequence. Remove this job from *E* and place it in *L*. Revise the completion times of the jobs remaining in *E* and return, to Step 2.

This algorithm is demonstrated using the following problem.

ILLUSTRATION 4 *A computer systems consulting company is under contract to carry out seven projects, all with deadliness assured in days from now. The consultants are a small group and they work together on each project, so that the project will be started and completed sequentially. Under the terms of contract, the consultants will receive Rs. 24,000 for each project completed on time, but they will incur Rs. 40,000 in penalties for each project completed late. Each project has an, associated duration, which is the anticipated number of days required to carry out the project as shown below.*

How should the projects be sequenced in order to maximize net revenues?

Project ID	1	2	3	4	5	6	7
Duration (D_j)	2	4	6	8	10	12	14
Deadlines (d)	6	12	30	19	12	18	24

SOLUTION: From the statement of the problem, one can identify that the objective is to maximize net revenues. This can be achieved by simply obtaining a sequence, which will minimize the number of tardy jobs *(NT),* Hence, we apply Hodgson's algorithm to minimize *NT*.

Step 1: The earliest due date order is shown below:

a_{ij}	2	12	12	18	19	24	30
Project (j)	1	2	5	6	4	7	3

Place the above sequence of projects which is in EDD order in set *E*. Therefore,

$$\text{Set } E = (1, 2, 5, 6, 4, 7, 3)$$

$$\text{Set } L = \text{(Empty)}.$$

Step 2: The lateness of the projects are checked as shown below:

Project (j)	1	2	5	6	4	7	3
Duration (t_j)	2	4	10	12	8	14	6
Completion time (C_j)	2	6	16	28	36	50	56
Due date (d)	6	12	12	18	19	24	30
Tardy/non-tardy (1/0)	0	0	1	1	1	1	1

In the above table, in the last row, 0 means that the project is non-tardy and 1 means that the project is tardy.

As per the sequence in the set *E,* there are five tardy projects. The first tardy project is 5, which is in the third position [3].

Step 3: The project with the largest duration among the first-three projects in the sequence is 5. Remove this project and append it to *L*. Therefore

$$L = \{5\}$$
$$E = \{1, 2, 6, 4, 7, 3\}.$$

The completion times of the projects in the set *E* are revised as shown below:

Project (j)	1	2	6	4	7	3
Duration (t)	2	4	12	8	14	6
Completion time (C_j)	2	6	18	26	40	46
Due date (d)	6	12	18	19	24	30
Tardy/non-tardy	0	0	0	1	1	1

Step 2: From Step 3, it is clear that there are three tardy projects. The first tardy project is 4, which is in the fourth position of the sequence in the set *E.*

Step 3: The project with the longest duration among the first-four projects is 6. Remove the project-6 from the set *E* and append it to the set *L.* Therefore

$$E = \{1, 2, 4, 7, 3\}$$
$$L = \{5, 6\}.$$

The completion times of the projects in the set *E* are revised as shown:

Project (j)		1	2	4	7	3
Duration (t_j)		2	4	8	14	6
Completion time (C_j)		2	6	14	28	34
Due date (d_j)		6	12	19	24	30
Tardy/non-tardy		0	0	0	1	1

Step 2: From the table shown in Step 3 it is known that there are two tardy projects. The first tardy project is 7, which is at the fourth position in the set *E*.

Step 3: The project with the longest duration. Among the first-four projects in the set *E* are 7.

Remove this job from the set *E* and append it to the set *L*.

$$E = \{1, 2, 4, 3\}$$
$$L = \{5, 6, 7\}.$$

The completion times of the projects are revised as shown below:

Project (j)	1	2	4	3
Duration (t)	2	4	8	6
Completion time (C_j)	2	6	14	20
Due date (d_j)	6	12	19	30
Tardy/non-tardy	0	0	0	0

Step 2: From the table in the previous step, it is clear that all the projects are non-tardy jobs. Hence, we reached the optimal sequence in E.

Now merge E and L to get the complete sequence.

Final sequence = E∪L={1,2,4,3,5,6,7}

In the above optimal sequence, total number of tardy projects is 3, which is the minimum value.

10.8 FLOW SHOP SCHEDULING

In flow shop scheduling problem, there are *n* jobs; each require processing on *m* different machines. The order in which the machines are required to process a job is called process sequence of that job. The process sequences of all the jobs are the same. But the processing times for various jobs on a machine may differ. If an operation is absent in a job, then the processing time of the operation of that job is assumed as zero.

The flow-shop scheduling problem can be characterized as given below:

1. A set of multiple-operation jobs is available for processing at time zero (Each job requires *m* operations and each operation requires a different machine).
2. Set-up times for the operations are sequence independent, and are included in processing times.
3. Job descriptors are known in advance.
4. *m* different machines are continuously available.
5. Each individual operation of jobs is processed till its completion without break.

The main difference of the flow shop scheduling from the basic single machine scheduling is that the inserted idle time may be advantageous in flow shop scheduling. Though the current machine is free, if the job from the previous machine is not released to the current machine, we cannot start processing on that job. So, the current machine has to be idle for sometime. Hence, inserted idle time on some machines would lead to optimality.

For example, consider the following flow-shop problem:

Job	Machine 1	Machine 2
1	5	4
2	3	1
3	6	2
4	7	8

If the sequence of the job is 2-1-4-3, then the corresponding makespan is computed as shown in Fig.10.1. Here the makespan is 25. Also, note the inserted idle times on machine 2 are from 0 to 3, 4 to 8 and 12 to 15.

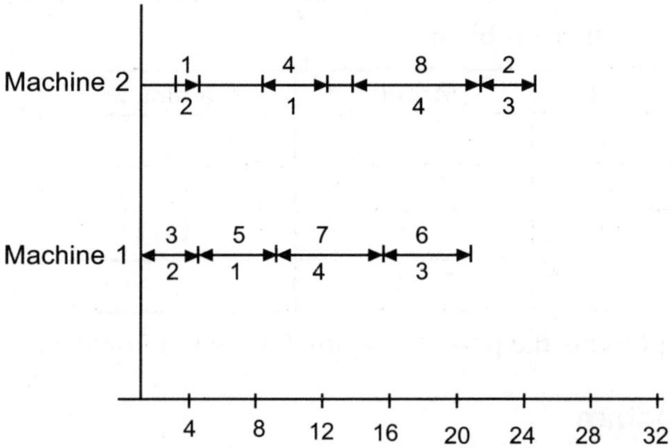

Fig. 10.1 Gantt chart for sequence 2-1-4-3

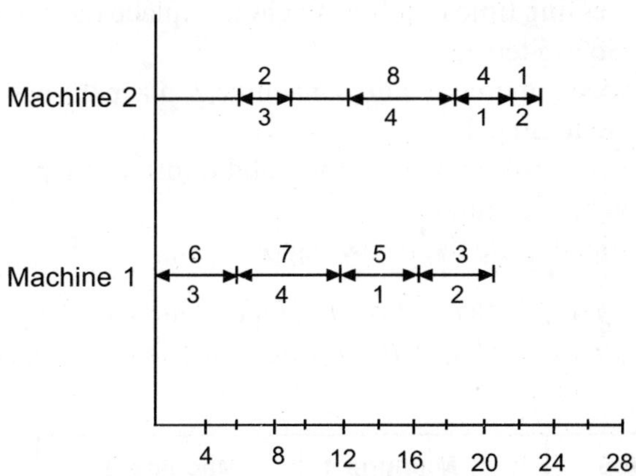

Fig. 10.2 Gantt chart for sequence 3-4-1-2

Consider another sequence say 3-4-1-2. The Gantt chart for this sequence is shown in Fig 10.2. The makespan for the schedule in Fig. 10.2 is 26. The machine 2 has idle time from 0 to 6 and from 8 to 13.

This problem has 4 jobs. Hence, 4! sequences are possible. Unlike in single machine scheduling, in flow shop scheduling, inserted idle time would minimize the makespan.

In the above two sequences, 2-1-4-3 and 3-4-1-2, the first sequence has lesser makespan. Like this, one can enumerate all 4! sequences, then select the sequence with the minimum makespan as the optimal sequence. Since, $n!$ grows exponentially with n, one needs some efficient procedure to solve the problem. For large size of n, it would be difficult to solve the problem. Under such situation we can use some efficient heuristic.

10.9 JOHNSON'S PROBLEM

As mentioned in the earlier section, the time complexity function for a general flow shop problem is exponential in nature. This means, the function grows exponentially with an increase in the problem size. But, for a problem with 2 machines and n jobs, Johnson had developed a polynomial algorithm to get optimal solution, *i.e.*, in a definite time, one can get the optimal solution.

Consider the following flow shop problem:

Job	Machine 1	Machine 2
1	t_{11}	t_{12}
2	t_{21}	t_{22}
3	t_{31}	t_{32}
n	t_{n1}	t_{n2}

In the above table, t_{ij} represents the processing time of the job i on the machine j.

10.9.1 Johnson's Algorithm

Step 1: Find the minimum among various t_{i1} and t_{i2}.

Step 2a: If the minimum processing time requires machine 1, place the associated job in the first available position in sequence. Go to Step 3.

Step 2b: If the minimum processing time requires machine 2, place the associated job in the last available position in sequence. Go to Step 3.

Step 3: Remove the assigned job from consideration and return to Step 1 until all positions in sequence are filled. (Ties may be broken randomly.)

The above algorithm is illustrated using the following problem:

ILLUSTRATION 5: *Consider the following two machines and six jobs flow shop-scheduling problem. Using Johnson's algorithm, obtain the optimal sequence, which will minimize the makespan.*

Job	Machine 1	Machine 2
1	5	4
2	2	3
3	13	14
4	10	1
5	8	9
6	12	11

SOLUTION: The workings of the algorithm are summarized in the form of a table, which is shown below:

Stage	Unscheduled jobs	Minimum tik	Assignment	Partialsequence
1	1, 2, 3, 4, 5, 6	T42	4 = [6]	×××××4
2	1, 2, 3, 5, 6	T21	2 = [1]	2 ××××4
3	1, 3, 5, 6	T12	1 = [5]	2×××14
4	3, 5, 6	T51	5 = [2]	25××14
5	3, 6	T62	6 = [4]	25×614
6	3	T31	3 = [3]	253614

The optimal sequence is 2-5-3-6-1-4. The makespan is determined as shown below. In the following table:

[Time-in on M/c 2 = max *[M!c* 1 Time-out of the current job, M/c 2 Time-out of the previous job]

Job	Processing time				Idle time on machine
	Machine 1		Machine 2		
	Time-in	Time-out	Time-in	Time-out	
2	0	2	2	5	2
5	2	10	10	19	5
3	10	23	23	37	4
6	23	35	37	48	0
1	35	40	48	52	0
4	40	50	52	53	0

The makespan for this schedule is 53.

10.9.2 Extension of Johnson's Rule

Consider a 'three machines and *n* jobs' flow shop scheduling problem as shown in Table 10.1.

Table 10.1

Job	Processing time		
	Machine 1	Machine 2	Machine 3
1	t_{11}	t_{12}	t_{11}
2	t_{21}	t_{22}	t_{11}
3	t_{31}	t_{32}	t_{11}
4	t_{41}	t_{42}	t_{11}
5	t51	t52	t11
.	.	.	.
i	t_{i1}	t_{i2}	t_{i3}
.	.	.	.
.	.	.	.
n	1	t_{n2}	t_{n3}

One can extend Johnson's algorithm to the problem shown in Table 10.1 if anyone of the following two conditions is satisfied.

$$\text{If } \min t_{i1} \leq \max t_{i2}$$

or

$$\text{if } \min t_{i3} \leq \max t_{i2}$$

If anyone of the above conditions is satisfied then, we can extend the Johnson's algorithm in the following way.

Create a hypothetical problem with two machines and *n* jobs as shown in Table 10.2.

The objective is to obtain optimal sequence for the data given in the Table 10.2. Later, the makespan is to be determined for the optimal sequence by using the data of the original problem shown in table.

This concept of extending Johnson's algorithm to this type of problem is demonstrated using an example problem.

Table 10.2 Hypothetical problem for the problem in Table 10.1

Job	M/c c–A	M/c c–B
1	$t_{11} + t_{12}$	$t_{12} + t_{13}$
2	$t_{21} + t_{22}$	$t_{22} + t_{23}$
3	$t_{31} + t_{32}$	$t_{32} + t_{33}$
.	.	
i	$t_{i1} + t_{i2}$	$t_{i2} + t_{i3}$
.	.	
n	$t_{n1} + t_{n2}$	$t_{n2} + t_{n3}$

ILLUSTRATION 6: *Consider the following 3 machines and 5 jobs flow shop problem:*

	Processing time		
Job	M/c–1	M/c–2	M/c–3
1	8	5	4
2	10	6	9
3	6	2	8
4	7	3	6
5	11	4	5

SOLUTION

In the above table,

Min (t_{i1})=6 Max $(t_{i2}) = 6$

Since the condition min $(t_{i1}) \leq$ max (t_{i2}) is satisfied, we can extend the Johnson's algorithm to this problem. So the modified problem may be given as follows:

Job	Machine A	Machine B
1	13	9
2	16	15
3	8	10
4	10	9
5	15	9

The following is the optimal sequence for the above problem:

3-2-5-1-4

The makespan of the above sequence is determined as shown below:

	Processing time (in hour)							
	M/c-1		M/c-2		M/c-3		Idle time on M/c-2	Idle time on M/c-3
Job	In	Out	In	Out	In	Out		
3	0	6	6	8	8	16	6	8
2	6	16	16	22	22	31	8	6
5	16	27	27	31	31	36	5	0
1	27	35	35	40	40	44	4	4
4	35	42	42	45	45	51	2	1

The makespan for this problem is 51 units of time.

10.10 CDS HEURISTIC

For large size problems, it would be difficult to get optimum solution in finite time, since the flow shop scheduling is a combinatorial problem. This means the time complexity function of flow shop problem is exponential in nature. Hence, we have to use efficient heuristics for large size problems.

CDS (Campbell, Dudek and Smith) heuristic is one such heuristic used for flow shop scheduling. The CDS heuristic corresponds to multistage use of Johnson's rule applied to a new problem formed from the original processing time.

At stage 1

$$t^1_{j1} = t_{ji} \text{ and } t^1_{j2} = t_{jm}$$

In other words, Johnson's rule is applied to the first and *mth* operations and intermediate operations are ignored.

At stage 2

$$T^2_{j1} = t_{ji} + t_{j2} \text{ and } t^2_{j2} = t_{jm} + t_{j\,m-1}$$

That is, Johnson's rule is applied to the sum of the first two and the last two operation processing times. In general at stage *i*,

$$t^i_{ji} = \Sigma_{ji} \text{ and } t^i_{j2} = \Sigma t_{j,m-k+1}$$

For each stage *i* ($i = 1, 2, \ldots m - 1$), the job order obtained is used to calculate a makespan for the original problem. After $m - 1$, stages, the best makespan among the $m - 1$ schedule is identified. (Some of the $m - 1$ sequences may be identical).

ILLUSTRATION 6: *Find the makespan using the CDS heuristic for the following flow shop problem:*

Job j	t_{j1}	t_{j2}	t_{j3}	t_{j4}
1	4	3	7	8
2	3	7	2	5
3	1	2	4	7
4	3	4	3	2

SOLUTION

Job (j)	M/c–1 t_{j1}	M/c–1 t_{j2}
1	4	8
2	3	5
3	1	7
4	3	2

The optimal sequence for the above problem is as shown below:

3-2-1-4

The makespan calculation for the above schedule is shown below:

Processing time (in hour)								
Job	M/c–1		M/c–2		M/c–3		M/c–4	
	In	Out	In	Out	In	Out	In	Out
3	0	1	1	3	3	7	7	14
2	1	4	4	11	11	13	14	19
1	4	8	11	14	14	21	21	29
1	8	11	14	18	21	24	29	31

Makespan of this problem = 31.

Stage 2

Job (j)	M/c–1 T_{j1}	M/c–2 t_{j2}
1	7	15
2	10	7
3	3	11
4	7	5

After applying Johnson's algorithm to the above problem, we get the sequence, 3-1-2-4. The makespan calculation is summarized in the following table:

Processing time (in hour)								
Job	M/c–1		M/c–2		M/c–3		M/c–4	
	In	Out	In	Out	In	Out	In	Out
3	0	1	1	3	3	7	7	14
1	1	5	5	8	8	15	15	23
2	5	8	8	15	15	17	23	28
4	8	11	15	19	19	22	28	30

The makes pan for the sequence 3-1-2-4 is 30.

Stage 2

Job	M/c–1	M/c–2
	T_{j1}	T_{j2}
1	14	18
2	12	14
3	7	13
4	10	9

The application of Johnson's algorithm to the above data yields the sequence 3-2-1-4. The determination of the corresponding makespan is shown below:

Job	M/c–1		M/c–2		M/c–3	
	In	Out	In	Out	In	Out
3	0	1	3	7	7	14
2	1	4	11	13	14	19
1	4	8	14	21	21	29
4	8	11	21	24	29	31

stage	sequence	Makespan
1	3-2-14	31
2	3-1-2-4	30
3	3-2-1-4	31

The best sequence is 3-1-2-4, which has the makespan of 30.

10.11 JOB-SHOP PROBLEM

In job-shop problem, we assume that each job has *m* different operations. If some of the jobs are having less than *m* operations, required number of dummy operations with zero process times is assumed. By this assumption, the condition of equal number of operations for all the jobs is ensured. In job-shop scheduling problem, the process sequences of the jobs are not the same. Hence, the flow of each job in job-shop scheduling is not undirectional.

The time complexity function of the job shop problem is combinatorial in nature. Hence, heuristic approaches are popular in this area.

Unlike the flow shop model, there is no initial machine that performs only the first operation of a job nor there is a terminal machine that performs only the last operation of a job.

In the flow shop, an operation number in the operation sequence of a job may be same as the position number of the required machine. Hence, there is no need to distinguish between them. But, in the job shop case, different jobs will have different operation sequences. So, we cannot assume a straight flow for the job shop problem. Each operation *j* in the operation sequence of the job *i* in the job shop problem will be described with triplet *(i, j, k)* where *k* is the required machine for processing the *jth* operation of the *ith* job.

Consider the following data of a job shop scheduling involving four jobs, three operations and hence three machines.

The first table consists of operation processing times and the second table consists of operation (process) sequences of the jobs. The set of machines required for a given job constitute a routing. For example, job 4 has a routing of 1-3-2.

Processing times (hrs)			
	Operations		
	1	2	3
Job 1	2	3	4
Job 2	4	4	1
Job 3	2	2	3
Job 4	3	3	1

Routing			
	Operations		
	1	2	3
Job 1	1	2	3
Job 2	3	2	1
Job 3	2	3	1
Job 4	1	3	2

10.12 TYPES OF SCHEDULES

In general, infinite number of feasible schedules is possible for any job shop problem, because one can insert any arbitrary amount of idle time at any machine between adjacent pairs of operations. These idle times are not useful in any sense. In fact, these will lead to non-optimal solution while minimizing makespan measure.

In the Gantt chart shown in Fig., one should try to move various operation blocks to the left as much as possible on each machine. This will help us to have a compact schedule, which will generally minimize the famous makespan measure. Adjusting the start time of some operations towards left without affecting the operations sequences will minimize the unwanted idle time. Adjusting the start time of some operations this way is equivalent to moving an operation block to the left of the Gantt chart while preserving the operation sequences. This type of adjustment is called **local-left -shift**, or a **limited-left-shift**. Given an operation sequence for each machine, there is only one schedule in which no local-left-shift can be made. The set of all schedules in which no local-left-shift can be made is called **the set of semi-active schedules** and is equivalent to the set of all schedules that contain none of the unwanted idle time described above. This set dominates the set of all schedules, which means that it is sufficient to consider only semi-active schedules to optimize any regular measure of performance.

The number of semi-active schedules is finite and is less than the total number of possible schedules. In a semi-active schedule, the start time of a particular operation is constrained either by (a) processing a different job on the same machine or (b) by processing the directly preceding operation on n different machines. In the former case, where the completion of an earlier operation on the same machine is constrained, it may still be possible to find obvious means of improvement. Even when no local-shifts are possible, a better schedule can obviously be devised by shifting operations to the left and beyond other operations already scheduled on some machine. This type of adjustment in which some operation. is begun earlier without delaying any other operation is called a **global left-shift** or **simply a left-shift**. The set of all schedules in which no global left-shift can be made is called the set of active schedules. It is clearly a subset of the set of semi-active schedules.

The set of active schedules dominates the set of semi-active schedules in terms of optimizing any regular measure of performance. So it is sufficient to consider only active schedules.

If no machine is kept idle at a time when it could begin processing some operation then it is called a **non-delay schedule**. We can identify a subset of schedules from the set of active schedules satisfying this property, which is known as a **set of non-delay schedules**.

All non-delay schedules are active schedules, since no left-shift is possible. There is no guarantee that the non-delay subset will contain an optimum. The Venn diagram showing the relative sizes between different types of schedules is shown in the following Fig. 10.3. There will be at least one optimal schedule in the set of active schedules.

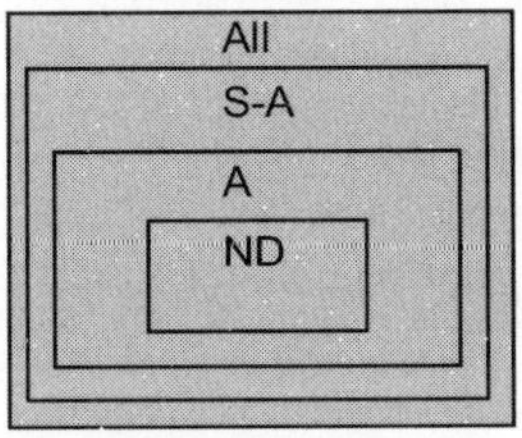

Note:
All–All the schedules
S–Sem-active Schedules
A–Active schedules
ND–Non-delay schedules

Fig. 10.3 Venn diagram showing different schedules

10.13 HEURISTIC PROCEDURES

Since, the job shop problem comes under combinatorial category, the time taken to obtain optimum solution will be exponential in nature. In this type of problem, the number of feasible schedules will grow exponentially, even for small increment in problem size. As a result, it will be impossible to solve large size problems optimally. Hence, we should resort to heuristic approach to get near optimal solution.

10.14 PRIORITY DISPATCHING RULES

In complete enumeration procedure or branch and bound procedure, the number of schedules generated before reaching an optimal schedule would be enormous. But, heuristic procedures will generally aim to generate only one full schedule. Whenever, there is a tie (conflict) in selecting an operation from among competing operations, we will have to use a priority rule. If there are ties at different levels, then we need more than one priority rule to break deep ties. For a given priority rule *R*, a heuristic based on the active schedule generation is given below:

Heuristic Active Schedule Generation

Step 1: Let $t = 0$ and assume $Pt = \{\phi\}$.
$S_t = \{$All operations with no predecessors$\}$.

Step 2: Determine $q^* = \min \{q_j\}$ and the corresponding machine m^* on which q^* could be realized.
j E S.

Step 3: For each operation which belongs to *S*, that requires machine m^* and satisfies the condition $Pj < q^*$, identify an operation according to a specific priority and add this operation to PI as early as possible, thus creating only one partial schedule, $PI+1$ for the next stage.

Step 4: For each new partial schedule $PI + 1$ created in Step 3, update the data set as follows:

(*a*) Remove operation *j* from *SI*.

(*b*) Form SI + I by adding the direct successor of operation *j* to *SI*.

(*c*) Increment *t* by one.

Step 5: Repeat from Step 2 to Step 4 for each $PI + 1$ created in Step 3 and continue in this manner until all active schedules are generated.

Similarly, another heuristic can be devised from the non-delay schedule generation algorithm by replacing the condition $Pj < q^*$ with $Pj = p^*$ in Step 3. These two heuristic algorithms (one for active dispatching and the other for non-delay dispatching) may construct different schedules. The quality of the solution obtained by these heuristics mainly depends on the effectiveness of priority rules which are used in them.

A sample set of priority rules are presented below:

(*a*) **SPT (shortest processing time):** Select the operation with the minimum processing time.

(*b*) **FCFS (first come first served):** Select the operation that entered SI earliest.

(*c*) **MWKR (most work remaining):** Select the operation associated with the job having the most work remaining to be processed.

(*d*) **MOPNR (most operations remaining):** Select the operation that has the largest number of successor operations.

(*e*) **LWKR (least work remaining):** Select the operation associated with the job having the least work remaining to be processed.

(*f*) **RANDOM (Random):** Select the operation at random.

10.15 TWO JOBS AND M MACHINES SCHEDULING

Two jobs and M machines scheduling is a special problem under job shop scheduling. The problem consists of 2 jobs, which require processing on M machines. The processing sequences of the jobs are not the same. Since, this is a special kind under the job shop scheduling like, Johnson's problem (*n* jobs and 2 machines) under flow shop scheduling, we have a graphical procedure to get optimum schedule.

The graphical procedure consists of the following steps:

Step 1: Construct a two dimensional graph in which *x*-axis represents the job 1, its sequence of operations and their processing times, and *y*-axis represents the job 2, its sequence of operations and their processing times (use same scale for both *x*-axis and *y*-axis).

Step 2: Shade each region where a machine would be occupied by the two jobs simultaneously.

Step 3: The processing of both jobs can be shown by a continuous line consisting of horizontal, vertical and 45 degree diagonal lines. The line is drawn from the origin and continued to the upper right corner by avoiding the regions. A diagonal line means that both jobs can be performed simultaneously. So, while drawing the line from the origin to the top right corner, we should try to maximize the length of diagonal travel (sum of the lengths of 45 degree lines), which will minimize the makespan of the problem.

Using trial and error method, one can draw the final line, which has the maximum diagonal portion. This concept is demonstrated using a numerical problem.

ILLUSTRATION 8: *Use graphical method to minimize the time needed to process the following jobs on the machines shown (i.e. for each machine, find the job which should be scheduled first). Also, calculate the total time elapsed to complete both jobs.*

Job 1	Sequence	A	-	B	-	C	-	D	-	E
	Time (hrs).	3		4		2		6		2
Job 2	Sequence	B	-	C	-	A	-	D	-	E
	Time (hrs)	5		4		3		2		6

SOLUTION: As per the procedure stated, the above data is presented in the form of a graph as shown in Figure 10.4.

The line from the origin to the top right corner shows the processing details and makespan. The makespan (time taken to complete both the jobs) is 22 hours. The start and completion times for both jobs are given in Table 10.2.

Start and completion times of jobs

Start and completion times of jobs					
	Job 1 (time)			Job 2 (time)	
Machine	Start	End	Machine	Start	End
A	0	3	B	0	5
B	5	9	C	5	9
C	9	11	A	9	12
D	14	20	D	12	14
E	20	22	E	14	20

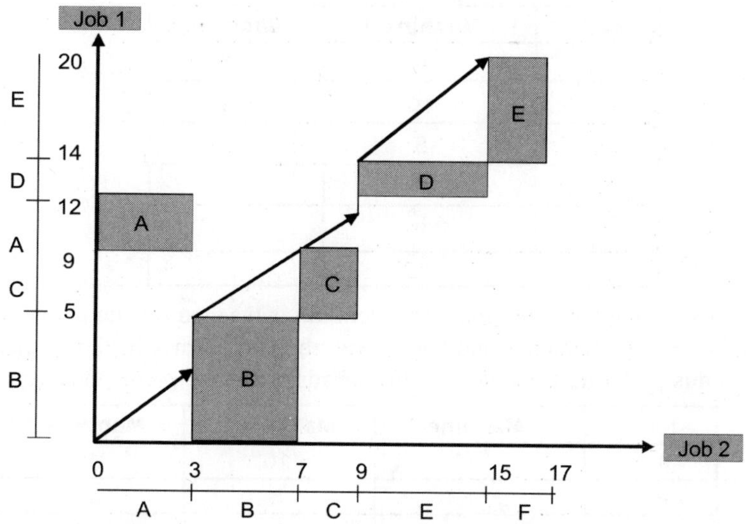

Fig. 10.4 Schedule for 2 jobs and % machines

Based on Figure and Table one can easily observe that the total idle for job1 is 5 hours (2+3). Hence the total for completing the job 1 is its sum of the processing times plus its idle time, *i.e.* 17 hrs + 5hrs = 22 hrs.

For job 2, there is no idle time. Hence the total time taken to complete the job 2 is its sum of the processing times, *i.e.* 20 hrs.

The makespan is the maximum of these two quantities.

Therefore, Max (22,20) = 22 hrs.

EXERCISE

1. Briefly discuss different measures of performance in single machine scheduling with independent jobs.

2. Consider the following problem in single machine scheduling with independent jobs.

job	1	2	3	4	5	6	7	8
Processing time (t_j)	5	12	8	10	3	15	8	6
Due date (d_j)	10	16	11	16	6	25	12	14
Weight (w_j)	2	1	1	2	3	4	2	3

Obtain the optimal schedule for each of the following performance measures:

(*a*) To minimize mean flow time.

(*b*) To minimize the maximum lateness.

(*c*) To minimize weighted mean flow time.

3. Distinguish between single machine scheduling and flow scheduling.

4. What are the assumptions in flow shop scheduling?

5. Consider the following two machines and 6 jobs flow shop problem.

Job	Machine 1	Machine 2
1	5	7
2	10	8
3	8	13
4	9	7
5	6	11
6	12	10

Obtain the optimal schedule and the corresponding makespan for the above problem.

6. Consider the following 3 machines and 5 jobs flow shop problem. Check whether Johnson's rule can be extended to this problem. If so, what is the schedule and the corresponding makespan?

Job	Machine 1	Machine 2	Machine 3
1	11	10	12
2	13	8	20
3	15	6	15
4	12	7	19
5	20	9	7

7. Consider the following flow shop problem:

Job	Machine 1	Machine 2	Machine 3
1	10	15	23
2	8	10	7
3	12	7	10
4	15	20	6

Find the optimal schedule for the above flow shop problem using branch and bound technique. Also, determine the corresponding makespan.

8. Explain the following:
   (*a*) Active-schedule.
   (*b*) Semi-active schedule.
   (*c*) Non-delay schedule.
9. Write short notes on dispatching rules.
10. Use graphical method to minimize the needed to process the following jobs on the machines shown (*i.e.* for each machine find the job which should be scheduled first). Also, calculate the total time elapsed to complete both jobs.

Job 1	**Sequence**	A	-	B	-	C	-	D	-	E
	Time (hrs)	2		6		5		4		7
Job 2	**Sequence**	C	-	B	-	D	-	A	-	E
	Time (hrs)	6		5		7		4		8

REFERENCES

1. Everett, E. Adam, Jr. Ronald J.Ebert, *Production and Operations Management*, Prentice-Hall of India Private Limited, 5th Edition, 1994.
2. R.Pannerselvam, *Production and Operations Management*, Prentice-Hall of India Private Limited, 9th print, 2004.
3. Joseph, G.Monks, *Theory and Problems of Operations Management*, Tata McGraw-Hill Publishing Company Limited, 2nd Edition, 2004.

GLOSSARY

ABC classification: Classification of inventory into three groups: an A group comprising items with a large dollar volume; a B group comprising items with moderate volume and moderate dollar volume; and a C group comprising items with a large volume and small dollar volume.

Acceptance number: The number of sample units specified in a sampling plan that must conform to specifications if the shipment is to be accepted.

Acceptance sampling: A statistical quality control technique used in deciding to accept or reject a shipment of input or output.

Accounting life: Length of an asset's life determined for the purpose of a depreciation schedule.

Action bucket: In the MRP record for the current week, a cell calling for immediate action to meet the MPS goal.

Activity: In PERT, project work needed to be accomplished, symbolized by an arc.

Activity charts: A graphic tool to analyze and time the small, physical actions of worker and machine in performing a routine, repetitive, worker-machine task so that idle time can be identified.

Adaptive exponential smoothing: An average method in which a smoothing coefficient is not fixed but is set initially and then allowed to fluctuate over time based upon changes in the demand pattern.

Aggregate capacity planning: The process of testing, the feasibility of aggregate output plans and evaluating overall capacity utilization.

Aggregate output planning: The process of determining output levels (units) of product groups over the coming 6 to 18 months on a weekly or monthly basis; the plan identifies the overall level of outputs in support of the business plan.

Allocated quantity: The quantity of an item in inventory that has been committed for use and is not available to meet future requirements.

Allowance fraction: The fraction of time lost on a job because of workers' personal needs, fatigue, and other unavoidable delays; the remaining fraction of time is the available fraction.

Andon: A warning light used as a visible control technique in total quality control.

Applied research: Research for the advancement of scientific knowledge that has specific commercial uses.

Appraisal costs: Costs of evaluating, measuring, or inspecting for quality at the plant and in the field.

Arc: In network modeling, an arrowed line segment; the symbol for a project activity.

Assembly line technology: A process technology suitable for a narrow range of standardized products in high volumes.

Assignment algorithm: A linear program to assign jobs so that a specific criterion is optimized.

Attribute characteristic: A product characteristic that can be measured by a rating of good or bad.

Available fraction of time: The fraction of time remaining after accounting for time lost on a job because of worker's personal needs, fatigue, and other unavoidable delays.

Available quantity: The quantity of an item expected to be: available at the end of a time period to meet requirements in succeeding periods. Calculated as scheduled receipts plus planned order receipts minus gross requirements for the period, plus amounts available from the previous period.

Back orders: Outstanding or unfilled customer orders.

Backward scheduling: Determining the start and finish times for waiting jobs by assigning them to the latest available time slot that will enable each job to be completed just when it is due, but not before.

Base stock level: The inventory level up to which stocks are replenished, fixed by a periodic inventory control operating doctrine.

Basic research: Research for the advancement of scientific knowledge that is not intended for specific commercial uses.

Batch production: American Production and Inventory Control Society (APICS) defines batch production as a form of manufacturing in which the job pass through the functional departments in lots or batches and each lot may have a different routing define batch production. It is characterized by the manufacture of limited number of products produced at regular intervals and stocked awaiting sales.

Batch technology: A process technology suitable for a variety of products in varying volumes.

Behavioral management: One of three primary theories of management, emphasizing human relations and the behavioral science.

Behavioral science: A science that explores how human behavior is affected by variables such as leadership, motivation, communication, interpersonal relationships and attitude change.

Bias: A forecast error measure that is the average of forecast error with regard to direction and shows any tendency consistently to over or under forecast; calculated as the sum of the actual forecast error for all periods divided by the total number of periods evaluated.

Bill of materials: A document describing the details of an item's product build-up, including all component items, their build-up sequence, the quantity needed for each, and the work centers that perform the build-up sequence.

Blanket rule: A general policy for inventory control that can be modified as needed in light of total inventory costs.

Bottleneck operation: The station on an assembly line that requires the longest task time.

Break-even analysis: A graphical and algebraic representation of the relationships among volume of output, costs and revenues.

Break-even point: The level of output volume for which total costs equal total revenues.

Breakthrough: A solution to a chronic problem; a dramatic change for the better in quality, stimulated by concentrated, analytic, company-wide quality improvement programs.

Buffer stock: Inventories to protect against the effects of unusual product demand and uncertain lead-time.

Business plan: A statement of an organization's overall level of business activity for the coming 6 to 18 months, usually expressed in terms of dollar volume of sales for its various product groups.

Capacity: A facility's maximum productive capability, usually expressed as volume of output per period of time.

Capacity planning: Design of the production system involves planning for the inputs, conversion process and outputs of production operation.

Capacity requirement planning (CRP): A capacity requirement planning is an iterative process of modifying the MPS or planned resources to make capacity consistent with the production schedule.

Cardex file system: A manually operated inventory control system in which an inventory card represents each stock item with transactions kept on the card.

Carrying (holding) costs: Costs of maintaining the inventory warehouse and protecting the inventoried items.

Causal forecasting models: A statistical forecasting model based on historical demand data as well as on variables believed to influence demand.

Cellular layout: The arrangement of a facility so that equipment used to make similar parts or families of parts is grouped together.

Central limit theorem: A statistical hypothesis that the sampling distribution approaches normality as the size of the samples increases, regardless of the distribution of the measurements of individual sample units.

Chance event: An event leading potentially to several different outcomes, only one of which will definitely occur; the decision maker has no control over which outcome will occur.

Change agent: The facilitator of change; the role of the production/operations manager in bringing about behavioral changes in other people.

Chronic problem: A long-term problem that causes continually poor quality, usually addressed through breakthrough measures.

Classical management: One of three primary theories of management, emphasizing efficiency at the production core, the separation of planning and doing work, and management principles and functions.

Codification: It is a process of representing each item by a number, the digit of which indicates the group, the sub-group, the type and the dimension of the item.

Combination layout: This is also called the hybrid or mixed type of layout usually a process layout is combined with the product layout. For example, refrigerator manufacturing uses a combination layout. The process or functional layout is used to produce various operations like stamping, welding, heat treatment are carried out in different work centres as per the requirement. The final assembly of the product is done in a product type layout.

Company-wide quality control (CWQC): A management philosophy and set of activities characterized by mobilizing the entire work force in the pursuit of quality, by statistical thinking, and by preventing errors.

Computer search: A set of directions that systematically guides a computer in evaluating alternative aggregate plans.

Computer-aided manufacturing (CAM): Manufacturing systems utilizing computer software programs that control the actual machine on the shop floor.

Computer-aided design (CAD): Computer software programs that allow a designer to carry out geometric transformations rapidly.

Computer-integrated manufacturing (CIM): Computer information systems utilizing a shared manufacturing database for engineering design, manufacturing engineering, factory production, and information management.

Consumer's risk (type II error) (b): The risk or probability of incorrectly concluding that the conversion process is in control.

Continuous operations: Operations characterized by standardized, high-volume, capital- intense products made to store in inventory; by small product mix; by special purpose equipment; and by continuous product flow.

Continuous technology: A process technology suitable for producing a continuous flow of products.

Control chart: A chart of sampling data used to make inferences about the control status of a conversion process.

Control limits: (Cl) Upper (UCL) and lower (LCL) boundaries defining the range of variation in a product characteristic such that the conversion process is in control.

Controlling: Activities that assure that actual performance is in accordance with planned performance.

Conversions process: The process of changing inputs of labor, capital, land, and management into outputs of goods and services.

Continuous production: Production facilities are arranged as per the sequence of production operations from the first operations to the finished product. The items are made to flow through the sequence of operations through material handling devices such as conveyors, transfer devices etc.

Critical fractile: In ratio of shortage costs to the sum of shortage and overstock for the perishable goods inventory situation.

Critical path: In PERT, a path whose activities are expected to consume the most time.

Critical ratio: The ratio of inspection costs to per cent defective.

Custom-shop service technology: A process technology suitable for capital intensive, high customer contact services.

Cycle counting: Counting on-hand inventories at regular intervals to verify inventory quantities shown in the MRP.

Cycle time: Time elapsing between completed units coming off an assembly line.

Decision tree: A diagram used to structure and analyze a decision problem; a systematic, sequential laying out of decision points, alternatives, and chance events.

Decision variable: A numerical, controllable parameter that, if modified, yields a variety of results.

Decoupling: Using inventories to break apart operations so that the supply of one operation is independent of the supply of another.

Degeneracy: A quality of a linear transportation-programming problem such that there are too few occupied cells to enable evaluation of the empty cells.

Delphi technique: A qualitative forecasting technique in which a panel of experts working separately and not meeting, arrive at a consensus through the summarizing of ideas by a skilled coordinator.

Demand pattern: General shape of a time series; usually constant, trend, seasonal, or some combination of these shapes.

Demand stability: Tendency of a time series to retain the same general pattern overtime.

Demand-based forecasting models: A statistical forecasting model based solely on historical demand data.

Deming's 14 points for management: Guidelines for improving quality proposed by Dr. W. Edwards Deming, as part of total quality control.

Dependent demand: Demand for an item that can be linked to the demand for another item.

Depreciation: An accounting procedure to recover expenditures for an asset over its lifetime.

Design specifications: The important, desired characteristics of a product or service specified in detail during the design phase.

Designated truncation time: Predetermined length of time a job is allowed to wait before it is assigned top priority for processing (see truncated-shortest-processing-time rule).

Detailed capacity planning: An iterative process of modifying the MPS or planned -resources to make capacity consistent with the production Schedule.

Detailed scheduling: Determining start times, finish times, and worker assignments for all jobs at each work centres.

Deterministic model: A model in which variable values are known with certainty.

Development: Technical activities concerned with translating basic applied research results into products or processes.

Direct time study: A work measurement technique that involves observing the job, determining the job cycle, stopwatch-timing the job cycle, and calculating a performance standard.

Disaggregation: The process of translating aggregate plans for product groups into detailed operational plans for individual products.

Double sampling: Acceptance sampling based on a first, small sample and, if results are inconclusive, a second, larger sample.

Dummy activity: In PERT, a fictitious activity consuming no time, symbolized by a dashed arc.

Earliest beginning time: In PERT, the minimum amount of time that must be consumed before an activity can begin.

Earliest-due-date rule (EDD): Priority rule that gives top priority to the waiting job whose due date is earliest.

Economic life: Length of time an asset is useful.

Economic order quantity (EOQ): The optimal order quantity, fixed by a Q/R inventory control operating doctrine.

Efficiency: A measure (ratio) of outputs to inputs.

Empirical-rational change strategy: A strategy for change that assumes people change their behavior when they believe it is in their own self-interest to do so.

Ergonomics (human engineering): ILO defines human engineering as — 'The application of human biological sciences along with engineering sciences to achieve optimum mutual adjustment of men and his work, the benefits being measured in terms of human efficiency and well-being.

Event: In PERT, the beginning or ending of an activity, symbolized by a node.

Expected beginning time (T_B): In PERT, the amount of time expected to be consumed before an activity can begin.

Expected completion time (Tc): In PERT, the amount of time expected to be consumed once an activity begins.

Expected time (te): In PERT, the amount of time an activity is expected to consume

Expediting: Tracking a job's progress and taking special actions to move it through the facility.

Exponential smoothing: An averaging method that exponentially decreases the weighting of old demands.

Factory building: Factory building is a factor, which is the most important consideration for every industrial enterprise. A modem factory building is required to provide protection for men, machines, materials, products or even the company's secrets.

External failure costs: Costs attributable to the failure of products in the field.

Factor ratings: A decision procedure in which each alternative is rated according to each factor relevant to the decision, and each factor is weighted according to importance.

Feasible (infeasible) solutions: Solutions that satisfy (do not satisfy) the restrictions of a linear programming problem.

Feedback: Information in the control process that allows management to decide whether organizational activities need adjustment.

Finite loading: A scheduling procedure that assigns jobs into work centers and determines their starting and completion dates by considering the work centers' capacities.

Firm planned order: A planned order release scheduled within the MRP time fence.

First-come-first-served rule (FCFS): Priority rule that gives top priority to the waiting job that arrived earliest in the production system.

Fishbone (cause and effect) diagram: A schematic model of quality problems and their causes; used to diagnose and solve these problems.

Fixed-position layout: The arrangement of a facility so that the product stays—in one location; tools, equipment, and workers are brought to it as needed.

Flexibility: The capability of a manufacturing system to adapt successfully to changing environmental conditions and process requirements.

Flexible manufacturing system (FMS): A computer controlled process technology suitable for producing, a moderate variety of products in moderate volumes.

Flow diagram: Flow Diagram is a drawing, of the working area, showing the location of the various activities identified by their numbered symbols and are associated with particular flow process chart either man type or machine type.

Flow process chart: A graphic tool to analyze and categorize interstation activities so that the flow of the product throughout the overall production process is represented.

Flow time: The total time that a job is in the system; the sum of waiting time and processing time.

Forecast: Use of past data to determine future events, an objective computation.

Forecast error: The numeric difference of forecasted demand and actual demand.

Forward scheduling: Determining the start and finish times for waiting jobs by assigning them to the earliest available time slots at the work center.

Fraction defective: The ratio of defective units to total units.

Gang process chart: A graphic tool to trace the interaction of several workers with one machine.

Gantt chart: A bar chart showing the relationship of project activities in time.

Gantt load chart: A graph showing work loads on a time scale.

Gantt scheduling chart: A graph showing the time requirements of waiting jobs; scheduled for production at machines and work centers.

Governmental industrial planning: Activities of the Japanese Ministry of International Trade and Industry that formulate industrial policy and determine the patterns of future growth and decline among the various industries, comprising the Japanese economy.

Gradual replacement models: A deterministic inventory model characterized by demand being withdrawn while production is underway; no stockouts, constant and known demand, lead time and unit costs.

Graphical planning procedure: Two-dimensional model relating cumulative demand to cumulative output capacity.

Gross requirements: The overall quantity of an item needed during a time period to meet planned output levels. Planned output for end items is obtained from the MPS. Planned output for lower-level items is obtained from the MRP.

Group technology: A way of organizing and using data for components that have similar properties and manufacturing requirements.

Heuristic: A procedure in which a set of rules is systematically applied; an algorithm.

Histogram: A bar graph of frequency distributions.

Homogeneous resources: Resources for which units supplied by one source are qualitatively equivalent to units supplied by any other source.

Human relations: Phenomenon recognized by behavioral scientists that people are complex and have multiple needs and that the subordinate-supervisor relationship directly affects productivity.

Implementation: Activities concerned with designing and building pilot models, equipment, and facilities for, and with initiating the marketing channels for, products or services emerging from research and development.

In-control process: A process for which all variations are random.

Indented bill of materials: A chart showing an end item's components, level by level, with increasing indentations to reflect the lower levels.

Independent demand: Demand for an item that occurs separately of demand for any other item.

Individual risk taking propensity: The degree to which an individual tends to take or avoid risks.

Infinite loading: Assigning jobs to work centers without considering the work center's capacity (as if the capacity were infinite).

Initial solution: The feasible solution tested first using the simplex method in solving a linear programming problem.

Input/output control: Activities to monitor actual versus planned utilization of a work center's capacity.

Inputs: Labor, capital, land, or management resources changed by a conversion process into goods or services.

Inspection: The observation and measurement of inputs and outputs.

Intermittent operations: Operations characterized by made-to-order, low-volume, labor intense products; by a large product mix; by general-purpose equipment; by interrupted product flow; and by frequent schedule changes.

Internal failure costs: Costs attributable defects in production at the plant.

Internal rate of return: Interest rate at which the present value of outflows equals the present value of inflows.

Intuitive forecasts: Forecasts that essentially are a manager's guesses and judgments concerning future events; qualitative forecasting methods.

Inventory: Stores of goods and stocks, including raw materials, work-in-process, finished products, or supplies.

Inventory control: Activities that maintain stock keeping items at desired levels.

Inventory modeling: A quantitative, method for deriving a minimum cost operating doctrine.

Inventory status file: The complete documentation of the inventory status of each item in the product structure, including item identification, on-hand quantity, safety stock level, quantity allocated, and lead-time.

Iso-profit line: Points in the solution space of a linear programming problem whose corresponding profits are identical.

Item level: The relative position of an item in the product structure; end items are upper-level; preliminary items in the product structure are lower level.

Job: A group of related tasks to activities that needs to be performed to meet organizational objectives.

Job design: Activities that specify the content of each job and determine how work is distributed within the organization.

Job enrichment: Redesigning jobs to give more meaning and enjoyment to the job by involving employees in planning, organizing, and controlling their work.

Job rotation: Moving employee into a job for a short period of time and then out again.

Job satisfaction: Employee perceptions of the extent to which their work fulfills or satisfies their needs.

Job shop production: Job shop production are characterized by manufacturing of one or few quantity of products designed and produced as per the specification of customers within prefixed time and cost.

Job shop technology: A process technology suitable for variety of custom-designed products in small volumes.

Just-in-time (JIT): A manufacturing system whose goal it is to optimize processes and procedures by continuously pursuing waste reduction.

Kaizen: The Japanese concept of continuous improvement in all things.

Kanban: Literally a 'visual record' a method controlling material flow through a JIT manufacturing system by using cards to authorize a work station to transfer or produce materials.

Labor efficiency: The ratio of outputs to labor input, the labor-actually worked to achieve their output; a partial factor productivity measure.

Labor standard: A quantitative criterion reflecting the output expected from an average worker under average conditions for a given time period.

Labor turnover: A measure of the stability or change in an organization's work force; the net result of employee terminations and entrances.

Latest beginning time (T_L): In PERT, the maximum amount of time that can be consumed before an activity begins, if the project is to be completed on time.

Layout: Physical location or configuration of departments, work centers, and equipment in the conversion process; spatial arrangement of physical resources used to create the product.

Lead-time: The time passing between ordering and receiving goods.

Lead-time demand: Units of stock demanded during lead-time; can be described by a probability distribution in stochastic situations.

Lead-time offsetting: The process of determining the timing of a planned order release; backing off from the timing of a planned order receipt by the length of lead-time.

Least slack rule (LS): A priority rule that gives top priority to the waiting job whose slack time is least; slack time is the difference between the length of time remaining until the job is due and the length of its operation time.

Level output rate plan: An aggregate plan calling for a constant rate of output for all time periods of production.

Line balancing problem: Assigning tasks among workers at assembly line stations so that performance times are made as equal as possible.

Linear decision rules (LDRs): A set of equations for calculating optimal work force, aggregate output rate, and inventory level.

Linear programming: Mathematical method for selecting the optimal allocation of resources to maximize profits or minimize costs.

Load: The cumulative amount of work currently assigned to a work center for future processing.

Load-distance model: An algorithm for laying out work centers to minimize product-flow, based on the number of loads moved and the distance between each pair of work centers.

Longest-operation-time (LOT) rules: A line-balancing heuristic that gives top assignment priority to the task that has the longest operation time.

Lot splitting: Processing only part of a job at one time, then the rest of the job at a later time.

Lot-for-lot ordering: A lot sizing policy in which order quantity equals net requirements for the period.

Machine life: Length of time an asset is capable of functioning.

Management coefficients model: A set of equations that represent historical patterns of a company's aggregate planning decisions.

Manufacturing resources planning (MRPII): An integrated information system that shares data among and synchronizes the activities of production and the other functional areas of the business.

Manufacturing accounting and production information control system (MAPICS): IBM's computerized common data base system for manufacturing information and control.

Marginal efficiency of capital (MEC): A concept from finance espousing that a firm should invest in opportunities whose return is greater than the cost of capital.

Markup: The ratio of profits to sales.

Mass production: Manufacture of discrete parts or assemblies using a continuous process are called Mass production. This production system is justified by very large volume of production. The machines are arranged in a line or product layout. Product and process standardizations exist and all outputs follow the same path.

Mass service technology: A process technology suitable for labor intensive, low customer contact services.

Master production scheduling (MPS): A schedule showing week by week how many of each product must be produced according to customer orders and demand forecasts.

Material requirements planning (MRP): A system of planning and scheduling the time-phased materials requirements for production operations.

Material handling: Haynes defines 'Material handling embraces the basic operations in connection with the movement of bulk, packaged and individual products in a semi-solid or solid state by means of gravity manually or power-actuated equipment and within the limits of individual producing, fabricating, processing or service establishment'.

Materials management: Activities relating to managing the flow of materials into and through an organization.

Mathematical modeling: Creating and using mathematical representations of management problems and organizations to predict outcomes of proposed courses of action.

Matrix organization: An organization that combines functional and project bases for groupings of organization units.

Maximum allowable cycle time: Maximum time allowed to elapse between completed units coming off an assembly line, if. 9 given capacity is to be achieved.

Mean absolute deviation (MAD): A forecast error measure that is the average forecast error without regard to direction; calculated as the sum of the absolute value of forecast error for all periods divided by the total number of periods evaluated.

Mechanization: The process of bringing about the use of equipment and machinery in production and operations.

Method study: is the systematic recording and critical examination of existing and proposed ways of doing work, as a means of developing and applying easier and more effective methods and reducing costs. According to British Standards Institution (BS 3138): "Method study is the systematic recording and critical examination or existing and proposed ways or doing work as a means or developing and applying easier and more effective methods and reducing cost."

Methods time measurement: A widely accepted form of predetermined time study.

Ministry of international trade and industry (MITI): The unit of Japanese government responsible for industrial planning for the activities that formulate industrial policy and determine the patterns of future growth and decline among the various industries comprising the Japanese economy.

Mixed strategy: Aggregate planning strategy that incorporates or combines some elements from each of the pure aggregate planning strategies.

Modeling management: One of three primary theories of management, emphasizing decision-making, systems, and mathematical modeling.

Modular design: The creation of products from some combination of basic, preexisting subsystems.

Most likely time (t_m): In PERT, the single best guess of the amount of time an activity is expected to consume.

Multiechelon inventories: Products stocked at various levels—factory, warehouse, retailer, customer in a distribution system.

Multiple activity chart: It is a chart where activities of more than subject (worker or equipment) are each recorded on a common time scale to show their inter-relationship.

Multiple sampling: Acceptance sampling based on many small samples.

Multistage inventories: Parts stocked at more than one point of the sequential production process.

Natural limits: Three standard deviations above and below the average of sample unit measurements.'

Net change method: Method for updating the MRP system in which only those portions of the previous plan directly impacted by informational changes are reprocessed.

Net present value: The result of discounting all cash flows of an investment back to their present values and netting out the inflows against the outflows.

Net requirements: The net quantity of an item that must be acquired to meet the scheduled output for the period. Calculated as gross requirements minus scheduled receipts for the period minus amounts available from the previous period.

Network: in PERT: the sequence of all activities, symbolized by nodes connected by arcs.

Network modeling: Analyzing the precedence relationships of project activities and depicting them graphically.

Next-best rule (NB): A priority rule that gives top priority to the waiting job whose, setup cost is least.

Node: In network modeling, a circle at one end of an arc; the symbol for the beginning or ending of a project activity.

Noise: Dispersion of demand about a demand pattern.

Nominal group technique: A qualitative forecasting technique in which a panel of experts working together in a meeting, arrive at a consensus through discussion and ranking of ideas.

Normal time: The average cycle time for a job, adjusted by a worker rating to account for variations in normal performance.

Normative-reeducative change strategy: A strategy for change that assumes people change their behavior only after changing their attitudes and values.

Objective function: A mathematical equation that measures the value of all proposed decision alternatives, a linear programming equation.

Occupational safety and health administration (OSHA): A division of the U. S. government created by the Williams-Steiger Occupational Safety and Health Act of 1970 to develop and enforce standards for job-related safety and health.

Office automation (OA): Computer-based systems for managing information resources.

Open order: A customer order (job) that has been launched into production and is in process.

Operant conditioning: A technique to modify behavior by direct rewards and punishments.

Operating characteristic (OC) curve: Given a sampling plan, the graph of the probability of accepting a shipment as a function of the quality of the shipment.

Operating doctrine: Inventory control policies concerning when and how much stock to reorder.

Operating system: An operating system (function) of an organization is the part of an organization that produces the organization's physical goods and services.

Operation chart: A graphic tool to analyze and time elementary motions of the right and left hand in performing a routine, repetitive task.

Operation set-back chart: A time-scaled chart showing the sequence, component, of product build-up.

Operations management: Management of the conversion process, which converts land, labor, capital, and management inputs into desired outputs of goods and services.

Operations splitting: Processing part of a job at one work center and the rest at another.

Operations system: The part of an organization that produces the organization's physical goods or services.

Operation process chart: It is also called outline process chart. An operation process chart gives the bird's eye view of the whole process by recording only the major activities and inspections involved in the process.

Opportunity costs: Returns that are lost or forgone as a result of selecting one alternative over another.

Optimistic time (t_0): In PERT, the least amount of time an activity is expected to consume.

Organization development (OP): Managing organizational change by applying knowledge from psychology, sociology, and other behavioral sciences.

Optimized production technology (OPT): A production planning system that emphasizes identifying bottleneck work centers, and careful management of materials and resources related to those bottlenecks, to maximize output and reduce inventories.

Order quantity: As part of the operating doctrine, the amount of stock that should be reordered.

Organizing: Activities that establish a structure of tasks and authority.

Out-of-control process: A process for which some variations are nonrandom (sporadic).

Outputs: Goods or services changed by a conversion process from labor, capital, land or management resources.

P- chart: A control chart using sample fractions defective.

PERT language: The terms and symbols specific to PERT.

Pareto analysis: Frequency distributions of quality cost sources.

Part-period method: A lot sizing policy in which order quantity varies according to a comparison of holding versus ordering costs.

Path: In PERT, a portion of the network, including the first and last activities, for which each activity has a single immediate successor.

Path time (Tp): In PERT, the amount of time expected to be consumed by activities on a path.

Payback period: Length of time required to recover one's investment; the ratio of net income to net annual income from investment.

Parameters of purchasing: The success of any manufacturing activity is largely dependent on the procurement of raw materials of Right quality, in the Right quantities, from Right source, at the Right time and at Right price popularly known as five 'R's' of the efficient purchasing.

Pegging: The process of tracing through the MRP records and all levels in the product structure to identify how changes in the records of one component will affect the records of other components.

Percent defective: The per cent of units that are defective.

Periodic inventory system: An operating doctrine for which reorder points and order quantities vary; stocks are replenished up to a fixed base stock level after a fixed time period has passed.

Pessimistic time (t_p): In PERT, the greatest amount of time an activity is expected to consume.

Physical distribution: Activities relating to materials management as well as to storing and transporting finished products through the distribution system to customers.

Planned order: A customer order (job) that is on the books and planned for production but that has not yet been launched into production.

Planned order receipts: The quantity of an item that is planned to be ordered so that it will be received at the beginning of the time period to meet net requirements for the period. The order has not yet been placed.

Planned order release: The quantity of an item that is planned to be ordered and the planned period for releasing this order that will result in the order being received when needed. It is the planned order receipt offset in time by the item's lead-time. When this order is placed (released), it becomes a scheduled receipt and is deleted from planned order receipts and planned order releases.

Planning: Activities that establish a course of action and guide future decision-making.

Planning for operations: Establishing a program of action for converting resources into goods or services.

Planning the conversion system: Establishing a program of action for acquiring the necessary physical facilities to be used in the conversion process.

Plant layout: Plant layout refers to the physical arrangement of production facilities. It is the configuration of departments, work centres and equipment in the conversion process. It is a floor plan of the physical facilities, which are used in production. According to Moore, "Plant layout is a plan of an optimum arrangement of facilities including personnel, operating equipment, storage space, material handling equipment and all other supporting services along with the design of best structure to contain all these facilities."

Poke a yoke: Literally, "fool proofing." Total quality control techniques that foolproof production from defects.

Power-coercive change strategy: A strategy for change that makes use of political, economic, or other forms of influence to force behavioral changes in other people.

Pre-automation: An analysis that is performed before automating a production process to reveal unnecessary equipment and activities so that they can be eliminated rather than automated.

Predecessor task: A task that must be performed before performing another (successor) task.

Predetermined time study: A work measurement technique that involves observing or thinking through a job, recording job elements, recording reestablished motion units, and calculating a performance standard.

Prediction: Subjective estimates of the future.

Prevention costs: Costs of planning, designing, and equipping a quality control program.

Preventive maintenance: (PM) JIT philosophy espousing daily, extensive check ups and repairs for production equipment, lengthening their useful life well beyond the traditional time frame.

Principles of motion economy: A broad set of guidelines focusing on work arrangements, the use of human hands and body, and the use of tools.

Priority sequencing rule: A systematic procedure for assigning priorities to waiting jobs, thereby determining the sequence in which jobs will be processed.

Probabilistic PERT: A modification of PERT to consider the variance $\mathbf{s}_e^2$ and the mean $\mathbf{m}_p$ of the expected times.

Process layout: The arrangement of a facility so that work centers or departments are grouped together according to their functional type.

Process capability: The ability of a conversion process to produce a product that conforms to design specifications; a range of variation from the design specifications under normal working conditions.

Process design: Process design is a macroscopic decision-making of an overall process route for converting the raw material into finished goods.

Process management: One of several theories of classical management, emphasizing management as a continuous process of planning, organizing, and controlling to influence the others' actions.

Process technology: Equipment, people, and systems planning activities that establish a course of action and used to produce a firm's products and services.

Product layout: The arrangement of a facility so that work centers or equipment are in a line to afford a specialized sequence of tasks.

Product explosion: The process of determining from the product structure and planned order releases the gross requirements for components.

Product group (family): A set of individual products that share or consume common blocks of capacity in the manufacturing process.

Product life cycle: Pattern of demand throughout the Product's life; similar patterns and stages can be identified for the useful life of a process.

Product mix problem: A decision situation involving limited resources that can be used to produce any of several combinations of products.

Product reliability: The probability that a product will perform as intended for a prescribed lifetime under specified operating conditions.

Product structure: The levels of components to produce an end product. The end product is on level 0, components required for level 0 are on level, and so on.

Production smoothing: Production planning that reduces drastic period-to-period changes in levels of output or work force.

Productivity: Efficiency; a ratio of outputs to inputs. Total factor productivity is the ratio of outputs to the total inputs of labor, capital, materials, and energy; partial factor productivity is the ratio of outputs to one, two, or three of these inputs.

Productivity gain-sharing: Rewarding employees for increases in organization-wide group performance.

Production management: Deals with decision-making related to production processes so that the resulting goods or services are produced according to specifications, in the amount and by the schedule demanded and out of minimum cost.

Production planning and control: Production planning and control can be defined as thc process of planning the production in advance, setting the exact route of each item, fixing the starting and finishing dates for each item, to give production orders to shops and to follow up the progress of products according to orders. The principle of production planning and control lies in the statement 'First Plan Your Work and then Work on Your Plan'.

Production system: The production system of an organization is that part, which produces products of an organization. It is that activity whereby resources, flowing within a defined system, are combined and transformed in a controlled manner to add value in accordance with the policies communicated by management.

Product development and design: is the process of developing a new product with all the features, which are essential for effective use in the field, and designing it accordingly. At the design stage, one has to take several aspects of design like, design for selling, design for manufacturing and design for usage.

Professional service technology: A process technology suitable for labor intensive, high customer contact services.

Program evaluation and review technique (PERT): An application of network modeling originally designed for planning and controlling the U.S. Navy's Polaris nuclear submarine project.

Progress reporting: Monitoring the time and cost variances during the progress of a project and depicting them graphically, including actual costs of work completed (ACWC), budgeted costs of work completed (BCWC), and budgeted costs of work scheduled (BCWS).

Project: A one-time-only set of activities that have a definite beginning and ending point in time.

Project planning: Activities that establish a course of action for a project.

Project scheduling: Activities that establish the times and the sequence of project tasks.

Project technology: A process technology suitable for producing one-of-a-kind products.

Pull manufacturing system: A system of production in which products is produced only as they are ordered by customers or to replace those taken for use. A JIT system.

Purchasing: Activities relating to procuring materials and supplies consumed during production.

Push manufacturing system: A system of production in which products are produced according to a schedule derived from anticipated product demand. An MRP-based or EOQ based system.

Q/R inventory system: An operating doctrine for which an optimal reorder point R—the trigger level—and an optimal order quantity Q—the economic order quantity are fixed.

Quality: The degree to which the design, specifications for a product or service are appropriate to its function and use, and the degree to which a product or, service conforms to its design specifications.

Quality circle (QC): A small group of employees who meet frequently to resolve company problems meet frequently to resolve company problem.

Quality control (QC): Quality Control may be defined as 'a system that is used to maintain a desired level of quality in a product or service'. Quality control can also be defined as 'that industrial management technique by means of which product of uniform acceptable quality is manufactured'. It is the entire collection of activities that ensures that the operation will produce the optimum quality products at minimum cost.

Quality loss function (QLF): A qualitative measure of the effectiveness of quality control, often in terms of the economic losses a customer suffers after purchasing an imperfect product.

Quality motivation: Programs to motivate workers to improve quality, including incentive and merit pay systems.

Quantity discount: A policy of allowing item cost to vary with the volume ordered; usually the item cost decreases as volume increases due to economies of scale in production and distribution.

Quasi-manufacturing technology: A process technology suitable for capital intensive, low customer contact services.

Queue: A waiting line.

Queuing theory: Concepts and models to describe and measure patterns of job arrivals and patterns of servicing customers and to evaluate the effectiveness of serving customers who wait in lines (queues) to be served.

R-chart: A control chart using sample ranges.

Random fluctuations: Unplanned or uncontrollable environmental influences (strikes, floods, etc.) that cause planned and actual output to differ.

Receiving inspection: The inspection of inputs.

Regenerative method: A procedure, used at regular intervals, to update the MRP by completely reprocessing the entire set of information and recreating the entire MRP.

Regression analysis: A causal forecasting model in which, from historical data, a functional relationship is established between variables and then used to forecast dependent variable values.

Reinforcement schedule: A more or less formal specification of the timing of a reinforcer for a response sequence.

Reorder point: As part of the operating doctrine, the inventory level at which stock should be reordered.

Research and development (R&D): Organizational efforts directed toward product and process innovation; includes stages of basic research, applied research, development, and implementation.

Restrictions: Restraints on the values of the decision variables of a linear programming problem.

Robot: A programmable machine capable of moving materials and performing routine, repetitive tasks.

Robust product: A product that can perform under a wide range of environmental conditions without failing.

Rough-cut capacity planning: The process of testing the feasibility of master production schedules in terms of capacity.

Route sheet: A document that shows the routing of a component, including the work centers and operation times, tough its production processes.

Routing: The processing steps or stages needed to create a product or to do a job.

Salvage value: Income from selling an asset.

Sample: A set of representative units of output selected and measured as part of sampling.

Sample range: The arithmetic difference of the highest and lowest measurement for a sample.

Sample unit: A representative unit of output selected and measured as part of sampling.

Sampling: The process of selecting and measuring representative units of output.

Sampling inspection: In this method randomly selected samples are inspected. Samples taken from different patches of products are representatives.

Sampling plan: A plan for acceptance sampling specifying the number of units to sample and the number of sample units that must conform to specifications if the shipment is to be accepted.

Scheduled receipts: The quantity of an item that will be received from suppliers as a result of orders that have been placed (open orders).

Scientific management: One of several theories of classical management, emphasizing economic efficiency at the production core through management rationality, the economic motivation of workers, and the separation of planning and doing work.

Service level: A treatment policy for customers when there are stockouts; commonly established either as a ratio of customers served to customers demanding or as a ratio of units supplied to units demanded.

Setup cost: The cost of revising and preparing a work center for processing a job.

Shingo's seven wastes: Seven sources of manufacturing wastes identified by Shigeo Shingo as targets for reduction through continuous improvements in the production process.

Shop floor control: Activities that execute and control shop operations; includes loading, sequencing, detailed scheduling, and expediting jobs in production.

Short processing time rule (SPT): A priority rule that gives top priority to the waiting job whose operation time at a work center is shortest.

Simple average: Average of demands occurring in all previous periods; the demands of all periods are equally weighted.

Simple lot size formula (Wilson formula): A deterministic inventory model characterized by one stock point, no stockouts, and constant and known demand, lead time, and unit cost.

Simple median model: A quantitative method for choosing an optimal facility location, minimizing costs of transportation based on the median load.

Simple moving average: Average of demands occurring in several of the most recent periods; most recent periods are added and older ones dropped to keep calculations current.

Simplex method: An algorithm for solving a linear programming problem by successively choosing feasible solutions and testing them for optimality.

Single sampling: Acceptance sampling based on a single sample.

Slack time: The difference of the length of time remaining until a job is due and the length of its operation time.

Slack time (T_s): In PERT, the amount of leeway time an activity can consume and still allow the project to be completed on time.

Slack variable: A variable in a linear programming problem representing the unused quantity of a resource.

Smoothing coefficient: A numerical parameter that determines the weighting of old demands in exponential smoothing.

Solution space: The possible (meaningful) values of variables in a linear programming problem.

Specialization of labor: Breaking apart jobs into tasks and assigning tasks to different workers according to their special skills, talents, and tools.

Specification limits (SL) upper (USL) and lower (LSL): Boundaries defining the limits of variation in a product characteristic such that the product is fit for use; output measuring outside these limits is unacceptable.

Sporadic problem: A short-term problem that causes sudden changes for the worse in quality, usually addressed through control measures.

Standard: A quantitative criterion established as a basis for comparison in measuring or judging output.

Standard time: The ratio of normal time to the available fraction of time.

Standard usage: An established industrial engineering time standard.

Statistical forecasting models: Casting forward past data in some systematic method; used in time series analysis and projection.

Statistical process control (SPC): The use of sample statistics to detect and eliminate nonrandom (sporadic) variations in the conversion process.

Stepping stone procedure: An algorithm of the transportation method of linear programming that uses a set of occupied cells to evaluate the effect on costs if an empty cell was to become occupied.

Stochastic model: A model in which variable values are probabilistic.

Stock (storage) point: A location of inventory stock keeping an item of inventory.

Stockless production system: A system of production that allows no (or as small as possible) inventories of raw materials, work-in-process, or finished goods; goes hand in hand with JIT philosophy.

Stockout costs: Costs associated with demand when stocks have been depleted; generally lost sales or backorder costs.

Stores management: This involves physical control of materials, preservation of stores, minimization of obsolescence and damage through timely disposal and efficient handling, maintenance of stores records, proper location and stocking.

Strategic planning: A process of thinking through the organization's current mission and environment and then setting forth a guide for tomorrow's decisions and results.

String diagram: The string diagram is a scale layout drawing on which, length of a string is used to record the extent as well as the pattern of movement of a worker working within a limited area during a certain period of time.

Subculture: Regional or ethnic variations of a culture.

Sunk costs: Past expenditures that are irrelevant to current decision.

System: A collection of objects related by regular interaction and interdependence.

System dynamics: A computer-based simulation methodology for developing and analyzing models of systems and their behavior.

Taguchi method of quality control: A method of controlling quality, developed by Dr. Genichi Taguchi that emphasizes robust product design and the quality loss function.

Task: The smallest group of work that can be assigned to a workstation.

Task sharing: Assigning one task each to two workers and assigning a third task to be shared between the two, thereby reducing idle time.

Technology: The level of scientific sophistication in plant, equipment, and skills in the conversion process.

Templates: Two-dimensional cutouts of equipment drawn to scale for planning the facility layout.

Thaw-move-refreeze model: A widely accepted model of the change process that accounts for the need to thaw the environment, that is, get it ready for change, and to refreeze the environment, that is, make the change take hold.

Theory Z: An approach to management preffered by William Ouchi that synthesizes traditional American and current Japanese methods, and stresses the contribution of every employee in solving problems through group consensus.

Throughputs: Items going through the conversion process, contrasted with outputs coming out of the conversion process.

Time fence: A designated length of time that must pass without changing the MPS, to stabilize the MRP system; afterward, the MPS is allowed to change.

Time measurement unit (TMU): A unit of time, equivalent to 0.00001 hours, used as a basis for methods time measurement (MTM), a widely accepted form of predetermined time study.

Time series analysis: In forecasting problems, analysis of demand data plotted on a time scale to reveal patterns of demand.

Time value of money: The potential for money to generate revenue over time.

Total quality control (TQC): The Japanese approach to quality control, stressing continuous improvement through attention to manufacturing detail rather than attainment of a fixed quantitative quality standard.

Transportation method: A special linear programming formulation for determining how sources should ship resources to destinations so that total shipping costs are minimized.

Trigger level: The optimal reorder point, fixed by a Q/R inventory control operating doctrine.

Truncated-shortest-processing-time (TSPT) rule: A priority rule that gives top priority to the waiting job that has waited longer than a predetermined designated truncation time; if no job has waited that long, the SPT rule applies.

Turnover: The ratio of sales to assets.

Uniform load scheduling (level scheduling): A method of scheduling in which small quantities of each product are produced each day, throughout the day.

Value system: An individual's beliefs or conceptions about what is desirable, good, or bad.

Value-added: When blending inputs into a product or service, the increased value of outputs compared to the sum of the values of inputs.

Value analysis is defined as 'an organised creative approach, which has its objective, the efficient identification of unnecessary cost—cost which provides neither quality nor use nor life nor appearance nor customer features'.

Value-added manufacturing: A method of manufacturing that seeks to eliminate wastes in processing, adhering to the edict that a stage of the process that does not add value to the product for the customer should be eliminated.

Variable characteristic: A product characteristic that can be measured on a continuum.

Variable output rate (chase) plan: An aggregate plan that changes period-to-period output to correspond with the demand fluctuations.

Visible control: A total quality control technique to make defects, as well as records of quality control, clearly visible to all employees so that company resources may be brought to bear on problems as they arise.

Visual load profile: A graph comparing workloads and capacities on a time scale.

Weighted moving average: An averaging method that allows for varying weighting of old demands.

Work breakdown structure (WBS): A methodology for the level-by-level breakdown of a project into successively more detailed subcomponent activities and tasks.

Work center: A facility, set of machines, or workstation that provides a service or transformation needed by a job (order).

Work measurement is the application or techniques designed to establish the time for a qualified worker to carry out a specified job at a defined level or performance.

Work sampling: A work measurement technique that involves defining the state of 'working,' observing the job over time, and computing the portion of time the worker is 'working'.

Work-study is a generic term for those techniques, method study and work measurement which are used in the examination of human work in all its contexts. And which lead systematically to the investigation of all the factors which affect the efficiency and economy of the situation being reviewed, in order to effect improvement.

Worker rating in determining normal time, a factor of adjustment to account for variations in 'normal' worker performance.

Work-in-process inspection: The inspection of a product at one or more stages of production.

X-chart: A control chart using sample averages.

Zero defects: A program to change workers' attitudes about quality by stressing error-free performance.